The Changing World of Soviet Russia

Books by the Same Author

Soviet Russia's Foreign Policy
Russia and Postwar Europe
The Big Three. The United States, Britain, and Russia
   (*out of print*)
The Real Soviet Russia (*out of print*)
Soviet Russia and the Far East
The Rise of Russia in Asia
The New Soviet Empire
Soviet Espionage

In Collaboration with B. I. Nicolaevsky

Forced Labor in Soviet Russia

The Changing World of Soviet Russia

by DAVID J. DALLIN

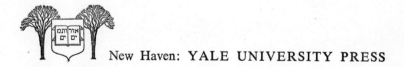

New Haven: YALE UNIVERSITY PRESS

LONDON : GEOFFREY CUMBERLEGE, OXFORD UNIVERSITY PRESS

1956

Preface

THIS BOOK has grown out of a volume written by me in 1944 and published under the title *The Real Soviet Russia,* a revised edition of which was published three years later, when the second World War was over and its effects on Soviet policy could to a certain extent be assessed. The world stood on the threshold of what later came to be called the cold war, in the course of which we witnessed the rising tide of Soviet antagonism toward the United States, Moscow's active role in the upheaval in China, its guiding hand in the Korean war, its conflict with Yugoslavia, its successes in the field of rearmament, and the appearance of its nuclear weapons. These events alone would have made changes in the book necessary.

Stalin's death opened a new era in the history of the Russian people—an era of successes and failures, suffering and privation, oppression, and longing for freedom. A slow process of deterioration and the crumbling away of the old system began with Malenkov's accession to power in March, 1953, and the subsequent Khrushchev-Bulganin era witnessed the resumption of the anti-West offensive, though in changed forms. These developments have called for a fundamental replanning of, and substantial additions to, the material in *The Real Soviet Russia.*

As for the basic ideas of the original work, however, there has been, I regret to say, no reason to negate or retract anything said in 1944–47. I have never shared the optimistic attitudes and high expectations in regard to Soviet policies that were widespread at the time the first two editions of *The Real Soviet Russia* appeared. Opposing these attitudes and hopes, I emphasized the narrow limits set by history to the so-called

v

evolution of Communism and its intrinsic antagonism to democracy. The fable of "equality" in Russia, which was uncritically believed by so many in this country, could not be accepted; the fact that the appalling poverty of the "ruling" workers and peasants had not come to an end had to be stressed; and I pointed to forced labor as a component part of Russian Socialism. I would be happy to have to withdraw any of the statements made in respect to any of these questions; the facts, however, have not refuted my views.

Events described in the present edition go up to 1955. On each Soviet problem dealt with I have tried to give the most important facts and figures. The task, I set myself, however, often proved difficult to achieve because official Soviet reports and statistics are becoming more and more meager. Moscow pretends that the Iron Curtain has been lifted in recent days; it points to the multitude of foreigners who are now permitted to visit the Soviet Union. But neither hurried tourists nor "delegates"—nor even United States senators and congressmen—are in a position to learn the truth about a regime which continues to conceal the real state of affairs, prohibits honest research, and offers the world nothing but slanted and twisted reports and pictures. The Curtain is still down.

In addition to material retained from the original book, parts of the present work have previously appeared in print, in *The Yale Review, The Reporter, The New Leader,* and *Middle Eastern Affairs,* to all of whom I am indebted for permission to reprint.

DAVID J. DALLIN

December, 1955

Contents

Introduction: KLYUKVA

THE GREAT ATTENTION focused on Russia today has produced
a sizable library of reports, articles, and books, but the quality
of the output has not always been on a par with the quantity.

A century ago a certain French traveler, visiting Russia,
was intrigued by what the Russians called *klyukva,* a cranberry
plant growing on small low bushes and used in the manufacture of a popular beverage. On his return to France, the ex-
plorer related how he had drunk tea with Russian grandees
"under the shade of a majestic *klyukva.*" His report provoked
loud laughter in Russia, and the word came to mean a certain
kind of ridiculous misinformation.

Klyukvas concerning Russia have not been limited to the
last century. Their production flourished in the Soviet era, especially in the years of the second World War, during which there
was a tendency among writers on the subject to overlook the
negative aspects of Soviet home and foreign affairs. Our press,
our envoys, our missions, and our foreign correspondents in
Moscow lauded Russia, eulogized Stalin, and minimized the
ominous trends of his policy. "Stalin is no more dictator than
was Mr. Churchill," wrote one authority. Another reported that
the Russian railway system had increased during the war from
a mere 58,500 to 1,143,700 kilometers. The average Soviet
worker, wrote still another, "has living quarters of from one to
three rooms, depending upon the size of his family; he pays
rent on the basis of his earnings; he has education, recreation
and medical privileges . . . and when his days of work are
over he can look forward to a comfortable pension as long as
he lives."

According to one of these "authorities," the "military com-

1

missars" in the Soviet army (who were appointed to watch, take coercive measures, and secure the morality and loyalty of officers and men) are a "mixture of padre, welfare officer and officer appointed for education." The NKVD, wrote a British correspondent, is something like a combination of "our Ministry for Home Security and the road transport department of the Ministry of War Transport." By the executions of "deviationists" like Bukharin and Zinoviev, Russia was "purged of fifth-columnists." An American ambassador asserted that "the word of honor of the Soviet state is as sure as the Bible," and "Soviet leaders . . . will go the whole way as high-mindedly, as altruistically, and as unselfishly as any nation of the world."

Another authority was certain that "Stalin is too smart to plan for a Soviet Germany, because he is fully aware that such a Germany would eventually dominate Russia." An American correspondent wrote: "In all the countries which the Red Armies have entered, the Russians . . . have not shown any particular favor toward the local Communists." With great self-confidence a political writer affirmed that "never have Russian and American foreign policies conflicted."

The years 1947–48 marked the beginning of a new period in international relations, especially in respect to East-West relations. The literature on Russia became more serious, conscientious, and objective. It was thought that, among other things, the errors in our assessment of the Soviet system were at the root of our failures in foreign affairs, and that better understanding of the Soviet Union was imperative. Scholarly studies of Russia were felt to be needed, and many institutes and research centers emerged, with the result that a number of books of good quality were published. The improvement extended also to the popular source of knowledge about Russia, the daily press.

Yet the few foreign correspondents who still remained in Moscow sometimes supplied strange items of news. Handicapped by Soviet regulations and censorship, dependent in every move on officialdom, unable to mix with the Russian population, their assistance in piercing the iron curtain was negligible. The advent of Malenkov, for example, inspired exaggerated expectations in some correspondents: "A Malenkov legend is already widespread," reported one, to the effect that he had "left philosophy to the philosophers" and "introduced a moratorium on the world revolution and on Communism." The same correspondent took pains to deny, from Moscow, that Stalin's "labor camps" contained millions of human beings.

After Beria had been executed on charges of serving British intelligence, a well-known columnist informed American readers that behind the backs of his comrades Beria had "made an overture to the British" in 1953, after Stalin's death, and that about five years earlier he had privately approached a high American official with a view to putting an end to the Soviet blockade of Berlin.

Another correspondent reported that "speculation regarding a possible Malenkov-Khrushchev rift" was without basis (this was written late in 1954 when, behind the scenes, Malenkov's stock had already sunk very low). "Malenkov," the correspondent asserted, "is the leader of the government group, and all of them, including Khrushchev, regard him as their leading member." Malenkov "has a winning smile and just a touch of Little Lord Fauntleroy about him."

Despite a large amount of information of this caliber, the general tone of the press and of scholarly research remained sober and realistic, and the prospects of Soviet internal evolution and Soviet-American relations were assayed cautiously.

The third period of postwar affairs began immediately after the "summit" conference of July 1955. The Soviet authorities opened the gates to visitors, and hundreds of curious foreigners flocked to Moscow. Americans who visited Russia included congressmen, senators, businessmen, farmers, judges, and, of course, a large number of correspondents. Traveling in the opposite direction, Soviet "delegations" came to the United States to study specific—mostly technical and economic—problems. The difference between the two streams of tourists was substantial. The Soviet delegations to this country refrained from making sweeping statements about or voicing approval of conditions in America: industrial progress, the standard of living, political freedom, or democracy. They behaved with dignity and remained what they were—loyal Soviet Communists. Some Americans in Russia, on the other hand, after a short stay were eager to acclaim what only a short time before they had been so critical of; their statements were often reminiscent of the war and postwar era. Before leaving Moscow, after a brief visit there in the summer of 1955, Senator George W. Malone of Nevada, up to then a vigorous supporter of Senator Joseph McCarthy, made a statement to the effect that "there is no evidence the people are going to rise against the Soviet regime," that therefore United States propaganda must be reduced and that, moreover, the supply of strategic materials to the Soviet bloc should be approved. Another senator, Allen J. Ellender of Louisiana, arriving in Vienna after a trip to Russia, reported that Soviet cornfields "rival anything we have in the United States"; not without satisfaction he communicated to the world press that he was fed "bread and cheese, the finest tomatoes you would imagine, chicken soup, fried chicken," etc., etc.

There is much confusion today about the alleged "lifting of the iron curtain." Short or even prolonged visits to the Soviet Union help little to understand the country, if only because there is not and cannot be genuine and protracted contact between the visitors and the Russian people; even newspaper reporters, as we have seen, make grave blunders in their interpretation of current developments because being isolated they are not permitted entry into all phases of Soviet private and public life.

A political system which makes a secret of elementary statistical data, such as those on census of social groups, distribution of income, births and deaths, and even train, plane, and automobile accidents; which does not report honestly on important political developments, such as the execution of a supreme leader; which conceals from its own people the truth about the outside world—such a system cannot be studied by the usual methods of visiting the country and interviewing people. A foreigner cannot understand Russia unless he can live with the people, work at a Soviet job, study in Soviet colleges, attend Soviet meetings and parties, work in a cooperative, even spend time in a Soviet jail.

What the free world wants and expects is to find ways of gaining a better understanding of Russia, opportunities to study her social system, to learn the attitudes and feelings of the people, their attitude toward their government and that of other nations, their satisfactions and dissatisfactions, and the degree of their loyalty to their government. Not even the most enlightened tourist or the best reporter is in a position to shed light on these questions, when they concern a totalitarian country. The granting of visas and provision of facilities for tourists and the extension of privileges to newspaper correspondents do not dissolve the "curtain."

Under normal conditions it is the political opposition, the nonconformist parties and their press, which has the function of criticizing the regime, of exposing its weaknesses, of appealing to the conscience of the nation and of evaluating the people's response. No foreign visitor or newspaper correspondent, by occasional interviews and the gathering of scattered impressions, can substitute for native political movements.

An understanding of the nature of Soviet Communism is the first prerequisite for an understanding of the changing world of Soviet Russia.

PART ONE: Social Revolution in Russia

Chapter 1. THE NEW SOCIAL STRUCTURE

Two main principles have been at the base of all Soviet policies throughout the nearly four decades of their existence: universal state economy and exclusive political power. Throughout all the moves and countermoves, throughout the genuine psychological evolution and the faked maneuvers, despite all the zigzags and turns in all possible directions, these two pillars of Sovietism have proved stable and resistant.

Decades will go by; generations will pass. Storms will be weathered and passions will quiet down. And then the history of that revolution will stand out as a gigantic endeavor to establish a system of social justice by means of political upheaval—a system of justice different from and contrary to all systems of political freedom known heretofore.

Marxism, Populism, Maximalism were theories and philosophies of some importance before and during the revolution. But philosophies and concepts are for the few. To the great majority of adherents the appeal of Sovietism lay in its strong moral nature—its goal of making an end to the misery of the masses. The principle of state economy was and remains the highest principle of Soviet policy; it continues to determine not only its economic policy but its policy in all other spheres. Individual economy continues to be regarded as an evil, even when it does not involve employment of hired labor and its limits are reduced to a minimum. Private enterprise employing hired labor is considered a crime with which there can be no compromise; this has been particularly true since the great economic upheaval of 1929–34.

9

ϟ   The second inviolate principle of Soviet policy is the preservation of all power in the hands of the political group which is determined to make impossible any restoration of individual economy; the preservation of that power by any and all means of internal policy, however ruthless; and the pursuit of a foreign policy which will facilitate the development and expansion of the system of integral state economy.

A great deal has changed in Russia during the Soviet era, but the government has never abandoned the two basic principles: state economy and the strong totalitarian political regime. We may say that Russia's misfortune consists in the firmness with which these two principles have been retained, in the lack of realism and refusal to compromise in this respect.

It is not the "realism" of Soviet policy but its narrow application which constitutes the main evil.

Equality and Inequality

One day in 1919 the head of a Red Guard detachment in the city of Voronezh confiscated Professor Dukelsky's second bed. "He demands," wrote Professor Dukelsky to Vladimir Lenin, "that I sleep with my wife in one bed." To this Lenin replied to Dukelsky that the Red Guard chief was quite right. "Of course," wrote Lenin, "the desire of intellectuals to have two beds, one for the husband and another for the wife, is quite legitimate," but "the average Russian citizen has never had as much as one bed."

ϟ   That was the period of the religion of equality, of equality of human beings practiced to its uttermost limits. It was not an intellectual concept, a theory, a scheme—it was the reflection of a most elemental emotion emanating from a tremendous moral urge. It was the embodiment of the idea of Supreme Justice, which was to be attained with the complete destruction of the "shameful" foundations of the old regime. The people were to govern themselves and to establish justice upon earth: the

Great Darkness was at an end, the Millennium had begun. In like manner did the Levelers and Diggers of the English revolution believe that the Kingdom of God was at hand. In like manner, also, did the mighty voices of equalitarianism resound in the French revolution, with their program of "the agrarian law" and of equality "worthy of the natural condition of man."

Everything that stood in the way of equality was to be abolished, at once, completely: that was the spiritual crux of the November revolution and of the ideology of the early period of the Soviet regime. Equality in consumption and strict rationing were to eliminate inequality in the distribution of food supplies. The floor space of houses and apartments was carefully measured and the available space equally distributed among the population. The peasants divided landlords' estates, the workers seized the factories and drove the old owners into the street. Expeditions from the cities requisitioned grain supplies from the villages for the hungry cities. Soldiers tore shoulder straps from officers' uniforms. All ranks were abolished to make sure that not a vestige of the old inequality would be left. Instead of the aristocracy the workers and peasants were to rule the country, and "every housemaid must learn how to govern the state," for all were now to be equal. Political democracy, in its accepted sense, was found to be inadequate because it did not guarantee social equality. Lenin hailed the Paris Commune because it had equalized the pay of state employees and workers, and he promised for Russia "the reduction of the pay of all, without excepting government leaders, to the regular wage scales of the worker." How distant all this now seems . . .

No less ghostly is the sound now of the decrees and manifestoes of those early years; thousands of human beings died for those ideas and thousands of enemies of them were maimed, tortured, and killed.

"Henceforward the Army of the Russian Republic consists of free and *equal* citizens bearing the honorable calling of Soldier of the Revolutionary Army," and, therefore, "all privileges associated with former ranks and ratings, as well as all insignia of rank (epaulettes), are abolished. All titles are eliminated. All decorations, etc., are eliminated. All separate officers' organizations are dissolved."

A decree promulgated a month or two later declared, "All titles and ranks of civil officials are abolished." All were to be equal.

Every army is held together as a cohesive whole either by a great cause or by rigid discipline. The discipline of the Red Army in its early years was not very considerable, despite the strict regime; but it was strengthened by one of those simple, naïvely elementary ideas which alone are responsible for great upheavals. This idea was not scientific Socialism, or Marxism; no theory at all guided the development. It was indeed simple, like the Cross of the Crusades, like the abolition of slavery in the American Civil War. The reign of equality, of justice, and happiness for all had arrived. The selfishness of the landlords and capitalists stood in the way of the coming of the Millennium. It was necessary, therefore, to destroy them, and no sacrifices were too great. Every sacrifice was considered justified, and every cruelty, however great, was believed endowed with high human purpose. In this idea lay the germ of the future ruthless terror.

Besides, grim reality compelled the realization of general equality as speedily as possible, independent of all theory. The economic catastrophe of the first years of the Soviet regime, 1918–22, had reduced living standards, even without benefit of ideology, to the lowest possible level of subsistence, and, at some moments, even below that. Money lost almost all value, rations were more or less equal. The bourgeois and landlords went to work as employees of state institutions, while state employees lived no better than the workers. In April, 1922, investigation disclosed that the workers were earning 5.71 "commodity rubles" per month, and government employees, 5.74. Equality was attained—on the basis of the lowest minimum subsistence.

The same degree of puritan frugality applied to the ruling party. Party officials did, to be sure, enjoy greater material opportunities than common citizens. The party leaders enjoyed privileges, believing that the interests of the Communist cause gave them the right to a certain measure of comfort, "essential to work." However, this was done quietly, shamefacedly, for it involved a breach with popular sentiments. The young Vyacheslav Molotov was among those who insisted upon the need of limiting the wages and salaries of Communists, especially those Communist employees who were in the higher income brackets. On his initiative, a party conference in 1922 decided—that, too, was a sign of the times—that "Communist employees whose monthly earnings are above the scales set for the 17th category must contribute from one quarter to one half of the surplus to a relief fund. Communists receiving above set scales are obliged to contribute to the fund the entire amount above the set scale." Molotov would have been incredulous if he had been shown a picture of himself as he was destined to appear in a gold-trimmed diplomatic uniform, as prescribed by decree twenty-five years later.

BUT the enthusiasm of equalitarianism soon ebbed. Equality in material conditions may be good if it is achieved on a high level, but equality in hunger led to disappointment. When the process of economic reconstruction began in the 'twenties, the Soviet government found that it could not take a single step forward without breaching the surface cover of equalitarianism in a thousand places. Otherwise economic progress in Russia would have been impossible. When the peasants were given the right to sell their products in the free market, the inevitable consequence was a considerable differentiation in earnings. Distinctions developed between workers and state employees. Finally, the new wage scales introduced for the workers created marked differences between the higher and lower brackets.

The reaction against equalitarianism was in swing. At first this reaction was confined to narrow economic spheres, but it soon spread beyond these limits. In contemporary phraseology this was a manifestation of "realism," but a realism limited by principles and habits of thought. Inequality inevitably proved victorious in practice, while equality was remembered only as a synonym for misery. *But it was very difficult to incorporate the idea of inequality into the framework of Communist ideology.*

After 1921 the retreat from the initial system of universal equality was for a certain time manifest; but the concessions were confined to the field of economics (commerce, wages, foreign concessions); there still remained a good deal of simplicity and emphasized novelty in human relations between superiors and subordinates, between officers and men, between chiefs and employees. Even in regard to individual income, the retreat was considered to be of a strictly temporary nature—a matter of expediency rather than a new civilization *sui generis,* or a new Soviet system of a class society.

Lenin, Trotsky, and Stalin ventured to adopt the NEP with all its deviations from equality in 1921, admitting it to be a retreat from the Communist achievements of the earlier Soviet period. But a year later, in March, 1922, Lenin proclaimed "the end of the retreat." A little later Nikolai Bukharin addressed the peasants with the slogan, "Enrich yourselves"; but he came to regret these words, which continued to plague him to the very day of his execution.

A new period began with the second Soviet revolution—the sweeping industrialization and collectivization. The instructions given from above were, "Down with equalitarianism!" Those who attempted to resist were ruthlessly eliminated. In his conflict with the "left-wing factions," Josef Stalin frequently denounced in sharp terms the "nonsense that money was unnecessary" and "trade was a dead letter." He assailed the demand for social equality by dubbing it ironically the *uravnilovka*—contemptuous Russian slang for equalitarianism.

"These people think that Socialism requires equality, equality in the needs and personal life of the members of society," Stalin declared in January, 1934. "These are petty bourgeois views of our left-wing scatterbrains. We know how greatly our industry has been injured by the infantile exercises of our left-wing scatterbrains. The left-wingers do not understand that money and moneyed economy will remain with us for a long time."

Mikhail Tomsky, leader of the Soviet trade unions, objected to any further differentiation in wage scales, to any additional distinctions of wages between higher and lower paid workers. He was removed and his place taken by the more subservient Nikolai Shvernik; Tomsky ultimately committed suicide.

"More inequality!" was now also the cry in the army; officer ranks were restored, fraternizing between higher and lower ranks was forbidden, and the authority of officers over privates was extended. The idea was adopted of "Distinguished Men in the Soviet Land," that is, persons who had distinguished themselves in one way or another, and had thus won the right to a higher standard of living. This new aristocracy *in spe* won its rights by labor and sacrifice; it was more reminiscent of those ancient conquerors from whom, through storm and stress, stemmed the future lords, junkers, and noblemen, than of the modern men of property. But the new Soviet aristocracy no longer engaged in the coquetry of unselfishness and equality with the "common man." It demanded earthly compensation, at once and as much as possible. Let each be paid for his deeds, and in accordance with the deeds.

A new class society was in the process of development.

"SOCIALISM IS INEQUALITY"

IT BECAME Stalin's task to bring this chaos of ideas into some sort of unity, to reconcile the new system of inequality with Communism, and to combine the new concepts with the traditions of Lenin's epoch. This task appeared all the more difficult because in the late 'twenties it was no longer possible to blame the ugly reality, the great poverty of the overwhelming majority, upon the avarice of capitalism, or to charge that this reality was the legacy of capitalism. The inequality now in force was a *new* inequality.

Stalin's concept was based on a distinction between Socialism and Communism.

When the Communist League was founded over a hundred years ago, and Marx and Engels proclaimed their "Communist Manifesto," the term "Communism" was used in reference to the future classless society. Later, for various reasons, the term "Socialism" came to mean the same thing. Particularly in Russia, since the beginning of this century, the term "Socialism" alone was used to express the ideal of a harmonious, happy, just social order—an order without poverty, war, and violence.

To be sure, there have been many efforts, in political literature, to distinguish between Communism and Socialism. Marx and Engels themselves (and later, Lenin) spoke, in passing, of the "lower" and "higher" stages of Communism as a matter of the near future, the realization of which required only the attainment of a certain technological level. "Communism," Lenin said, "is the Soviet power plus electrification," i.e., a matter of a few years as far as its realization was concerned.

It became Stalin's task, proceeding from the ideas expounded by Lenin, to develop the theory of Socialism as a specific social order, distinct from both capitalism and Communism. According to Stalin's theory, the order now existing in Russia represents complete Socialism. In such an order there is no private economy, there are no persons who live without working, but social equality does not exist. People are paid not "according to need" but "according to deed." In November, 1935, Stalin declared in an address that "the distinction between intellectual and manual labor continues to exist," and that "the productivity of labor is not yet so high as to insure an abundance of consumer goods."

Communism will represent a higher stage of development, he

said: "Communism means that in a Communist society everyone works according to his abilities and receives consumer
goods not in accordance with what he produces but in accordance with his needs as a culturally developed human being."
He assailed those who thought of "material equality on the basis
of poverty."

According to Stalin, the transition from Socialism to Communism would be a "painless" process, i.e., without revolution
and without a change in government, for the Soviet government
(unlike the preceding Russian governments) was not an obstacle to the realization of complete Communism (contrary to
the allegations of the Trotskyites). It is the best possible government for its realization. According to Stalin, it was quite
possible to build Socialism in one country alone, and the transition from Socialism to Communism, he maintained, was likewise possible, theoretically, in one country (theoretically—because other countries were considered likely to rise to the
Socialist level before Russia reached the next stage of its
development). Stalin would not recognize any internal economic impossibility of attaining complete, ideal Communism
in one country.

Speaking at the party congress of 1939, Stalin clearly indicated this possibility: "We are moving forward, to Communism," he declared; nor did he regard the "capitalist encirclement" of Russia as an obstacle. Communism, like Socialism, could exist in one area. This pronouncement was
immediately taken up by Professor Mitin, the principal commentator on Communist sociology, who developed and emphasized Stalin's new idea. "In his address before the 18th
Congress," said Mitin, "Stalin demonstrated the possibility of
the transition from Socialism to Communism in one country."

Neither Stalin nor his professors dwelt on these questions
more concretely. Their idea, never clearly developed, was to
raise production to levels which would bring abundance and
surpluses in all spheres; distribution would then become possible

not by means of exchange of commodities or through money, but without limitation, just as water is delivered to everyone in unlimited quantity. Such a path to Communism would not impinge upon the welfare of "Distinguished Persons"; for this would not be equalization downward but the elevation of the lower spheres from existing levels. Only a detail was missing— the necessary gigantic production, such as has not been even remotely attained by any country in the world. As regards Russia, she was, on the eve of the war, endlessly removed from any such possibilities. Stalin's scheme bore no relation to the facts. Its important element was that the existing poverty and social injustice were attributed to Socialism as, in the past, they had been ascribed to capitalism. Socialism as an imperfect system was now juxtaposed to the mysterious, nebulous ideal of a perfect Communism, which, to be attained, required only the loyalty of the citizens of Russia to their government.

With Communism, as a social ideal, receding into a nebulous future, like a Moslem paradise in a future life, the reality —termed Socialism—was a new class society, profoundly distinct from previous social systems (capitalism, feudalism, and others) but, like all these systems, remote from the ideal of a classless community. The rigid political system had the function of preventing the emergence of a class struggle within the new society.

The Melting Pot and the New Social Classes

The social revolution in Russia lasted about two decades. Starting in 1918 it passed through various stages—the civil war, the purges of the 1920's, the elimination of the kulaks, the purge operation of 1935–38—and by the end of the 1930's it was virtually completed. Subsequent developments brought about only partial changes but not a profound transformation of the substance of the new system. This is why facts, charts, and figures throughout this chapter show the social composition of prewar Russia as compared with 1940.

The period of equalization, embracing the first three to four years, marked the melting into one mass of all classes and groups of the old society. All classes were thrown like so much scrap into a melting pot beneath which burned the fires of the revolution dissolving all the old identities. Countesses in dirty aprons served tea to workers and employees in Soviet institutions, court ladies cleaned the streets of snow, steel barons functioned as members of house committees and together with porters and shoemakers solved questions of keeping toilets clean and obtaining firewood. Workers moved to the villages and became peasants, while peasants migrated to the cities to try their luck. Poor people were moved into mansions, while professors and generals had to find room in modest quarters. Medals, epaulettes, ranks, fortunes disappeared, and new ones had not yet been created. Everything was topsy-turvy.

But gradually new shapes began to emerge from this socially amorphous mass. There was a differentiation within the new mass, and new classes began to appear in the historical arena.

It was a painful process, at times encouraged, at other times delayed by directives from above; complicated, at some moments, by monstrous repressions, or supported, as it suited the will of the powers-that-be; progressing silently at some points or giving rise to bitter factional conflict. There was, for example, a weak effort to facilitate the rise of the class of "nepmen"— private traders and small industrialists; later they were liquidated. At one time well-to-do peasants were promised certain rights; subsequently these rights were abrogated. At one point foreign concessionaires were invited into the country, with offices, staffs of employees, bank accounts; later they were expelled and lost their money. Each of these classes, as it appeared, provided itself with clients, quarters, comforts; money was utilized on occasion in an effort to establish contacts with government institutions, and to create a favorable social atmosphere. Later all such people, their entourage, and the *décor* they had managed to create around them were hurled back into the melting pot, and the new class, before reaching maturity, disappeared in a flash. Most of these embryos of privileged elements perished in 1929–31 in the new outburst of the revolutionary flame. They perished, but there was no turning back any longer to any primitive equalitarianism; the process of differentiation proceeded hesitatingly along a new line of development.

This differentiation continued in the 'thirties, with the development of industry and the collectives. The process had not yet been concluded by the end of the 'thirties; nor was it interrupted by the war. However, a new pattern of society had emerged after about two decades of profound transformation, to replace what was called a "capitalist-landlord" type of social order. Gradually and rather slowly acquiring traits of stability, the type of a Soviet society was reestablished in the postwar era.

SOVIET society as it appears today consists of four principal classes:

The highest class is that of state employees. It comprised at the beginning of the war from 10 to 11 million people, about 14 per cent of the active population; its size today is somewhere between 18 and 20 million. However, since no population statistics have been published by the Soviet Union for the last fifteen years, we have, in the main, to rely on prewar data.

Workers, rural and urban, comprised from 18 to 20 million people. Industrial workers, the basic element of this class, numbered about 8 million.

Peasants, nearly all collectivized, totaled about 40 million, i.e., about half of the working population.

The forced labor class, the exact extent of which is not known and the number of which has fluctuated at frequent intervals, may be estimated at from 7 to 12 million in the late 'thirties, less at the present time.

These are the four principal elements of the new Soviet

society.[1] In addition, there are the armed forces, pensioners, etc., whose significance is of secondary importance in the social structure. A comparison of the social pyramids of 1914 and 1940 would appear as follows:

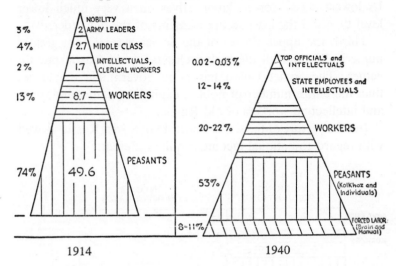

1914   1940

The distinction between the social structure of 1914 and 1940 may be reduced to the following points:

First, the Soviet pyramid is lower, never having attained the upper limits of the social structure of old Russia. There are no millionaires of the old type, there is no court, there are

1. The above figures, as well as the diagrams, are based on the available material and are drawn with all possible objectivity; however, they must be regarded as rough estimates. Although Russia has an income tax and account is taken annually of the income of the various classes, the results are kept a strict state secret. Information divulged by official sources concerning the class structure of the country likewise leaves many questions unanswered. In 1937, for example, official sources reported that the peasantry comprised 61 per cent of the population; in 1939 these sources placed the figure at 46 per cent. The official sources failed to explain the discrepancy.

Official statistics do not of course mention the category of forced labor. The workers of this category sometimes appear in the column "Workers," and thus add to the numerical strength of free labor, or they do not appear at all. For these reasons the actual numerical strength of the different social classes as given above does not necessarily coincide with the figures of the official statistical tables.

no magnates of the old industry, and even the highest elements of Soviet society enjoy a standard of living lower than that of former "capitalists."

✗   Second, the Soviet pyramid begins at a lower social point. Its lowest class—forced labor—lives on a very much lower level than did the least secure elements of the old order.

✗   Third, the upper classes of the Soviet pyramid are greater numerically than all the higher classes of old Russia put together. The Soviet Union has more government employees than the entire number of nobles, capitalists, state employees, and intellectual workers of old Russia.

But the picture of the social structure of Soviet Russia viewed with regard to national income is quite different.

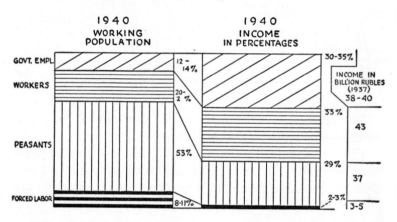

The highest class, comprising from 12 to 14 per cent [2] of the population, receives from 31 to 35 per cent of the national income (that is, of products distributed and not retained for the state's various needs). The share of the workers is about the same despite the fact that they number almost one-quarter of the population. The peasants, who comprise over half the population, receive a share less than that allotted to the employee class. The least secure, of course, is the class of forced

2. See below, p. 59, n. 7.

labor, whose share in the national income is insignificant, although its place in the national economy is important.

The proud assertion then of Paragraph 4 of the Soviet Constitution that "exploitation of man by man has been wiped out in the USSR, because private ownership of the instruments and means of production has been abolished" is unconvincing indeed. To be sure, there is no private ownership; but how can it be asserted that the system as it has developed in Soviet Russia, with its social extremes, is devoid of the elements of exploitation, particularly in the Communist-Marxist sense of the term? "Payment for work according to deed" has rapidly developed into a flexible formula that sanctions the payment of large salaries, monetary awards of hundreds of thousands of rubles, and luxury for the few. The goods consumed by the few are the product of the labor of the many. This may be inevitable; but then the system is not at all devoid of "exploitation."

Even living without working is theoretically not impossible under these conditions. The huge interest paid on government loans represents a striking example of "unearned increment," making it possible for the beneficiaries to live without the need of working, or at least to live by the work of others. The guaranty of the right of inheritance is another example.

"Payment according to the quality of labor" is the formula adopted by the Soviet government to justify in Marxian terms its new concept of exploitation.

The methods of "exploitation" used are as old as the world, and the Soviet system has added nothing new to hoary experience. These methods are: first, wage labor; second, an unfree peasantry; third, slave labor. What *is* new in the Soviet system, distinguishing it from capitalism, is the universal application of these methods by the state. There are no slave owners, industrial magnates, feudal landlords in Russia. But the state is the employer of the free workers, as well as the slave owner and feudal lord. Only the state has the right to use all the historical methods of exploitation, while distributing the product as it sees fit.

It is a false conception that since everyone works for the state, he is himself a co-owner, a shareholder in the great enterprise, and hence cannot be considered exploited. Actually the state is a center of redistribution of goods and wealth in accordance with the wishes of its ruling elements; the state appoints the "associates" to their particular jobs and determines the conditions of their unfree work.

This "socialist system" differs radically from capitalism, and Soviet economists are unquestionably right when they emphasize this distinction. Whether it is a better system for the people is another question.

INDUSTRIAL EXPANSION ON COMMUNIST LINES

"EVERY new plant," said Stalin in inaugurating the program of industrial expansion, "represents another fortress of the working class, which strengthens its positions in the struggle with capitalist elements." Every new plant increases the number of workers in the country and decreases the number of individual artisans and peasants; the establishment of a new plant increases the number of that portion of the population which the government regards as most devoted to it, or, at any rate, most obedient. The political objective of expanding the numerical weight of the workers was the main motive behind this policy of rapid industrialization. Military and world-revolutionary considerations were added later.

In every country industrial development is based on well-calculated business considerations. A new plant must produce more cheaply than other plants, or, at any rate, its operating cost must not exceed those of other plants—otherwise it cannot function. This is a simple fact of progressive industrial development.

But there are occasions, for instance in time of war, when problems of accounting and price are forced back to secondary consideration by political necessity. Bombers must be produced at any cost, even in plants which produce at greater cost than is necessary; strategic railways must be built even though they may have no economic justification for the future. The deficit is borne by the state, that is, by the people, whenever political considerations require new industrial construction.

Soviet industrial development in peacetime offers a model of the *political* development of an economy. Its leading principle is not the highest possible productivity but productivity under a universal state economy, regardless of whether such productivity is more or less expensive. The development is guided by political principle, not by the calculation of surpluses, cost, and price; although every new plant must, of course, take into consideration the factors of cost of construction and production, these calculations do not have any great significance. Only rarely has the cost of construction been kept down to the figure originally set for the erection of new or expansion of old industrial units, involving the expenditure of hundreds of millions of rubles. In nearly all instances huge additional appropriations were required, and this was considered a matter of course. The problem of the cost and selling price of the product was regarded as secondary—for did not the state have the right to fix prices arbitrarily, and were not the deficits covered from its resources?

Political considerations demanded the development of industry—that was enough. The village shoemaker was able at times to produce shoes from local raw materials more cheaply than were huge shoe factories, but this convincing economic consideration had to give way before political principle. The small storekeeper could sell his wares cheaper than the Commissariat of Internal Trade; but freedom of individual economy was contrary to principle. Small private shops may produce radios, while big plants are unable to meet the demand;

the same is true of many other commodities. But this was strictly forbidden. Everywhere realism had to give way to principle.

Some Soviet "industrial giants," representing the achievements of the most modern techniques, are located in the most distant regions. During the war they unquestionably proved useful, but they had been built and had operated for a long time also for the purposes of a peacetime economy. In the opinion of many experts, some of the big plants in the Urals, in Siberia, and other distant places are not economical in the customary sense of the term because of natural circumstances —distances, inaccessibility. Their construction and operation were due not so much to reasons of military preparedness as to political considerations of a general Soviet character.

Before the first World War, for instance, at a time of high protectionist tariffs the industry of Leningrad operated with English coal. Its delivery by sea made it cheaper than Ukrainian coal. The Soviet government, however, in order to stimulate the development of the Russian coal industry, refused to buy coal abroad. For this reason, coal from the Don Basin delivered over a long distance to Leningrad proved more expensive, not in money (for prices were arbitrarily fixed) but in the amount of labor power expended, railway cars employed, and readjustments necessitated by the needs of production and transport. The result was an additional expense covered by the state. But the resources of the state, in the final analysis, come from the people—from taxes, prices, wages. Once more realism gave way to principle.

Another instance was the mechanization of Russian agriculture. Nowhere in western Europe or America was agriculture so backward technically as in prerevolutionary Russia. But nowhere in the world on the eve of the second World War was there such an abundance of agricultural machinery, including the most complex appliances, as in Soviet Russia. This great transformation, most of which took place during the 'thirties, was carried out rather for political than for economic considerations. In the United States only 21 per cent of agicultural units used tractors, in Russia 93 per cent; in the United States there were 75,000 combines, in Russia 154,000; in France there were only 100, in Germany 15!

The organization of the peasantry into collectives in 1929–34 could not have lasted had the old agricultural system remained unchanged. Only after the horse had been to a great extent supplanted by the tractor, and the tractor had become the property not of the peasants or the collective but of the nearby state tractor station, did the newly established economic system in the villages begin to correspond to the political purposes set by the government. The disappearance of individual economy, the transformation of Russia into a land of large-scale agriculture, once it was accomplished, constituted a finished, rounded system. But did this represent a saving of labor power, or, on the contrary, an increased expenditure of labor power for the production of wheat, meat, and other food or raw materials? Was the transformation rational in the most realistic sense of the word, i.e., as measured in terms of prices? These questions were relegated to the background. Even if it had been demonstrated that the new economy was not rational, political considerations would have demanded it imperatively.

Yet, the question of the collectives remains one of the most important in Russia, where half the population still works on the land. In prerevolutionary times the peasant spent only a few rubles annually for the purchase of tools and implements; he was often unable to buy even the most necessary, the cheapest tools. His product was almost wholly the result of his own labor. The new system presents an entirely different, extremely complex picture.

To gather the grain in the fields under the new system it is necessary that many thousands of workers first obtain the necessary metal in the mines of the Ukraine or the Urals. Others must dig coal. Still others carry the coal and iron ore on the railroads to huge plants. In these plants thousands of workers make steel and iron. Then other trains carry the metal to plants manufacturing agricultural implements, where additional thousands of workers and engineers manufacture the machines, machine parts, and repair material. These machines are distributed by rail, water, and trucks across the country, into all corners where there are machine-tractor stations. At the same time masses of workers employed in the oil wells of Baku or Grozny dispatch the oil to refineries. The oil is then transformed into gasoline and sent all over Russia by means of various types of transport. At machine-tractor stations and on Soviet state farms millions of people are occupied in the operation and maintenance of the machines.

Everywhere, in all these mines and plants, a large personnel of technicians, bookkeepers, overseers, watchmen, directors is required, in addition to the thousands of workers directly employed in production for the needs of agriculture. Other requirements include the operation of stores, with their managers and salesmen; houses or barracks for handy men and repair men, carpenters, furniture makers; technical schools for training of workers, with their own teachers, directors, guards, and so on.

This colossal apparatus turns out no greater volume of production than the peasants formerly produced almost entirely with their own labor: in general, grain crops, which had continuously increased before the revolution, have not shown a substantial increase in the past thirty years, especially if we consider grain production *per capita* of the population. This ominous trend lay at the roots of the agricultural crisis which became evident after Stalin's death when the Malenkov and the Khrushchev regimes had to turn much of their attention to farming, husbandry, kolkhozes and sovkhozes.

Under the new system agricultural production proceeds on two levels: the first is operated by that portion of industry, from the mine to the machine-tractor station, necessary to keep agriculture going; only the second level is operated by the collectivized peasants. Quite naturally, their share of work is smaller than before and for this reason the population of the villages has decreased without injury to agricultural output. Millions of people, transferred to industry, continue, however, to work for the needs of agriculture: they constitute the human material required by industry to make possible the operation of agriculture. Their remuneration and their living in the cities is more costly than before. This constitutes precisely the effect of the social revolution called the collectivization: the diminution of the peasant class, unreliable politically and, therefore, dangerous for the regime, and an increase in the number of city workers.

Is the new economic system more profitable, that is, have the commodities produced become cheaper (in terms of gold or hours of labor)? Research to date has failed to provide an answer, but there is reason to believe that the answer is no. The sweeping mechanization was carried out not because of economic necessity but because of political considerations.

Russia has been not only industrialized but superindustrialized. Her agricultural economy has been not only mechanized but supermechanized. She has been protected from outside competition by a system of superprotectionism. For this reason her population has been compelled to make sacrifices which were not merely temporary. Despite the great investments, the people have not improved their standard of living. If ever realism in the national economy gains the upper hand over "principle"—that is, if the needs of the "common man" begin to dictate policy—Russia will inevitably be compelled to reexamine the economic validity of many industrial plants, to curtail the mechanization of agriculture, to reduce production costs and the utilization of excessive machinery, to increase the agricultural population, and, in this manner, to expand the amount of commodities available for popular consumption.

The Population Problem

THE population problem in Russia is more political than in any other country. Biological phenomena, the normal rate of births and deaths, have less influence upon the evolution of the population than anywhere else. Wars and internal social and political upheavals play a far greater role. The growth of population in the face of an almost stationary population in western Europe has political and military implications. The Soviet government itself has made the task of facilitating population increase an important feature of its political program.

How strongly political factors determine population growth in Russia may be seen from a few figures. In 1914 Russia had a population of about 170,000,000 (with Finland, Bukhara, and Khiva); a quarter of a century later, in 1939, after suffering territorial losses, after an alternating decrease and increase in population, the figure remained at 170,000,000. Had Russia experienced a normal development under conditions of peace after 1914, had the rate of population increase continued on the level preceding the first World War, Russia's population would have been over 320,000,000 today.

Actually in 1946, the population of the Soviet Union in its prewar borders amounted to less than 170,000,000; adding the approximately 25,000,000 in the reannexed and newly acquired provinces and the natural increase, the total population today is probably between 210,000,000 and 215,000,000.

Three hundred twenty million in theory and 210,000,000 in reality! Political phenomena responsible for this deficiency of 110,000,000 include:

1. Losses in the first World War.
2. Epidemics and an accelerated death rate in the period from 1914 to 1920.
3. Civil war, 1918–20.
4. Famine, 1921–22.

5. High mortality among deported elements of the population, 1929–34.
6. Famine, 1932–33.
7. Second World War, direct losses.
8. Mortality among war prisoners and excess civilian deaths.
9. Deficit of births because of war conditions.

In the first World War the total of killed and dead from battle wounds amounted to about 9,000,000. Of these, four powers on the European continent bore a nearly equal share: Russia, France, Germany, and Austria-Hungary. Each lost approximately 1,500,000 men. Russia's share of the total was 20 per cent. The casualties of England, Serbia, Belgium, and the United States were below the million mark.

Yet, total population losses due to the first World War, including the deficiency of births, as estimated for 1925, amounted to 1,800,000 in England and 5,600,000 in Germany; the losses suffered by Russia (including civil war losses) totaled 28,000,000.[3] The effect of political developments is clearly visible from these figures. In the intrawar period, 1920–40, political factors continued to dominate the population problem in Russia. Finally, the losses in the second World War (including military and civilian deaths, birth deficit, loss through excess of emigration over immigration) reached 37,500,000.[4]

In the second World War, the total number of killed and dead in the European campaigns for all countries except Russia was about 1,000,000 for the Allied belligerents and 3,500,000

3. According to Frank Lorimer, whose unpublished manuscript on Russian population is quoted in the publication of the League of Nations, *Future Population of Europe* (Geneva, 1944), of the total deficit of 28,000,000, 2,000,000 are attributed to emigration, less than 10,000,000 to birth deficits, and more than 16,000,000 to military and civilian deaths. One-third of the losses occurred during the first World War, two-thirds during the revolution.

4. N. S. Timasheff, "The Postwar Population of the Soviet Union," *American Journal of Sociology, 54* (1948–49), 153, makes the following estimate: deaths of military persons 7,000,000; civilian deaths (in excess of normal) 18,000,000; birth deficit 10,700,000; migration (excess of emigration over immigration) 1,300,000.

for Germany, with probably another 500,000 for its allies. But how great were Russia's human losses in the war? There is no exact answer to this question.

When the war ended, no official data on human losses were published in Russia. Material losses were accurately computed and announced as amounting to 679 billion rubles. Hundreds of men in local and state institutions, economists and statisticians, must have toiled over statistics and other material. Everything was taken into account—livestock, furniture, household goods. But no account of the losses in men in the course of a long and bloody war. Stalin, in his reply to Churchill's Fulton, Mo., speech, mentioned that "the Soviet Union sustained irreparable losses of about seven million men," but his figure included only "direct losses in battle, under German occupation, and from forced labor in Germany." His total, in accordance with Soviet tradition, fails to take account of deaths among Soviet prisoners of war as well as deaths from starvation during the siege of Leningrad and the great number of those listed as "missing" in official reports. In the past the missing, the prisoners, and the sick in the Russian Army have constituted the major part of human losses. After the first World War the number of Russian dead was at first set at 750,000, though it actually reached 1,700,000–2,000,000.

The available data make possible the approximate estimates in the table on page 33.

In the first World War, Russia bore 33 per cent of the Allied losses in Europe. In the second World War her share amounted to about 80 per cent. Of the total military losses of all belligerents in Europe, Russia's share was 20 per cent in the first, 60–68 per cent in the second World War.[5]

The widespread notion that the second World War was more bloody and required greater human losses than the first is both

5. Taking into account civilians killed and dead, the share of Russia in the total of human losses of both Allied and Axis countries amounts to about 60 per cent; Poland lost five million civilians and is second only to Russia in civilian losses.

KILLED AND DEAD (EUROPEAN CAMPAIGNS)

COUNTRY	FIRST WORLD WAR	SECOND WORLD WAR Military	SECOND WORLD WAR Military and Civilian
ALLIES			
United States	126,000	202,000	202,000
Russia	1,700,000	6–8,000,000	12–16,000,000
France	1,350,000	165,000	400,000
British Empire	900,000	400,000	450,000
All others	1,060,000	450,000	5,000,000
Total	5,136,000	7,217,000–9,217,000	17,052,000–21,052,000
(Russia: Percentage of total)	33%	83–87%	76–80%
GERMAN BLOC			
Germany	1,775,000	3,100,000	3,500,000
Austria-Hungary	1,200,000	—	—
All others	400,000	400,000	500,000
Total	3,375,000	3,500,000	4,000,000
Grand Total	8,511,000	10,717,000–12,717,000	21,052,000–25,052,000

correct and incorrect. It is true of Russia; it is not true in regard to the other great nations of the coalition. The total losses of France and Britain were smaller than in 1914–18; there is no Allied nation except Russia whose losses in the second World War reached even half a million in Europe. Russia's losses reached figures unprecedented in world history. Russia alone lost more than all the other nations together.

As far as figures of German losses are known, the total of Germans killed on the eastern front amounted to 1,700,000. In order to kill this number of Germans, the Red Army had to sustain far greater losses. The ratio is three Russians to one German, or even higher; if civilian dead are counted, at least six Russians had to die for one German. This represents the true scale of the efficiency of Stalin's defense of the nation.

To these "permanent losses" must be added millions of cripples, of legless, armless, and blind veterans and civilians. The number of these has not been made public, but it certainly exceeds considerably the number of invalids and disabled in the other countries. These cripples and invalids of war and the millions of widows and orphans are now a constant feature of Russian life.

Material losses were likewise on an unprecedented scale. According to Molotov, the invaders destroyed or burned 1,710 cities and more than 70,000 villages and hamlets. Six million people were left homeless; 31,850 industrial enterprises, employing a total of 4 million factory and office workers, were destroyed or damaged; 7 million horses, 17 million head of cattle, and tens of millions of hogs and sheep were slaughtered or shipped to Germany. The Soviet Extraordinary State Commission, as mentioned above, estimated the direct loss to the national economy and private citizens at 679 billion rubles.

RUSSIA bore the brunt of the war burden. All nations of the world must be grateful to Russia for her sacrifices. But from the Russian point of view it is more than doubtful whether the government's policy, which resulted in Russia's assuming the major share of the burden, deserves endorsement. Political motives and Communist ideology were the real causes of Russia's enormous losses. It was political, not military leadership that led to the sad record of losses and sacrifices.

Motives of internal policy were the cause of the disorganization of the army known as the "Great Purge." The purge ended only on the very eve of the war. The best and most experienced military leaders were replaced by newcomers. Therefore, when the war began, the military leadership proved inadequate. After a few months a reshuffling of the high command became necessary, but it did not take place until after enormous losses had been sustained by the armies.

Russian prisoners of war perished by the thousands in camps in Germany because, for political reasons, the Soviet government persisted in its refusal to adhere to the Geneva Convention; in this way it gained a free hand in the treatment of German war prisoners in Russia. But the millions of Russians were written off the moment they gave evidence of "lack of heroism" by falling into German hands. Their government never cared for them. A report read at the Nuremberg trials stated that during the last four months of 1941, 500,000 Russian prisoners died in German camps. Out of about 4,000,000 Russian prisoners, only 1,300,000 were considered able to work after a few years in captivity, and only 400,000 were actually working. The rest were dead or seriously ill. Hunger and typhus reaped a rich harvest. Another German report on Russian prisoners, quoted in Nuremberg, stated that "there is no sense in transporting manpower in open and unheated cars because in such instances we have to unload corpses only."

It is rightfully claimed that the absence of the "second front" during 1941–44 was another reason why many millions of soldiers and civilians had to die on the fields of Russia. The absence of the second front was, however, the result of the Soviet policy of collaboration with Germany between 1939 and 1941. At the time of Hitler's attack, the Soviet government had maneuvered itself into an impossible political situation. The "first front" in France had succumbed as a consequence of this policy. Because of the foreign policy Russia had pursued, Germany was able for a period of eighteen months to advance in Russia and ravage her lands. By political means the Soviet government was destroying what its armies would have been able to defend in warfare.

In every coalition war each of the partners strives to keep his losses at a minimum, and, consequently, to shift the burden onto his allies. No government can be blamed for taking such a course; no people will willingly bear greater sacrifices than necessary. In the first World War, many an angry dispute arose between France and Russia on this account. "One's own shirt —a Russian proverb says—is closest to one's skin." Stalin's government would have been glad to see the danger of Hitlerism removed by the Western powers without Russia's participation in the war. Once Hitler's armies were advancing in Russia, however, no alternative was left, and no separate peace was possible. The failure to foresee these developments was due to more than the personal shortsightedness of the Soviet leaders. It was the direct result of theories and principles that have dominated Soviet policy for decades and continue to dominate it today.

This was no mere strategic error by Soviet Russia. It was a political crime. Uncritical minds took seriously Stalin's allegation that by concluding the nonaggression pact with Germany, "we secured for a year and a half the opportunity to prepare our forces to repulse fascist Germany." But the Germany which attacked Russia after its victories in the West was far stronger than at the time the nonaggression pact was signed. On the other hand, the "preparation of our forces to repulse Germany" between 1939 and 1941 was much less effective than superficial observers were inclined to believe.

In this year and a half Soviet troops occupied the Baltic countries and eastern Poland in order to create a buffer against a possible German attack. At least, this is how this policy has been presented to the world. However, this "buffer" was overrun by Germany in a fortnight, and by the middle of July, 1941, when the Germans had crossed the prewar borders of Russia, they had already captured a considerable number of troops stationed in the Baltic States and Poland. How this situation was misunderstood by Stalin himself is obvious from his speech of July 3, 1941—eleven days after the start of the war—when he stated that "the enemy's best divisions and his best aviation contingents are already smashed." Actually Hitler's army was exceedingly strong at the time, and eighteen months of death and destruction were to pass before the first decisive defeat could be inflicted upon it. Actually the seizure of the Baltic

States and eastern Poland, while creating animosity against Russia in the West, was of little help in the eventual war with Germany.

It seems as though every nation develops some kind of instinctive guiding policy in matters affecting population. France, for instance, with her declining birth date, placed Maurice Gamelin at the head of her armies at the outbreak of the second World War; his policy in 1939–40 was "to spare the blood" of French troops. In practice this meant capitulation rather than fighting bloody battles and incurring the consequent losses. Russia, at the other extreme, with her enormous birth rate, has produced war leaders who despised economy in the expenditure of lives and were prepared to offer gigantic sacrifices.

SOVIET theory holds to the idea that the more favorable the material circumstances of life the more the population multiplies, and that for this reason the growth of population in the land of Socialism should, and indeed does, proceed at a rapid pace. According to this theory cessation or retardation of population growth is a sign of decay, i.e., it is a product of capitalism. This is what ails Europe. In Russia the "might and power of Socialism finds clear expression in the unprecedented rapid tempo of population increase"—15 per cent in twelve years.[6] During the same period, according to *Pravda*, the population of Italy increased only 9 per cent, of Germany 7 per cent, and even of the United States only 11 per cent.

For this reason, "in order to liquidate radically the crisis of population," in other nations, "it is necessary to liquidate capitalism and to establish a Soviet regime."

The first drafts of the Five-Year Plan envisaged a rapid growth of the Soviet population. It was assumed that the annual increase would be 3,000,000 to 3,500,000, and that the total by 1930 would be 160,000,000; in 1933 Stalin proudly asserted that the figure was already 168,000,000, and in 1937,

6. *Pravda*, June 2, 1939, on the 1939 census.

according to him, it was to be 180,000,000, for "the death rate has declined, the birth rate has risen, and the net growth is immeasurably greater . . . we now have an annual increase of population of 3,000,000." If this development had proceeded uninterruptedly, Russia would have had a population of more than 192,000,000 in 1941; together with the new regions (the Baltic States, Bessarabia, etc.) it would have exceeded 220,-000,000 in 1946—and this would indeed have been a fabulous growth.

But in 1937 a census was taken in Russia and it showed such a deficiency compared with Stalin's predictions and the assumptions of the Five-Year Plans that the directors of the Census Bureau were executed. The results of the census were not made public, and a new census was ordered in 1939. But the new census also showed a deficiency of 10,000,000 to 12,000-000. The government had to recognize it as official. Its results have been erroneously interpreted both in Russia and abroad.

Erroneous, first of all, is the theory that cultural and material improvement necessarily leads to rapid growth of population. On the contrary, the most rapid increase of population is observed frequently among the most backward peoples, who have many families of eight to ten persons. On the other hand, cultural development usually leads to a decline in the birth rate. The most rapid population growth ever experienced by Russia, greater than in the Soviet period, was not in the cities but in the villages in the nineteenth and early twentieth centuries, before the first World War. It may safely be assumed that there will be a decline in the Russian birth rate if and when living conditions for the general population improve.

At the end of the eighteenth century the population of European Russia amounted to 25 per cent of that of the whole of Europe. It has remained approximately at that level until today; namely, 26 per cent in 1880, 28 per cent in 1900, 24 per cent in 1930, 25 per cent in 1940. (It is about 28 per cent in 1955, along with the new territories acquired by Russia.)

Those inclined to belief in mystical forces may draw relief and support from this amazing constancy. For a period of 150 years Europe had experienced many bloody wars with different population losses for individual nations; there was an enormous decline in the birth rate in the West, and Russia's frontiers have changed several times during this period. West and East traveled their separate courses of development, but Russia's proportion remained almost constant.

In order to evaluate correctly the future political-military power of Russia, two important factors must be taken into consideration.

Since the end of the nineteenth century Japan's growth has added a new potential front for Russia and has increasingly absorbed her forces. Like the United States, which has been compelled to build a two-ocean navy instead of the one which had guarded her "Atlantic Front" of the nineteenth century, Russia moved into the difficult position of a nation with two fronts, a position analogous to Germany's. Before that, Russian manpower and industry had been concentrated almost entirely on the European side of the international balance of power. Since 1900 she has been able to use only part of her economic resources and manpower in the task of counterbalancing other European forces.

Asiatic Russia has grown with astonishing rapidity. At the end of the eighteenth century the population of Siberia and Russian Central Asia amounted to 1,000,000; in 1914 it was 21,000,000, and in 1939 it had risen to 33,000,000.[7] Today it is about 40,000,000. The population of the whole of Asiatic Russia, including Transcaucasia, was about 41,000,000 in 1939. In 1951 Russia and her new territories had a population of approximately 161,000,000. Together with the satellites, she had a population of 254,000,000—almost exactly the population of non-Soviet Europe.

But European Russia, as distinct from all other regions of

7. Bukhara and Khiva are included in 1914 as well as in 1939.

the vast country, has always been and will remain for a long time the soul of the nation. The entire population of European Russia (within her 1921–39 frontiers) was about 112,000,000 in 1914; twenty-five years later, at the last census, it numbered 129,500,000.

The weight of a nation in international-military affairs depends *first and foremost* on her adult male population. The male population of Russia in Europe (within the frontiers of 1921–39) had grown less rapidly: it was about 54,000,000 at the time of the revolution, about 55,000,000 nine years later, and about 60,000,000 in 1939. (Although in possession of all the exact data, the government has refrained from making public many features of the census which would have helped clarify this question in details.)

Even before the first World War, Russia, like most other countries, had more women than men—the women predominating by less than 1 per cent. Naturally, more men than women died during the war period. In all belligerent countries the considerable predominance of women over men at the end of the first World War had gradually declined as the older generation disappeared and the new came into being.

Russia presents an astonishing exception. In 1914 there were 67,700,000 men and 67,900,000 women in Russia (the future Soviet territories of European and Asiatic Russia of 1921–39). The difference was insignificant. In 1926 there were 71,000,000 men and 76,000,000 women—a difference of 5,000,000; in part this was explained by the efforts of the war and civil war. The most significant feature of the situation, however, was that subsequently, from 1926 to 1939, a period of peace when a gradual normalization was to have been expected, the actual development was in reverse. In 1939 there were 81,600,000 men and 88,800,000 women in the territory of European and Asiatic Russia, a difference of 7,200,000. The excess of women over men had increased tremendously. It was a development unprecedented for any country.

This excess of women over men was even greater when considered from the viewpoint of European Russia alone. For Asiatic, and particularly non-Slavic peoples, have always had more men than women. In European Russia the excess of women over men was probably 9,000,000 at the time of the last census in 1939. (No official figures are available and one must fall back upon indirect deductions.)

Adult men die off more rapidly in Russia than women, a fact constituting the most serious population problem for the Soviet Union. The economically active sex lives under much greater dangers to life and health in Russia than anywhere else, for in addition to occupational hazards there are also wars and political hazards, such as the deportation of millions of kulaks in 1930–34, which affected for the most part the male population of the villages. Their deportation to the east and north resulted in a high death rate among the males. (According to available information women constitute only about 10 per cent of inmates in labor camps.) The expansion of the deportation system contributed to the population increase of many regions in Siberia, but this also explained the decrease of the male population in European Russia and the increased death rate of males.

Hitler has said, "Let us not forget that the Slav East is more fertile than all the rest of Europe." Napoleon said, "In a century Europe will become Cossack." But the fact is that until now wars and the domestic policies of Russian governments have belied these predictions.

Chapter 2. THE NEW UPPER
CLASSES. I. Their Rise

WHILE the old classes were making their last efforts to resist the new regime in Russia, a new class of government employees was taking shape—a class without precedent in any other country either in point of numbers or in significance. In the cities, where political life was concentrated, there remained, apart from the silent workers, only the employee-intellectuals. Nowhere and at no time had such a phenomenon been known before. All those who had previously performed the functions of tradesmen, salesmen, agents, middlemen, journalists, doctors, lawyers, actors, artists, manufacturers, engineers, and parliamentarians now entered into the composition of the new class. In the villages, too, administrative and economic functions now began to be taken over by the growing cadres of the new employees. A new social class, remotely resembling the old Russian intelligentsia, was coming into being.

This new intelligentsia, made up of state employees or state officialdom, constitutes the highest class of Soviet society.[1] It governs the state, administers the economy, conducts the schools, directs the army, takes care of the sick, creates literature, runs the press, and concerns itself with science. The differences that exist between the various sectors of this new great social class—income, ideological, and political differences—do not disturb a certain harmony of this unique class of intellec-

1. Before the revolution the term "intelligentsia" was rather vague; it meant chiefly members of the liberal professions. In the Soviet period it is being applied to all white-collar workers, thus embracing not less than 80 per cent of employees in the government's offices. The terms "intelligentsia" and "government employees" became almost identical and are so used in this book.

tual workers. Its growth under the Soviet regime, its influence, its relation to the government, and its political orientation become increasingly significant year by year.

Those who would foresee the future of Russia must first make a careful study of the new intelligentsia. In postrevolutionary periods in all countries, when popular movements subside and political struggles become restricted to the activities of limited social circles, it has always been the intelligentsia that came forward as the fountainhead of new ideas and creative instrument of public opinion. The "middle estate" had more leisure and wealth than the lower classes, i.e., those engaged in manual labor; and the intelligentsia had more knowledge. The "middle estate" and the intelligentsia were the decisive elements of public opinion in western Europe in the nineteenth century, and their conservative or oppositionist tendencies have frequently determined the course of political development. Later, with the growth of industry, the old propertied middle classes of the cities ("the petty economy") diminished in size, but there was no polarization of the population. Between the "highest 50,000" and the lower millions there always evolved a "new middle estate," possessing, to be sure, neither capital nor its own economy, but continuing, in many other respects, the political functions of the urban amalgam composed of artisans, storekeepers, poets, scientists, and orators. Like its predecessor, the old middle estate, it enjoyed a standard of living higher than that of manual workers. Its position in society, the national economy, and the state, and its intellectual life and interests often made it one of the decisive elements in politics.

In no country, however, is the role of this class so great as in present-day Russia, and for the following reasons: first, in Russia, as distinguished from other countries, it is not only the middle estate in the accepted sense of the term, but also the highest class, for above it there is no landed aristocracy, nor are there any financial or industrial magnates; second, the lower elements in Russia are inarticulate; and third, as regards its numbers, the new middle estate has assumed unprecedented proportions.

COMMUNISM AND THE INTELLIGENTSIA

THE deep ideological and political antagonism which, in the early period of the Soviet regime, divided Bolshevism and all the propertied and middle classes of old Russia applied particularly to the intelligentsia, upon whose members Communism wielded little influence. From the ranks of this old intelligentsia came the more capable and skillful leaders of all the anti-Communist movements, political, religious, and philosophical. There were in its midst few supporters of the old prerevolutionary Russia; its tendencies found expression in ideas ranging from moderate-liberal to left-wing Socialist. This old intelligentsia resisted the new regime before submitting; and even in submitting, after a struggle of three or four years, it remained a source of protest and discontent.

At the same time the dissolution of the old social order was proceeding rapidly. The higher classes disappeared one after another, and by the end of 1920 there were no more landlords, industrialists, private bankers, or big businessmen in Russia. After another ten or fifteen years most of the small traders and individual peasants had likewise disappeared. The intelligentsia alone survived, despite its antagonism to the regime in the early period of the new order. It proved impossible to wipe out the intelligentsia, even though the government had the power to do so. The intelligentsia was needed more than ever—in the wrecked industry, in the medical profession struggling desperately against disease and epidemics, in the field of education, in the new military academies, and in the army. All government institutions were being filled with new people, and many posts, except the very highest, had to be entrusted to the oppositionist intelligentsia. It constituted the government machine and—such was the paradox during those early years—it sent anti-Communists to the Soviets at every opportunity that offered. The fact is that the Soviet regime was governing through an anti-Communist administrative apparatus.

"The bourgeois intelligentsia," said Lenin, "does not represent an independent economic class and therefore does not constitute an independent political force." His theory was that the intelligentsia would remain the enemy of Communism as long as there were higher classes to utilize its services, but that it would veer to the support of Communism after capitalism had been abolished. According to Lenin, the intelligentsia had no place of its own in the great battle of history. It was entirely possible to move it to the side of Communism, but in any case it was "necessary to learn from it without making, however, the slightest political concessions to these people."

In those days promises of material advantage alternated with threats. Despite the fever of equalitarianism raging at that time, Lenin promised privileges to scientists, engineers, and the "bourgeois intelligentsia" in general. He offered "these people" inducements to build great new laboratories, to expand the universities, and to create working conditions for scientists superior to those of any other country. But he frequently added that the resistance of the intelligentsia must be ruthlessly broken.

He carefully followed the fluctuations in the sentiments of the intelligentsia and looked forward to the time when it would be possible to bring it wholeheartedly to his support. More than once he declared prematurely that the change had come in the sentiments of the intelligentsia, when, as a matter of fact, the evolution had barely begun. "Tens and tens of thousands [of intellectuals] have served us faithfully because they were moved to our side," said Lenin. "They came to us from the other camp, having been transformed into our conscious supporters." [2]

2. Address, December 5, 1920; Lenin, *Works*, 3d ed. Vol. *10*, 207 ff.

In reality, without consciously joining the ranks of Communism, the intelligentsia gradually withdrew between 1918 and 1920 from active participation in politics; it seemed hopeless to fight, and, besides, there was inner disillusionment combined with loss of faith in former political ideas. What came to dominate the intelligentsia was not so much a Communist orientation as a general disorientation.

The political vacillations of the regime with respect to the intelligentsia continued with remarkable regularity, but the basic attitude was one of distrust. Neither the restoration of industry in the 'twenties, accomplished with the aid of the technological intelligentsia, nor the expansion of scientific institutes and other institutions, nor the great expansion of the state apparatus, providing a place for everybody, including even the least capable of the intellectuals, their wives, mothers, and children—nothing could convert the intelligentsia to active support of Communism. Some intellectuals to be sure eventually found their way into the Communist party, but this fact only increased the regime's distrust of the rest.

Periods of moderation were regularly succeeded by periods of ruthless repression. In 1928 came the great Shakhta trial, which ended in the conviction of forty-nine "wreckers"—engineers and technicians—five of whom were shot. They were accused of having deliberately disorganized and wrecked the coal industry, of having been in contact with foreign governments and émigré counterrevolutionists, of having flooded the mines, and, in general, of having committed sabotage with the object of turning the workers against the Soviet regime. The trial had all the earmarks of a political demonstration, and was viewed as a signal for a new attack upon the intelligentsia. Far-reaching conclusions were drawn from it. "The bourgeois intelligentsia," declared Stalin, "is infected with the disease of wrecking . . . The malicious wrecking on the part of the top elements of the bourgeois intelligentsia constitutes the chief form of resistance by the moribund classes of our country."

Another trial staged by the government concerned sections of the food industry. It was not held in public, but forty-eight food specialists were shot.

Those were the years of collectivization, of the first Five-Year Plan, of mass exile. Several thousand engineers and intellectuals were arrested, and from these prisoners were created the cadres of engineers and directors employed on the great public works built by the labor of inmates of forced-labor camps. Two years after the Shakhta trial there took place the similar trial of the so-called Industrial party, in which another group of influential intellectuals was accused of wrecking.

The case of the "Academicians" occupied public attention from 1929 to 1931. This involved more than 150 scientists and professors, who were scattered through various prisons, the case being concluded, without a public trial, only in the summer of 1931. Many were executed and others sentenced to various terms of exile.

The fear that dominated the intelligentsia, together with its uncertainty as to its status and rights, reacted unfavorably upon the progress of economic construction. The situation, however, soon took a new turn.

FLUCTUATIONS IN POLICY

A NEW crop of intellectuals made its appearance. Young people of the Soviet generation were being graduated from secondary and higher educational institutions. They were carefully sifted before being admitted to study courses, and most of them were members of the Communist Youth League who had no recollection or knowledge of either the old regime or democracy. Ignorant of the traditions of the old intelligentsia, but familiar with the required Soviet political terminology, these people at first evoked no suspicion or fears on the part of the regime. On the contrary, the road to the solution of the accursed problem of the intelligentsia now appeared to have been opened through the succession of generations, and through selection and training. Among the new elements there were many children of workers, and this served as an added guaranty of "loyalty." Many of the new young intelligentsia joined the party, increasing the percentage of Communist engineers, lawyers, doctors, and educators.

Six months after the trial of the Industrial party, the regime's anti-intelligentsia attitude was succeeded by another policy: the government seemed to turn its face toward the intelligentsia. In June, 1931, Stalin declared that whereas, only two years before, the intelligentsia "had been infected with the wrecking disease," leaving the government no recourse but ruthlessness, "new sentiments among the old technological intelligentsia" had now taken shape. "Even the confirmed wreckers of yesterday are beginning to cooperate with the working class," said Stalin. "The attitude of the old technological intelligentsia has already begun to change."

For this reason Stalin promised a new policy. "Our policy now," he said, "must be to attract the intelligentsia and show concern for it." "We must alter our attitude toward the technological intelligentsia of the old school." This was an attempt at rapprochement with the old as well as the new intelligentsia, for it was the period of feverish industrial construction and collectivization.

Half a year later, however, Stalin again thundered public threats against wreckers and saboteurs, including those "professors who in their wrecking go to the length of infecting cattle in collectives and on Soviet farms with plague germs and the Siberian anthrax, spreading meningitis among horses, and so on." He accused them of "organizing mass looting and theft of state property and of the property of cooperatives and collectives." "Theft and plunder in plants, warehouses, and commercial enterprises—these are the main activities of these people," he charged. Addressing his associates, Stalin accused them angrily of "gazing indifferently upon such manifesta-

tions." This time the accusations and repressions fell upon both
the old and new intelligentsia.

Soon after came still another change. From 1934 to 1936
arrests among the intelligentsia diminished, and working conditions improved. The general policy was directed toward the
promotion of national unity and class collaboration; the lack
of legal status of various Soviet social groups, as reflected in
the former constitutions, gave way to nominal equality before
the law. For the intelligentsia, this appeared to indicate a readiness on the part of the regime to overlook past sins: the sins of
bourgeois origin, of earlier sympathy with oppositionist parties
and groups, past offenses that had led to arrests, and other dark
spots in biographies. Indeed, in his address dealing with the
new Constitution (November, 1936), after speaking of the
status of the workers and peasants, Stalin declared: "The intelligentsia has suffered many changes . . . It is now united in
its roots with the working class and peasantry . . . The intelligentsia is now a full-fledged member of Soviet society, and
participates together with the workers and peasants in the
building of the new classless society."

Nevertheless Stalin retained his doubts. The intelligentsia
had by now developed into a potentially powerful force; even
numerically it had become larger than the industrial working
class, while its social significance was out of proportion to its
numbers. During the discussions of the new constitution
(1935–36), a proposal was brought forward—with the apparent purpose of emphasizing the final rapprochement between the regime and the intelligentsia—to add to the first
article of the Soviet Constitution (the one stating that the Soviet Union "is a state of workers and peasants") the words
"and of the toiling intelligentsia." [3]

But Stalin opposed this. "The intelligentsia," he said, "has

3. This proposal was offered very cautiously, for the word "toiling" left
room for future persecution of "capitalist restorationists," i.e., of any group
of the intelligentsia.

always been, and remains, but a layer between two classes, a *prosloika*. Previously it was recruited from the nobility, the bourgeoisie, and, in part, from the peasants and workers. In our time the intelligentsia is recruited primarily from the workers and peasants. But it remains a layer between two classes, not a class." The proposal to mention the intelligentsia in the Constitution was rejected.

Lenin's concept of the intelligentsia as an intermediate layer might have been justified at a time when it was numerically a handful. But at the end of the 'thirties this argument, coming from Stalin, was an anachronism and served only to accentuate the continued distrust of the intelligentsia, even of its loyal portion, including that belonging to the Communist party.

Indeed, at the very moment that the new Constitution went into effect (1936), the regime launched the operation which was generally known as "the Great Purge." The purge affected intellectual circles almost exclusively; it struck primarily the Communist portion of the intelligentsia, but also nonparty circles. At the end of the purge, Stalin declared that 500,000 new employees had been added to the government apparatus during that period; most of them replaced those who had been purged. The mass character of the purge, the severity of the punishments inflicted, the senselessness of the arrests, and the unbridled power of the NKVD served to determine for a time the relations between the regime and the intelligentsia.

Theories hostile to the intelligentsia, especially to the party intelligentsia, again prevailed in party circles. Only those can be considered true champions of Communism, it was said once more, who live by manual labor, in mines, plants, and fields; but when they "break away from their class" and move up to nonmanual occupations, when they attend universities and technical schools, they begin to think and feel differently: they become unreliable from the Communist point of view.

The Great Purge ended at the beginning of 1939, and was

followed by a new swerve in the direction of the intelligentsia.
At the party congress in March, 1939, Stalin said:

"There are widespread views in our party hostile to the Soviet intelligentsia . . . There is a careless, contemptuous attitude toward the Soviet intelligentsia, which is treated as a stranger, even as an element hostile to the working class and the peasantry. The intelligentsia has experienced a radical change . . . These comrades continue to regard the intelligentsia and to treat it in a manner that was justified in the past, when the intelligentsia served the landlords and capitalists."

Interpreting in his own way the history of the dissolution and death of the former intelligentsia, Stalin concluded: "Hand in hand with the process of differentiation and break-up of the old intelligentsia went the stormy process of formation, mobilization, and gathering of forces of the new intelligentsia. Hundreds of thousands of young people, children of the working class and peasantry, went into the schools and technological institutes. A new Soviet intelligentsia, closely bound to the people, was thus created. But there are those in our party who assert that workers and peasants cease to be human beings, or become human beings of an inferior kind, when they pass through educational institutions."

Then came the second World War and, nine months later, the fall of France. A military-industrial fever seized Moscow, the general situation again grew tense, and new blows began to descend upon the intelligentsia, directed this time particularly against their numbers in industry. The decrees of the second half of 1940 placed upon the directors of plants, engineers, and technicians responsibility for bottlenecks and failures for which the persons in question, directors of enterprises or their branches, could not possibly have been responsible. The penalties imposed were very severe. A series of trials resulted in jail sentences of from five to eight years. They were demonstration trials designed not so much to punish the accused as to put fear in the hearts of others.

The wartime policy with respect to the intelligentsia since the middle of 1941 was again a dual one. The war, on the one hand, facilitated collaboration among all elements and classes of the population; officially the bourgeois origin of some and even the anti-Communist record of others were forgotten. The new intelligentsia was encouraged, advanced to prominent positions, acclaimed. At the same time, the intelligentsia was kept under rigid control. The close watch maintained over the military intelligentsia was only one aspect of the general system.

Very soon after the end of the war, Soviet policy again took a sharp turn against that part of the intelligentsia which it considered to be not 100 per cent Stalinist. The purge of intellectuals and writers of great standing became sweeping and widespread. Literary magazines, theaters, and movies were among the victims of this reversal to prewar Communist orthodoxy. Leaders of the Soviet Army, even the popular marshals, disappeared almost completely from press and publicity. They were once more degraded to the level of military specialists, with no political influence at all.

Stalin's death eased the strain somewhat and inaugurated, as far as the intelligentsia is concerned, a period of less severity and less persecution; more criticism was permitted. This was, however, the beginning of a slowly approaching crisis rather than a system resulting from a new policy. The problem of the intelligentsia remained unsolved.

A Strange Amalgam

If we may judge the political physiognomy of the new intelligentsia by its origins, it appears to be a curious conglomerate of all classes of old and new Russia, with a strong admixture of the old elements.[4]

4. As was indicated before, Russia's social transformation was virtually completed by 1940. Since then, despite war and postwar developments, the basic elements of Russia's social structure have remained the same. This is why, in charts showing the process, the social composition of prewar Russia is compared with 1940.

Only an insignificant percentage of the propertied classes of old Russia transferred to manual labor after the revolution—that is, became workers or peasants. Among the latter there are no former nobles, big businessmen, or intellectuals. On the contrary, these elements of the population went into the government service, for the most part in accordance with their special capacities. Moreover, in consequence of economic necessity, the members of their families, including their wives and mothers, who had not had to work, also became Soviet employees, though only rarely workers. In this manner the former propertied classes joined the ranks of the new intelligentsia, whose composition follows.

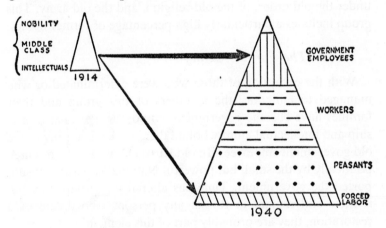

1. *Prerevolutionary Government and Communal Employees*

Before the first World War these numbered between 600,-000 and 700,000. The number increased in the first half of the first World War; if we include communal and other public service employees, the total before the revolution was about 1,000,000. After the revolution some of these remained in the Baltic States, eastern Poland, and Bessarabia after those regions had been lost by Russia, while others, particularly higher-ranking employees, emigrated to other countries. We have no figures showing the effects of these changes, but it is probable that more than 500,000 former government employees remained in the Soviet Union.

The Soviet revolution destroyed the old government machine, but the former state employees remained part of the new higher class.[5] As their numbers were diminished by death, their children gradually filtered into economic and administrative life as Soviet employees. Many had abandoned their old traditions, while some had been sincerely converted to Communism. On the whole, however, these elements retain recollections of the old regime, of old Russia, of the security of their families under the old order, of the old religion, and the old army. This group includes a particularly high percentage of former nobles.

2. *The Former Gentry*

With the exception of those who were exterminated or who managed to emigrate, the members of this group and their families have become government employees. Personal friendship and intellectual affinity bound them to the first group—the old government employees. In old Russia they were represented politically by the small but powerful Nationalist party that supported the government. Time has altered this group, too, but if there still remain in Russia any persons who dream of a restoration, they are probably part of this element.

Before the first revolution, there were 114,000 persons with estates of more than 100 *desiatins* (270 acres); they and their families totaled about 400,000.

5. For example, Kaganovich created something of a sensation when he reported at the 16th Party Congress, thirteen years after the November revolution, that there were 251 former nobles, businessmen, theologians, and former employees of the ministry of finance employed in the Commissariat of Finance, comprising no less than 41 per cent of the higher staff. He disclosed also that there were 39 "strangers," including 15 nobles, landlords, priests, etc., employed in an important division of the Central Committee of Trade Unions.

The old Russian gentry, which included practically all the great landowners and many government employees, represented about 1½ per cent of the population—that is, about 2,500,000 persons of all ages at the time of the revolution. If we exclude from this number minors, émigrés, and those who perished in the civil war or later, there remain no fewer than 1,000,000 former nobles or their descendants who have been incorporated in the Soviet administrative apparatus. It is paradoxical but true that the number of state employees originating from the old landlords' families is greater under the Soviet regime than it was before the revolution.

3. *Prerevolutionary Military Elements, Mainly Officers*

At the time of the revolution there were about 300,000 army officers. Many of these joined the White armies, and later emigrated. A great many were killed in the civil war. On the other hand, the Soviet government tried hard to enroll former officers in its military service, and many old generals received important posts in the Red Army. Their children also belong to the apparatus of Soviet officialdom, partly military but for the most part civil (except during the war period). They probably total between 100,000 and 150,000 persons, who still wield some influence despite their limited numbers.

4. *Former Priests and Their Children*

At the time of the revolution Christian priests and their families numbered between 500,000 and 600,000. The ministers of non-Christian religions numbered 50,000. Very few remained in their profession. A great many were either exiled or executed. Probably about 200,000 or 300,000 became state employees. Since the new religious course was announced in 1943, a new clerical intelligentsia has been permitted to emerge on a limited scale. For a number of obvious reasons, however, it is in no position to evolve an independent political course.

The four groups just discussed were the pillars of old Russia. Between 1,500,000 and 2,000,000 persons originating from those groups are now part of the Soviet administration.

5. Commercial and Industrial Elements of Old Russia

This was a class made up of various elements, from small traders to bankers and industrial magnates. They numbered together with their families between 5,500,000 and 6,000,000 persons. Few of them emigrated; some remained in regions that Russia had lost and regained again between 1940 and 1945.

Some of the former large and small capitalists who remained in Russia tried for some years to continue their independent economy, and felt rather hopeful during the short period of the NEP. But every year, in increasing numbers, they joined the army of Soviet state employees, and their children made no effort to follow the bourgeois line. Within ten years all opportunities for private industrial and commercial enterprise had disappeared.

A very small percentage of this class became workers or peasants; a great number went into the government service. No fewer than 2,000,000 or 3,000,000 persons of "bourgeois origin" were in the state apparatus on the eve of the war. Some filled minor positions as salesmen, stenographers, etc., but the majority were brain workers—that is, they belonged to the intelligentsia.

6. The Old Intelligentsia

In addition to state and municipal employees the old intelligentsia included doctors, lawyers, journalists, actors, teachers, artists, engineers, and a great many others engaged in a variety of analogous occupations (sometimes called "professions").

The transformation of these social groups into Soviet state employees was easier and more rapid than in the case of other classes. Those formerly employed in private enterprise adjusted themselves automatically to the government service with the transfer of industry and trade to the state. Engineers remained at their old posts and became Soviet employees. Opportunities for private practice were gradually reduced also for doctors, lawyers, and writers, and all of them eventually found themselves incorporated in the Soviet administrative machine.

These groups (5 and 6) totaled between 1,000,000 and 1,300,000 at the time of the revolution, or, together with their families, from 3,000,000 to 4,000,000 people. They constituted in old Russia the bulwark of the liberal but not of the revolutionary opposition. For years after the revolution, the majority of Soviet employees were recruited from them.

7. Workers

After the November revolution, many workers went into government service. The first to do so were members of the Communist party, who, in many instances, now received important jobs; then came nonpartisan workers and, last, workers belonging to other parties. They received posts in the offices of newly formed organizations—trade-unions, plant committees, cooperatives, and various commercial and industrial institutions. For workers, transfer to the government service meant great social advancement. This was even truer of their children, who now began to prepare themselves for intellectual occupations offering greater opportunities.

The number of workers and persons of "proletarian origin" in the government service continued to grow in the 'twenties and 'thirties. Many workers, however, received posts not in the economic but in administrative and other government bureaus. The special confidence accorded by the government to persons of proletarian origin facilitated their administrative careers. The number of workers who became government employees amounted to scores of thousands at the very outset. The numbers grew in the course of time but no exact figures have ever been published. Their entry into the government service involved a loss to industry of the more intelligent and better qualified elements. Only in 1940, almost on the eve of the war, did the Soviet government begin to take measures to stop this depletion of industry.

8. *Peasants*

Soviet employees of peasant origin are to be found in considerable numbers among the lower grades of the government apparatus, particularly in the field of agriculture. Many peasant youths who went to the cities managed to get through various schools and even higher educational institutions. Many of them took their places in the ranks of the Soviet intelligentsia as agronomists, veterinarians, teachers, etc. Official statistics afforded an interesting contrast between the prerevolutionary period and that preceding the present war. Before the revolution peasants made up from 14 to 20 per cent of the students in colleges and universities; the children of workers were almost entirely absent. In 1938, on the other hand, the children of peasants and workers totaled between 50 and 53 per cent of all such students.

RAPID INCREASE

TO UNDERSTAND the fantastic growth of the new higher class, we must bear in mind that the total number of government employees, about 1,000,000 at the time of the revolution, had reached 2,767,000 by 1924. Ten years after the Soviet revolution, when industry had barely been restored to prewar levels, although Russia meanwhile had lost 20 per cent of her population by being deprived of the territories previously mentioned, the number of government employees had reached 4,000,000. Neither the workers nor the peasants had increased in number during that ten-year period; only the total number of government employees had increased fourfold. It was strange to see the army of intellectual workers overtaking all others numerically. Two years later their number rose to 4,600,000.

But then came the years of "the great upheaval," 1929–33, the period of industrialization and collectivization. The number of industrial workers began to grow rapidly, but the hosts of government employees remained far in advance. By 1933 they had reached the gigantic total of 8,011,000, and by 1935, 8,780,000.[6]

The 1937 census disclosed the fact that the intelligentsia had reached a total of 9,591,000, or between 13 and 14 per cent of the population. Its numbers continued to rise, reaching more than 10,000,000 by June, 1941.[7]

To understand the significance of these figures, we must remember that all the higher classes of prerevolutionary Russia, including the government apparatus and private industry, totaled about 7 per cent of the population. If we add to this the prerevolutionary intelligentsia and the office workers, the total came to 8 or 9 per cent. These were the organizers of the national economy and the administrators of the old empire.

The present situation indicates that the state and economic apparatus, organizing and directing the physical labor of the masses, has more than doubled. To support the apex of the social pyramid was a great burden before the revolution, when

6. These figures are actually underestimates, for they do not include the figures covering the following state agencies: NKVD; the apparatus of the Communist party and the Komsomal; the Commissariat of Defense. These three groups added several hundred thousand to the army of government employees. The exact figures are a state secret.

7. There were an additional 2,000,000 employees, or 3 per cent of the population, who cannot be included either in the intelligentsia or in the ranks of manual labor; these are minor employees. The total number of government employees on the eve of the war was therefore between 12,000,000 and 13,000,000, or about 17.5 per cent of the population.

it was necessary to maintain from 10,000,000 to 12,000,000 members of the propertied and middle classes. But far greater was now the burden of maintaining from 18 to 20 million government employees, including their families (exact data are not known) simultaneously with intensified investment in industry.

What is the explanation of this phenomenon? Is it the fact that the government is now spending more money and using more people in education, science, medicine, and sanitation? True, the number of teachers has considerably increased. But all these changes in policy, education, and public health do not begin to solve the riddle of the many millions of government employees.

What is more, despite their constant increase, their numbers were never sufficient; new cadres were being sought uninterruptedly. Even during the period of great industrial unemployment in the 'twenties, government employees were never discharged. "We have no people!" is the cry heard from the provinces whenever instructions covering new tasks and new plans arrive "from the center." The shortage of manpower for the Soviet machine was a constant subject of discussion in the Soviets and at party meetings. Young people graduated from secondary and higher schools were snapped up without delay; tens of thousands were thus poured annually straight from the schools into the administrative and economic machine. But it was like drinking salt water; the greater the amount swallowed, the greater grew the thirst, and again and again rose the cry to Moscow: "We have no people." Moscow replied angrily: "You must find them! Seek and ye shall find!" And once more the search was resumed.

Efforts were also made to reduce the dimensions of the monstrously swollen machine, for it constituted an intolerable burden on the state budget. Although the matter was not discussed publicly, the higher circles understand perfectly that the millions of government employees weigh very heavily upon the national economy, for 12 or 14 per cent of the population consumed as much as 30 or 35 per cent of the national income. "Reduction of the apparatus" was constantly discussed by the central and provincial authorities. Periodically draconic measures were resorted to with a view to achieving this purpose, when by a stroke of the pen chiefs were ordered to cut their staffs 10 to 20 per cent. There were scores of such orders. But, contrary to many other decrees of the Soviet government, these failed to produce results. At first the orders were obeyed, but the work began to suffer and then, gradually, almost imperceptibly, new cadres of employees were engaged, and frequently the new total exceeded the old in many a Soviet institution. The central authorities, their attention being engaged in other drives, could only shrug their shoulders.

For example, there was a big leap forward during the first Five-Year Plan, when the total number of government employees increased from 4,000,000 to 8,000,000. The plan had modestly envisaged that the "number of government employees will increase by 6 to 10 per cent during the five-year period"; in reality, the increase was unprecedented. The second Five-Year Plan provided for a reduction of 600,000 in the number of government employees. Instead of the prescribed decrease, there was a marked increase.

This applied not only to government institutions but to all other organizations, such as the trade unions.[8] When he ap-

8. The range of the trade unions' activities is very large, particularly since the liquidation of the Narkomtrud (Labor Department) in 1933. Its functions, among them Social Security, have been transferred to the trade unions. Sport, recreation of workers and employees, rest homes, a system of schools, and lectures are in the province of the trade unions. The "shop committees" and "plant committees" with their thousands of members, technically elected by the workers, and their thousands of office employees are a component of the Soviet trade-union system. Finally, in every political campaign special duties and functions fall to the trade-union apparatus: they recruit workers from among the peasantry; they help advance Stakhanovism; they participate in state and communal projects, such as building homes, observing "weeks of cleanliness," accelerating industrial production, fulfilling the five-year plans, getting food, distributing allotments of garden land; they do everything, in fact, except perhaps exert real influence on wage policy and working hours.

peared before the Central Committee of Trade Unions in December, 1934, Shvernik, then head of the trade unions, spoke with horror of the "inflated apparatus of the trade unions in industrial plants": 117 paid employees in the plant committee of a rubber factory in Leningrad, 87 in the Frunze plant, 77 in the Gorkunov plant, 74 in the Petrovsky jute plant, and 84 in the Tsuriupa club. Moscow demanded that the trade unions cut their staffs. But two years later it was disclosed that "the trade unions have 76,500 paid employees, in addition to cultural workers." Expenditures for maintenance of the apparatus amounted to three-quarters of the paid-up dues. Because of this, it was ordered in 1937, though not for the first time, that "expenditures for maintenance of the apparatus must not exceed, depending upon the union, 25 to 50 per cent of the paid-up dues." But in August, 1940, the Central Committee of Trade Unions again decreed: "Cut the apparatus in half or down to a third and also stop paying trade-union officials out of plant funds." This order contained certain figures illustrating the general problem presented by Soviet employees:

The Moscow automobile plant had 931 paid trade-union employees; the Gorky automobile plant, 648; the Kolomensky plant, 183; and the Moscow Hammer and Sickle plant, 203. In 1938 the Union of Employees in the Commissariat of Trade had 2,807 paid employees; after its division into six independent unions, the number of paid trade-union officials increased to 3,546. The Union of Coal Miners had 444 paid employees in 1938 and 742 in 1940. Additional trade-union employees were paid by the plants; for example, 103 trade-union employees were on the payroll of the Moscow automobile plant.

The Leviathan

THE unprecedented expansion of employees in the government service is rooted in the insolubility of the basic problem—the impossibility of controlling from a single center the administration of the whole economic, political, cultural and scientific, material and intellectual, urban and rural life of a great country. The more the functions of the state expand, the more difficult becomes their performance. When they become all-embracing, the Soviet state makes gigantic efforts to cope with them. The growing pressure finds expression in the recruiting of new cadres of employees and directors. The greater the burden upon the state, the more numerous the bottlenecks and the more frequently does it seek extraneous remedies.

The frequently unsatisfactory performance of the state machine has given rise to chronic shake-ups and readjustments, transfers and regroupings. There have been a great many of these in the history of the Soviet government, but they have never produced adequate results. For this reason another measure resorted to has been the establishment of new divisions, sectors, institutes, and commissariats, whose task it has been to correct mistakes. These new institutions soon developed their own shortcomings, and they, in turn, were subdivided, expanded, or multiplied, adding new masses to the army of government employees.

Taken by itself, every state function seemed logical and normal. If all private stores, for example, are closed, the Commissariat of Trade must substitute its own outlets. But private trade, particularly in Russia, consisted mainly of thousands of small stores, in the cities and villages, with their own small "capital" of microscopic dimensions, each with its single owner, who was also his own bookkeeper, salesman, economist, and statistician. Only in the cities did some stores employ salesmen. When the state took over all private trade, it appointed an employee for each store; in some cases the appointee was the former owner. But it was necessary to control the employee, to keep a record of goods bought and sold. Furthermore it was necessary to supply the thousands of stores, to check the quality of the goods, to systematize prices, and to perform scores of other functions. For these purposes there was born at the top the grandiose brain of the Commissariat of Trade. And as the task of distributing the goods in a country like Russia is an unusually difficult and thankless one, the Commissariat of Trade was constantly being subdivided and expanded.

The Commissariat of Domestic Trade was created in 1924. Within a year, quite logically, it embraced foreign trade also, and became the Commissariat of Trade. At the end of the 'twenties came the liquidation of the NEP, with the abolition of private trade of every description. The Commissariat of Trade was thereupon divided into two departments, domestic trade being placed under the jurisdiction of the new Commissariat of Supply. The latter set up a number of vast subdivisions having to do with retail trade, produce, industrial commodities, consumer goods, the maintenance and operation of stores and local trade networks, the supplying of health resorts, hospitals, hotels, the regulation of prices, and a great many other duties. A year and a half later this Tower of Babel was condemned. A new organization was created, with another expansion of the apparatus. Soon each of the sixteen republics of the Soviet Union had its own Commissariat of Trade, operating under the direction of the All-Union Commissariat of Trade in Moscow. In 1940 the mammoth state trade apparatus ran 152,700 stores and 6,300 restaurants and other eating places. The number of its employees reached 1,400,000 in 1941.[9]

No one in particular bears the responsibility for the development of this monstrous machine. On the contrary, most of those directing it are reasonable people, able, devoted to their work, unsparing in their efforts, even to the extent of not sparing their health. Every step they take is carefully thought out, including the unification or division of bureaus, the formation of new agencies and the enlistment of scores of thousands of employees. If, in spite of everything, this incongruous system has been built up, the fault is not that of individuals or their motives. The underlying trouble is the insolubility of the basic

9. *Large Soviet Encyclopaedia* (2d ed. 1952), *12*, 298.

problem—centralized organization and control by the state of all Russian business and of the country's economic and social life as a whole.

Many more illustrations could be cited to emphasize this situation. Even in large-scale industry, more amenable to state control than small business, one sees the same phenomena. The number of engineers and technicians has naturally increased under the Soviet regime, keeping pace with the great industrial expansion. They totaled 1,400,000 on the eve of the Russo-German war. But there were and are many more of them than would be the case in private industry under analogous conditions.

The Soviet economic journal *Problemy Ekonomiki* gave a comparison between two electric stations, one in the United States, at South Amboy, New Jersey; the other in the Soviet Union, at Kemerovo. Each produces the same amount of electricity. The American station employs 51 persons, 17 of them office workers. The Soviet station employs 480 persons, of whom 91 are office workers, 106 are in the "division of fuel and transport," 98 in the "boiler room," etc. In Russia, 11 men are required to produce 1,000 kilowatts of electricity; in the United States, 1.3.

The same Soviet journal presents a comparison of two mines, one of the Pittsburgh Coal Company; the other, bearing the name of Lenin, in the Urals. "The American mine employs 8 persons in the office, the Russian 67. The production of the Pittsburgh mine is three times as great as that of the Soviet mine, which employs 48 engineers and technicians, 6 of whom direct operations, 8 are employed above ground and 29 in various sectors; in addition there are 22 foremen (one for every 10 miners), who supervise but do not participate in production. The mine bearing the name of Lenin employs eleven times as many technicians as the American mine."

The number of workers in Soviet industry increased 17 per cent from 1932 to 1936, but during the same period the number of government employees increased 25 per cent. In the Soviet machine industry the number of workers decreased 5 per cent between 1937 and 1939, while the number of employees increased 13 per cent.

A Soviet industrial official, the same journal reports, visited an electric station in Switzerland. On one of the doors he saw a sign "Director." He found the director sitting behind his desk. The following conversation took place:

"Where is your chief engineer?"

"I am the chief engineer."

"Where is your secretary?"

"I have no secretary."

"But who receives daily reports, etc.?"

Instead of replying, the director opened a cabinet, explaining that those in charge submitted all material to him.

"But who conducts your correspondence?"

"I have very few letters to write."

"But what do you do when you have to write a letter?"

"When I do have to write occasionally, I do the writing"— and the director opened a drawer in his desk and pointed to a typewriter.

In view of all this, one can readily understand some of the reasons for the unprecedented expansion of the employee class in Russia. If we look more closely, we see the basic groups that make up the intelligentsia. Engineers and technicians, for example, numbered 207,000 in 1926 and 1,400,000 in 1941. But those who benefited most by this policy were the bookkeepers and their next of kin, the statisticians and economists; in 1926 they constituted a very large group numbering about 1,000,000; thirteen years later this typical category of the secondary bureaucracy had expanded to 2,000,000, running far ahead numerically of all other elements of the intelligentsia. The bookkeepers alone numbered 1,700,000! No country has such a large army of bookkeepers and statisticians as Soviet Russia.

Together with their families, they constitute a population greater than that of Texas or Sweden, and perhaps thrice that of Ireland. The bookkeepers are divided into ranks, like army men: there are chief bookkeepers, senior bookkeepers, just plain bookkeepers, and keepers of accounts. The statisticians, too, comprise several divisions.

THE trend continued after the second World War. At the same time open and accurate reporting ceased; the secrecy maintained under Stalin was strictly followed by his successors. Not only were the state and party machines prohibited from revealing anything about their size and configuration, but even data concerning the trade unions were tightly concealed. The Soviet labor force, the growth of which during the postwar decade was noted with considerable pride by Moscow, comprised both manual and white collar workers. In 1933, when the total membership of Soviet trade unions amounted to 17,-120,000, the number of white collar workers was over 8,000,-000 (47 per cent). On the eve of the war, trade union membership rose to 25,000,000; in 1949 (including the newly acquired territories) it reached 28,500,000; and at the time of the Eleventh Trade Union Congress in 1954 it numbered 40,400,-000.[10] Calculating the white collar group at from 45 to 50 per cent of the total membership, it numbers today from 18,000,-000 to 20,000,000.

10. In 1953 the total number of workers and employees, including nonmembers of trade unions (in particular the working population of the corrective labor camps) has amounted, according to *Pravda* (July 10, 1953), at 44,800,000.

Chapter 3. THE NEW UPPER
CLASSES. II. Their Future

RIGID HIERARCHY

THE new Soviet intelligentsia is destined to play a decisive role in the internal changes confronting Russia. Its experience has made it the only great social force capable of initiative and activity. It is already the dominant element in the social life of the country, though not in political leadership. Future developments, despite the fact that they may involve a series of crises, are bound to bring it to the fore in politics also.

In Soviet literature, art, and science the intelligentsia is both the creator and the theme. Russian novels are now being written by intellectuals, for intellectuals, on themes dealing mainly with the life of the intelligentsia. Shakespeare's principal characters were lords, counts, gentlemen, and merchants; Tolstoy's and Pushkin's were princes, counts, nobles, and officers. Today the Soviet reader wants to see himself, the Soviet intellectual, in literature; and the writer, his confrère, willingly satisfies this demand. Some writing is still being done, by order of the government, about peasants, soldiers, and, rarely, workers. But for the past two decades these heroes have surrendered first place in interest to the intelligentsia. The magazines take their themes principally from the life of Soviet employees; the best satires reflect the life of the Soviet state apparatus. The theaters rarely produce plays about workers or peasants. Even the great political newspapers, so dull to the average reader, with their endless articles on purely economic themes both in peacetime and in wartime, become understandable when we remember that they are written with a view to instructing Soviet employees in their activities.

The Soviet employee has come into literature not only as a reader but as an active force. Though he has broken through the barbed-wire barriers, he has not yet broken through the censorship. Literature and the theater, in his eyes, suffer from the fact that they are required to please the party authorities. For the censorship is one of the party's weapons in its struggle against the political rise of the intelligentsia.

Not everything is aboveboard in the personal and social conduct of the component elements of this new great class. Many of these people have reached their present status after suffering great privations and by ruthlessly overrunning their associates. In the long years of the Soviet regime, many saved their own skins by betraying their closest friends. All of them grew up in an evil, nerve-racking, dangerous period, when men stopped at nothing in order to survive. Because of all this there is a great deal of toughness and crudity in the upper circles and much meanness below. The crudity at the top is frequently accompanied by humiliating servility below. Higher-ups are addressed as "you," and the reply is frequently "thou." This appears to be in the order of things, one of those old, persistent traditions which return by themselves, without resort to artificial means.

To establish oneself, to learn the entrances and exits, to master the formulas, to obtain contacts—in short, to find one's place and to hold it—is the course to be pursued, for upon this depends life itself, one's own and one's family's. Under such circumstances all those questions which formerly occupied first place in the life of Russian government employees and which have always concerned officialdom in all countries assume primary significance: salary, expenses, per-diem compensation, allowances for quarters, extra allowances, and so on; added to these, in Soviet Russia, are extra payments in cash—bonuses and rewards—as well as in foodstuffs, quarters, hospitalization facilities, and trips to summer resorts, to the Volga, the Crimea, and the Caucasus. Thousands of medals and ribbons grace human breasts, each carrying with it certain rights and privileges. But most important of all is advancement up the administrative ladder, the kind of success that gives a person inner satisfaction, a sense of dignity, a feeling of pride, for advancement signifies recognition of one's services by the omnipotent state.

A hierarchical society like that of Soviet Russia needs all this not less but more than any other. Rigid subordination, strict differentiation of rank, glorification of discipline—all the devices on which the old Prussian and Austrian idea of government service was based—find even greater application under the Soviet order: the chief of department and his subordinate; the army commander and the rank-and-filer; the general and the colonel; the director and the staff man; the secretary and the clerk; the people's commissar and the vice-commissar; in the party apparatus, first secretary, second secretary, and third secretary; in the theater, "people's artist" and "distinguished artist."

IF ONE may speak of the "class interests" of millions of government employees, these interests would appear to be of a dual character. Politically all these people, nonpartisans and Communists alike, dream of security, in their private and public lives, from unwarranted interference—security from arrest, purges, unjust demands, and demotion in rank. They find it intolerable that almost every family has some member who is being subjected to repression at home or is confined in a concentration camp; that one's every step is watched not only by superiors but also by someone else; that though someone is prying through one's office desk, one is not permitted to protest that one is held responsible for the mistakes of one's superiors; that no allowance is made for objective causes of failure to carry out instructions; that somewhere behind one's back, behind the wall, lists of suspects are being drawn up; that one is

judged by a "fixed" court. What is truly unbearable is not so
much the state of general lawlessness as a man's own inability
to explain, to defend himself, to call things by their real names.
Unbearable, too, is the fact that one cannot lead a quiet life
even though one has not committed a single crime. And a quiet
life is the dream of millions of average government employees
after all the revolutionary upheavals and wars.

Since it is an amalgam of various social strata, the new class
of government employees cannot be considered to be wholly
democratic in its political sentiments. The majority are people
under forty years of age who have never known any form of
rule other than stern dictatorship, and who are accustomed to
associate Western democracy with all sorts of evil. Yet dissatisfied with this or that feature of the regime, they cannot,
without some ideological concert and group discussion, give
concrete political expression to their sentiments. What they
would like to have is a government based on law, not a police
state, even though a government based on law is not necessarily a perfect democracy. But the prerequisites for great political programs have not yet come into being in Russia. Any
outbreak that may occur will revolve round specific questions
of limited significance; the deeper significance of any such
outbreak will become clear only after the event.

In the economic sphere the new intelligentsia at first glance
does not seem to disagree with the Communist system of universal state economy. The official press and scientific institutions
never tire of asserting that every class of the population in favor
of private property has been abolished in Russia, and that the
restoration of capitalism, in whole or in part, has no supporters
in a single social group. This claim rests on the fact that except
for a few old people no one in Russia is likely to express any
such desire, either privately or publicly; but the situation is not
so simple as all that.

There is a substantial difference in the attitudes of orthodox
Communism and of the Soviet intelligentsia on the subject of

the state versus private economy. The first regards the state
economy as a boon to Russia and the rest of the world, in fact
as the main bulwark of progress, for the attainment of which
all else should be forgiven.

As far as the Soviet intelligentsia is concerned, the state economy is an established fact, but not a question of principle. The
mass of government employees see no reason to prefer the
state economy to a private economy where the latter seems
more reasonable and economical. They do not possess that
Communist enthusiasm which demanded the liquidation of
every little private store even though the surrounding population was deprived, in consequence, of necessary commodities.
Nor is there any mass enthusiasm for collectivized agriculture.
On economic as on political questions, the intelligentsia has no
clear program. Should a policy determined by the interests of
this class gain the upper hand, it would have to follow new
roads in the sphere of economics.

The same is true of many other Russian problems. On the
question of religion, for example, Communist policy was in
principle actively godless, deviating only from time to time
toward neutrality. Most government employees, however, were
never militantly antireligious. Many, perhaps the majority, considered religious marriage a necessary complement to civil
registration, had their children baptized, and observed funeral
rituals. The antireligious campaigns provoked their displeasure.

The attitude of the majority of government employees, even
of party members, toward the Communist parties abroad has
been very cool. They regarded the Comintern as representing
a few hundreds or thousands of foreigners, "leeches and para-
sites," residing in Russia. The Hotel Lux in Moscow, which
housed the Comintern, was the butt of nasty jokes and protests.
The dissolution of the Comintern in 1943, brought about primarily by considerations of foreign policy, was at the same
time a concession to these sentiments. The idea of world Communism, though never abandoned by the high party hierarchy,

was never popular among the great masses of Soviet employees; it is now less in favor than ever.

Insofar as Communist expansionism does influence the government's foreign policy, it does not meet with the approval of the Soviet intelligentsia. The military defense of Russia is accepted as a matter of course, but any further plans and programs are not regarded as equally axiomatic. The Soviet intelligentsia, including even its Communist element, viewed very coldly the Stalin-Hitler pact of 1939. This attitude may be duplicated in connection with some further zigzag in foreign policy. The attitude of the Soviet intelligentsia toward England and the United States has never corresponded to the traditional Communist antagonism, which at times has been nothing short of hatred.

Such is the inarticulate program of the Soviet intelligentsia. However modest and limited it may be, it differs radically from the attitude of the regime. A government founded on law would mean especially the liberation of the vast majority of prisoners from jails and concentration camps and the abolition of forced-labor camps. The introduction of realism in economic policy would mean greater liberty for the economic activities of the peasantry. These reforms would put into effect what millions of Soviet citizens dream of only silently.

In connection with this program, the Soviet intelligentsia—and this is most important—reflects the hopes and interests of every other class of the population. The peculiar role of the Russian intelligentsia as the focus of the political needs of all classes of the population is by no means new in Russia. On the contrary, it was this tradition that in the past made the Russian intelligentsia a unique phenomenon in world history. Now it once more confronts the state power as the main embodiment of popular interests and sentiments. Having been transformed from a small group of "old intellectuals" into a class comprising many millions of government employees, and having lost its one time revolutionary fervor, it now reflects, in its hopes and sentiments, the general urge for what might be termed the end of the revolution.

It longs for a peaceful, wholesome life. It is being glorified with slogans, lauded to the skies, honored with the titles of heroes of labor, heroes of war, heroes of Socialist construction. But they themselves, these millions of employee-intellectuals, do not want to be heroes. They are tired of heroism, of stress and strain, of sacrifice and suffering, of persecution and war and death. They want to come home from work, relax, and play with their children. They do not want to have meetings and conferences every night; they want to sleep. They want to buy things without having to stand in queues, to read without being watched, to converse without fear, to love without danger, to obtain an apartment without having to play the sycophant. Two generations of Russians have not known the meaning of normal living. The people now on the scene want to live.

The ending of the revolution, after four decades of great experiments, transformations, and achievements; after wars, foreign and civil, unprecedented for Russia and the world; after countless sacrifices; after immeasurable sufferings, famines, epidemics, and unutterable misery; after repeated manifestations of extraordinary heroism and moral degradation; after the promulgation of great ideals and sweeping programs; after the imposition upon the nation of great lies and deceptions —after all this, the ending of the revolution would reflect the general need of the tortured, desperately tired people. The ending of the revolution would not involve a return to the past. Hardly anyone dreams of the restoration of old Russia. But the revolution must be ended. All that is beautiful in it, and all that is ugly, must be relegated to history.

In realizing this, the Soviet intelligentsia expresses the urge of virtually every class of the population.

ABOUT 20 per cent of government employees are members of the Communist party. The majority, especially the most in-

fluential members of the party, live and work in close proximity
to the mass of government employees. All share the everyday
problems of Soviet life; there is a constant exchange of things
and ideas between them. The party is always trying to indoc-
trinate the elements that surround it with its own ideas and to
win them over to its side. The party exerts influence on its sur-
roundings, on the mass of nonpartisan employees, but the surrounding social elements also influence the party. These elements, their needs, ideas, fears, and hopes, penetrate, in spite
of all obstacles, into the great mass of party members, infect it,
and tend to disorganize it. Thus, silently, does the class of government employees poison the party. True, it has no freedom of
speech, no ideology, and no capacity for active resistance.
Nevertheless it does resist, to a considerable extent, psychologically, passively. At times there ensues an apparent armistice,
but never for long. Up to now the party has always managed,
after making some concessions, to turn back to its former policy.
But this, in turn, has tended to estrange the party from those
whose labor built the national edifice.

Official reports and textbooks on the history of the Russian
Communist party touch only lightly upon the role of the intelligentsia in the party. Formal statistics on this question have
long ceased to be published. The newspapers print accounts of
party meetings in the army, in plants, and in collectives. But
almost nothing is said about the activities of party organizations
in government institutions. Indeed, the facts do not fit into the
framework of a "workers' party."

The first census of the Communist party membership, in
1922, showed that 8.2 per cent of Soviet employees belonged
to the party. The highest percentage of Communist officials,
43.4, was in the GPU. Five years later another census disclosed
11.7 per cent of Communists among the intelligentsia, 6.1 per
cent among the workers, and less than 1 per cent among the
peasants.

But the 12 per cent of Communist employees in 1927 already

included at that time the leading personalities of the Soviet state machine. The directors of all departments were all members of the party; all were people's commissars or vice-commissars, both in the central government and in each of the affiliated republics. The directing personnel in industry in the middle 'thirties was made up entirely of party members: between 95 and 100 per cent of the heads of enterprises and their immediate assistants, the directors of trusts and their immediate assistants.[1]

To the 20 per cent of Communists in the Soviet intelligentsia should be added about 10 per cent of Komsomol members.

STANDARDS OF LIVING

THE new intelligentsia is the highest class of Soviet society by virtue of its earnings and its standard of living. Nevertheless there is a wide differentiation in earnings and living standards within the intelligentsia. There is a vast gap between the village teacher in some distant province and the Stalin laureate or

1. A striking parallel between the quantitative growth of the party and the increase in the number of government employees is shown by the following figures:

Year	Number of Employable Intellectuals		Number of Party Members
1920	About 2,000,000		612,000
1929	4,600,000		1,532,000
1932	About 8,000,000	Before the purge	3,170,000
1939	9,600,000		3,200,000
1941	10–11,000,000		3,900,000
1953–55	18–20,000,000		7–8,000,000

The increase in percentages over 1920 run almost parallel:

1920	100	100
1929	230	250
1932	400	518
1939	480	523
1941	500–550	637
1953–55	1,000	1,100

ballerina in Moscow. This, however, does not alter the fact that a sense of unity exists among all elements of this class, from the lowest to the highest—a sense of unity more keenly felt than in any other country.

The earning capacity of intellectuals is lowest in the villages, where employees in administration, education, and rural economy are paid no better than industrial workers. The higher the administrative center, the higher the earnings. The average earnings of intellectuals are about twice the average of workers; particularly high are the earnings of engineers, which are many times those of workers. A few engineer groups earn several thousand rubles a month as compared with the average monthly wage of from five to seven hundred rubles for workers.

Still higher are the earnings of picked groups of writers, actors, and scientists, who, in addition to their salaries of many thousands of rubles per month, receive all sorts of special grants, are given the use of automobiles, are occasionally exempted from paying taxes, etc. The higher aristocracy of Soviet society, consisting of artists, engineers, technicians, and some of the highest officials and comprising no more than twenty or thirty thousand persons, is the apex of the Soviet pyramid.[2] It is not entirely Communist; but its welfare depends closely upon its loyalty. Being in the forefront it is constantly watched. It is unqualifiedly devoted to the regime, with a devotion which relegates conviction and political opinions to second place.

Fixed monthly salaries are not the only source of income for many, particularly those employed in the economic field. All

2. One criterion of the change is the increase in the number of domestic servants. At the beginning of the 'twenties, practically no one could afford to have a house servant, and the number of "domestic workers" (1,500,000 before the revolution) fell to 150,000 in 1923–24. Later it began to rise rapidly. By 1927 there were already 339,000 domestics, and the government's plans envisaged further increases: to 398,000 in 1929 and 406,000 in 1932 (see *The Five-Year Plan*, Moscow, 1930, p. 17). In the latter part of the 'thirties, with the rapid rise of the new aristocracy and oligarchy, the number of domestic servants increased so greatly that official sources became silent on the subject.

sorts of bonuses—for economy, for efficiency, for quality, etc. —increase incomes very considerably. Rewards frequently take the form of lower vacation costs and trips to vacation resorts. But all salaries and incomes-in-kind combined leave the standard of living of most of the intelligentsia extremely low in comparison with living standards in the United States or western Europe.

Despite the inner differentiation, the class of government employees has a keen sense of solidarity; its differentiation from the "common man" has reached an extreme completely unknown in the United States. The bourgeois-intellectual origin of some, the snobbishness of others—parvenu elements that have sprung from peasants and workers—weariness from many years of privation, of imposed impoverishment, followed by the government's encouragement in the middle 'thirties to "live merrily"—all this has resulted in the development of hierarchical forms known only to medieval feudal society. Not to mix with "the people," to have fine clothes and fine furniture, to own a victrola and a radio, to ride in "soft" railway cars regularly used only by government employees, to enjoy vacations in "rest homes" as distinguished from the places frequented by workers, to eat in restaurants operated for the special use of Soviet employees—all this serves to give them a sense of superiority. Even in theaters, the old workers' shirts, *kosovorotki,* at one time in the front rows, have been banished to the rear of the gallery.

All this suggests a marked reaction against the epoch of the *kosovorotki* and the *uravnilovka,* like the revenge for the years of imposed privations. The encouragement by the government of these changes is officially explained in economic terms: as a reward for valuable services. The "happy life" enjoyed by some is designed to encourage others to follow their example.

The intelligentsia has not been able to satisfy its basic political aspirations. But one thing it has won is the right to a decent living for the small number of its élite.

FUTURE DEVELOPMENT AND DIFFERENTIATION

THE process of formation of new classes had not yet been completed when the war broke out. It is going on now, after the war. The fate of the higher classes, in particular, will depend, as heretofore, upon the course of inner political development, to wit:

1. So long as the political system remains unchanged and retains the basic principles of an all-powerful state economy, the evolution of the higher class will proceed along the road of hierarchism. This development would mean the widening of the gulf dividing the members of the higher class from those performing physical labor. The transition of lower elements to higher levels would become more and more difficult. The expansion of hierarchism would imply an inner differentiation of the higher class into groups and subgroups, and their advancement up the social ladder would be circumscribed by rigid rules of government service.

2. If political developments result in changed economic principles—if, for example, freedom of small business is restored—the new small tradesmen and petty industrialists will arise from the ranks of the same higher class. Thousands of employees now working as salesmen in state-owned stores or performing duties on the lower levels of the industrial machine will leave the government service; former store managers, for instance, will become independent owners.

The employees in question possess great practical knowledge, versatility, and the necessary minimum education; many are greedy beyond description. These people will seize the new positions before any elements from the ranks of the workers and peasants have a chance to come forward and become a new class of small tradesmen and capitalists. The more room the state permits for private initiative, the greater will be the numbers that break away from the class of government employees and the more rapid will be the formation of a new commercial-industrial class.

3. If, theoretically speaking, the capitalist economy should be restored, with private heavy industry, trade, and banks, the new capitalist class would emerge wholly from the ranks of government employees. Only from these ranks could come the cadres of businessmen, promoters, directors, pioneers of foreign trade, department store owners, and bankers. The great scope developed by Soviet industry is the product of human imagination; this imagination, in such a case, would serve the cause of private economy.

The present upper class will remain (socially, *although* albeit not politically) at the head of the nation, with changes of one kind or another, for a long time. It will continue to show differentiations, to develop, to learn, to change its political attire; eventually it may even drive political regimes from power and put others in their place. It may divide into parties. But it will stand for Russia in the eyes of the world.

Chapter 4. THE WORKING CLASS

It is usually assumed that the revolution destroyed or decimated only the propertied classes of old Russia. In reality, however, this applies also, though in a different sense, to the Russian industrial and agricultural workers. The working class that now exists in Russia must be thought of as something entirely new. It came into being after the revolutionary period and is to be sharply distinguished from its earlier counterpart. Workers of the prerevolutionary era and members of former workers' families constitute but a small minority, probably less than 10 per cent of the contemporary Russian working class. This is a fact of cardinal importance.

It must be remembered that the industrial workers constituted, in a political sense, the most important part of Russia's former working class. For various reasons, the agricultural workers, as well as the relatively small number employed in petty trade, played a small role in comparison with the workers in plants and factories. After their famous march to the Winter Palace in 1905, the industrial workers of St. Petersburg, as Leningrad then was called, gave the signal for the first revolution. The wave of strikes in 1905 culminated in barricade battles in sections of Moscow inhabited by industrial workers. The labor conflict and the suppression of the strike in the Siberian gold fields in 1912 were events of great political significance, and marked a turning point in history. Finally, it may be said that both the revolution of March, 1917, and the November revolution would have been impossible but for the intense political activity of the Russian workers, especially in the two capitals. Neither the mutinies in the army nor the agrarian disorders could have amounted to much or resulted in the victory of the new government without the impetus derived from the political movement of the workers.

On the eve of the first World War, however, industrial and railroad workers in Russia numbered only about 3,500,000. To be sure, there were some 3,000,000 part-time agricultural laborers, and several million in trade and business offices, but the industrial workers constituted the heart of the Russian working class. Women workers were not very active politically, and, if we exclude apprentices and minors along with them, we come to the conclusion that what has been called the Russian labor movement before the revolution comprised about 2,500,000 workers. This was only 2 per cent of the adult working population of old Russia.

Of these 2,500,000 human beings, a great many went to war in 1914–16. Some were killed, others wounded, and still others went back to their native villages after demobilization. Thousands of workers were drafted into the armies of the civil war between 1918 and 1920; their mobilization assumed considerable proportions because the new regime, for political reasons, preferred to mobilize workers rather than peasants, whom it did not trust. Hundreds of thousands of workers were sent to the front, and many never came back to their jobs. Industrial production was declining, there were no raw materials, cities were starving. All those who had any ties with the villages— and most of the Russian workers were of peasant stock—tried to leave the cities, particularly because the division of the land was under way and workers were eager to help their families in the villages get their share. The wars, hunger, and the industrial depression thus combined to drive workers from the plants and sharply reduced their numbers.

Of the total number of workers in the prerevolutionary period, only half remained in 1921–22, and even these were only partly employed. By that time, according to certain statistics, industry had declined 83 per cent. Its revival, begun in the 'twenties, brought new elements into the plants and factories, in addition to the old workers, including former independent artisans, employees in small trade, former minor government employees, members of the old police force, and young people. But the dissolution of the old working class continued.

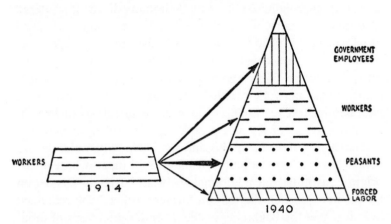

The process was accentuated by the influx of many workers into the ranks of the newly developing economic and administrative bureaucracy. This phenomenon assumed a mass character. In line with official ideology, the Soviet press and literature of the period exalted the spiritual and moral qualities of the workers: the working man was the symbol of all that was lofty and great. The worker's courage and heroism, the worker's heart and the worker's soul, proletarian culture, and proletarian art—all this filled the columns of the Soviet press and inspired Soviet orators. Many poets and writers who had scarcely set foot in an industrial plant sang the praises of the worker in all sincerity, though their knowledge of these people was altogether theoretical; others joined in the exaltation in order to be in step. This worship of the worker, which was essentially self-praise on the part of the regime, continued for about ten or fifteen years.

Meanwhile the real workers, who had experienced on their own backs what factory labor was like in Russia, were deserting the plants by the thousands, the very same plants where the new human beings of the poets' songs were being forged. New managers were needed to replace the old and their number grew in proportion to the inexperience of the newcomers. The new administrative economic staffs, with their many divisions scattered all over the country, required additional human material, some of which was supplied from workers in the same industries. The trade unions were developing rapidly into a great state apparatus. The same thing was true of the Communist party machine, whose network reached into every nook and corner. A new administrative organization was being set up in the villages, and many of the new posts were being filled by workers.

Thousands of vacancies became available, with able, shrewd people, particularly workers, rushing to fill them, whose social origin constituted an additional, substantial recommendation for the new jobs. Of the million former workers who remained in industry at the beginning of the 'twenties, hundreds of thousands soon moved up the social ladder.

Many of the children of the former workers sought to escape the hardships of industrial labor. Free education enabled workers to send their children into the engineering and teaching professions, to military schools, and into scientific fields. Thousands of girls took business courses or became saleswomen; many went into medicine or teaching. The end of the 'twenties brought the first mass graduations of young people from educational institutions, men and women who had never worked in industry; and, beginning with the 'thirties, this new type of Soviet intellectual was to be seen everywhere. The old workers were dying off, many of them satisfied to know that their children were facing a better life than their own, not troubled by the question whether this was true Communism.

At the same time, however, the economic chaos was being overcome, and the number of new workers was increasing. By 1927 the number of industrial workers had been restored to the prerevolutionary figure of 2,600,000; in 1930 it was

3,670,000; and by 1935 it had doubled, reaching the figure of 5,620,000. Before the outbreak of the war it had increased to 8,000,000.

Along with these millions of new workers, there were probably no more than a few hundred thousand of the old ones. The government, although it was in possession of the pertinent data, refrained from publishing the complete figures, for it sought to create the impression of the continuity of the Russian labor movement. It wanted to have it believed that the working class responsible for the revolution of 1917 had continued to function as the main foundation of the new regime. The few workers of the old category who remained at their jobs were the least capable element, devoid of initiative: even before the revolution they had been considered on the whole a backward, docile group.

Why No Labor Movement in Russia?

THE source from which the millions of new workers were recruited was the old Russian reservoir which in the past had supplied the Russian mercantile class, the army, and all former cadres of workers—the virtually limitless reservoir of the peasantry. During the eight years from 1928 through 1935 the cities absorbed 17,686,000 men and women who had come from the villages, or about 2,000,000 persons annually. The urban population, which was 28,000,000 in 1929, increased to 56,000,000 within ten years.[1]

Without this great new labor force there could not have been any successful industrialization. For a period of ten years an endless procession of trains filled to capacity carried this mass of labor in unprecedented numbers from the villages to the cities. Neither Europe nor America had ever known such an intensive mass migration. It was as if some giant pump had lifted millions

1. See pp. 31–41. In 1953, along with the newly annexed areas, the urban population reached 80,000,000.

of human beings from their ancient habitats and transplanted them thousands of miles to factories and public works of which they had never even heard before. Most of the new workers migrated to the cities voluntarily, hoping to find better working conditions. In the two famine years of 1931 and 1932 some 7,000,000 people went to the cities. More or less compulsory enlistment of peasants in industry played a substantial part in this migration during the years immediately preceding the present war. In 1940, for example, a new law mobilized a large part of Russia's peasant youth for training in technical schools by obliging the collectives to supply 400,000 boys and girls annually.

This was how the new Russian working class was formed. There were, of course, other elements in this great tide, such as former domestics, who now moved into industry, and the remainder of the former unemployed. But these urban reserves were soon exhausted, and had been completely used up by about 1933, which marked the beginning of the second Five-Year Plan. The new Russian working class constitutes essentially a part of the peasantry transported to the cities for employment in plants and factories.[2] Many a memory and hope bound them, and continued to bind them, to the villages.

They remain in the cities, but their transformation in the industrial cauldron is proceeding very slowly; it will be a matter of decades before the process is complete. They have brought to the cities all the characteristics of the Russian village, the paradoxically contradictory, enigmatic features of the "Russian soul," so mysterious to the outside world. Boundless subservience to fate, amazingly low living standards, and an endless capacity for enduring privation have been the characteristics

2. In 1933–34 a trade-union investigation produced some interesting figures. The metallurgical industry disclosed that the percentage of former peasants or children of peasants employed before 1917 was 31 as against 62 per cent in 1931–32. In the flour-mill industry, the comparative percentages were 48 in 1917 and 72 in 1931–32. In the building trades the respective figures were 56 and 78.

of these people who have formed the mainstay of first-class armies, as well as the solid foundations of monarchies and dictatorships. And, coupled with this, there have been periodic outbursts of the wrath of millions, cruel and bloody peasant uprisings, with their sudden terrible vengeance for humiliation and whippings, for oppression and poverty, for undernourishment, for years of famine. And later, after merciless suppression of such uprisings, have followed periods of pacification. There have been heroic self-sacrifice and silent submission; mutiny and obedience; revolt and loyalty; the village community, *obshchina*, and cunning individual calculation; anticlericalism and religious devotion. The rational West always regarded all this as the extreme of the irrational.

It is not surprising, therefore, that until 1905 the Russian peasantry had never been able to develop the forms of life, habits, and action which have characterized the American worker and farmer and the workers of western Europe: the capacity for systematic, consistent building of their own organizations, from month to month, from year to year, without stormy disturbances followed by apathy, without sweeping upheavals followed by loss of faith in themselves. How could the Russian peasants ever have developed any such characteristics? Having emerged from serfdom at about the time of the abolition of Negro slavery in the United States, they had only found themselves caught in the toils of a rigid police system.

This also explains the tardiness of the old prerevolutionary working class in making its appearance on the political scene. That working class was composed primarily of former peasants who had migrated to the cities with the development of Russian industry during the fifty years preceding the revolution. Those workers, too, bore uncomplainingly the burden of poverty and dirt. There were no trade unions of any kind, for their existence would have been impossible, before the first revolution. Collective action by the workers was inconceivable, strikes were illegal and were punished by mass whippings and bloody suppression. It required much heroism to register any protest on economic questions. Very few were capable of displaying such courage. Before 1895 even sporadic, short-lived strikes were rare events. They grew more frequent later, but only the year 1905 brought the first great strike wave that swept the whole country.

Only then did the Russian worker begin to develop the characteristics that mark trade-union and political labor organizations and that require a relatively high degree of urban culture. This was facilitated, in addition to the experience gained in the cities, by the influx of thousands of intellectuals into the young Russian labor movement, with their enthusiastic faith in the liberating mission of the working class. The group of intellectual élite born of this development supplied the leaders who, in the period between the two revolutions, 1905–17, built the first solid trade unions in the face of police repression and founded all sorts of workers' relief organizations and educational institutions. Those twelve years constituted the only period when Russia had any genuine trade unions. Heroic efforts and a great deal of idealism were required to build them, and hundreds of persons spent a total of thousands of years in prison for this experiment in the Europeanization of the Russian peasant-worker.

The new postrevolutionary working class, which also sprang from the peasantry, was not a continuation of the old. It brought with it to the cities subservience and loyalty to the powers that be, long-concealed discontent, the tendency to be satisfied with little, and no knowledge of, or feeling for, social organization. The molding of this mass in the industrial cauldron was an exceedingly slow process, particularly because it no longer had the cooperation and encouragement of idealistic intellectuals and also because the more capable elements of the new workers, distinguished by some measure of originality, speedily left the ranks in an effort to gain advancement in the economic scale. For them, roads were opened for advancement, without any collective improvement of the general level of life. The relatively high pay enjoyed by the more skilled made the idea of any collective action, so far as they were concerned, seem quixotic and foolishly altruistic.

This is one reason why the development of a labor movement has proved impossible under the Soviet regime. There have been outbursts of revolt in factories, of the kind known before, marked by primitive anger and passion. These outbursts, easily suppressed, have been scarcely noticed by the country as a whole; indeed, they have been nothing more than sporadic phenomena. There is still a great deal of dissatisfaction among the workers, but it has taken the form of a dull, chronic pain.

Another reason why the revolution has failed to develop a new labor movement must be sought in the peculiar qualities that have marked the new Russian working class.

In all countries, and under all conditions, the most active workers in the labor movement have been adult men; the role of women, as members of unions and particularly as initiators and leaders, has been comparatively limited, and even less important has been the role of minors. Women constitute about 15 per cent of industrial workers in the United States (24 per cent of the total labor force), and 20 to 30 per cent in western Europe.

The situation in prerevolutionary Russia was to a certain extent analogous. Before the first World War, adult men made up 62 per cent of the workers, women 27 per cent, and minors 11 per cent. On the eve of the second World War, the composition of the industrial workers was quite different. Women numbered about 40 per cent in industry, while young workers (below 23) numbered 35 to 40 per cent of the men. Thus adult men constituted from 35 to 40 per cent. In 1937 there were approximately 7,800,000 workers employed in Russian industry, but of these only 3,000,000 or fewer were adult men.

This relatively active part of the working class thus grew rather slowly. It bore no relation to the generally known figures showing the fantastic increase in population of the cities (100 per cent in twelve years), the increase in production (fivefold in twenty years), and the increase in the total number of wage earners. While the general mass of industrial labor increased from 300 to 400 per cent, the number of adult male workers grew very slowly. Even before the present war, the Russian working class consisted for the most part of women and youths.

THE STANDARD OF LIVING

THIS thoroughgoing transformation of the Russian working class during the period of the revolution makes a comparison of earnings under the old and new regimes almost pointless. The whole matter is political rather than economic. Of political significance is the question: What benefits have been derived from the social reconstruction by the class that enjoyed special privileges during the first period of that reconstruction? This question has played a vital part in the conflict of parties in Russia, and particularly in the factional struggle within the Communist party.

There are two answers, both official. The first explains why real wages for the Russian workers could not be substantially raised. It calls attention to the fact that Russia's unprecedentedly speedy industrialization required tremendous efforts on the part of a poor nation and called for sacrifice of immediate welfare for the sake of the future. It recalls also the need of military expenditures, which increased greatly in the 'thirties and then again in the 'fifties, using up immense sources that could have been employed to better advantage. Guns and tractors instead of butter, electrical stations instead of meat— such was the explanation, an explanation not without some measure of truth.

But along with this explanation we have assertions from the same sources that claim an unprecedented increase in earnings, not only of individuals, but of the whole laboring mass. Allegedly Russia has achieved the impossible: a simultaneous expansion of industrial investment and of military-industrial preparedness, coupled with a substantial improvement in the workers' standard of living.

According to official statistics, wage scales, which had fallen very low at the beginning of the 'twenties, reached the prewar level in the second half of the 'twenties. In 1930 Stalin reported to the party congress that "real wages have already risen 167 per cent, in comparison with the prewar period." In 1934 he reported that wage scales again had risen, on an average, from 991 to 1,519 rubles per year. This meant that by 1934 they had already reached two and a half times their prewar level. Judging by official figures, wages continued to rise after that period. According to Molotov, "real wages doubled during the second Five-Year Plan [i.e., from 1933 through 1937]." If we combine the data given by Stalin and Molotov, we may conclude that wages had increased 450 per cent by 1938, as compared with prewar scales. Finally, a further increase of 35 per cent was contemplated under the third Five-Year Plan (i.e., before 1943). Thus, if we are to credit the official figures, real wages at the beginning of the second World War were five times as great as those which prevailed on the eve of the first World War.

If this miracle were true, it would justify a great deal of what has occurred under Communism. It would mean that millions of men who had barely subsisted under the old regime, and millions of new workers who had flocked from the villages to the cities after the revolution, attained within the short period of fifteen or twenty years a level of material well-being such as had never been enjoyed either by the workers of western Europe or by those of the United States, the highest paid in the world. If it were true that the wage scales of the Russian workers had increased fivefold by the outbreak of the second World War, as compared with prerevolutionary levels, it could not be denied that Russia had caught up with and overtaken the capitalist nations.

ᕁ The fact, however, is that these claims are sheer propaganda. It is well known that any estimate of real wages is not a mere arithmetical process, and that all such statistics are likely to be unreliable, particularly under conditions of violent price fluctuations in times of inflation.

Not only were prices rising rapidly in Russia during the 'thirties but the same commodities commanded a variety of prices, depending on whether they were bought in the state co-operative stores, in the open market, or elsewhere. Contradictory conclusions may be drawn in any price studies under such conditions, according to the figures used. Moreover, official statistics included in the calculation of wages the benefits of social services, which are usually excluded in any wage computations: social insurance against illness, the cost of lectures provided by the government, maintenance of clubs, and other things; [3] this was referred to as the "socialized portion of wages." The workers, however, might easily have preferred to receive cash instead of lectures and similar things. It was by such methods that official statistics yielded their optimistic conclusions.

For purposes not of propaganda but of real work, however, the state adopted a very different procedure. Every ruble that could possibly be saved had to be devoted to expansion of the basic capital of the Soviet economy. According to this concept the Soviet state has the right to demand from its workers the maximum of sacrifice for the sake of their future well-being. In fixing wage scales it pays the workers only as much as it considers absolutely necessary. The Soviet government has no intention of generally raising living standards until the program of reconstruction is completed, and until the "Americanization" of Russia permits a reduction in the tempo of economic accumulation and thus makes possible the increase of real wages to unprecedented levels. Such is the official concept. Whatever

3. Funds for "cultural services" alone covered 39 per cent of wages in 1933 and 35 per cent in 1935, and around 38 per cent after the second World War.

one may think of the ultimate aim sought, this concept, at any rate, expresses more correctly the official policy on the wage question than does the propaganda concerning the fivefold enrichment of the Russian workers during the twelve-year period under discussion.

One of the best-informed and most objective of Russian economists, the late Sergei Prokopovich, came to some interesting conclusions. He found that during the period of the first Five-Year Plan (1928–32) "there was less per capita production of foodstuffs and consumer goods than before the war"; thus, "wages at the end of the First Five-Year Plan were below prewar scales." He found that "in the course of the years 1935–39 real wages gradually went up"; however, the average real wage of workers and employees at the end of the 'thirties was "below the prewar level and below the level of the last years of the NEP," i.e., 1927–29. "The war in central and western Europe [from 1939 to 1941, when Russia was not a belligerent] produced another fall in real wages."

In general, it may be said that the wages of workers and other employees had risen considerably in the 'twenties after the years of famine and civil war and the first period of the NEP; later beginning with 1930, they fell considerably during the period of collectivization and the first Five-Year Plan; and they began to rise again about 1935, but the increase was uneven for the various categories of workers and other employees. At the end of the 'thirties the higher, more skilled groups, as well as limited circles of Soviet "specialists," had attained and even passed the prewar level, while the lower mass of workers and other employees had at the most reached the prewar level, which, incidentally, constituted a considerable improvement over the early 'thirties.

On the basis of a detailed and objective study of Soviet wages, Mrs. Janet Chapman [4] has arrived at the following con-

4. Janet G. Chapman, "Real Wages in the Soviet Union, 1928–1952," *Review of Economic Statistics, 36* (1954), 134–56.

clusions: The 1928 level of real wages was the highest reached during the Soviet period, but was below the 1913 level. The fluctuation since 1928 is shown in the following figures, taken from Mrs. Chapman's study:

1928—100
1937— 81
1948— 56
1952— 90
1954—100 (approximate)

Beginning about 1930 wages dropped sharply. They rose again in the middle 'thirties and attained a prewar peak of 81 in 1937. They dropped again during the war and early postwar period and then rose again, reaching the highest level of the Soviet era in 1954–55.

The term "average wage" is often misleading because it does not reflect the large and growing differentiation in remuneration of various classes of workers. Real wages in the upper brackets (Stakhanovites and others) are sometimes higher than in 1913, while in the lower brackets wages are on much the same level or even below the level of those on the eve of the first World War.

The new Russian workers are divided into many groups, with all the local economic differentiations that constitute the difference between poverty and sufficiency. Many a dramatic struggle revolved round this question during the first fifteen years of the revolution, many a utopia perished in the course of these conflicts, and many a person was "liquidated" for trying to preserve some semblance of equalitarian relations, to prevent the lower grades of workers from falling too low, and the higher categories from developing into a "labor aristocracy." These Communists of the old school could not understand why it was necessary to have a revolution only to return later to the old system of unequal wages and to restore the higher class of wage earners whom the Communists of all countries had detested as a manifestation of the "capitalist corruption" of the workers.

What triumphed in the end, as is well known, was that "realism" which has subjected everything to the task of expanding industrial production. Under the prevailing conditions of scarcity, higher earnings naturally provided the strongest incentive to better, more productive work. For this reason, piecework became the prevailing system, and, what is more important, the wage scales set by the state for the skilled began to exceed many times the scales of the lower, unskilled workers. The distance between maximum and minimum wages was intentionally and systematically widened. This soon led to the development of that class of workers which, under Soviet conditions, is repeating the history of the "labor aristocracy" of England and other countries at the end of the nineteenth century. The "Stakhanovites" of the 1930's and the "advanced workers" in general who make up this aristocracy, though not very numerous, are at the present time the most virile, determined, and skillful of all the workers in Russia. Not only are the wages of the Stakhanovites many times larger than those of the rest of the workers, but they also enjoy many special privileges and advantages. We need only refer to summer "rest homes" and sanatoria, to which Stakhanovites have a priority.

On the basis of two Soviet studies published in Moscow in 1949–50 Harry Schwartz has compiled the following listing of salaries and wages in Russia in 1949–50 (in rubles a month): [5]

Director, scientific institute	4,800–6,000
Senior scientific researcher	2,800–3,500
Head of elec. pwr station	2,500–3,000
Chief engr., Magnitogorsk iron and steel plant	2,500–3,000
Head of steel-making shop in large Urals plant	2,040–2,520
Assistant head of above shop	1,740–2,220
Director, national administrative office	1,700–2,200
Production foreman, Urals steel-making shop	1,500–1,920
Production foreman, steel-making shop in western area	950–1,200

5. *New York Times,* April 3, 1952.

Economist in large plant   790–1,000
Bookkeeper in large plant 410– 600
Driver of medium-size bus 550– 600
Driver of 2½-ton truck 360– 410
Stenographer 450– 600
Telephone operator 410– 525
Typist 410– 525
Rural kindergarten teacher 250– 350

THE best criterion of the standard of living of workers in all countries is the extent to which female labor is used, especially that of married women and mothers. Factory work is hard on women in general, resulting, as it does, in a higher degree of illness and other burdens; it is particularly hard on married women and mothers. Under ordinary circumstances only necessity drives the wife of a worker and the mother of a family to take a job. Work in a plant or factory involves neglect of the home; obviously it means that children must remain without their mother for many hours.

Housekeeping in Russia takes up much more time than in other countries. An interesting study of the time required for this purpose by the wife of a worker was made at the beginning of the 'thirties. It was shown, for example, that a woman wage earner can donate less than a quarter of the time to caring for her children that a housewife who is not earning wages can give. The former spends 470 hours in preparing food, the latter 997 hours. The former stands in line for purchases 152 hours, the latter 182 hours.

Especially interesting are the figures showing how the worker's home and clothing suffer when the woman of the house has to go to work; the nonwage-earning housewife devotes 228 hours to the care of the home and the family clothing, while the wage earner spends only 110 hours, or half as much time. In addition, work in the little family garden, so necessary and so widespread in Russia, demands much effort, too much for a woman burdened with factory labor as well as with housekeeping. For mothers of small children the necessity of working in a plant is frequently a personal tragedy.

So much ideological nonsense has been uttered on the subject of female labor that it has become difficult to grasp the elementary facts. Many journalists and travelers have pictured with great enthusiasm the expansion of female labor in Russia; they often represent it as a great achievement. "Women are guaranteed equality of opportunity, but they have also to accept the responsibilities. . . . The changed position of women in the Russian social structure was wholly good, both for them and for the country: crèches, nurses in uniform . . ."

These phrases are but unvarnished repetitions of what the writers have been told by Moscow guides, and parallel official declarations. "The woman works on a basis of equality with the man, both in industry and in the collectives," writes Sautin, chief Soviet statistician. "Such are the brilliant results."

No, factory work by women does not constitute, contrary to the opinion of many, any degree of progress. For most women it does not mean participation in social life. Their employment, to any great extent, is the consequence either of extraordinary political events, such as war, or of extreme poverty. Most ardent advocates of female labor have no conception of the pain and struggle which it entails for the mother of a family. Many writers who have visited Soviet Russia point to the network of day nurseries where small children are kept all day long; Soviet journals frequently take pride in the number of such nurseries. But this relatively cheap institution, found in some measure in almost every country, cannot possibly serve as a substitute for the home. It is particularly widespread in Russia not because of the nature of the "progressive" Soviet economy but solely because female labor is nowhere so common as in Russia. The wide use of government-operated eating places is no more inspiring. Of course, these are necessary when the wife works in a factory, but she and her family never cease to dream of having their own home in the true sense of the word.

Therefore, the percentage of working wives and mothers among higher social elements is much smaller than among Soviet workers.

The number of female workers in Russian industry at the beginning of this century was about 400,000 or about 18 per cent of the total of industrial workers. As in all countries, the number grew rapidly until the first World War, and reached 635,000 in 1913. Under the Soviet regime, female labor expanded to proportions unprecedented in any country. There were 28 per cent of women in industry in the 'twenties, but in 1933 they numbered 1,826,000, or 35 per cent, and in 1937 3,300,000, or 40 per cent.[6] There are no official figures on the growth of female labor during the next six years until the outbreak of the war. Even if the increase was not very great, it is certain that the percentage of women workers in Soviet industry immediately before the war was more than 40.

During the period 1941–45, according to official figures, the percentage of women in industry exceeded 70. However, this has no relation to any preceding data. The percentage of women workers naturally declined after the war, but in view of the tremendous loss of life of males at the front, it remains near 50 or more.

There are no figures to show the number of married female workers. However, the total number of women workers, running into millions, indicates in itself how large the percentage of wives and mothers must be. Another indication is afforded by the ages of these workers. At the beginning of the 'thirties, 80 out of every 100 women workers were more than 20 years old, while 60 were 24 or over. It may be fairly assumed that married women predominate in the general mass of female workers.

The percentage of female workers in Russia is higher than in any other European country or in the United States; except

6. In 1923, 404,000, or 28 per cent; in 1927, 700,000, or 28.2 per cent; in 1928, 769,000, or 28.6 per cent.

for China, it is probably the highest in the world. The United States presents the opposite extreme; western Europe occupies an intermediate position. Similiar significance attaches to the unprecedented increase in the employment of minors in Soviet Russia.

These facts throw more light than any statistical tables could on the question of the standards of living and wages of the workers. The mere physical existence of the workers is possible only because the number of breadwinners in each family is now greater than before; this constitutes the principal means of defense against inadequate wages. The number of nonworkers in each family has declined considerably.[7] Only by increasing female labor and that of minors is it possible to exist at all.

THE WORKERS AND THE COMMUNIST PARTY

IN THE light of the aforementioned facts, it is easy to imagine the relations existing between the working mass and the Communist party. The majority of workers, particularly those in the lower brackets, take no interest whatever in the party. Neither the discontented nor the obedient, loyal workers feel that they can derive any benefit from membership in the party.

But the top layer, which strives for advancement and has some reason to hope for success, derives marked advantages from party affiliation. Every plant has groups of workers who are released from their jobs, temporarily or indefinitely, for such tasks as organizing plant clubs, for "cultural-educational work," for the business of the plant committee, and so on. There are hundreds of workers who perform governmental or quasi-governmental functions—in the *Dosaaf* (Defense against Gas War and similar tasks) or collecting membership dues. Finally there are the Stakhanovites and "distinguished people," who have

7. Official statistics on this point reveal the following facts: In 1930 there were 2.05 dependents for each worker in a family; in 1934, 1.66; and in 1935, 1.59.

already moved forward. They are in the forefront; they find
the party membership card useful and sometimes necessary,
for it serves to open many doors.

The party, in its turn, follows a similar line of reasoning.
It has no need for the millions of average workers, except perhaps as evidence, for propaganda purposes, of its tie with the
working class; this was especially true in the periods of struggle
against the opposition. What the party now requires is the inclusion of the more active elements in its ranks. Even if these
remain at the bench, they are carefully husbanded, their activities are watched, and they are utilized for various forms of
activity as need arises.

In sum, about three-quarters of the industrial workers are
nonpartisans, about 15 per cent are in the Komsomol, and only
from 5 to 10 per cent belong to the party. The party has long
refrained from publishing data concerning this question; but
the fact is that the percentage of Communists among the workers has not increased.

An occupational census taken in 1933, at the end of the
first Five-Year Plan, disclosed that the proportion of all members of the Communist party and of candidates for membership among the workers, including apprentices, ranged from
8.4 per cent in the ceramic industry to 17 per cent in the machine industry. In the metallurgical industry the percentage was
13.9, in the building trades 6. The percentage of men was
double that of women. In the Komsomol, however, men made
up 13.8 per cent and women 18.6 per cent.

During the eight years between 1933 and Russia's involvement in the war, the number of workers doubled. During those
eight years the working mass was expanded largely by the influx
of peasant elements, the newcomers into the party having
worked as peasants only a short time before. These worker-
peasants showed no greater enthusiasm for joining the party
than the other groups.

DURING the war, from 1941 to 1945, the working class of Russia, particularly the men, underwent another transformation. Mobilization into the Red Army, embracing the youngest and the oldest age groups, took an immense toll of workers. Many did not return; others lost or had impaired their capacity for work. A number of industrial plants were moved to the east during the first years of the war and the plant workers were obliged to move with them. After the war many of the industrial establishments thus transplanted were ordered to remain at their new locations, and only a part of the workers returned home. Millions of women were drawn into the industrial apparatus and many thousands of adolescents and children had to work in plants.

During the course of the war working conditions became hard to the point of being unbearable. The working day was extended to ten, eleven, and at times twelve hours. The accident rate rose to ominous proportions. Food was scarce and often only private truck gardens (planted mainly to legumes) saved worker families from famine.

Real wages sank to the lowest minimum. There were three sources of food, as far as the worker was concerned: rationed food, which although cheap was insufficient and consisted mostly of bread; the canteens organized by individual plants, which sometimes were able to obtain the meats and fats almost totally lacking in the rationed food; and the individual truck gardens of the workers. The free market existed everywhere during the war, but its prices were prohibitive for the workers, and only in exceptional cases were workers able to obtain a few pounds of "luxuries" from this source.

The end of the war brought a speedy restoration of certain labor standards, for example the 48-hour week; vacations were again permitted; small children were excluded from factory work. As far as the standard of living is concerned, however, the improvement has been very slow.

Among those who returned from the war to the factories were men with a great deal of political experience, a fresh outlook, and new ideas. They have seen foreign countries, and what they observed of conditions in the West surprised and astonished them. They were now able to compare, from their own experience, standards of living in the West with those in Russia. They told hundreds of stories at home about what they discovered abroad. The famous Soviet solicitude for the well-being of its working class, about which they had been told for years and decades, was contradicted by their own observations of other countries. A great many workers, nonpartisan before the war, returned from the army as members of the Communist party; party membership, among other awards, was almost automatically conferred on every soldier who had distinguished himself in military exploits. Returning from the wars, these Communist freshmen had to undergo series of lectures in which they were imbued with ideas concerning the superiority of Russia over other nations. However, personal experience cannot be erased by persuasion, words, and press dispatches.

Meanwhile a great shortage of manpower, due to the war casualties, begins to haunt Russian industry. The lack of manpower is the greatest problem of Soviet economics today. The millions of women who have been drawn into the industrial process are no substitute for a normal recruitment of industrial labor. Lack of manpower is driving Soviet economy toward a rigid system of obligatory labor. The struggle against frequent changes of jobs on the part of workers was a constant preoccupation of the industrial managers in the 'thirties. Such workers, contemptuously labeled "fliers," were decried and sometimes punished for breaking their promises. Changing positions was but a substitute for the improvement of working conditions in the absence of real collective bargaining by trade unions. After 1940, when the war danger began to increase, the fight against these shifts assumed great proportions. In June, 1940, immediately after the fall of France, a law against "unauthorized quitting of employment" was adopted. The punishment was two to four months in jail. Two months later it was ordered that jury trials not be granted in these cases, since the jury was often inclined to sympathize with the defendant worker. In December, 1941, a decree raised the punishment in such cases during wartime to five to eight years of imprisonment; workers became "plant-bound" in the full sense of the word. In July, 1945, workers and employees previously sentenced for breaking labor laws were pardoned. The law itself, however, was not repealed and there is apparently no intention of repealing it. The press once again began to demand a "strengthening of labor discipline" and compliance with the law, reiterating its complaints concerning "fluctuations of labor" despite the severity of punishment.

Under other conditions this shortage of manpower would result in enabling the Russian worker to conduct a successful labor union movement, and many a strike would be bound to be successful. To prevent such a development, the Soviet trade unions have to be held down as before, and no free trade union movement is possible so long as the political system remains unchanged.

A return to the system of free labor, meaning the worker's freedom to choose his place of employment and leave it as he desires, is not possible at present. Precisely the contrary must be expected: because of the manpower shortage and the poor compensation for work, the search for other and better opportunities on the part of the worker will have to be fought by the state and it will make the labor system more rigid and severe.

While one part of the labor force has to perform compulsory labor in concentration camps, even the better-off class of "free" workers must gradually lose much of the freedom it formerly enjoyed.

THUS the Russian working class represents an entirely new,

very large, and rapidly expanded social class. The peculiarities of the Russian working class are the recent peasant origin of a considerable majority and the inevitable retention of the habits, traditions, and memories of the Russian village; a very low wage scale for the majority; the rise of a top layer with good earning capacity; a deep cleavage between the higher and lower elements. In addition there are the opportunities for the advancement of the docile; the helplessness of the mass; a network of "informants" in every shop and plant.

The result of these conditions is a vast social passivity, the absence of any kind of open or illegal organization, and, finally, a docility on the part of the great majority.

The Communist party has no fear of great political difficulties or danger from the workers. It may be right as far as the threat of hostile political movements is concerned. The first signal for any such movement will hardly come from the workers. But any political movement that might arise in other social strata would find a sympathetic response among many Russian workers discontented with the low standard of living, the unbridled power and control exercised by plant officials, and the unlimited power of the police in private life.

Chapter 5. THE PEASANTRY

For no other class in Russia have the consequences of the revolutionary upheavals been so tragic and disappointing as for the peasantry. This is true of their material comfort as well as their political aspirations.

After the first decade of revolution, at the end of the 'twenties, it became apparent that the NEP experiment, a private trade system within a Communist state, had already yielded all it could. After its potentialities had been exhausted, a new turn in Soviet policy became imminent. Two roads were open. For several years the "Leftists" had advocated a great program of industrialization and collectivization and an integral program of Communism. The "Rightists," with Nikolai Bukharin and Alexei Rykov at their head, continued to advocate private enterprise for the peasantry for the next period, and were prepared for new economic concessions. The government—Stalin—had to decide which way to go. It was a decision fraught with destiny.

The introduction of the NEP had brought a degree of pacification in the villages; the peasant uprisings ceased. Because of the primitive production methods of Russian agriculture, the peasant economy was being restored more speedily than that of industry. The new food tax on agriculture provided considerable foodstuffs for the cities, complemented by private trade.

The economic revival of agriculture was accomplished by a process of social differentiation among the peasants. Some peasants rented their holdings and moved to the cities, others rented more land and expanded their operations. The leasing

105

or renting of agricultural implements and machinery became a growing practice. The sons of large families left their homes to take jobs as agricultural laborers, while other peasants became their "capitalist" employers. Some had bad crops; others, having sold their products profitably in the market, returned from the cities with articles of "luxury" and added a second or third cow to their inventory.

All this was "within the law" but very dangerous. The members of the party and the Komsomol looked with animosity upon the new "capitalist" tribe, and the less opportunity the law gave them to combat this capitalist breed, the greater became their urge for a change in policy. "This is not what we fought the revolution for!" What was worse, the majority of the peasants, fearing a new antipeasant maneuver, refrained from expanding their economy. Having restored it more or less to the prewar level, they had acquired a modest measure of security as far as their own immediate needs were concerned, plus a small surplus for disposal in the market and tax payments. To have gone beyond that would have meant rising from the status of *seredniaki*—middle peasants—to that of kulaks, and exposing themselves to possible reprisals in the event of a political shift. In many places the peasants feared to sow too much, or to increase the number of their cattle; they purposely divided their land among their children in order not to be thought to have too much property. In this way the number of peasant households artificially increased from 16 million at the beginning of the revolution to 25 million in the middle 'twenties.

Thus the economic development of the villages was greatly limited by political conditions. The area of grain cultivation, which had fallen from 232 million acres in 1913 to 163 million in 1922, rose speedily under the NEP to 232 million in 1926. At that point, however, it remained stationary: the acreage was 232 million in 1927 and 227 million in 1928. The crop yield likewise remained stationary: in 1926 it was 76.8 million tons; in 1927, 72.3 million; and in 1929, 71.7 million.

The NEP could not last: either the peasantry would break through the outer political crust of the new order to create a new political system more compatible with its character and needs, or, in the event of the peasants' failure to mobilize the forces necessary to achieve this, the existing political regime was bound to remold the peasantry, transforming it from a class of private owners into an element of state economy.

The first-named course was essentially the program of the Rightists. To be sure, the "Right Opposition" was not a peasant party; both in its ideology and in its policy it was a group within the Communist party whose leaders had been Lenin's close lieutenants and regarded themselves as representatives of the working class. But, paradoxically enough, it was in the persons of these and other "working class representatives" that the peasants' hopes for a liberation from their new yoke found their last expression. The Right Opposition termed the policy of collectivization "military-feudal" in character; it issued warnings against its severe economic consequences. It opposed the mass extermination of the so-called kulaks. It considered individual peasant economy the key to the reconstruction of agriculture.

What the Right Opposition wanted was a great expansion of private agriculture—a road that every noncommunist government would choose. It did not consciously fear the growth of a peasant capitalism with all its implications for a Communist state.

The Leftists, on the contrary, were strongly opposed to any new concessions to the peasant. A huge industrialization was point one on their program, and they saw no other sources for new industrial funds than the village. To this end a reconstruction of the peasant economy was necessary. "Petty economy," Lenin had written, "gives birth to capitalism and to the bourgeoisie—constantly, daily, hourly, in elemental fashion and on a mass scale." "If we continue, as before, to maintain small economies, we shall inevitably be threatened with destruction," for "agricultural economy under the system of commodity production cannot free mankind from mass poverty and oppression." Until his death Lenin adhered to this idea; he declared that in Soviet Russia "the peasantry was the last capitalist class."

There was no difference between the positions of Lenin and Stalin on this point. "Is the restoration of capitalism possible in our country?" asked Stalin in 1928. "Yes," he replied, "it is possible. This may seem strange, but small production gives birth to capitalism and to the bourgeoisie, especially under the conditions of the NEP." When the food crisis came at the end of the 'twenties, Stalin drew the following conclusion from his theory: "The task is to transform the USSR . . . into a land of large agricultural economy, furnishing the market with a high percentage of its produce. . . . The rate of expansion of commodity grain production is lower than that of our increased grain requirements. Industry is growing. The cities are growing. The different regions are growing. Yet, production of commodity grain is growing at an extremely slow tempo." [1]

Despite his hatred of Trotskyism, Stalin maintained that "the greatest danger confronting us comes from the Right." Indeed, in setting up the collectives, Stalin was in reality putting into effect a plank of the Trotskyite program; he justified this before the perplexed party by saying that no adequate forces had been available to wage a war with the kulaks when Trotsky demanded it.

"In 1926–27," Stalin declared, "the Zinoviev-Trotsky opposition had sought to impose upon the party a policy of immediate offensive against the kulaks. Was it possible for us to undertake such an offensive with any hope of success five or

---

1. According to Soviet statistics, before the first World War the landlords and well-to-do peasants supplied the market with an average of fifteen million tons of grain annually. Now the landlords had vanished, while the number of well-to-do peasants and the size of their establishments had been reduced. In consequence, at the end of the 'twenties, the amount of grain reaching the market from these "capitalist" sources was only two million tons.

even three years ago? No, it was not!" And the fact that the establishment of the collectives involved the extermination of part of the peasantry failed to impress Stalin. "What's bad about it?" he asked. "Why not apply extraordinary measures against the kulaks if it is all right to arrest hundreds of speculators in the cities and exile them to the Turukhansk region?" He denounced the Right Faction as pursuing a "liberal bourgeois policy."

The establishment of the kolkhoz system in the course of three or four years and the transformation of Russian peasants into members of collectives constituted the most radical upheaval known in history. Its effects were more profound and distressing than the expropriation of the propertied classes in 1918–20. There were, however, instances of resistance to an extent and in forms of which neither Russia nor the outside world had any adequate conception. The Soviet press, of course, did not report them, and the cities heard only fragmentary reports of riots, of their suppression, of mass exile. As a matter of fact, there were a great many uprisings embracing whole regions, revolts, ruthlessly suppressed by GPU troops. Tanks were let loose upon the peasants, whole villages burned to the ground and even bombed by government planes. The execution of captured rebels was resorted to with the object of intimidating and terrorizing the population, and was therefore of a mass character. But even where uprisings did not take place, the authorities systematically exiled kulaks, that is, better situated peasants, the term being applied also to many of the politically more conscious, more intelligent peasants apt to express protest. They were exiled to the far north and distant east, chiefly to Siberia. The instructions from Moscow demanded the complete "liquidation of the kulaks as a class." These, with their families, numbered in 1928, according to official statistics, 5,859,000 human beings. Some day we may learn how many of them were exiled; perhaps all were.[2]

2. See p. 138.

The reaction of the peasantry did not always take the form of uprisings. Even more threatening, perhaps, was their passive resistance. Under the new policy, the peasants were required to hand over to the collectives their livestock and implements; they preferred, however, to kill the cattle, sell the meat, or consume it themselves. In many instances, moreover, they wrecked their own equipment. The number of cattle, which had risen in the 'twenties, fell between 1929 and 1934 from 30.4

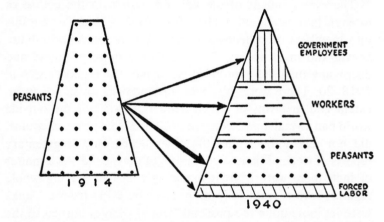

million to 19.5 million, the number of horses from 34.6 million to 15.6 million, etc. As a consequence of the general disorganization (and in part because of unfavorable weather), wheat production in 1931 declined 17 per cent. Since the state insisted on collecting its own share first, there was a terrible famine in many agricultural regions, with millions of dead.

The new system had taken definite shape by the middle of the 'thirties.

THE KOLKHOZ

ACCORDING to its rules, a kolkhoz is essentially a cooperative society, in which each individual participates with his own labor. Theoretically, the collective governs itself, introduces new machinery as it pleases, sells its grain on the free market, and, as circumstances permit, may earn considerable money. The collective contains the seeds of capitalist development, if taken hypothetically and independently of the political system.

But first of all the kolkhozes were designed as instruments for the extraction of agricultural products. From its crop the administration of the collective must pay to the state the required taxes in kind and money; it must pay also for the services of tractor stations, accumulate necessary reserves for seeds and other funds, retain a portion for feeding the cattle of the collective, and so on. Nearly two-thirds of the crop is consumed for these purposes. The rest is divided among members of the collective, but only after deductions have been allotted to managers, technicians, and other officials.

The cash proceeds derived from that portion of the crop and other products which the collective sells in the market are likewise subject to various deductions, including taxes payable in cash. The administrative personnel must also be paid from these proceeds. From the sum thus received by the individual peasant, he pays an income tax, as well as other levies. In 1937, one of the most profitable years enjoyed by agriculture, members of the collectives received 48 per cent of the collectives' receipts, the remaining 52 per cent having been used to cover various expenditures.[3] From the 48 per cent, the peasant has to pay at least 8 per cent in taxes, leaving him 40 per cent. This 40 per cent is further reduced by the fact that, in buying goods for his own use, the peasant must pay sales taxes sometimes amounting to more than 50 per cent of the prices he is obliged to pay.

The part played by the collectives as an instrument for the extraction of agricultural products is stressed in the minds of the peasants by the enormous apparatus of officialdom func-

3. A decree promulgated in 1937 required that at least 60 per cent of the cash income be divided among the members of the collectives. It is not known how this decree has been applied.

tioning in the villages. Neither Russia nor any other country had ever had such a huge swarm of officials. According to official statistics, there were 384,389 chairmen and vice-chairmen of collectives in 1938, 248,390 bookkeepers, and 232,421 chairmen of inspection committees. The whole personnel numbered nearly 1,000,000. In addition, there were 1,530,000 chauffeurs and mechanics employed at tractor stations. The total number of employees paid out of the peasants' labor was about 2,500-000. This, of course, did not include employees outside the economic administrative apparatus in the villages, such as treasury officials, police, teachers, and others.

It is easily understood why the peasant pays more attention to his own small individual holding than to the business of the collective: small though it may be, it serves as an important foundation for his existence. A great part of all cattle in the Soviet Union were to be found in these meager holdings. But even the 10 per cent of the grain crop produced by these holdings constitutes a tremendous help to the peasants.

At first the government had no intention whatever of permitting the peasants to retain any land for their own use; later, after the famines of the early 1930's, came a concession, formally recognized in 1934–35. But the amount of land granted for private use was kept down to a minimum, from one-quarter to one-half of a hectare.[4] Within a few years, however, these small holdings, into which the peasants had begun to put their labor, became not only a part of the source of food for their personal use but, in part, the mainspring of supplies for the cities; paradoxically, these small plots furnished, within three or four years, a considerable part of the country's agricultural production.

Before the outbreak of the war (1937–38) the average member of a kolkhoz put in 47 per cent of his labor hours in the kolkhoz, 33 per cent in his private plot or away from home, and the rest in his household. Millions of peasants began to

4. One hectare = 2.471 acres.

avoid working in the collectives. In 1937, according to official figures, 13,100,000 peasants worked less than fifty days a year in their collectives, and, of this number, 4,600,000 did not work a single day.

For this reason new repressions were hurled against the individual peasant holdings in 1939. It was discovered that in some districts such holdings had expanded to the gigantic size of three hectares, and that in others some peasants employed in collectives had two private holdings, while others were selling theirs. Orders were then issued limiting the right to such holdings and the right to keep cattle; at the same time, and quite naturally, the state increased its demands upon the members of the collectives. In some districts every peasant was required to work in his collective not less than sixty days a year; in others not less than eighty days. Failure to meet these requirements entailed the loss of all the peasant's rights, including the right to his own holding. This compulsory labor minimum showed that the system of dividing the product of the collectives in proportion to each peasant's labor was inadequate, and that compulsory labor was an added necessity.

From the peasants' point of view, the collectives are a tremendous pump for draining the product of their labor through many channels; while the machine and tractor stations, with their political divisions, party cells, and propaganda activities, represent a state apparatus for political and police control over the villages.

OLD WINE IN NEW BOTTLES

THE establishment of this system was novel to the point of being sensational. The government had counted on speedy acceptance of the new conditions by the peasantry because of the marvels of technical progress introduced in the collectives. Critics, both in Russia and abroad, expected a catastrophe in Russian agriculture. It soon became apparent, however, that both the government and the critics had been mistaken, for they had failed to take into consideration certain old and tried methods known throughout Russian history, which were retained in the Communist system of agriculture.

To be sure, the peasants who had long been accustomed to use the primitive plow and to fertilize the soil with manure suddenly came into contact with the wonders of foreign machinery, and in such quantities as were unknown to the best-ordered landed estates of old Russia, or even to the most efficiently regulated farms of western Europe. But behind the new brilliant façade of mechanized agriculture, there was a noticeable revival of old traditions. It was this tradition that the Rightist leaders had in mind when they called the kolkhoz system a revival of the feudal-military economy or the old serf system.

Throughout Russian history the peasant had enjoyed but a few brief moments as a free proprietor—thirty to fifty-five years, beginning with the 'sixties, in some cases with the 'eighties, of the last century, and until 1918. Before that, continuing for centuries, social relations in the villages followed this pattern: the majority of peasants were obliged to work for landlords; most of the land belonged to the latter, the peasants controlling only a portion. The peasants were compelled to work a certain number of days a week, in most cases three of six working days, on the landlord's estate. They lived only from the labor on their own land, and their objective was to reduce the amount of unpaid labor they were required to perform for the landlord.

This type of *corvée* labor on the landlords' estates was called *barshchina*. Another form of bondage was the *obrok* system; the *obrok* was a compulsory cash payment of the peasant to the landlord.

Peasant labor was compulsory, and the peasant was a serf. At the base of these economic relations was the state's need of a great army and of manpower, most of which, from the sixteenth to the eighteenth centuries, could be supplied only by the peasantry, the estates of the landlords serving as organizational centers.

Even after the emancipation of the serfs under Alexander II in 1861, the system of *barshchina* continued in some places for about twenty years, the peasants being required to work thirty-five to forty days each year on the estates. This system was abolished in 1883. What remained in many places until the revolution were the forms of share-cropping known as *otrabotki* and *ispolshchina,* as well as various other types of burdensome tenantry.

Characteristic of all these forms of peasant-landlord relations was the peasant's obligation to work for the landlord either without pay or in return for the lesser share of the product. For centuries Russia lived under this system; the nation expanded, grew more powerful, and achieved many a military success. But the foundation remained unchanged, and attempts at reform, undertaken from time to time, were unsuccessful.

The peasants themselves tolerated this economic regime for many generations, though not without complaint or efforts at resistance. In the seventeenth and eighteenth centuries great uprisings took place, sweeping entire regions, in addition to many local mutinies. In the middle of the nineteenth century the number of local revolts grew from year to year until the end of the 'fifties. All these mutinies were suppressed by local forces or by the army, which was itself composed of peasants.

For the regime of a vast country these sporadic outbreaks presented no real danger. They never threatened to develop into one united political movement, which presupposes determination and some degree of continuity. They were merely isolated protests against individual manifestations of cruelty, exploitation, and injustice—protests which died down as fast as they occurred and were soon succeeded by the same state of unquestioning obedience and submission to fate.

For the peasantry the system of collectives meant a return, in many respects, to the old order. To be sure, the private landlord was no more; instead there was the state-master; serfdom had vanished, and there were many other distinctions. History knows no perfect analogies. But there are also elements of the old in the new situation of the peasantry: a large economy, which requires "hands" and which the peasants give their labor to; the obligation to work diligently, without attempting to shirk one's duty; outside domination of one's household and labor; a pay system dictated from above; and, finally, the right to own a small plot of land. The small plot is one's own bit of land—small, to be sure, but precious. The collectives have been pictured as the most modern achievement of the twentieth century. But their chief elements are derived—and not accidentally —from the hoary past. "A feudal-military system," said the Right leaders to Stalin.

Of course, Soviet policy has not followed the old track because it deliberately wanted to revive the old Russian customs; on the contrary, the Soviet regime considers its policy extremely progressive. But there is small choice between economic systems, especially in questions involving the interrelationship of state and peasantry. Having repudiated the satanic principle of individual economy because of its inherent capitalist potentialities, but at the same time being in need of constantly increasing quantities of the peasants' products, the Soviet state really had no other way than to amalgamate the peasants into great administrative-economic units and to make labor compulsory. At the same time it was compelled to reduce the private holdings of each peasant to a minimum, in order not to lose his labor on the big landed estate known as the collective; and the hidden conflict between the state and the members of the collectives has continued uninterruptedly over the issue of the peasants' right to their own holdings and their obligation to work in the collectives.

A SIGNIFICANT social differentiation among the peasantry has been taking place since the middle of the 'thirties. First, a growing differentiation among the kolkhozes became discernible, and, second, a differentiation among the members of each kolkhoz.

Differences in the achievements of the kolkhozes were a natural consequence of differences in the fertility of their soil, in the quantity of land at their disposal, in their produce, in prices and other market conditions. They were the outcome of the long history of Russia's colonization, and similar to the former prerevolutionary differentiation between the peasantry of the crowded poor regions of central and western Russia and the more recently populated provinces of the south and east. Before the reforms of 1951–52 the sown area of an average kolkhoz amounted to 131 hectares in the Leningrad region, 273 in the Moscow region, 781 in the Ukraine, 1,414 in the Azov-Black Sea province, and 1,931 in the Saratov region. A prosperous kolkhoz does not, however, necessarily mean that its members are prosperous.

More significant is the second line of development, the differentiation among members of the kolkhozes, and the polarization of their poor and well-to-do elements. This evolution, which had naturally started before the war, has been accelerated by it. A member of a fortunate kolkhoz, working with his wife and three or four sons on the kolkhoz farm as well as on his own plot of land, has greater opportunities than, say, a poor widow. If a city lies nearby he has a free market to sell a part of his products—sometimes at fancy prices. He is not a kulak in the strict sense, since he is a member of a collective and does not hire labor; but if he is as clever and capable as a member of the liquidated class, he slowly climbs up the social ladder. However, these opportunities are limited.

Unlike the well-to-do elements of the cities, kolkhoz peasants play no part in the formation of public opinion and exercise no political influence. It may be that in their hearts they dream of other political conditions, that they fear the possible consequences of their comparative prosperity, and that they would prefer private enterprise to the present system. But their secret thoughts are of no real consequence at the present time.

THE COMMUNIST PARTY IN THE VILLAGE

IT is not difficult to understand why the peasants have played so insignificant a role in the Communist movement throughout the history of the Soviet regime.

In 1926 statistics of a party census showed that Communist peasants engaged solely in agricultural work were almost non-existent. In the whole of the Ukraine there were only 10,240; in Byelorussia, 1,350; and in all Great Russia, 51,000.

The beginning of collectivization was marked, on the one hand, by the dispatching from the cities of many thousands of party and Komsomol members for the purpose of setting up the new economic organization, and, on the other, by intensified recruiting of party members in the villages. New state institutions were being set up in the villages, offices with masses of employees, and these were naturally filled, as far as possible, by members of the party and the Komsomol. As for the collectives, they numbered more than 200,000. Only in part of the kolkhozes were the chairmen Communists.

For this reason the number of party members in the villages increased from 404,000 in 1930 to 790,000 in 1934. But this did not at all signify any rush of the peasants into the Communist organizations. On the contrary, Lazar Kaganovich reported to the party congress in 1934 that "50 per cent of the collectives had no Communists at all."

This complaint was repeated time and again. Two years later it was reported to the conference of the Komsomol that it had no organizations in 149,000 collectives.

At the 1939 party congress, the last before the war, Andreyev reported that "in 243,000 collectives there were 12,000 party groups with a total membership of 153,000"; that some collectives had only Komsomol groups but no party groups;

and that "in more than 100,000 collectives there were neither party nor Komsomol groups." Some of his figures astonished even the pessimists. In Byelorussia, for example, there were 9,665 collectives but only 44 party groups with a membership of 614; in the Vologda region there were 5,970 collectives but only 31 party groups, with a membership of 442; in the Perm region there were 3,314 collectives with 16 party groups and 274 members. Another delegate reported that in the Yaroslav region there were 36,000 party members but that only 2,500 were peasants.

In the Moscow region, a third delegate reported, there were about 250,000 Communists, but of the 6,556 collectives in this large region only 304, or 4.6 per cent, had any party units, while only 25 per cent of the collectives boasted units of the Komsomol. In 1938 the party had 27,000 condidates for membership, of whom only 334 came from collectives. A delegate from Leningrad reported that his party organization had admitted 28,217 members from the end of 1936 to March, 1939, but that of this number only 1,177 had come from the collectives.

Notwithstanding the intense efforts subsequently made to recruit party members, the results in the villages were insignificant. A year and a half later, the official organ of the Komsomol again complained that "in 90,000 collectives there were no Komsomol organizations." Immediately before the war, in the spring of 1941, the official organ, *Partiinoye Stroitelstvo,* reported that there were only 610,000 party members in the villages, or 19 per cent of the entire party membership, and these 610,000 embraced, in the main, the bureaucracy of the collectives.

Thus, after a quarter of a century, about 5 per cent of the urban population belonged to the party (not counting the Komsomol), while in the villages the ratio was 5 per 1,000; even this included the administrative apparatus of the state. The peasantry continued to stand aloof.

This was the reply of the Russian village to the claim that the kolkhoz peasants had reconciled themselves to the new system.

THE WAR AND AFTER

THE wartime policy of the government, as far as agriculture and the peasantry were concerned, was a direct continuation of the prewar system. Many expected that the Soviet government would call on the private initiative of the farmers and that a "realistic" encouragement of their private economy, particularly in the devastated and liberated areas, would follow. The aim of such a reversal could lie in a real reconciliation with rural Russia, a kind of new NEP in a war and postwar world. These expectations were soon shattered.

The government left no doubt that it was determined to travel the old roads. It was natural that the obligatory grain deliveries of the kolkhozes and the private economies as well were doubled; but the discrimination against private economy was discernible. Private peasants in the liberated areas were now obligated to deliver 30 per cent more products than the neighboring kolkhozes (before the war the difference amounted to between 5 and 10 per cent according to the decree of 1933). Animals, which were returned to southern and western areas after the expulsion of the Germans, went almost exclusively to kolkhozes, although private cattle, for example, exceeded the collective ownership by 50 per cent before the war. A decree provided for further increase of the number of kolkhoz cattle at the cost of private economies.

Obligatory work in the kolkhozes has been augmented since 1942. Before the war it amounted to 60 to 80 work days a year, but in 1942 the minimum was fixed at 100 to 150 days. Youths 12 to 16 years of age were made liable to work at least 50 days. People violating this decree had to bear the consequences: first, prosecution; second, the loss of all their kolkhoz privileges; and third, the loss of their plots.

All these decrees aimed at the restoration and strengthening of the kolkhozes and at further curtailment of private economy for the war and postwar period. Sometimes a paradoxical situation would arise. The collective economy is generally based on machines, tractor stations, repair shops, supply by industry, not to mention a steady supply of gasoline. This complicated system was disturbed when the automobile industry had to concentrate on war material, when gasoline transport was upset, and when workers were drafted for army service. The situation in the great area liberated from the invasion was naturally worst of all.

To a great extent agriculture had to return to old and at times primitive devices, since even horses were mobilized. Manual labor and work with horses and cattle more and more took the place of machines. Small economies were better adapted to the new conditions. Peasants worked on their plots, and workers and employees created millions of small subsidiary gardens of their own. However, the government adhered to its policy.

THESE conditions were strongly reflected in the attitude of the peasantry toward the war. This attitude, at first glance, was almost incomprehensible.

The Army, which was rapidly expanded after 1939, absorbing a large part of the adult male population, was from 70 to 80 per cent peasant in composition. It fought bravely, enduring without complaint unheard-of privations. The peasants who remained at home, however, reacted differently to the military situation. When the German troops invaded Byelorussia, and particularly the Ukraine, the peasants in the villages hoped for some improvement in living conditions under the regime of the invaders; they thought the Germans would probably dissolve the "Bolshevik collectives." At the same time, the behavior of the Germans in the occupied territories of Russia had begun to shatter the peasants' hopes. The seizure of grain, meats, and fats from the peasants; the many cases of violence, rape, and murder committed by the Germans; and the disappointment suffered by some Ukrainian intellectuals who had hoped for the establishment of an autonomous Ukraine under a German protectorate brought disillusionment. It also became abundantly clear that the Germans had no intention of abolishing the collectives. They soon perceived their value as a means of draining food supplies from the villages; knowing little of Russian village life, they preferred to deal not with millions of small economic units but with large agricultural organizations. They drove thousands of peasants and masses of cattle from the villages, while being unable to provide the Russian villages with machines and gasoline. Only in rare instances, by way of rewarding individual villages for acts of collaboration, did they grant special permission to break up collectives into individual holdings. Such occasions of division of land were marked by great celebrations, prayer meetings, military music, and other signs of general rejoicing.

Some pro-German illusions that might have existed in the minds of peasants in occupied territories were quickly shattered, while in the unoccupied regions, particularly in the east and in Asia, there was experienced the beginning of that typical wartime prosperity which is tantamount to impoverishment: a rise in the prices of foodstuffs sold in the "free market," with corresponding huge profits. Even before the war, peasants were permitted by law to sell their meat, milk, butter, and lard in the cities. This trade had been small in comparison with that conducted by the state, but in view of the terrific wartime shortages it assumed significance for the elements of the population that could pay high prices.

Prices increased with the catastrophic speed that characterizes periods of food shortage. City dwellers would hasten to offer hundreds and thousands of rubles for lard, meats, and potatoes; others, less prosperous, were frequently compelled to sell their clothing and domestic furnishings in illegal city markets at high prices in order to buy food. Peasants who went to the cities with small supplies of their products would return home with thousands of rubles in their pockets.

Who was the winner in this competition between city and village? The urban population was naturally irritated by the peasants' "avarice." "The villages are waxing rich on the misery of the people," the cities complained.

The peasants were amassing huge quantities of paper rubles. At times they understood the unreality of this wealth: "we give the cities goods and get paid in worthless paper"; at other times they made purchases with this money, but there was little to buy. The government endeavored to reassure them by pointing out that the state, which would continue to dispose of the bulk of commodities after the war, would sell to them at stable, relatively low prices, and that the peasants would be able to buy these goods in large quantities with their accumulated money, thus making a large profit. But such arguments were unconvincing in the light of the hard experience gained in Russian and other European inflations in the past.

The peasants were also urged to invest their accumulated savings in government loans, and huge amounts flowed into the State Treasury, accompanied by letters expressing devotion to Stalin. All this was pictured as a purely voluntary patriotic campaign. Letters from inflation millionaires were published in the Soviet press as manifestations of peasant patriotism.

At the same time, the collectives continued to supply the cities and the Army to the extent of their ability; in many cases they did so beyond their means. Whenever the government was confronted with instances of extreme need, the respective divisions of the party's committees would call upon its organizations in the villages to launch a campaign of patriotic offerings for the cities in the guise of voluntary contributions.

Such has been the strange picture of peasant activities during the war: self-sacrifice on the part of peasants in uniform; doubt and frequent hesitation on the part of their people at home; the delivery of large supplies to the cities and the army, both by collectives and individuals; the investment of part of the money in bonds for the benefit of the state.

Viewed as a whole, the picture may seem incongruous, but

such it was. The peasantry remained what it has always been—
the chief material source of great armies and supplies. As ever,
it gave to the state, without adequate compensation, its labor,
its products, and its sons. But, as was the case for centuries, the
peasantry remained deprived of its own independent political
or other organizations. There have been many stormy outbreaks of protest, but they have all died down, and obediently,
silently, and frequently against its own interests, the peasantry
continued to meet all the demands of the state.

IN 1945 the sown area in the liberated territories amounted to
69 per cent of the prewar acreage; crops were of course at an
even lower level. The kolkhozes had lost millions of men, and
the loss of manpower was not made good in 1945–46. The
yield per acre had diminished considerably. Many a kolkhoz
was slowly disintegrating; and they tended to serve mainly state
needs. The members were losing interest in kolkhoz agriculture and instead turned their main attention to their small
private plots. This was officially conceded to be true in large
areas, such as the Kuibyshev Region, Uzbekistan, and others.
"A weakening of the kolkhozes" was reported.[5] Still more profound was the crisis in the Ukraine, where under the Germans
many a kolkhoz had disintegrated and private peasant economy re-emerged.

But the government did not choose to follow the road of
pro-peasant "liberalism" and NEP. Restoration and strengthening of the kolkhoz system became the immediate program
for the postwar period. Party groups in the villages were instructed not to relax the system established before the war;
moreover, certain wartime measures, such as obligatory work
for the kolkhoz, were to remain in effect after the war. Privately
owned cattle were to be "commandeered" for the collectives.

The first postwar years were hard ones. The Germans had
caused great destruction of industrial machinery and the harvest

5. *Bolshevik*, No. 5, 1946.

of 1946 had been poor; in addition, the rigid system of collective economy was reintroduced. Over the years collectivization was gradually restored in its old form and even applied to newly acquired Soviet areas. The machinery of the MTS (Machine-Tractor Stations) was rehabilitated, destroyed homes were rebuilt, and the rural economy gradually emerged from the worst stage of its paralysis. The improvement, however, was appallingly inadequate. Seven years later, Stalin's successors, Malenkov and Khrushchev, revealed to what a low level agricultural production had dropped in those days. Production of meat and dairy products, they noted, still lagged—a state of affairs that reduced the majority of the urban population to a low living standard.

Nevertheless no retreat from the kolkhoz policy was contemplated. On the contrary, new measures were taken to achieve a high degree of government control of the peasantry. We have seen how before the war most of the collectives had no Communist party units; this situation now had to be remedied. In 1950 a sweeping drive was launched to "aggrandize the kolkhozes"; within two years the 254,000 collectives had been reduced to 94,000. The new, larger units averaged 1,693 hectares in size as compared with the previous 589 hectare average. It goes without saying that a unit of the Communist party, agency of the Central Committee, has since been at work in almost every kolkhoz.

Another important measure was the great purge of chairmen of the collectives; in the summer of 1955 Khrushchev replaced 30,000 former kolkhoz chairmen by new people from the cities. Carried out with fanfare and the support of the press, the sweeping operation [6] was rooted in the conviction that the basic principles of Soviet economy are sound and that failures are the fault only of the personnel. The degree of success in the field of agriculture to be expected from the reforms instituted under Khrushchev will be no greater than that achieved by his predecessors.

6. See below, p. 345.

SHOULD Russia experience any great domestic upheavals in the near future, the peasantry will not initiate them. It has at present neither the strength nor the ability nor the experience for any political initiative. The most it can do is to throw the weight of its influence on the side of an opposition movement after an upheaval, though without playing any independent role. New upheavals would be certain to affect the villages and lead to the restoration of an individual peasant economy in place of collectives. A new division of the land would become inevitable in the event of violent political clashes, and regardless of the programs put forward by the conflicting elements.

But should developments take a less violent form, without a popular revolution or counterrevolution, events in the villages would take a different turn. Under such circumstances the state would retain its authority, and its requirements would continue to play an important role. The development of the agricultural economy would then proceed along evolutionary lines— through gradual expansion, for example, of individual peasant holdings at the expense of the collectives, the lowering of prices of commodities manufactured in the cities, the reduction of taxes, and granting the peasants the right to expand their activities in any direction. The final effect would be the same, as in the first instance—a redistribution of land.

The interests of the peasantry, however silent and obedient though it may be, are bound to assert themselves very loudly in any political crisis. It will long continue to make up the most numerous section of the Russian people. And the economic requirements of the state and nation demand the speediest possible solution of the problem presented by Russia's hundred million pariahs.

Chapter 6. FORCED LABOR

Until only a decade ago the issue of forced labor in Russia was not recognized by the general public in this country. Vague reports about mysterious "labor camps" were viewed with doubt; eye-witness accounts were considered anti-Soviet propaganda. It was indeed extraordinary that in the middle of the 'forties this author was obliged to begin a chapter about a numerous social class of a great country by demonstrating that it exists and constitutes one of the most important factors in the development of the nation's economy. But the conscious blindness of some and the false information disseminated by others contributed to the fact that this class remained a mystery to many readers.

To be sure many books and personal memoirs have been written on the subject but there were, of course, no official data. Much that was pertinent had been mentioned by American and British correspondents. For example, here is what Quentin Reynolds wrote in 1942 in *Only the Stars Are Neutral:*

"A few miles outside of Kuibyshev we passed one of the big concentration camps reserved for political prisoners. Beyond that we saw a long line of them working on a new road. There were about 800 of them . . . On their faces there was no sign of hope. A few soldiers with rifles guarded them carelessly, for there was no place for them to run. Steele and I looked at each other and winced . . . We winced, I think, because these 800 prisoners were women."

In 1943, upon his return from Russia, Wendell Willkie published a series of articles as well as his book. He refrained from saying anything very unfavorable of the Soviet government; nevertheless, he recalled the astonishment he had felt when,

after visiting some Russian cities, he had failed to find a concentration camp in the suburbs of Yakutsk, an exception to
the rule:

"We drove into Yakutsk in a heavy black Soviet limousine.
Between the airfield and the town we looked for the usual concentration camp we have seen in some other cities—half barbed
wire fences, with sentry boxes at the corners. But there was
none, or at least we never came across it."

Wendell Willkie's articles appeared in the *Reader's Digest*.
Before their publication in book form, Willkie was persuaded
by influential people in Washington to omit the paragraphs on
forced labor quoted above.

Walter Graebner, an objective and accurate correspondent,
reported in *Round Trip to Russia:*

"On the way we passed hundreds of . . . barracks inhabited
by labor battalions and political prisoners. It is impossible to
get any accurate reports as to the number of prisoners, why they
were arrested, etc. In many places I noticed high roofed platforms, on which rifle-bearing guards stood to see that no one
escaped."

In *Blind Date with Mars* Alice Moats told of a conversation
with a Soviet citizen, who said to her:

" 'Do you realize that as a result of the great purge, there
is not one person in this country who has not either been locked
up himself or has had some member of his family in a concentration camp? Right now there are some fifteen million people
in work-camps and prisons!' Later a person in a position to
obtain accurate figures set the number at twenty millions."

The British journalist, Philip Jordan, who called his book
Russian Glory, wrote:

"It was at Ryazan that we saw something which, had I seen
it at home, would have filled me with indignation and disgust,
but which, because its victims seemed not to care or to object,
was no concern of mine. Standing beside our train was a long
line of flat cars intercepted here and there by barren prison vans.

On the flat track opposite our window were perhaps thirty women guarded by an NKVD man with a tommy-gun. They were squatting like dummies there, and had not moved for hours, for against their exposed flanks the first snows of winter had driven, and there they now rested. One of the women had a baby in her arms . . . The others were monoliths of sorrow hatched rudely out of some shabby but enduring stone. There was something terrible about them. They looked like the last inhabitants of a world they could remember to have once been populated by a race of happy men who existed no longer."

The correspondent of the *New York Herald Tribune*, Walter Kerr, told in his book, *The Russian Army*, of the reception received in Murmansk by the large convoy in which he arrived in Russia:

"As we came alongside the pier we saw hundreds of Russian workmen waiting to unlash the planes from our decks and to hoist the tanks from our holds.

" 'Let's give them a cheer!' shouted one of our Scotsmen, and after the men had cheered they stared in amazement at the blank, disinterested faces of the Russians on the dock. There was perhaps a half minute of awful silence, and then the mouth of the Scotsman hardened and he screamed out, 'All right. Go to hell then!' And he turned his back and went below, followed by the rest of the crew. A few hours later we found out why the Russians had failed to acknowledge the cheer. They were prison laborers, far from their homes, guarded by police with rifles and fixed bayonets. I suppose they did not care whether any country sends supplies to Russia."

The British economist Leonard Hubbard, who had studied labor conditions in Russia, remarked:

"The quantity of labor at the disposal of the GPU in their various convict camps throughout the USSR ran into millions . . . The use of convict labor in the '30s has certain similarities with the use of serf and forced labor by Peter I."

Hubbard estimated the number of prisoners in Soviet concentration camps at "millions." There are, of course, no accurate figures. Those we have are subject to violent fluctuations. Reports current in Soviet Russia place the number at 15 to 20 million. These reports were the sources of Miss Moats' information cited above. But neither the Russian people nor those abroad can possibly have a clear idea of the situation. The subject is veiled in deep secrecy.

The late Polish Socialist Victor Alter spent about two years in Soviet jails as a political prisoner. He was released through the amnesty granted to Poles in 1941 and lived in Kuibyshev for several months before his execution in December of the same year. Alter was intensely interested in the subject of concentration camp prisoners. He concluded that their number was between 8 and 12 million. On the other hand, a person who had been an inmate of a concentration camp in northern European Russia, writes in a report as yet unpublished:

"Soviet officials contradicted sharply the statement that the figure [of prisoners] was above 20 million, but they did not object to a figure within the limit of 20 million."

The American engineer John Littlepage, who was employed by the Soviet Gold Trust in Siberia for a period of ten years, until 1937, estimated the number of forced-labor workers as "from one to five million," and stated that "the recent purges, which affected hundreds of thousands of persons, undoubtedly added to the labor army."

Boris Souvarine, French authority on Russia, in his biography of Stalin, estimated the number of prisoners in concentration camps at 5 million, exclusive of forced-labor groups such as "inhabitants of isolation camps and the exiles." As of 1937, he declared, "15 million condemned in the various categories would probably be the number most in accord with the facts."

Victor Kravchenko, in his *I Chose Freedom*, reported that "in official circles, twenty millions became the accepted estimate of this [prisoner] labor reservoir; the estimate did not

include the boys and girls forcibly torn away from their parents
and assigned to regions and industries in which manpower
shortages were sharpest. The war industries of the USSR rested ⟨
primarily on slave labor."

In 1945 the Polish authors Sylvester Mora and Peter
Zwierniak published a book, *La Justice Soviétique,* which included numerous firsthand reports of former prisoners of Russian labor camps. The authors of this well-documented book
rejected all exaggerated estimates of the population of the labor
camps, by prisoners and guards alike, yet reached the conclusion that the 38 camps known to them include a total of 9,500,-
000 prisoners; a multitude of smaller camps situated outside
these larger units may contain another five million men and
women. "We are convinced that the number of 15 million
prisoners is rather modest for the years 1940–42."

The official census returns for 1937 have not been published at all, and of the returns for 1939 only a few summarized
figures appeared. They include, naturally, no indication as to
the labor camps. In statistical tables these inmates, as well as
all other groups of exiled or deported people, were registered
just as "Wage Earners" in addition to officials and free workers.
From 1934 to 1939 members of this wage-earners group, with
their families, allegedly increased at a rate which even in the
Soviet Union is impossible: from 45 to 84 million. The veil
has not been lifted so far, but there can hardly be any doubt
that the inclusion of all deported people in the great class of
wage earners in 1939 is partly responsible for the statistical
miracle.

LABOR AS AN INSTRUMENT
OF CORRECTION

THIS extraordinary historical phenomenon of the creation of
a great social class by the methods of exile, imprisonment, and
compulsion has had its ideological inception in high principles

of humanity and love of one's neighbor. Faith in labor, in the enlightening effect of labor, in the correction of the human being through labor, in treatment of criminals by the therapeutic use of labor, the appeal of the all-embracing poetry of labor, gave rise to concepts in Soviet Russia which ultimately found expression in hard and bitter experience. One can think of no greater paradox than this transformation of the most advanced ideas of the science and morals of recent centuries into a cruel system of compulsory labor for millions.

The road to hell is paved with good intentions. The contemporary world is given to forgetting rapidly and it no longer remembers the furor and resentment provoked, before the revolution, by the soul-shattering description of life in Russian prisons and places of exile; few, indeed, remember George Kennan and his *Siberia and Exile,* the books of Emil Dillon, Peter Kropotkin, and the thousands of pamphlets and articles published in the world press concerning the sufferings, horrors, the barbarism practiced in Russian prisons. Until 1917 the Russian penal regime occupied an increasingly prominent place in the political literature of the world, as the Russian revolutionary movement expanded and thousands of intellectuals, writers, and political leaders passed through the gates of Russian jails.

However, the number of prisoners in the old Russian *katorga* (penal servitude) was much smaller than in the Corrective Labor Camps today. In 1900–05 there were 15,000 such prisoners; in 1910, 28,742; in 1913, 32,757, with only 5,000 political prisoners.

All members of the Bolshevik old guard had experienced imprisonment, and like all other revolutionists, they had reached the firm conviction of the need of radical prison reform: abolition of the accursed *katorga,* of "prison companies"; the need of humane treatment of prisoners, as long as prisons remained necessary for a short "period of transition"; the recognition of the human rights and human dignity of prisoners. The principle generally accepted was "correction rather than punishment." And labor in prisons was considered to be the best means of correction. Systematic work, particularly for professional criminals, was regarded as good training for a useful social life, because it made possible the acquisition of new habits, of technical skills, and facilitated the criminal's transformation into a useful member of society. These ideas, derived from the non-Communist science of the nineteenth and twentieth centuries, had been incorporated in the general ideology of Bolshevism, whose leaders wrote the word "labor" in capital letters, a word that played the role of a universal moral principle. The basic program of Bolshevism guaranteed to all "the right to work," and only those who toiled were to enjoy political rights: "He who toils not shall not eat."

The penal policy of Bolshevism constitutes perhaps the most interesting monument of the early years of the Soviet regime: it was a striking mixture of the cruel "Red terror" and liberal concern for the "care of prisoners." Occasionally, innocent people—even hundreds of them—were executed, but those who escaped execution could reasonably hope to be released from prison. The famous Cheka, which later developed into the all-powerful OGPU, at first had no right of sentencing prisoners but merely had the duty of conducting preliminary investigations; the sentences were imposed by special tribunals, which as early as two months after Lenin's assumption of power had received the right of condemning prisoners to "corrective labor."

But the first years, judging by decrees and official instructions, were marked by the highest, most humane intentions. According to instructions promulgated in 1918, a prisoner, while "obliged to do physical labor," received compensation commensurate with trade-union wage scales, including overtime pay. The laws for the protection of working women and minors and for inspection of industrial plants were proclaimed applicable to prisons as well. Vocational training of prisoners was made obligatory. It was forbidden to address prisoners with the familiar "thou"; prisoners were permitted to smoke; occasionally they were granted "leaves" and were permitted to live in private quarters; finally, it was intended to make wide use of the parole system.

"Punishment must be devoid of any semblance of torture and must not subject the prisoner to useless and unnecessary suffering," declared the Commissariat of Justice in a document issued in the heat of the civil war, in December, 1919.

Concentration camps, first introduced in the autumn of 1918, were intended for "the counterrevolutionary bourgeoisie." But at the same time, the Communist Party Congress (March, 1919) adopted a program calling for the replacement of prisons by corrective establishments, reaffirming the principle that "labor is the chief method of correction and training." Recalling the French revolution and Voltaire—"make a man diligent and he will be honest"—the promulgated reforms called for abolition of "fetters, handcuffs, solitary confinement, deprivation of food, interviews through bars."

The criminal code of 1922, seeking to draw a contrast with the capitalist world, limited imprisonment to a maximum of ten years. This was more humane as compared not only with old Russia but with the most democratic countries. Regarding the United States, in particular, Soviet textbooks and lectures on criminology sought to expose the cruelties of its prisons and drew comparisons between the principles—the principles, to be sure, not the practice—of the American and Soviet penal systems. All this was sincere at that time: the Soviet leaders believed that the time was not far distant when crime would quickly decline in Russia, the prison population would be radically reduced, and the penal system would become the model for the entire world.

Meanwhile practice remained strangely remote from principle. The civil war had ended but the prison population grew from year to year, and rather rapidly. The police apparatus, political and criminal, was expanding and becoming more efficient; new types of punishable offenses made their appearance. In 1922 the prison population totaled 57,200; in 1927 it was 122,700. In 1929 it rose to 242,000. The number of administrative punishments imposed (i.e., without trial) increased sixfold from 1923 to 1926. The prisons became congested, for there was room for only 80,000 persons.

And with the end of the 'twenties the government entirely ceased publishing figures concerning the number of prisoners in jails and concentration camps.

Still greater was the disappointment with respect to education and training of prisoners. Resolutions of party congresses, articles in the press, the instructions of the Commissariat of Justice, direct court orders—none found any expression in practice. There were no workshops in most prisons and the few that did exist were without tools and equipment. Moreover, there was still much unemployment at the end of the 'twenties and any increase in prison labor naturally reduced the available job opportunities for the unemployed. In some instances sentences of forced labor were carried out fictitiously: the prisoners remained at work at their former places of employment, spending their nights in jail, and were eventually released altogether because of the prison congestion. These privileges were not accorded to political prisoners, however.

According to official figures only a third of forced labor sentences were carried out at the end of the 'twenties, despite considerable efforts to put them into effect.

THE FIRST LABOR CAMPS

THE first true Corrective Labor Camp appeared in 1923 and soon became the model for many such camps. Modest in size, it was established on the Solovetsky Islands, in the White Sea. The inmates of the Archangel concentration camp were transferred to this new institution. Unlike most prisons, the Solovetsky camp was placed from the very beginning under the authority of the OGPU. It was shortly abbreviated to SLON—the Russian initials for "Northern [Forced Labor] Camps for Special Assignment." Its location in the far north had the advantage of requiring only a small guard, because escape was almost impossible, and the distance from all centers, especially those abroad, permitted the introduction of a rigorous regime which in an even harsher form became the rule in the 'thirties.

The Solovetsky camp had 6,000 prisoners in the middle 'twenties, a figure which remained stationary until 1926–27. Most of the prisoners were "politicals," i.e., members of non-Communist parties, priests and monks, professors, "nepmen," and many lawyers of nepmen. So-called "wreckers" appeared somewhat later, as did hunger strikers from other prisons, and "anecdotists," that is, persons exiled for spreading political anecdotes critical of the Soviet regime and its leaders. Then came many Trotskyites and other Communist dissidents. From 1928 on, the number of "campers" increased rapidly to 30,000; soon the Solovetsky camp and adjacent annexes expanded, part of it toward the mainland. In 1929 the Northern Camp Administration embraced seven concentration camps, of which the Solovetsky camp was only one. The total population of these northern camps on May 1, 1930, was 662,257, according to N. Kiselev, a former OGPU official. This figure is confirmed from other sources.

At first the northern camps had no great economic significance, and originally they had no economic aims. Because of climatic conditions there was no agriculture on the Solovetsky Islands, the prisoners being occupied primarily in lumbering and fishing. But this type of forced labor no longer had any relation to the idyl prescribed by the Corrective Labor Code. Trade-union wage scales, the eight-hour day, and labor inspections no longer existed. In reality, it represented the revival of the old Russian system of hard penal labor under a cruel, uninhibited administrative regime. Food supplies from the mainland arrived irregularly and were always inadequate; in the matter of clothing the situation was even worse. The death rate through cold, disease, and suicides was very high. Kiselev reports 183,-490 deaths for the five-year period of 1925–29. Particularly difficult was the situation of the comparatively small number of women. "I did not know a single woman [in the camps], unless she was old, who in the end had failed to give herself to the Chekists," writes Kiselev. "Otherwise, she would quickly and inevitably perish."

The years 1929–30 mark a turning point in the history of the concentration camps. It was the period of the second revolution, and its reverberations were felt in the most remote human settlements. From the initial experimental labor camps of the 'twenties there developed a great class of forced labor at the beginning of the 'thirties.

Many factors contributed to this process. The vast program of industrialization, begun in 1928, required huge numbers of additional workers, such as industry did not have at its disposal. The construction of railways, highways, and canals, which constituted a very substantial element of the various Five-Year Plans, required millions of workers, largely unskilled. The production of lumber for export had to be stepped up considerably because of the decline in production of wheat and oil, formerly the chief commodities of Russian export, due to the mechanization and collectivization of agriculture. It was hard to enlist workers voluntarily for the difficult jobs of metal, mineral, and coal mining in the far north and east. New industrial centers were being built in the east, particularly in Asia —Magnitogorsk, Kuzbas, and others. Everywhere there was the problem of recruiting masses of unskilled labor for the speedy construction of new cities. Finally, as part of the war-preparedness program, it was necessary to build new railway lines, many airdromes, barracks, thousands of miles of military roads, and much else. Where were the necessary labor forces for all this construction to be obtained in the face of the labor shortage in the expanding plants and factories?

But then came the collectivization of agriculture, which the government coupled directly with the "liquidation of the kulaks." This liquidation, as we have seen, meant the exile of millions of peasants from the villages to forced labor. The collectivization campaign continued for four to five years, from 1929 to 1934. The enormous network of Corrective Labor Camps developed precisely during that period. Built on the Solovetsky model, they now became an economic enterprise of first-class importance. Their boss, the OGPU, became the greatest employer in the USSR and in the world: not a single branch of heavy industry, not even the Commissariat of Heavy Industry or the Commissariat of Transport, commanded such an army of "hands" as was at the disposal of the OGPU at the beginning of the 'thirties.

To meet the problem of the increased need of labor power, the government passed new legislation and issued a number of new instructions. In 1928 the Soviet of People's Commissars intensified the "measures against hostile class elements." In November, 1929, it decided to alter radically the entire penal system, to abolish imprisonment in general as a means of punishment in favor of the system of Corrective Labor Institutions. The Soviet of People's Commissars ordered that all those "sentenced to deprivation of liberty for a period of more than three years be exiled to Corrective Labor Camps in distant parts of the USSR"; those sentenced to shorter terms were to be sent to Corrective Labor Colonies (reserved, as a lighter measure of punishment, "for toilers only"). Judges were strictly forbidden henceforth to mete out short prison sentences without hard labor.

The consequences made themselves felt immediately. In 1927 hard-labor sentences totaled 18.6 per cent; three years later they rose to 56.5 per cent. Short-term sentences in 1927 were 32.1 per cent; in 1930, 1.9 per cent. Limited deprivations of liberty amounted to 8 per cent in 1927, and only 2.6 per cent in 1930. Publication of the actual number of sentences was discontinued because of the enormous totals. The population of the forced labor camps grew rapidly.

The general political climate became intensely grim. In August, 1932, the government promulgated a law concerning the "protection of state property," characterized by unprecedented severity and directed principally against peasants who refused to turn over their property to collectives. The punishment prescribed for violations was either death or "deprivation of liberty for not less than ten years." This law was very widely applied, but the exact number of sentences remained unknown. In the midst of this stream of repressions, P. Postyshev declared in behalf of the Central Committee of the party at a congress of lawyers in 1931, "We will retain our penal system in all its ruthlessness, our repressions, our measures of suppression against the class enemy."

In July, 1934, the former OGPU was transformed into the NKVD, under which there was organized immediately the Chief Administration of Corrective Labor Camps and Labor Settlements (GULAG), whose duty it was to administer the many growing forced labor camps. The NKVD was vested with the right "to order without trial expulsions, exile, and imprisonment in Corrective Labor Camps for a period of not more than five years." A year later the NKVD was given charge of the construction of all highways. To put the police in charge of highway construction may appear incomprehensible in the United States, but it was quite natural in Russia under the prevailing conditions.

SUCCESSFUL DEVELOPMENT

THIS regime of ruthlessness operated in the same direction as the general trend of collectivization and industrialization. In 1928, as far as can be established, the class of forced labor was about 30,000; in 1930, about 650,000; and by 1934–35 it had reached millions.

These numbers continued to grow, in some years quite rapidly. They included: first, ordinary criminals, formerly maintained in prisons; second, kulaks, whose numbers were particularly large after 1931–32; third, participants in peasant mutinies, which at times had swept entire regions, and all of whose inhabitants suffered exile; fourth, "counterrevolutionists," that is, members of non-Communist parties and sympathizers; fifth, Communist-oppositionists, who comprised a very large number of exiles, particularly in the period of the great purge of 1936–38; sixth, national groups, exiled as a whole as a preventive measure, such as Soviet citizens of Polish nationality in the middle 'thirties (after Poland's *rapprochement* with Germany); [1] this category also includes Germans (Soviet citizens) exiled from various regions of European Russia and Siberia, especially after the beginning of the Russo-German war.[2] Added to the categories of exiles mentioned were "socially hostile elements" in the newly occupied regions in 1939–40. Hundreds of thousands were exiled from eastern Poland, the Baltic States, and Bessarabia. In addition there was the systematic exile of the population residing along the frontiers, as on the Finnish border, and from many places of the Far East; in other places, too, where fortifications were in the course of construction, tens of thousands of civilians were driven to the east and north.

In addition to these principal groups comprising the basic mass of forced labor, there were numbers of Chinese brought to the labor camps; Greeks from the Crimea and the Black Sea region; Kazakhs, Uzbeks, Tadzhiks from central Asia; Turks and Armenians from the Turkish and Iranian borderlands; "speculators" (black-market traders), smugglers, persons guilty of misusing state funds, of whom there were many in the 'thirties; and finally many former employees of the OGPU-NKVD.

---

1. There were approximately 626,000 Poles in Soviet Russia, but it is not known what part of the Polish population was exiled.
2. Germans in the Soviet Union numbered 1,423,000.

From all the foregoing it is apparent that there have been and are various categories of forced labor in Soviet Russia. Some have been condemned to direct exile; others are sentenced to Corrective Labor Camps; there are many groups not sentenced by the courts but exiled by way of precautionary action, such as those moved from frontier regions. Living conditions of the last category, that of the so-called "special migrants" and "voluntary migrants," are much more tolerable than those of the first-mentioned group. Of the national groups, for example, exiled to the east after the occupation of the Baltic States and eastern Poland, about one-third were sent as prisoners to concentration camps; the rest were domiciled, without sentence, in other camps. The "aristocrats" among those condemned to forced labor are not required to live in camps but may have their own private quarters, under strict supervision; frequently they are separated from their families. Because of the advantages they enjoy they come closer, however, to the class of free wage earners. At the opposite pole of the forced-labor system are the inmates of Corrective Labor Camps in the Far North.

All of them have constituted a gigantic reservoir of manpower for the Soviet economy.

THE FIVE-YEAR PLANS

THE great projects carried out during the period of the first Five-Year Plans were executed on the basis of the experience obtained through the Solovetsky labor camp. In 1930 it was decided to build the gigantic White Sea-Baltic Canal, the project being entrusted to Genrikh Yagoda, the notorious chief of the OGPU (executed in 1938). The work began in November, 1931, and was completed in 1933–34; the number of workers employed in the concluding period—all of them recruited from the labor camps—was nearly 300,000. The canal is situated along the Finnish border; some of the workers managed to escape across that frontier, and, in the middle 'thirties, made public descriptions of life in the labor camps; these writings, checked against one another, presented what seems to be a clear picture of the situation.

Thus, for example, a French engineer employed in Russia and sentenced to forced labor, having managed to escape across the Finnish border, published in the French magazine *Etudes* a detailed description of the conditions of life and work in the construction of the White Sea-Baltic Canal; his account coincided with many other descriptions.

"More than 200,000 prisoners were employed on the project," he wrote. "More than 50,000 died during a period of a year and a half. The work day was eleven hours. There were no Sundays or any days of rest. Interruptions occurred only during transfers of workers from one camp to another. The work tasks were set very high, and food rations very low. Those who carried out their prescribed task received 800 grams [29 ounces] of bread daily; those whose performance was only half of the prescribed norm received 300 grams [11 ounces]. Besides bread, a watery soup and salt fish were the only foods. Most of the work was done by hand, without mechanical appliances. Despite the terrible Karelian cold, prisoners were forbidden to build camp fires: 'You can warm up by working!' they were told. This camp was named by the prisoners 'Hell of Ice.' I myself saw dead people who had been frozen with axes or saws in their hands. From 25 to 30 men died daily in winter. Responsibility for discipline was placed collectively upon each company: if a prisoner escaped the rest were punished by extension of their terms of service. Those caught escaping were shot."

From a purely economic point of view the project was a success: the canal, 142 miles long, was completed on schedule, including many dikes, locks, dams, etc. The cost was comparatively low—95,000,000 rubles—which is not surprising considering the form of labor employed. The canal was named the Stalin Canal, and its official opening was marked by a great celebration, widely publicized in the press. Some fifteen Soviet writers wrote enthusiastic articles, emphasizing the social significance of the project in regard to the labor employed—the transformation of criminals into useful members of society. Some prisoners, particularly genuine criminals, spoke and wrote about the beneficent effects they had experienced under the fatherly influence of the OGPU—in the hope of obtaining clemency. When Maxim Gorky visited the project, the prisoners assembled to greet him sang the following lines:

> We are prisoners of a free land
> Where there is neither suffering nor torture,
> We are not being punished, but reformed.
> This is no mystery, no secret.

And, indeed, 72,000 prisoners—all of them criminals—were amnestied upon completion of the project.

The policy of "reforging" camp inmates became a prominent theme of Soviet press propaganda; in reality, this was an attempt to soothe the consciences of those who were compelled to witness the monstrous expansion of forced labor in Soviet Russia. The policy of "reforging" was put forward to justify the severity of the system, the extremely difficult conditions of life and work, and the actual revival of the old *katorga*. Camp papers published for the benefit of the prisoners by the prisoners themselves bore the title "Reforging." "Our principle," wrote thieves and robbers, "is: We give everything, we demand nothing." Also:

> Our slogan is—forget the past,
> Drop your former habits:
> Forget all dives and wine
> And drills and master keys:
> Get into the ranks of toiling men
> In the battle for the Five-Year Plan.

For the outside world and for the Russian public, in particular, this was to serve as a moral justification of the new institution.

Simultaneously with the construction of the White Sea-Baltic Canal, and particularly after its completion, the government launched a number of other projects. Among these was the Moscow-Volga Canal, technically a very complex undertaking, with pumping stations, hydroelectric works, and river depots. In 1932 this project was placed under the OGPU. Construction began in 1933 and was completed in 1937. About 200,000 workers were employed. Upon completion of the project, 55,000 prisoner-workers were released before expiration of their terms in view of their successful "reforging."

At the same time (1932–33) other projects were under way in the Vishera camps, in the Urals, where 300,000 workers were employed. Other great projects were also under construction, including chemical works on the Berezina, the great Siberian-Turkestan railroad, and the Baikal-Amur road. Construction was also under way in the Kuznetsk region in western Siberia, where a new industrial base was being established: coal and iron mines were opened in an almost deserted area without housing or workers; the population of this area grew from 128,000 to 770,000 within a period of eight years. An additional track of the trans-Siberian railroad was being laid to meet the military needs of the Far East. The government's task of establishing a separate supply system for the Far Eastern armies to make them as independent as possible of European industry required millions of hands. Added to all these projects were many others, including new mines, lumber mills, military works. Toward the end of the 'thirties a network of forced-labor camps embracing an enormous population was spread over northern Russia, particularly in the Archangel, Vologda, Olonetsk, and Kem areas, and the prisoners were employed on the great railroad construction from Kotlas to Vorkuta. There were also many camps in western and eastern Siberia.

Early in the 'thirties new gold deposits were discovered in northeast Siberia, and soon a network of labor camps emerged in this region. Conditions of climate and distances from inhabited settlements made them the hardest of all Soviet camps, fraught with the gravest danger to the lives of the prisoners.

In February, 1932, the steamer *Sakhalin* arrived at Nogayevo Bay, where only a few huts of native Tunghuzs stood. Jan Berzin, the chief of the Far Eastern camps of the NKVD, came ashore with a group of workers who carried with them construction material. They began to erect the city of Magadan— later the capital of an important region under the *Dalstroy*. Highways were built to the north and west; later several railroad lines were added.

The Dalstroy was an enormous kingdom of the MVD in which the free native population had become a small minority. A few steamers belonging to the MVD used to transport prisoners to Magadan from Vladivostok, where the prisoners arrived by train from European Russia; from Magadan they were distributed to the various camps. Each steamer made 12 to 15 trips a year (before the war) carrying thousands of men and women on each trip. Meanwhile Magadan became a city with large buildings, an electric power station, and a theater for the multitude of officials. During the war it was the residence of the Dalstroy's chief, Ivan Nikishov, member of the Supreme Soviet. The total population of prisoners in the Dalstroy region has been variously estimated; despite the lack of reliable figures, it seems likely that at the peak of the boom they totaled over a million men and women, who, in addition to mining gold, performed a great many other tasks, including construction of roads and air bases, fishing, and lumbering.[3]

"The number of inmates in the concentration camps," it was reported in September, 1938,[4] "has assumed astronomical

3. It is reported that gold and platinum were shipped to Russia proper from the Dalstroy by special MVD aviation units.
4. *Sotsialisticheski Vestnik*, Paris, 1938, No. 24.

proportions. Gigantic works are under construction: for example, the Verkhne-Kolymsk road, extending from the Sea of Okhotsk, is being built with bare hands, without any mechanical appliances. The center of this project is at Nogayev, where there is a huge labor camp to which thousands upon thousands have been exiled. People are dying there like flies, perishing in various ways, without anyone knowing about it, for the sentences dooming victims to prison and labor camps carry with them the notation: 'without right of correspondence.' This is how they live under horrible conditions of boredom, bad food, in complete isolation from the outside world, slowly dying from weakness and exhaustion, hunger and constant thrashing of the nerves. They are buried alive!"

During the war—that is, since June 22, 1941—the camps acquired an even greater significance. New buildings had to be erected for evacuated plants; great works were under construction in Arctic and White Sea ports; railways were hurriedly built in various sections of the country. These projects were also completed quickly and according to plan if they had direct bearing on the conduct of the war. All this involved, of course, a heavy cost in human lives. But the work was done, and this appeared to be the important thing. Those who believe that success justifies the means may point to the defeat of Germany as justification of the system of forced labor.

Between 1941 and 1945, the population of the labor camps was considerably depleted. A part of the prisoners were pardoned to be inducted into the Red Army; this mercy was not accorded to political prisoners, however. Another reason for the reduction of forced labor was hunger, particularly in the remote parts of the north and east. In many regions transportation broke down and even in the large cities there was enormous privation. As for the prisoners, they died in hordes. A large part of those who arrived at the camps in 1940 were Poles; these were freed late in 1941 in accordance with the agreement between General Sikorski and the Soviet government. For these reasons the labor camps toward the end of the war began to present a serious problem as far as their economic objective was concerned.

After the war Russia's gradual rehabilitation, and particularly the upsurge of her industry under the successive Five-Year Plans, benefited considerably from the forced labor system. Prewar mining, building, and industrial development sites, at which forced labor was employed, were renovated and expanded. New canals were built, new railroads constructed, new mines operated. In addition to the ambitious projects which had existed before the war, a number of new ones emerged; small units grew to tremendous size. Forced labor was required in great masses. Among the most important areas of development in the postwar era was the Vorkuta region in the Komi Republic, beyond the Arctic Circle, which attained importance as a source of coal for Leningrad. While the exact number of inmates of the Vorkuta camps remains unknown, they are estimated to total about 500,000. Another coal-mining region with much forced labor is the area in Central Asia where the Karaganda camps are located, which have grown considerably since the war. The formerly small camps of Norilsk, situated beyond the Arctic Circle in North Siberia, have become the center of a new "Yenisei industrial plant." Norilsk is now a booming city with a population of at least 120,000 prisoners. Founded in 1939, Norilsk served at first as a producer of nickel, copper, and platinum. After the war the northern part of the Yenisei River was closed to foreign travel; mining of uranium became the main activity of the camps.[5] The sweeping goal of the Five-Year Plans could not be fulfilled without a new influx of fresh labor to replenish the human losses sustained in the concentration camps. The replacements have come from various sources:

First, during the war, five small national Soviet Republics

5. *New York Times,* January 16, 1955.

were abolished because of the political unreliability of their population. These included the German Volga Republic, the Crimean Republic, and three others, with an aggregate population on the eve of the war of about three million. It is not known exactly what part of their population was deported when the territory was annexed to the neighboring Soviet Republics (chiefly the Russian SFSR).

Secondly, in 1945–46 the civil population of territories which had been occupied by the Germans supplied a considerable number of persons suspected of collaboration and fraternization with the occupation forces. Most of these were quickly sentenced to long terms of compulsory labor and shipped to labor camps.

A third source was Russian soldiers who had served in the German armies or in any way under German command after being taken prisoners—Vlasov troops and others—and considerable numbers of civilians, men and women, who, as deportees in Germany, had to some extent aided the German war effort. Many thousands of these who were in areas occupied by British and American troops were taken into captivity by the Western Allies and then forcibly returned to Russia under a special agreement concluded by the three governments. Public opinion in Britain and America was unaware, however, how many thousands of eventual forced labor prisoners were thus shipped to Russia by the civil and military authorities of the democracies.

A fourth source was the war prisoners from Germany and her satellites and, after September, 1945, also Japanese troops captured in Manchuria. This group was valuable not only because of their number but also because among them there were highly qualified workers, skilled engineers and technicians of great value to the Soviet economy. While the bulk of German prisoners of war, who had been living in special camps, were returned to their homeland after a few years, those among them who had been charged and often falsely, with crimes (mainly theft) were shipped to the general Soviet penal institutions; their sentences were often as long as twenty-five years. A large number of them were repatriated in 1953–54, after Stalin's death, and the rest in 1955–56.

The fifth source of recruits was found among the political deportees from Germany and other European nations, of whom there was an influx after the end of the war. Included were those who were found "unreliable" or opposed to the specific kind of "democratization" in East Germany and other Soviet-occupied areas.

A sixth source were anti-Soviet elements in the newly annexed territories in Europe, in particular those in the Western Ukraine and the Baltic states. For a number of years the guerrilla groups and civilian population suspected of sympathizing with and aiding the anti-Soviet underground supplied human material for Soviet deportation sites.

Finally, the unprecedented wave of crime that followed the war helped to fill the gaps in the old and new forced labor camps and colonies.

THE NETWORK OF LABOR CAMPS

THE class of forced labor was as essential to Soviet economy as are the free workers, collectivized peasants, and state employees. Without the armies of forced labor the state economy could not have attained the effectiveness which it had reached at the beginning of the war. Without them the army could not have been supplied. The Soviet social-economic system cannot exist without forced labor. One might as well expect a bridge to remain in use with half a frame. Optimism would be justified if the mainspring of class formations in Russia emanated from the caprice of a supreme leader; the fact is, however, that the development of the huge class of forced labor in Soviet Russia arose not from the good or bad will of individuals but rather as a consequence of the specific principles upon which the Soviet State has been founded.

The economic basis for this phenomenon is simple enough. The gigantic program of investments required of millions of human beings that they contribute many more values to the state than they were receiving; their daily labor had to produce a greater value than the value of the food, clothing, and shelter which they absorbed. The difference between the values they created and the values they used constituted the surplus utilized by the state for its construction purposes. To increase this surplus to a maximum has been the basic task of Soviet economy. If this sphere of Soviet economy were to be freely studied in the scientific works of Soviet economists or in Soviet universities, we would be told, in terms of Marxian economics, of the Soviet State's need of "surplus labor," that is of its requirement of large surpluses over the values consumed by the workers.

The lower their consumption the greater the surplus left to the state. But to reduce consumption below a minimum was considered irrational because of the consequent speedy decline in the productivity of labor. For this reason the system of labor introduced in the camps took into consideration both factors: the need of encouraging the worker's interest by making food allotments conform strictly to his output and the need of making his labor as cheap as possible—an objective attainable only under conditions prevailing in prisons and forced-labor barracks.

From the economic point of view, the labor camps embrace a huge army of labor operating under severe discipline and this army can be moved rapidly and efficiently in any direction. A leading feature of the organization is the utter mercilessness displayed with regard to the individual. Added to this is the aversion felt by the workers for their tasks, for the officials, for the regime, a loathing perhaps akin to that displayed in the labor relations that existed on some colonial plantations a hundred years ago.

Material at our disposal makes it possible to draw a picture of the conditions under which the class of forced labor lives.

The camps on which we have information comprise only a part of the total.[6]

I. RUSSIA IN EUROPE, *Northern Regions*

1. Abez'-Inta	23. Plesetsk
2. Archangel	24. Pokcha
3. Balychygan	25. Rugozero
4. Belomorsk	26. Savinobor
5. Belush'ye	27. Segezha
6. Franz Josef Land	28. Solovetsky Islands
7. Kandalaksha	29. Sortavala
8. Kargopol'	30. Suoyarvi
9. Kholmogory	31. Syktyvkar
10. Knyazh-Pogost	32. Tot'ma
11. Kotlas	33. Ust'-Kulom
12. Kozhva	34. Ust'-Shchugor
13. Kuloi	35. Ust'-Ukhta
14. Kur'ya	36. Ust'-Usa
15. Medvezhegorsk	37. Ust'-Vym'
16. Mezen'	38. Vaigach
17. Molotovsk	39. Vanz
18. Monchegorsk	40. Vel'sk
19. Nar'yan-Mar	41. Veslyana
20. Novaya Zemlya	42. Vorkuta
21. Pechora	43. Vytegra
22. Petrozavodsk	

II. RUSSIA IN EUROPE, *Central Region and the Urals*

1. Asha	5. Chkalov
2. Astrakhan'	6. Chusovoi
3. Borovichi	7. Elabuga
4. Chelyabinsk	8. Gorky

6. Of the various lists of Russian concentration camps the most recent has been compiled by B. Yakovlev and A. Burtsov. The authors were in a position to use information brought over in 1953–54 (*Kontsentratsionnyie Lageri SSSR*, Munich, Institute for the Study of the History and Culture of the USSR, 1955).

II. Russia in Europe, *Central Region and the Urals* (*cont.*)

9. Ishimbai
10. Ivanovo
11. Ivdel'
12. Izhevsk
13. Karabash
14. Kashin
15. Kazan'
16. Kirov
17. Kizel
18. Kopeisk
19. Kostroma
20. Krasnotur'insk
21. Krasnoural'sk
22. Kuibyshev
23. Kungur
24. Kustanai
25. Kuznetsk
26. Leningrad
27. Magnitogorsk
28. Miass
29. Molotov
30. Morshansk
31. Moscow
32. Nizhnyi Tagil
33. Orsk
34. Ostashkov
35. Penza

36. Ramenskoye
37. Rezda
38. Rezh
39. Sama
40. Saransk-Pot'ma
41. Shadrinsk
42. Shcherbakov
43. Solikamsk
44. Stalinogorsk
45. Starodub
46. Svirstroi
47. Syzran'
48. Tavda
49. Tetyushi
50. Tikhvin
51. Tula
52. Turinsk
53. Ufa
54. Uglich
55. Ulyanovsk
56. Ural'sk
57. Verkhne-Ural'sk
58. Verkhnyi Ufalei
59. Vologda
60. Volkhov
61. Yaroslavsl'

III. Russia in Europe, *Southern and Southeastern Regions*

1. Baku
2. Dnepropetrovsk
3. Krasnovodsk
4. Makhach-Kala
5. Nal'chik
6. Nikopol'

7. Sal'yany
8. Stalingrad
9. Stalino
10. Sukhumi
11. Tbilisi
12. Uman'

IV. Russia in Asia, *Northern Siberia*

1. Berezovo
2. Byugyuke
3. Gorali
4. Karaul

5. Kyusyur
6. Mirnoye
7. Nordvik
8. Noril'sk

9. Podkamennaya Tunguska
10. Pokur
11. Salekhard
12. Tura
13. Turukhansk
14. Ust'-Port

15. Ust'-Vorkuta
16. Vereshchagino
17. Verkhne-Imbatskoye
18. Veslyana
19. Vilyuisk
20. Yakutsk

v. RUSSIA IN ASIA, *Southern Siberia*

1. Abakan
2. Akmolinsk
3. Aktyubinsk
4. Aleksandrovskoye
5. Aldan
6. Bodaibo
7. Chita
8. Ekibastuz-Ugol'
9. Erofei-Pavlovich
10. Irkutsk
11. Kemerovo
12. Kokchetav
13. Kolbashevo
14. Krasnoyarsk
15. Kyzyl
16. Leninogorsk (form. Ridder)
17. Mariinsk
18. Narym

19. N. Shadrino
20. Novosibirsk
21. Olekminsk
22. Omsk
23. Petropavlovsk
24. Prokop'evsk
25. Semipalatinsk
26. Sretensk
27. Stalinsk
28. Taiga
29. Taishet-Bratsk
30. Tobol'sk
31. Tomsk
32. Tyumen'
33. Ust'-Kamenogorsk
34. Vitim
35. Zayarsk

VI. RUSSIA IN ASIA, *Central Asia*

1. Alma-Ata
2. Andizhan
3. Bureya
4. Chardzhou
5. Chelkar
6. Dzhezkazgan
7. Fergana
8. Frunze
9. Irgiz
10. Kagan

11. Karaganda
12. Karakas
13. Kazalinsk
14. Kurgan-Tyube
15. Kzyl-Orda
16. Pakhta-Aral
17. Taldy-Bulak
18. Tashkent
19. Turkestan

VII. RUSSIA IN ASIA, *The Far East*

1. Aim
2. Allaikha

3. Askol'd (island)
4. Ayan

VII. RUSSIA IN ASIA, *The Far East* (*cont.*)

5. Balychygan	20. Nizhniye Kresty
6. Birobidzhan	21. Ozhogino
7. Iman	22. Pomori
8. Izvestkovyi	23. Sakhalin
9. Kamchatka	24. Seimchan
10. Khabarovsk	25. Sredne-Kolymsk
11. Khonu	26. Stanchik
12. Kolyma	27. Stolbovoye
13. Komandor Islands	28. Suchan
14. Komsomol'sk	29. Tebyulyak
15. Kuril Islands	30. Tiksi
16. Magdagachi	31. Ust'-Kamchatsk
17. Maior-Krest	32. Ust'-Mil'
18. Nikolayevsk	33. Ust'-Srednikan
19. Nizhne-Tambovskoye	34. Verkhoyansk

There are forty thousand and more prisoners in each of the bigger camps. They are divided into *lagpunkty* (concentration points), *lagkolonii* (concentration colonies), and *lagtochki* (administrative centers).

Inmates characterized as kulaks, counterrevolutionists, mutineers, and "socially detrimental elements" are regarded as capitalist elements; the "purely criminal" cannot, of course, be characterized as such. The criminal elements in the camps consist almost entirely of confirmed professionals of the criminal world, dubbed "thirty-fivers" (from Paragraph 35 of the Criminal Code). The official view concerning the various class groups in the labor camps is as follows:

"Class differentiation in the camp: hostility between 'thirty-fivers,' on the one hand, and counterrevolutionists and kulaks, on the other. The 'thirty-fivers' insist that they are not opposed to the proletarian state . . . The kulaks, however, fear to be together with the thieves and do not consider them full-fledged humans. The 'thirty-fivers' are beginning to look upon the counterrevolutionists and kulaks as class enemies." [7]

For this reason the camp administration looks favorably

7. I. L. Averbakh, *From Crime to Labor* (Moscow, 1936), pp. 192–193.

upon the "thirty-fivers," from among whom overseers of the inmates are chosen. Among the professional criminals are many gangsters of great daring and initiative, natural leaders of criminal bands, called in prison slang *pakhans* and "Ivans"; eager to win the favor of the administration, they are prepared to do anything, without exception.

"This type of inmate yields the cadres of the commanding staff both in [prison] economy and educational activities. The administration relies upon this element for support" (Averbakh).

The northeastern camps of the Yakutsk region are situated even farther to the north than famous Turukhansk, the most terrible place of exile of the prerevolutionary era. Those exiled to Franz Josef Land have no hope at all. This island had been entirely unpopulated until recently, and under the Soviet regime it was originally only a meteorological station. Not much better is the situation in the Kamchatka camps or on Chukotka. Together with some camps in the extreme north of European Russia, this group constitutes the places of most severe imprisonment and forced labor. To these camps are sent delinquents from other camps, in accordance with OGPU instructions of November 28, 1933: "All chronic loafers, malingerers, and dissimulators are to be sent to distant northern camps."

Below is a description of one of the northern camps in the late 1930's, given by a person who himself was an inmate:

"I was brought to the Labor Camp on the Onega River. There I found about 35,000 prisoners. Like all other camps this camp is a purely economic institution. The prisoners work on undertakings and are supposed to be paid for their work. Bread is the basis of their food. The size of the bread rations depends on the output of their work. They get a hot meal twice daily: between four and five in the morning and between eight and nine in the evening. During the day you don't get anything but hot water. Sugar is unknown. No fruit or vegetables were ever given to us. Up to the outbreak of the war the bread ration amounted to 900 grams (as a maximum during the war the ration was reduced to 650 grams). No clothing was provided for the work, no mattresses, no blankets or pillows. We used to sleep on the floor in barracks or on dirty bunks.

"Our work was in the forests near Archangel. We had to cut trees. In our camp there were several hundred women, to whom the same rules applied. The younger tried to make up the low salary by selling their bodies: there were many prostitutes among them. The price was 500 grams of bread.

"We had to work in our own clothing. After two or three weeks our suits were torn to pieces: the prisoners were half naked. The temperature was very low: even in June we had up to twenty-five degrees of Celsius below zero [—13° Fahrenheit]. After twelve to thirteen hours of work in the snow-covered forests, we used to return to the barracks thoroughly drenched. In the same rags we went to sleep: there was nothing to cover ourselves with. Very often these rags were stolen. And after such nights we had to get up in the mornings in the same rags, cold, frozen, half dead.

"The prisoners could not wash. Men did not shave. There was no time for it; there was no need for it. We used to work without respite. Sunday was also a working day. Even May 1 was a working day. The majority of brigades in my camp had no rest during the entire period I spent there.

"The great majority of the inmates were political prisoners, divided into two groups: one of them was 'spies,' the other 'socially dangerous elements.' The first group consisted mainly of people from national minorities. In my camp, for instance, there were 400 Greeks, old inhabitants of the Kerch region in the Crimea, who had suddenly been arrested in 1937–38— they were sentenced to five to eight years in labor camp. Russians and Ukrainians used to get ten years as dangerous elements. The reason for their arrests was usually the occupation of their parents (middle-class people, rich peasants, civil servants, intelligentsia, and . . . Communist-oppositionists).

"The work is being done promiscuously—in day and night shifts: in subpolar conditions it makes no difference, as during the winter the day is only two to three hours long. Almost all prisoners are suffering from scurvy, loss of teeth.

"The penal labor camps are places of the greatest moral degradation: prostitution, thievery, swindles mark this struggle for existence."

The author of the report concludes as follows:

"A sad picture: slowly, almost invisibly the mass of silent, dirty men in torn clothing moves—going to work or returning from it. Every now and then someone in the crowd slips and falls on the snow or into the mud. Nobody stretches out a hand to the fallen: you have got to save your own energy. Only the guard helps with his rifle to get up."

And here is another description. It concerns the labor camps near Kolyma in eastern Siberia, in 1940–41.

"In the Kolymsk region there are many separate camps, scattered over hundreds of miles. For this reason the names of the camps are given as 'On the 400th Kilometer,' 'On the 1,000th Kilometer,' 'On the 1,500th Kilometer,' and so on.[8] These camps are hidden in the mountains or are situated along the River Kolyma, in the distant Tundra, extending northward to the shores of the Arctic Ocean. It is very difficult to reach them, approach being possible only by water. In good summer weather it takes seven days from Vladivostok to get there, in stormy weather fifteen days, in winter even longer. Before the war, however, there was communication by air.

"Winter begins at the end of September. In the camp 'On the 1,500th Kilometer,' for example, there was snow one meter high on September 20. The temperature was minus forty and

8. The mileage refers to the position of the camps along the course of the Kolyma River.

lower. The inmates, inadequately clothed, are dying in masses in such temperatures. They wear waistcoats of poor quality and trousers. At night they can cover themselves only if they have blankets of their own, and they wrap their heads in sacks. The two brothers M. died within five minutes of each other: they left their barracks in seventy degrees below zero and were almost instantly frozen.

"Russians are in the majority, but one also meets other nationalities—Germans, Greeks, Chinese, although these are few. I met an exceptionally large number of Poles of Russian citizenship, arrested merely on suspicion of espionage for Poland, or even without suspicion, as early as 1936–38.

"To Kolyma they send political prisoners, serious offenders, those condemned to death and then pardoned: among the non-political prisoners there were murderers, thieves, burglars, prostitutes. Nonpolitical male and female offenders are as a rule put together with the political prisoners, whom they are allowed to order about and to whom they often 'administer justice,' since political prisoners, unlike the criminal offenders, do not enjoy the protection of the authorities.

"Very often the chiefs of individual camps are recruited from among former prisoners, and the prisoners, whether they are political or not, are being treated according to the caprice of the chief. For example, in the Camp of A., where I worked in the fish industry, the chief was a former petty criminal. He used to treat us better and was more considerate to the prisoners. On the other hand, in O., the chief, also a former prisoner, treated prisoners horribly.

"The conditions of work for men: twelve working hours a day . . . Women's working hours: eleven hours; an hour's break for dinner counts as the twelfth hour. In the 'well run' camp in M., the best of the camps in Kolyma, the break for dinner lasted up to one and a half hours. Women prisoners are wakened at night if the exigencies of work require the bringing in of coal, cabbage, potatoes, firewood, no matter what the temperature may be—at night it is always very low; this extra work is demanded regardless of the number of hours worked in the daytime. Without taking into consideration the number of hours spent at work during such a night shift, the women are sent at daybreak to their normal work.

"In the camps of Bukhta Nakhodka [near Vladivostok] only people who worked were fed. As there were too many prisoners in that camp for the work available, a part of them, whether capable or incapable of working, were left behind in the barracks, where they were not given any food. Their overseers, recruited among the nonpolitical prisoners, collected money from those sent to work, thus making it possible for them to receive food. I arrived, for example, at Bukhta Nakhodka after a journey of sixty-one days in a railroad car of the NKVD, when we received only bread and water. The train was full, twelve to fifteen people in each compartment, lice everywhere; it was only possible to sit huddled up. A small space was always left free for those who wanted to stretch their legs (one at a time, in turn). There was no talk of food during the journey, although next door to us was the kitchen where food was being prepared for the guards and their commander. Even water was given to us only twice a day, in spite of the unbearable Siberian heat wave. Very often at some station or other our part of the train was simply sealed and moved to a siding, while the guards with their commanding officers went to the town for the whole day, leaving us without water and without any possibility of satisfying our physiological needs. Usually we were let out for this purpose three times a day if the convoy was good, and twice a day if they treated us badly.

"After this sort of a journey, lasting for sixty-one days, with some stop-offs, I arrived at Bukhta Nakhodka so weak that I was incapable of the smallest exertion. For this reason I was not sent to work, but as I was not working, I received no food. It was only owing to the help of an old Don Cossack (also a prisoner) that I managed to survive this part of my captivity.

"*Billeting conditions:*

"*Men.* In the '400 Kilometer Camp' the men made their own tents, covered with moss; in other camps there were wooden barracks, with crevices in the walls filled with moss, and leaking roofs. There were no sleeping accommodations, everybody slept on the floor; sometimes a few had a common bunk, if they were lucky. There were no blankets of any sort. Everybody was extremely cold. In the '400th km.,' which was considered an 'easy camp,' when the temperature fell more than forty-three below zero and there was a very strong wind, work was suspended and the prisoners were allowed to take shelter in their tents or barracks. Their clothing was abominable.

"*Women.* It depended upon the camp. In Arman, for example, they lived in new, very damp barracks, which leaked so badly that when it rained the women used to hang a blanket above their heads, but even that device helped very little. The barracks were comparatively clean. There were no mattresses. Each woman had a wooden bunk and was given a large bag which could be filled with shavings. They received also pillow cases (if they had pillows of their own) and a rug. The air was so damp and stale, the fog so heavy, that the women often did not undress at night. Only once a week they changed their underwear in the bathhouse.

"In Magadan [the center of the Siberian northeastern camps] two women's camps exist, only two streets distant from each other. In the first, there are half-decayed wooden barracks, inside a ruin of wooden bunks, and a dilapidated fireplace in which things could hardly be warmed up. After sundown there was no lighting. . . .

"One of the women's camps in Magadan was run by two young women leaders from the NKVD, both very pretty, energetic and hellishly tough and wicked. It was a sort of exemplary camp, perhaps even a show camp. Situated in a large area at the foot of the mountain, it was surrounded by barbed wire and a palisade.

"The stocks of clothing consisted not of the normal prison clothes, but mostly of garments confiscated from prisoners or those left by the dead, and of parcels sent by the families to prisoners who had died. I was witness myself of confiscation of personal property from newly arrived prisoners. I was myself ordered to surrender my sweater and old woolen underwear.

"During the summer season prisoners doing field work were sent out of the camp for a few weeks for haymaking. They live in tents or usually just under canvas stretched across poles. Men and women live together. Women who in this condition kept to themselves and went to sleep separately were made fun of and teased by the prisoners.

"Health, death rate:

"The prisoners were extremely weakened, exhausted by their long imprisonment and heavy physical labor. Owing to the cold and dampness most of them suffer from kidney trouble. They also suffer from swelling legs, open sores on legs, on arms, and around the ribs, as well as from scurvy. Many go blind. There are a great many cases of frostbite. Illnesses are spread because of the lack of recreation and any signs of civilized life. Many die of diarrhea [dysentery, a variety peculiar to that part of the world different from another type of dysentery, known in the north]; finally, people die from general exhaustion. How high the death rate is is difficult to ascertain, but I know from a prisoner who was in my company that in his camp he belonged to a special group whose duties consisted only of digging graves. Others told me that in the mountains where the soil was heavy and the temperature low, they did not dig graves, but just collected a number of corpses and left them in the snow, far from the camp. I heard similar accounts from other people from Kolyma.

"Women stood up to the new conditions relatively well.

They suffered only from their sores on legs and arms. On the legs the sores continued as far as the lower parts of the abdomen. The sores are difficult to cure, and the discharge of pus goes on for months. The scurvy makes the skin on arms and on legs crack. The fingers bleed from hard work. These sores do not exempt one from work. With hands covered with sores from scurvy and with pus, they are obliged to pack herrings into barrels, wearing only linen gloves, or rather something resembling gloves.

"The woman-prisoner B. suffering from lung trouble was forced to wash floors in the barracks despite a serious cut on her hand; this caused blood-poisoning. The commandant did not exempt her from work, despite her fever of 39 [102° F.]. Only when she lost consciousness was she sent to Magadan to the hospital: 'to her funeral,' the commandant said when she left.

"In the hospitals physicians, even university professors, treat the patients; all of the physicians are prisoners themselves. There are no physicians in the camps, except imprisoned doctors."

There were reports of mutinies in the camps, particularly in the Kolyma region—mutinies which were mercilessly suppressed. Riots have also been reported among prisoners evacuated from the Kola Peninsula. Other reports spoke of the death of 800 prisoners in the tundras of Pechora in the winter of 1941–42, while 1,800 prisoners and 110 guards were reported to have perished in a prison train in February, 1941. There was a report of the sinking of prison barges in the White Sea with a loss of 7,000 lives.

SINCE STALIN'S DEATH

FLUCTUATIONS in living conditions of the labor camps have been a regular feature of their history during the last twenty-five years. In the first two years after the war physical con-

ditions were at an unprecedented low, but about 1947–48 a
certain improvement set in which continued for the next five or
six years. Food allotments have improved since 1948, so that
for the working part of the labor population starvation has
ceased. By 1950–51 food was satisfactory as far as the relatively "well-paid" male working population was concerned.
The working time is now ten hours a day, with three or four
days off a month. Most of the old, filthy barracks have been
gradually replaced by new ones which, although primitive and
of wood construction, are usually clean. Beds, too, are clean,
and the elite among the inmates have the privilege of separate
beds. Medical care and medications, while insufficient, are
available in the larger camps. The attitude of the administration has improved, too; as a rule inmates are not beaten and
punishment by confinement in dungeons is not so frequent
as before. In the majority of the camps loudspeakers broadcast
news from Moscow, and Moscow and local papers are available. The prisoners, some of whom are politically intelligent,
are usually aware of world events.

A significant innovation was the separation of political prisoners from the criminals. Certain camps, the so-called "regime
camps," are restricted to political prisoners; the "general
camps," which maintain less rigorous rules, house the criminals
and some *bytoviks*.[9]

Two important factors made this improvement in labor
camp conditions necessary. One was purely economic. In the
chapter dealing with Russian population problems, the huge
loss in male manpower brought about by the internal policy
of the government during the 'thirties, and to an even greater
extent by the war, was noted. In addition, from three to five
million men were kept in the armed forces after the war.
Despite the vastness of the country, Russia's human resources

9. The term means "offenders against the mode of life"; the group comprises black-marketeers, officials taking bribes, and some others in nonpolitical categories.

are now nearly exhausted; the ambitious Five-Year Plans, the unprecedented development of war industries, and the ever-growing need of food make every able-bodied worker highly valuable. The traditional Soviet disregard of the individual and the waste of manpower since the first days of industrialization and collectivization have started to tell. A new policy in respect to the unfree labor in the concentration camps has been imposed on the government.

The second reason why living conditions in the camps had to be improved is rooted in political considerations. Since about 1947–48 the non-Soviet world has reacted to the Soviet forced labor system with such a flood of indignation and protests that Moscow could not remain indifferent. It was remarkable that Stalin had succeeded in building and maintaining an iron curtain around his concentration camps and that they remained almost unknown to the West for about fifteen years. But since 1942–45 one group after another of former inmates have appeared in various places abroad. Poles interned in Russia in 1939–40 and released in 1942 came to London and New York to tell their story. When the Allied armies occupied Central Europe in 1945 they found there thousands of displaced Russians, former prisoners of Soviet labor camps. American trade unions, in particular the American Federation of Labor, persistently demanded of the International Labor Office that forced labor in Russia be investigated. Since about 1948 slave labor in Russia has been a paramount topic of discussion in the United Nations. An *ad hoc* committee of that body was set up in 1951 to investigate and report on forced labor everywhere, including countries which would not permit direct investigation; its report was published in 1953. Though it did not take sides, it substantially confirmed the existence and the large extent of forced labor in Russia.

It would be no exaggeration to say that since the great purge of the late 'thirties there has been no other Soviet issue which has lowered Soviet prestige and provoked anti-Russian feelings to the extent that the system of compulsory labor has. Among the postwar inmates of the labor camps have been thousands of Germans, Japanese, and Italians, and smaller numbers of other nationals, including nationals of the Allied countries. It was clear to Moscow that one day most of these men would have to be repatriated, because not even under Stalin could they be summarily liquidated. Back home, these witnesses would inflict new wounds on Soviet prestige if the old attitude toward prisoners continued.

At the same time that living conditions have improved to some degree, the general Soviet punitive system has not become less severe since the war. While improvements were put in effect for able-bodied men and women, the lot of invalids and aged prisoners sometimes remains appalling.

On the island of Novaya Zemla there is now a camp which is a land of no return; because of climatic conditions, inmates of other camps sent to Novaya Zemla as punishment have little hope of ever seeing their homeland again.

In the prewar era the average term of a prisoner in a labor camp was five to six years. Since the war, in 1945–52, sentences under ten years have been rare; they vary from ten to twenty-five years, so that the average term has been doubled or trebled. This increase in severity, which was in line with the general political course, helped also to relieve the manpower shortage in the economy of the Far East and Far North and helped considerably to augment the population of the labor camps.

Camps for political prisoners are in the main composed now of four groups of inmates:

First, prisoners from the newly acquired Soviet territories, and especially the western Ukraine. The men and women in this group are excellent workers, industrious and clean; they hate Russia and the Russians and make little distinction between the Russian authorities and their Russian fellow inmates. Other important and influential national groups are Lithuanians, Latvians, and Estonians; only small groups of Germans and Japanese remain in the camps.

The second group is composed of "religionists" of both sexes—fanatic, self-sacrificing, often refusing to work, stoically enduring privation and punishment.

Third are the Communists and members of Communist families deported for various crimes. They are devoted to the regime and are willing to collaborate with the camp administration against the other prisoners.

The fourth group are the young intellectuals, students and ex-students, arrested and sentenced (most of them to from fifteen to twenty-five years) for political opposition to and political activity against the government. They constitute the most intelligent and politically educated element of the camp population. "They are unconditional believers in personal freedom," writes Dr. Joseph Scholmer, a former prisoner of the Vorkuta camp, "and are far more uncompromising in their defense of the rights of the individual than most Western liberals. These Russians have been at great pains to form an objective picture of the situation in the West today, and they are in fact the only resistance group in the camps that really approaches the problems of the twentieth century systematically and without prejudice. The men who lead these groups, mostly Russian intellectuals and ex-students, are of quite first-class character and intelligence and they and their counterparts in the other labor camp areas of the Soviet Union represent perhaps the biggest single hope for the future of the West and civilization today." [10]

ALTHOUGH the prospect of Stalin's death had been, at least since the war, a regular topic of discussion in the labor camps, the death of the dictator in March, 1953, provoked great commotion. The Communist minority was sad and depressed, and the devout Christians prayed and thanked the Almighty for

10. Joseph Scholmer, *Vorkuta* (New York, Henry Holt, 1955), p. 195.

relieving Russia of the "antichrist." Hopes rose high. The expected general amnesty materialized, but affected only some of the criminals and very few of the political prisoners. Soon the news arrived of the arrest of Lavrenti Beria, supreme chief of all concentration camps. Excitement mounted until a wave of strikes and local revolts spread over the Russian concentration camps. Reports on these strikes have reached the West from Vorkuta, Norilsk, Karaganda, and Kolyma.[11] Strike committees were elected, leaflets were distributed, programs of action were developed and carried out.

Although the strikes were put down by bloody measures they nevertheless had substantial consequences.

When the "iron curtain" was raised a little in 1955 and numbers of visitors from the West asked Moscow for permission to see Vorkuta, the large and well-known camp, permission was refused; but it was becoming obvious that sooner or later Western journalists would have to be taken to this polar forced labor settlement. Reforms were introduced: [12]

(1) There was a return to the system of *zachoty,* which had been in force in the 'thirties: those prisoners who produce more receive a reduction in sentence.

(2) Criminals with a bad record were separated from the general mass of inmates. This was felt to be an improvement for the rank and file of prisoners.

(3) In other parts of the huge Vorkuta camp, with the exception of the severe "regime" section, good workers received an occasional *"propusk* (pass), usually good for four to eight hours, which entitles them to leave camp to spend evenings on Sundays in the town of Vorkuta. The latter can be reached by bus in 15 to 45 minutes—depending on the prisoner's camp location—and has 70,000 inhabitants. Once

11. *New York Herald Tribune,* April 19, 1955; also, in addition to Dr. Scholmer's book, mentioned above: Brigitte Gerland, *Die Hölle ist ganz anders,* Stuttgart, Steingrüber Verlag, 1955; Wilhelm Starlinger, *Grenzen der Sowjetmacht,* Würzburg, Holzner-Verlag, 1955.

12. Rainer Hildebrandt, *The New Leader,* November 21, 1955.

there, the prisoner can move about freely, make friends and pay visits, and frequent theaters, cabarets and restaurants." [13]

(4) Prisoners who had completed two-thirds of their sentences and had fulfilled their quotas were made "half free": they lived as deportees but were not imprisoned; they were forbidden, however, to leave the district and were obliged to do the work assigned to them.

How important forced labor still is for the Soviet economy is evident from a cynical speech of the MVD general when he announced these reforms to the Vorkuta inmates: "We, the administration, understand you perfectly: you want your freedom. But I beg you to understand us as well: we need the coal."

13. *Ibid.*

PART TWO: The Soviet System

Chapter 7. THE SO-CALLED EVOLUTION OF COMMUNISM

RUSSIAN COMMUNISM has indeed experienced a great evolution during the almost four decades since November, 1917. It has repeatedly repudiated its former policies, changed leading ideas, conceptions, slogans. But a sense of proportion in judging this evolution is of paramount necessity in arriving at an understanding of it. There has been a multitude of variable elements in this development, but also some unalterable concepts that have remained constant throughout.

More than one writer has minimized the gradual changes within Russian Communism. Still more analysts and publicists have considered Communism to have been overcome and practically abolished in the course of its evolution. Both conceptions have proved to be wrong. Predictions and expectations based on them have proved faulty. Policies built on them might as well have been erected on sand. Endorsement of them has led to failures and inevitable disappointments, and many a reputation succumbed in the course of events.

While two principal elements of initial, orthodox Communism have remained unchanged throughout the entire history of Communism—state economy and political dictatorship—gradual changes have taken place. These changes may be divided into three types.

THE FIRST type of Communist evolution was the outcome of the natural maturing of man and movement. It was a coming of age that superseded the childish, puerile habits of thought and action and certain primitive ideas.

It began in the early 'twenties, when members of the Youth League used to discuss at meetings, heatedly and far into the night, the questions: Was it proper for a Communist to wear a necktie? Was it obligatory to wear the primitive Russian kosovorotka-shirt or should a Communist wear more modern clothes? In general, should a revolutionist attach importance to his attire in view of the fact that his task is to devote himself to fighting civil and international wars?

Very tense were the discussions among young Communists on the question of love. Was there not a contradiction between pure love and the materialism of a revolutionist? Between poetry and the Communist Manifesto? Does love interfere with work? Family responsibilities, kitchen work, and diapers make a sparrow of the eagle. Marriage ties are fetters.

There was much discussion about education. School discipline was the heritage of the old regime, sheer violence. Should the new, perfect state dictate the school curriculum and textbooks? Would it not be better for the students to take these matters into their own hands? From now on there was to be only "self-government of the students." They themselves were to determine the school regime, the system of education.

Hundreds of these and similar questions stirred the minds of the Communist youth, as well as the party in general in those early days. The party as a whole consisted in the main of young people; youth was its conscience. To adopt modern dress, to embrace pure love, to have a family, to plan rigid school programs, it was feared, would be to enter upon the path of a petty-bourgeois existence, to sow the seeds of surrender to capitalism. But how many were really prepared to travel the road to fanatical, uncompromising stoicism?

Time and nature asserted their claims. The moustacheless youths became fathers, the neophytes of Communism were transformed into veterans. The older party leaders came forward with the "petty-bourgeois" advice to be moderate. "Your enthusiasm is magnificent," said the leaders, "but you should apply it to other spheres—to industry, to the army, to propaganda." For those who demanded ideological explanations, it was added: "Communism is not a religious order, it is the road to a better life on earth, not in heaven."

The long series of reforms was thus the consequence of a natural, sincere evolution. "You are losing the revolutionary perspective," cried the extremists angrily. "You are traveling to Canossa, you are betraying the world revolution, as you betrayed the Chinese revolution." "You are Thermidorians," rang the cry, as sharp as a whip, in the middle 'twenties. But the opposition was in the minority.

The reformation of the way of life continued. The right of inheritance was restored. This necessarily included the right to property that a person had not earned by his own efforts. The family was strengthened, divorce was no longer encouraged, abortions were forbidden. Experimentation in education ended with a return to the old school system. Veneration of parents, insistently recommended from above, supplanted militant contempt for the "old fogies."

A SECOND group of reforms introduced by the Soviet government was not a genuine psychological evolution but rather a manifestation of political zigzags that had become necessary in the course of events; they were mostly of a temporary nature.

In 1921, for instance, free trade for peasants was reestablished, concessions were offered and granted to foreign capitalists, and it really looked as if Communism had started to evolve backward toward free enterprise. In Russia as well as abroad these reforms gave rise to interesting theories and speculation concerning Lenin's conversion to capitalism, a reconciliation with bourgeois society, and the actual abolition of Communism. Lenin's NEP, introduced in the early 'twenties, was, however, merely a means of rehabilitating Russian economy after the civil war. As soon as this goal was achieved, Stalin abolished the NEP. All the hopes and predictions of the various political groups abroad regarding the future evolution of Russia were upset when the "second revolution" began and individual peasant economy was abolished, free trade persecuted and concessions terminated by one means or another.

Unlike the natural evolution described above, free trade, capitalist economy, and the entire NEP were only a political zigzag on the part of the government.

Political movement has also been inherent in the wave of nationalism which has been encouraged and propagandized since the middle 'thirties. Not all of it was a maneuver; there were in it ingredients of genuine reorientation. But without the systematic patronage from above, and without the blessing afforded by the conditions of international relations, Russian nationalist emotions would never have been so successfully aroused as they were during and after the war. It was a series of systematic "campaigns," skillfully directed into the desired channels, sometimes held in check and sometimes let loose.

The religious policy of the Soviet government in all its zigzags never reflected a sincere evolution toward religious faith. Even in its most liberal moments, as in 1943–46, it remained a political necessity rather than a genuine turning toward God and Christianity.

A score of similar moves were at first interpreted abroad as a genuine development toward democracy, and only subsequent events served to clarify the real motives. The abolition of the Cheka in 1922 was accompanied by commentaries in which the end of the civil war was given as the main reason for the reform. Yet on the day the Cheka was abolished the GPU was created. The political system became more rigid rather than more liberal, all expectations to the contrary notwithstanding.

The Soviet Constitution of 1936 was never intended to

abolish and supersede dictatorship. It was never intended to enable the holding of free elections in which competition between parties and candidates would be permitted. While the Constitution was being discussed in the press, particularly abroad, the *Bolshevik* comforted the orthodox Communists in Russia with the promise that with the adoption of the new Constitution the party dictatorship would rise to an even higher level. In fact, the inauguration of the "democratic" Constitution coincided with the start of the most extensive and cruel of all the purges ever conducted by the party's leadership.

The thousands of speeches and statements about democracy during the war of 1941–45 bore the same characteristics. Not for one moment did the Soviet government intend to take any steps toward bringing about democratic liberty in Russia. The pronouncements on democracy were calculated to arouse hopes in Russia and expectations in the Western world; they fulfilled their purpose. Not discerning the real aims behind this move, public opinion abroad was misled to consider the zigzag as a real step forward toward freedom in Russia.

A THIRD chapter of evolution, psychologically sincere, was the gradually growing faith in the armed forces of the Soviet Union and their ability to perform social miracles in neighboring countries and to do the job of social revolution that had failed to materialize by other means. This question will be discussed in the pages that follow.

THE REVOLUTION IS NOT YET ENDED

THE theory that the Soviet regime was gradually and imperceptibly degenerating into a different political system was for the first time seriously developed by a group of rightist émigrés in 1921–24 (the group called "Changing Landmarks") and then by Trotsky, after the middle of the 'twenties. The first group reacted positively to the changes introduced by the

Soviet government in 1921–22—free trade for peasants, concessions to foreign capitalists, etc.; they considered these reforms as symptoms of a steady and gradual evolution of Lenin's government toward what seemed to them a normal, nationalist policy. They termed this evolution "Thermidorian" and were prepared to support it by all available means.

Trotsky, on the other hand, although he reached the same conclusion that the leadership of the Communist party after Lenin's death was developing in the "Thermidorian" direction, resented the growing independence of the bureaucracy from the people, the privileges of the "higher-ups," and the general trend, which he considered nationalist and anti-Communist.

For all of them, however—for the "Rightists" as well as the "Leftists"—the evolution of the Soviet regime was tantamount to the end of the revolution. They believed that out of this multitude of political acts and new slogans a new Russia was emerging under the Soviet government—a nonrevolutionary, at times even antirevolutionary, nation. They expected this "Thermidorian" tendency to prevail in the future, and they took their stand accordingly. This view—that a political system can evolve into its own opposite without crisis or upheavals, by a purely psychological development of its leadership, almost imperceptible to the ordinary eye—lay at the bottom of their policies.

The early period of the "ascending line of the revolution" in the French Revolution did have some resemblance to the course of the Russian revolution. At first came the substitution of a constitutional regime for the autocratic system; the monarchy was then supplanted by the republic; then came the execution of the king; the struggle among the republican parties brought to power the more extreme, more revolutionary tendencies. The terror grew apace; political killings and executions assumed a mass character. Economic decrees issued by the revolutionary governments violated the rights of property, introduced requisitions, and limited freedom of trade. The gen-

eral uncertainty, absence of personal security, and acute political tension found their expression in the political upheaval
of July, 1794, when the revolutionary dictator Robespierre
was overthrown. It was the upheaval of Thermidor.

That moment marked the beginning of the "declining line
of the revolution" in France. At first those who came to power
consisted of supporters of the revolutionary parties, but soon
they began to fade out. The system of ideologies developed in
previous years appeared to remain in force for a while, but
very soon it ceased to play any role. Fixed prices and requisitions were abolished; the fever of self-enrichment began. Much
of the old way of life and many of the old customs were revived. Finally, the republican regime itself began to give way
to the dictatorship of the former revolutionist Napoleon Bonaparte.

Trotsky applied this blueprint in his analysis of the course
of Russian revolution. He conceived of himself and Lenin as
the Russian Robespierres, the bearers of the pure ideals of the
revolution. Stalin's victory over Trotsky in the middle 'twenties
appeared to the latter as the triumph of "revolutionists grown
wise," of the practical elements, of realists who proceeded to
abandon everything to which they nevertheless continued to
give lip service: Communism, world revolution, social equality.
Trotsky never tired of denouncing the omnipotent bureaucracy
under Stalin as the party of Thermidor, with Stalin as its
leader. He pictured Stalin as an intellectual mediocrity, devoid
of ideas, one who had abandoned all ideological moorings
and principles after Lenin's death and who was guided solely
by the thirst for power.

Trotsky's supporters as well as many other Communist
dissidents accepted this concept. And it did, indeed, seem
easy to find confirmation of it in the evolution of Soviet society:
revival of the family, veneration of parents, restoration of the
old school system, privileges of the bureaucracy, and introduction of ranks and decorations were some of Stalin's reforms

which fitted into the scheme of Thermidor. The dissidents, like Trotsky himself, kept on repeating this accusation, so deadly to true Communism, for a period of years. But they failed to perceive that there were other facts diametrically opposed to this entire conception, that the years had failed to confirm their theory, and that, after more than fifteen years of "evolution," the world was still confronted by the old enigma of Russia—Russian Communism had not only survived this long period but had actually developed in another, non-Thermidorian direction.

There is little analogy between the Russian and the French revolutions, and still less between the Stalinist system and the French Thermidor. It is essential to make the difference clear, not as a matter of historical research but as a task necessary for understanding the policies of today and tomorrow.

"Down with the tyrant!" shouted the French crowds on the day of Thermidor. They could no longer tolerate the spectacle of executions and nightly killings. They feared the Revolutionary Tribunal. They yearned for more normal conditions of life, for security from the lawlessness of the revolutionary police. The peasants wanted an end to grain requisitions. Even in his last speech Robespierre had continued to demand a bloody "purge" (the Russian Communists did not invent this term); but those who were to have been the victims of that purge forestalled it by carrying out the Thermidorian revolt. Thermidor led to a gradual restoration of "normalcy." The Revolutionary Tribunal was first reformed and then abolished; the executions almost ceased; political persecutions declined; the economy began to improve. And even later, with the rise of Bonaparte, and despite the severe regime he instituted, there was no such terror as prevailed under Robespierre.

Thermidor marked a relief for France after the period of revolutionary stress. Can this interpretation be applied to Soviet Russia today? Can it be seriously asserted that political persecutions have ceased, that purges are no more, that executions have stopped? Have normal conditions been restored; do people feel more secure in their lives? Do collectivization and armies of forced labor constitute normalization of the national economy? One need only pose these questions to perceive how erroneous is the analogy with Thermidor.

The revolutionary process has not yet been concluded in Russia; the "ascending line of the revolution" continues. Whether we consider this good or bad, the fact is that the Russian train has not yet reached its "Thermidor."

The accompanying chart presents a graphic idea of the inner political development of Russia during the period of the revolution. It is not a diagram that pretends to specific scientific significance. It is offered merely because a graphic presentation frequently facilitates understanding of a question.

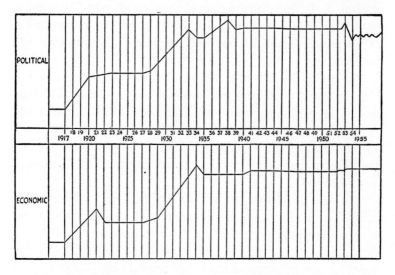

The line begins in 1917, the period of broad liberties and expansion of democracy. In the next years the revolutionary line moves steeply upward. The oppositionist press and parties are gradually liquidated; repressions are intensified; executions are begun. Then comes the civil war; the regime grows increasingly ruthless. At the end of the civil war the Cheka is established in all cities, grain is requisitioned from the villages, the capitalist classes are ejected.

The year 1921 brings some economic reforms. On an economic chart we see a decline of the revolutionary line—Lenin's concessions to the peasantry. But the main political line does not decline at that moment; on the contrary, the repressions are intensified. Economic concessions and freedom of trade do not in any way indicate an altered Communist policy. In fact just the reverse, for in order to stress its adherence to Communist principle, the Soviet government jails the members of all other political parties still at liberty. With the same purpose in mind it intensifies the antireligious and other campaigns. The line of the revolution moves upward. A measure of stability ensues for several years, marked by suppression of all non-Communist tendencies, while the Communist party continues to maintain a comparative degree of political freedom within its own organization.

But in the late 'twenties the revolutionary line makes a big leap upward, politically and economically. The period witnesses the beginning of mass persecutions of Communist oppositionists and ruthless purges, followed by collectivization with its mass repressions directed against the peasantry, against the church, and against many other groups. This continues until 1933–34.

The year 1934 brings a measure of political and economic relief. This is, however, relative. Although the peasants are no longer persecuted as ruthlessly as before, there are also virtually no more kulaks—and the stream of exiles declines. Note the very important feature of the entire revolutionary development in Russia: long and sharp swings upward, short zigzags downward, which, however, never indicate a return to the starting point.

In the middle 'thirties the economic line discloses a slight relief. In 1934 the peasants are accorded the right to own small bits of land adjacent to the collectives. But the main line, the political line, soon takes another leap upward. The remnants of Communist dissident factions are liquidated. The purges are accompanied by another outburst of terror. Persecutions of nonpartisans and of priests are resumed. The country lives in perpetual fear. The line reaches its zenith.

Again in 1939 it declines slightly, when the period of repressions ceases, but without indicating any return to the point preceding the purges. There can be no toleration whatever of any opposition, legal or semilegal. Literature, art, politics, science, everything is *gleichgeschaltet*. The dictatorship reaches its apogee. There is another upward swing in economic life; a new limitation of the rights of private economy in the villages. Ninteen-forty brings a feverish mobilization of industry with a new tightening of the screw. Neither the prewar era, however, nor the war years witnessed any discarding or even weakening of the main principles of Soviet Communism. The chaos and disorientation of the war years caused no voluntary and intentional relaxation of the political and police system or any substantial change in the agricultural economy.

The bar on the graph remains at the same level during the postwar era. In the early 'fifties the streamlining and enlargement of the kolkhozes (collective farms) mark new "progress" for Soviet Communism, an upward swing of the economic trend. On the eve of Stalin's death the political bar rises once more to signify the first stage in a projected new purge. It falls after Stalin's death and begins to zigzag, but at a high level; the system of political dictatorship remains in force.

But how are we to understand the revival of venerated heroes of Russian history, of Soviet patriotism, of "Russianism" in terminology, the restoration of ranks in the Army, of sympathy for Slavdom and the growing antagonism to the West? Are they not symptoms of a rising primitive, non-Communist nationalism?

First of all, the advent of any new party to power, including

the Communist party, tends to make it patriotic *ipso facto*.
Ridicule of and contempt for "defense of the fatherland" are
transformed into "defense of the Soviet fatherland" or "defense
of the revolutionary land" when those who formerly did the
ridiculing become the government. And, in truth, patriotism
in Communist ideology is not a product of recent years, as
many suppose. On the contrary, it has been dominant from
the period when Lenin was waging war against the Germans
in 1918, against Allied intervention in 1918–19, and against
Poland in 1920.

"We are now 'for the war,' since November 7, 1917," wrote
Lenin. "We stand for defense of the fatherland." In February,
1918, he wrote a proclamation in which he declared: "The
Socialist fatherland is in peril! Unqualified defense of the republic!" On another occasion Lenin wrote: "Are we, conscious Russian proletarians, devoid of the emotion of national
pride? Of course not! We love our language and our country
. . . We are filled with the sense of national pride, for the
great Russian nation has also created a revolutionary class."

Patriotism is, therefore, not a product of the last decade of
Bolshevism. To be sure, it was intensified in the 'thirties; it
found new soil under new conditions, and the government
has encouraged it enormously. Now it was no longer necessary
to add the word "Soviet" to the word "motherland," or "revolutionary" to the word "fatherland."

The second source of the new nationalism is to be found in
the stabilization and strengthening of the regime. This was a
psychological phenomenon. Before the revolution there prevailed widely a primitive but extremely revolutionary attitude
toward Russian history, not only in Bolshevist popular literature but also in the literature of other revolutionary parties.
The entire Russian past was portrayed as a dark history of
violence, stupidity, robbery, by scoundrel-tsars and idiots. Little pamphlets, published by the revolutionary underground or
abroad for circulation in Russia, presented in popular form the

history of tsarism in the Empire. Particular popularity was enjoyed, for example, by the little books of Leonid Shishko, which had sought to demonstrate that all the tsars "were concerned only with their power, and as for the people it was quite all right for them to die of hunger in the great state." It was all a manifestation of antihistoricity, of repudiation of the past. History begins with us!

This ideology was at first completely dominant under the Soviet regime. It exercised its most powerful influence during the civil war, which was waged as a struggle against the "restorationists of old Russia."

Everything was still fresh and novel in the 'twenties. Every speech and every article began with a description of how miserable life had been under tsarism, and how different it would be now. The newspapers painted contrasts between the old and the new that was now beginning. Repudiation of the past was the life blood of political literature in the first decade of the Soviet regime. Old Russia was pictured as the springboard from which the swimmer leaps into fresh water.

Eventually all this began to sound repetitious, monotonous, banal, annoying, and unconvincing. Old Russia began to recede into the dim distance of the past; some began to forget, others had not known it at all. The new regime achieved stability, the danger of a restoration of the old had passed. A new complex of ideas gradually supplanted the old antihistoricity. The new people now sought not mere repudiation of the past but affirmation of their own place in the long chain of successive historical epochs. It was no longer necessary now to denounce Peter I as a robber and Catherine II as an immoral woman. Now it could be declared that Peter I was great for his time, that Ivan the Terrible performed mighty deeds for his country, but that Stalin was no less a legitimate and no less a great leader for his epoch. It was no longer necessary to repeat that field marshals Mikhail Kutuzov and Alexander Suvorov were tsarist sycophants. No, they were great military leaders of their time, just as Zhukov and Konev were for theirs. His place in history is now of moment to the Soviet man. Moreover, these views fit properly into the framework of Marxist historical theory.

Communism does not cross itself out when it begins to recognize Russian history. This psychological need of placing oneself within the framework of history, of becoming part of the gallery of tsars and field marshals, is so potent that occasionally it leads to a childish repetition of the absurd. It would have been possible for the Communists to follow revolutionary or Napoleonic examples and to introduce novel decorations and marks of distinction for generals; but, no, Soviet generals were given red trouser stripes, just like those of the old days. History knows a wide variety of military rewards—from the laurel wreath to marriage to a distinguished bride—but in Russia the old decorations worn on the breast and named after famous tsarist generals were restored. Napoleon invented all sorts of new ranks, but Russia now again has her major-generals and lieutenant-generals, awkward-sounding foreign ranks but taken from the arsenal of old tsarist Russia. The title of Marshal, likewise, existed in Russia before the revolution in the common Russo-German form of *Feldmarschall*. Regiments and divisions fighting with distinction could have been given new names, but they were now known again as Guard Regiments. Shoulder straps and bars would not seem necessary to win military victories. But they were restored in their old forms. "Privileged" military schools, traditional in Russia, have been reestablished by a decree having to do with the rebuilding of reoccupied regions. For a few years it was as if a Commission of Restoration had been set up by the Commissariat of Defense for the purpose of restoring page by page the old military rules and decorations and adapting all the attributes of the old army to the new.

The last blows to the obsolete Soviet system of titles were struck in 1946, when it was decided to abolish the People's

Commissars, and the government of the Soviet Union adopted the prerevolutionary name of Council of Ministers. The explanation advanced in *Pravda* claimed that "the Soviet of People's Commissars was created at the time of the birth of the Soviet State. This was the period of its establishment . . . At present, however, we have a Soviet State which has successfully developed and withstood a great test." This explanation was insufficient. The same could have been said ten or fifteen years before. What *Pravda* failed to acknowledge was this intensive desire of every one of the hundreds of commissars to acquire new prestige and stability through the return to the age-old title of Minister. Somewhat later, in September, 1946, the Red Army was renamed the Soviet Army.

Thirdly, the new nationalism represented a political zigzag on the part of the Soviet government. In 1934, after the first year of the Hitler regime had failed (contrary to the expectations of Moscow) to provoke a revolutionary upheaval in Germany, it became clear that Russia had to prepare for war. The preparations consisted not only in doubling the size of the army, training the new commanding staff, and expanding the war industries, but also in taking certain ideological measures. The ideology of nationalism was one of the principal weapons at hand.

To make war and to be victorious it was necessary not only to stir the activity of party cells and regional secretaries but to enlist and move into action the dissidents, the malcontents, the formerly injured and oppressed. Above all, it was necessary to enlist those elements of the intelligentsia and government servants who would play the decisive role by holding commanding positions in the army, i.e., the new officers.

However, during the 'thirties, and as late as the outbreak of the war, problems of nationalist ideology and of the new nationalist policy had occupied but a small place in the press as compared with the attention given to problems of industrialization, the collectives, and administrative expansion. The schools and universities devoted a great deal more time and energy to problems of Communist science—to capitalism, Communism, the bourgeoisie and proletariat, the class war and social revolution—than was given the seedling national ideology. The upswing of nationalism, a natural phenomenon during the war, was greatly enhanced by the government's policy. The new trends did not cease, however, as the end of the war approached. When Russia emerged from the catastrophe as one of the greatest among the world powers, the Soviet leadership tried to combine the old type of Russian nationalism with Communist achievements and territorial expansion. Soviet science and Soviet literature, proclaimed Andrei Zhdanov in 1946–48, are the most progressive in the world, and there is no longer any reason for "idolization" of and "genuflection" before the West. The new nationalism was at the same time a new form of Communism.

THE STATE DOES NOT DIE

"THE state will wither away and die: once the exploiters are suppressed and re-educated to become toilers all 'pressures' by the state will disappear. The Red Army is a temporary army. It cannot be a standing army, for the civil war cannot continue forever."

This was written in 1920 by Lenin's disciples, Bukharin and Preobrazhensky, in a book called The A.B.C. of Communism, for years an obligatory textbook in Russian schools, and translated into many languages as the best exposition of Communist fundamentals. "When the exploiters cease to resist, the dictatorship of the proletariat will be increasingly ameliorated. The workers' state will gradually wither away."

The state is evil. For the state, as interpreted by Lenin, Bukharin, and the entire galaxy of Communist leaders of the early period, is not "a territory plus the population, plus the government," as is supposed in universities outside of Russia, but only the third element—the government. The state is the synonym of the state machine, of the state organization, of the apparatus by means of which the government governs. And the government and its machine constitute together an instrument of force; there can be no place for them in a Communist society. The principal elements of state force are the police and the army. They must disappear.

This concept differed from anarchism in that it presupposed a "transition period": the period of transition of the revolutionary government into the new system. The revolutionary government is created to liquidate capitalism, the bourgeoisie, economic exploitation. Only toilers will remain after the disappearance of the capitalist classes, and then there will be no more room for state force and violence. The anarchists wanted to begin with liquidation of the state. Lenin (in line with Marx) wanted to conclude the transformation of society by liquidating the state.

And the state of the "transition period," i.e., the temporary Soviet state, was pictured by Lenin in colors which, in the light of the Soviet experiment, now appear the extreme of liberalism and naïveté. Bureaucratism was to be rooted out radically; the entire population was to participate actively in the administration of the state. The state will "abolish the army, the police, the officialdom, and will supplant them with a more democratic state machine in the form of the armed working mass." Lenin's concept of the revolutionary state provided also for "completely free elections, recall of officials, without exception, reduction of their salaries to the customary earnings of a worker."

On the eve of the November revolution, in 1917, Lenin wrote:

"The workers, having conquered the power of government, will smash the old bureaucratic apparatus and will supplant it with a new one, composed of workers and employees, and measures will immediately be taken to prevent these from degenerating into bureaucrats." These measures were to include (1) "not only free elections but also the recall applicable at any time," (2) "a salary scale not above workers' wages." Since "all become bureaucrats temporarily it will be impossible for the state to become bureaucratic."

For Lenin the "state" was an abominable term. His state would be a "semi-state," he declared. The sooner it disappeared the better. He thought eagerly of the future that was to follow the transition period, a point which was not to be long delayed. And he painted the following picture:

"Liberated from capitalist slavery, from untold horrors, savageries, stupidities, abominations, capitalist exploitation, human beings will gradually become accustomed to observe the elementary rules of social life acquired through thousands of years of experience; to observe these rules without compulsion, without force, without subjection, without the special apparatus known as the state."

Only Communism will do away with the necessity of the state, declared Lenin, for there will be no one upon whom it will be necessary to use force. As regards the question of how to deal with "excesses committed by individuals," Lenin declared, "no special machine, no apparatus of force will be required for that, it will be handled by the armed people themselves"; moreover, he added, "the roots of the social causes of excesses are in the exploitation of the masses." With the removal of these roots the causes of excesses will begin to "wither away." With their elimination the state, too, will wither away. "The whole of society," wrote Lenin, "will be like one single office and one plant, with equality of labor and equality of pay."

In accordance with this principle, the program of the Russian Communist party in 1919 declared, after setting forth a series of demands: "Complete and thoroughgoing realization of these measures will lead to the abolition of the power of the state." Stalin declared at the same time: "We stand for the withering away of the state . . . Higher development of the state power for the purpose of preparing for and effecting the withering away of the state power—that is the Marxian formula."

This negative attitude on the part of Bolshevism toward the state in general and toward its own "semi-state" in particular was no mere abstract theory, borrowed from Marx. It was the inheritance of the long struggle of Russian revolutionists against the old state, with its police, its Okhrana, its agents-provocateurs. The subsequent revival of all these elements under the new Soviet state had to be justified not only to the conscience of the Communists and their supporters but also to the outside world. In all of Lenin's passionate attacks against "formal democracy," in hundreds of his speeches and articles after the establishment of the Soviet regime, there was evident this need of self-justification for the revival of the power of the state in its most rigorous forms. The question of the state appeared clear and simple: Why was it necessary to have the GPU, courts, jails, etc., in the Soviet State, after the revolution had been accomplished?

Cheliapov, a Communist authority on the state, wrote on the subject in two editions of the highly official *Soviet Encyclopaedia*, in 1929 and in 1935. In 1929 he declared:

"The apparatus of compulsion, the GPU, courts, prisons, and so on, is retained temporarily, only while the resistance of the bourgeoisie continues, but these instruments of struggle will wither away in proportion as the resistance declines. The state will disappear together with the disappearance of the division of society into classes."

Six years later he wrote quite differently. The "division of society into classes" and the "resistance of the bourgeoisie" had disappeared. The landlords, capitalists, and their parties had been eliminated. The "kulaks," too, were liquidated. Stalin had already declared that the Socialist order had been realized in Russia. But why does not the state, starting with the GPU, begin to "wither away"? Cheliapov now postponed this event to the vague distant future, when "the perfect Communist society" will have been established, "when a psychological transformation" will have taken place.

Bukharin's old views, which were the views of Lenin, were now explained by the assertion that Bukharin was a potential "fascist hireling": "Contrary to what was asserted by the fascist hireling Bukharin, punitive organs and the army will be only the last to wither away," it was stated now in the *Soviet Encyclopaedia*.

The reality, indeed, did not correspond to the theory. If it is true that all opposition to the Soviet political system can be explained by the play of class interests, who are the classes that must continue to be suppressed without cessation? Are they the workers, the collectivized peasants, the toiling intelligentsia? If so, then the future looked dark, indeed.

"The function of compulsion inside the country has ceased, has withered away," declared Stalin in 1939. "The exploiters are no more and there is no one to suppress any more." But the inevitable question arising after this utterance was: But why does the NKVD continue to be so active?

The answer to this question is provided in the theory assiduously cultivated by Stalin that as long as capitalism existed outside of Russia it would seek to recruit agents among unstable elements and to create opposition groups and movements with the purpose of destroying the Soviet state. In other words, there is no basis for opposition to Communism inside the country; the opposition constitutes merely a "fifth column."

"The capitalist world sends us spies and diversionists," declared Stalin repeatedly. The hundreds of thousands of people upon whose heads Stalin hurled his reprisals constituted only an "agency of foreign capital." At every demonstration trial the government found it necessary to establish a direct relation between the defendants and the outside world, particularly with the "intelligence services" of hostile countries. It was necessary to get "confessions" from every defendant to the effect that he had acted through inspiration from outside. The theory of the "fifth column," which some foreign writers have been so ready to accept, constituted one element of this concept: that there cannot possibly be any dissatisfaction with the Soviet government inside the Soviet land!

THE state was perpetuated as an "apparatus of force." Imperceptibly, without admitting it to itself, Russian Communism began to accept the old theory of the state as a complex of population, territory, and power. The Soviet press began to speak proudly of "our great state," of "the great prestige of our state." "Service to the state" became an honorable idea, the "needs of the state" were given priority. Stalin took another step forward when he applied to his state the formerly contemptuous term of a "great power." "We have become," he said, "a great industrial and kolkhoz power!" How removed from the time when Lenin spoke almost apologetically of his "semi-state"!

The term "Great Power" was rapidly adopted in the press, in textbooks, in Soviet science. It was a substitute for "empire." The point has now been reached when the proud term "Soviet empire" could well be adopted without qualification, and it is only the old theory of hostility to imperialism which has interfered with this remaining final step. There is no issue in world political affairs, Moscow now says, that is outside the sphere of interest of the Soviet government.

One more important element in the new worship of the state derived directly from the history of Communism in Europe. After the numerous disappointments, the unsuccessful uprisings, and the shattered revolutionary attempts in other countries, Russian Communists began to look upon the Soviet state as one of the chief instruments for effecting Communist transformations abroad. Therefore, the Soviet "apparatus of force," its military and diplomatic machinery, emerged as the great hope of Communism. The greater the new Great Power becomes, the more capable it is of substituting its weight for the revolutions that have failed to develop elsewhere. The Communist state becomes in a measure the substitute for the Communist revolution: such is the pattern of Communist evolution.

Communism remains its content, but it has absorbed also the heavy weight of the state machine. "We go forward [from Socialism] to Communism," declared Stalin at the party congress in 1939. "Will the state be retained by us also in the period of Communism? Yes, it will, if the capitalist encirclement is not liquidated."

The state is the main instrument for liquidation of the capitalist encirclement: this is one of the most important lessons drawn by Communism from its own experience. It cannot be expected, therefore, that in the near future the state, of its own will, will begin to "wither away," loosen its grip, reduce the role of the police apparatus and grant the people more liberty and civic rights.

RUSSIAN COMMUNISM IN THE WAR

DESPITE its perturbations and upheavals the war with Germany failed to alter either the principles of Soviet foreign policy or the economic regime of the country. Moreover, long before the war the government had determined upon a program for preserving inviolate the Soviet political and economic system in the event of a conflict.

Two hours after the first German air raids on Russia, on the night of June 22, 1941, the government ordered many arrests, which were carried out in accordance with previously prepared lists. Among those seized were many suspect Communists who had been permitted to remain at liberty and many nonpartisans who it was thought might become dangerous.

But the success of the German aggression in the first months of the war could not but confuse and bewilder many minds. It was asked: Had the policy of collaboration with Germany of the past two years been really wise? Were not the Soviet defeats to be attributed to the incapacity of the party leadership? All the springs of policy and ideology stood dangerously exposed.

This found particular expression in a decline in the prestige of the party, which appeared to have lost confidence in itself and in its philosophy. The doubts current abroad at that time concerning Russia's ability to resist were felt no less within the country itself. Stalin remained silent for almost two weeks after the German attack: This was the only instance in the annals of the second World War when the head of a government failed to address his people on the outbreak of hostilities. When he finally did venture to speak on July 3, 1941, it was an attempt to justify himself before the country, an effort to answer the doubters.

Concerning his 1939 pact with Hitler, he said:

"One may ask: How did it happen that the Soviet government entered into a nonaggression pact with such treacherous persons and monsters as Hitler and Ribbentrop? . . . A nonaggression pact is a peace pact between two states. Could the Soviet government have refused to accept the proposal?

"What did we gain by concluding a nonaggression pact with Germany? We secured for our country for a period of a year and a half an opportunity to prepare our forces."

This did not sound very convincing. Everybody knew that during that period Russia had lost an allied army in France, and everyone could observe how rapidly the German forces were advancing. To those who doubted Russia's capacity to resist, Stalin said: "The enemy is not so terrible as he is pictured by some frightened little intellectuals." But those involved were more than "little intellectuals." In the Army itself there was lack of confidence, as Stalin had repeatedly admitted.

Only rarely and in passing did Stalin refer to his party in his first war speeches. It was impossible, in the atmosphere prevailing during those months, to take pride in its policy. The party's own lack of confidence and bewilderment found expression in the immediate disappearance from the press, from public addresses, and from propaganda of the words "Socialism" and "Communism," as well as all acclamation of Soviet industry, of the collectives, and of military preparations. The ideological content of the war was reduced to an extreme minimum, to unusually modest terms. The official *Bulletin of the Agitator* in July, 1941, published a program of lectures to be delivered throughout the country. This program was entirely without Socialist or Soviet content. The subjects covered were: War Against Fascism—A War for the Fatherland; Lenin and Stalin on National Defense; Fascism; The Front and the Rear; Care of Soviet Soldiers; The People's Heroism; The Defeat of the Germans in the Ukraine in 1918; The Partisans; The United Front of Peoples; The Occupied Regions, etc.

Lectures on such subjects could have been delivered under any Russian government and in any country. "The war," wrote this organ of the Central Committee of the Communist party, "is a war for the preservation of the peoples inhabiting the USSR; a war for life or death of the Soviet State; it is to determine whether the peoples of the Soviet land are to remain free or are to be enslaved once more."

Anti-Communist and anti-Soviet sentiment found expression in various forms in this early period of the war. Officially, all difficulties were attributed to the activities of the fifth column, for all oppositionists were proclaimed to be pro-Hitlerites. But at the very time when persons abroad were writing with enthusiasm that there was no opposition left in Russia after the purges, the Soviet press and radio were reporting a different story.

A man named Andronov was executed in Leningrad in August, 1941, for talk "calculated to undermine measures taken by the Soviet Government." A group of grinders engaged in "counterrevolutionary propaganda" was liquidated in Alma-Ata. On November 15, 1941, the Moscow Military Tribunal sentenced to death two engineers, two technicians, and an economist of a certain plant for "spreading appeals" among workers. This was reported by the Soviet radio. The *Bolshevik* told how a certain Sirotin had discovered a man "with leaflets"; how a certain Novikova had turned over to the militia "a counterrevolutionist who was spreading lies." Although the press soon quit writing about opposition sentiments, there could be no doubt that these did not disappear.

Later came information dealing not with opposition but with a veritable fifth column eager to collaborate with Hitler Germany in the struggle against the Soviet regime. Many Orthodox priests in occupied regions of Russia entered into collaboration with the German authorities. This was significant because the priests would not have ventured to act contrary to the sentiments of their parishioners. Declarations in favor of Germany were published by high church dignitaries: Polikarp Sikorsky, Bishop of Vladimir in Volyn, who proclaimed himself head of the church in the Ukraine; Sergei Voznesensky, Archbishop of Riga; the Archbishop of Mitava; the Archbishop of Narva; the Bishop of Kaunas; the Metropolitan of Latvia. In August, 1942, they met in Riga and sent a telegram to Hitler expressing "admiration of the heroic struggle" he was waging, and promising to "pray to the All-Highest to bless the Axis arms with speedy and complete victory." Professor Okienko, former dean of Kharkov University, became archbishop of an "Independent Church."

These developments indicated the prevalence of many varied sentiments among the population.

Under the German occupation, especially in the beginning, dozens of Russian pro-Nazi newspapers were started, with their staffs of editors and correspondents. "On behalf of the intelligentsia" and "on behalf of the Russian people" the writers welcomed the "liberation from Bolshevism," often adding their joy of being freed from "Jewish rule." Names of well-known old

Russian writers, such as Ivanov-Razumnik suddenly appeared in the collaborationist Russian press. Other pro-German personalities accepted positions as local mayors and in various departments of local government: in industry, transportation, health, and elsewhere.

Long before General Vlasov assumed leadership over the "Vlasov movement"—before he was even captured by the Germans—the essential preconditions were present in the feelings of the people of every area from which Soviet authority and troops were withdrawing. All the latent hatred of the regime—indignation at the collectivization of the land, the purges, arrests, inquisitions, deportations, and shootings—suddenly erupted. This was a rebellion, but of a curious kind. It was a rebellion led by Communists against Stalin's Communism. What had occurred was a split in the Communist ranks—probably the only form political change could have taken under the repressive conditions of the Soviet Union.

General Andrei Vlasov, the leader of the dissidents, was a Communist of long standing. He had fought on the Red side in the civil war and had since been entrusted by the government with important military-political assignments. He had never been involved in any of the recurrent purges. In 1941 he was wounded but recovered.

General Vasili Malyshkin, one of General Vlasov's most important advisers, was a former professor at the General Staff Academy and an old Communist. Major General Feodor Trukhin was a graduate of the General Staff Academy. General Georgi Zhilenkov, another of Vlasov's associates, had been a high-ranking political commissar in the Red Army. Colonel Sergei N. Buniachenko had been personally decorated by Stalin for his part in the Manchurian border war with the Japanese in 1938–39. Mileti Zykov, actual author of some of Vlasov's manifestoes and proclamations, was likewise a Communist of long standing. Colonel V. Mal'tsev, a prominent aviator, held the title of Hero of the Soviet Union. This list could be extended indefinitely with the names of officers in the middle and lower ranks, many of them Communist party members.

Vlasov's program, which he set forth in speeches and proclamations, promised not only "the overthrow of Stalin's tyranny" but, in addition, "restoration to the peoples of Russia of the rights gained in the popular revolution of [February] 1917," and "abolition of the kolkhozes and forced labor."

THE battle of Moscow in October–December, 1941, ended with the retreat of the German armies. The government, which had prepared to evacuate to the Urals, felt first relief and then a sense of stability.

There was a revival of self-confidence in the party and renewed faith in its ideology, starting with 1942 and growing stronger in 1943 and 1944. Party committees gradually began to function more regularly. Articles in the press began increasingly to praise the party's wisdom and services. Publication of the *Propagandist,* which set the tone for propaganda throughout the country, was resumed in March, 1942, with an edition of 100,000 copies. Two channels of propaganda were indicated: emphasis on nationalism and stress on Communist ideology. Both were to be pursued simultaneously.

The development of nationalism was at first not so much a manifestation of a social movement as the result of a directive from above. National spirit and patriotism were necessary to overcome the initial "passivity and indifference" of the population and to strengthen discipline in the Red Army. A campaign against "indiscipline" and even desertions had to be waged until as late as the autumn of 1942. The press was filled with articles, reports, and stories exposing cowards and traitors at the front. Detailed accounts of German atrocities, public hangings—in the presence of tens of thousands—of Soviet citizens who collaborated with the Germans, extensive reports of the Krasnodar and Kharkov trials—these were intended to serve the same purpose as the creation of the orders of Kutuzov and Suvorov. Only gradually was the sentiment of anti-German nationalism transformed from official propaganda into a popular movement.

But simultaneously with the growth of nationalism the traditional Communist party line gained in strength. This gain was all the more striking in the light of the party's loss of prestige in the first eight months of the war. In April, 1942, the *Propagandist* wrote: "Propaganda work has declined considerably during the war. The party organizations had failed to understand that not only must there be no let-up in propaganda activity in wartime but it must be given even wider scope."

"In the first year of the war," we are told from the city of Gorky, "some party organizations paid less attention to problems of propaganda . . . The regional committee warned the party organizations of the need of stimulating attention to problems of party propaganda." Later, Emelian Yaroslavsky wrote that "many party organizations have failed to grasp the significance of mass party-political activity . . . What is needed is not a let-up but intensification of the work of lecturing."

In January, 1943, the Administration of Propaganda and Agitation attached to the Central Committee sent out a circular to party organizations dealing with "shortcomings in the work of party cabinets" (for consultations on Marxism-Leninism), which warned that there must be no weakening of "ideological-political training of cadres during the period of the war."

Increased activity of party-propaganda organs and thousands of lectures and articles gradually restored the once shaken prestige of "Marxist-Leninist science." In March, 1943, G. Alexandrov, director of the Central Committee's division of propaganda, issued new instructions explaining why the "study of Marxist-Leninist science is necessary, obligatory for all." In support he cited Stalin, who had repeatedly stressed the universal obligation to study the "Marxist-Leninist science of society, the laws of social development, the laws of the development of the proletarian revolution, of the victory of Communism."

Participation in propaganda activity was now proclaimed to be the duty of every active Communist. Many Communists had dodged this work for various reasons, but now it was declared that "the self-liquidation of many of our cadres in political work among the rural population cannot be tolerated." In 1943 it was declared menacingly that "some of our branches have failed to appreciate the importance of propaganda of the Marxist-Leninist theory in wartime, and have weakened in leadership in propaganda work . . . In a number of regions party and Soviet workers have ceased the study of Marxist-Leninist theory . . . They have failed to fight against the detrimental view that now is not the time to engage in political self-education."

In Soviet terminology the return to Communist party ideology meant the revival of study of the book, *History of the Communist Party, Short Course*. This book, published in 1938, was written in part by Stalin and was based mainly upon his speeches and articles; within its three hundred pages it contains the history of the Russian Communist party covering a period of forty years. Written in orthodox Communist style, it presented the official conception of Soviet Communism, its struggle against other parties and Communist factions, the official history of industrialization, of the collectives, and of Soviet foreign relations. It was translated into many languages and fifty-one million copies have been distributed. All Communist education was obliged to follow the line of this book. Constituting an adaptation of "Marxist-Leninist science" to Russian conditions, it was designed to serve as an antidote to the dangerous tendencies inherent in daily nationalist agitation.

Meanwhile victory followed upon victory at the front. The Germans were retreating from the Ukraine and from Leningrad; the prestige of the Soviet government rose to unprecedented heights throughout the world. Now the party began to demand recognition of its services. Who organized the peoples of the Soviet Union for struggle against the invaders? The answer: the All-Russian Communist party. Victory over Germany, it was concluded, was, therefore, the victory of Russian Communism. The newspapers broadcast the information that half of those who had received the distinction of "Hero of the Soviet Union" were Communists, that hundreds of thousands of Communists had been awarded medals and decorations. The party's prestige was rising.

Stalin made three regular public appearances annually during the war, no more and no less: on Red Army Day, February 23; on May Day; and on the anniversary of the November revolution, November 7. But it was not until November, 1943, after two years of war, that he devoted part of his speech to the party. He could now speak of it with enthusiasm:

"The leading and guiding force of the Soviet people has been the party of Lenin, the party of the Bolsheviks . . . Under the leadership of the party of the Bolsheviks, the workers, peasants and intelligentsia of our country have won their freedom and built a socialist society. In this patriotic war the party stood before us as the inspirer and organizer of the nation-wide struggle against the fascist invaders. The organization of the party's work has united and directed toward a common goal all the efforts of the Soviet people, devoting all our forces and resources to the cause of the enemy's defeat. During the war the party has cemented still further its kinship with the people."

The theory of the dictatorship of the proletariat, on which silence had been maintained during the early period of the war, reappeared in the press. The Old Bolshevik A. Badayev recalled Stalin's words: "The Red Army is the army of the emancipated workers and peasants, the army of the November revolution, the army of the dictatorship of the proletariat." A. Gorkin tried to demonstrate in the *Bolshevik* that the "historical consequence of the realization of the policy of the party of Lenin and Stalin

is the regime of victorious Socialism. Its base is the dictatorship of the working class in alliance with the peasantry."

If Russia had been victorious because of its Socialist order,
it follows that this order must also be best for every other
country. The objective of the war was to be the establishment
of such an order throughout the world, for it alone offers a
guarantee against wars. But as it was forbidden to speak of this
openly, the aforementioned Alexandrov wrote about it in veiled
terms:

"One of the most serious, one of the most important aims of
the present war must be the establishment of such a social
order upon earth, under which adventurists, provocateurs, and
imperialist parties would be deprived of the opportunity periodically to drag the majority of peoples and states into bloody
wars."

The overtones of Marxism-Leninism sounded at times louder
than the nationalist music. The one hundred twenty-fifth anniversary of Marx's birth was marked in 1943 with solemn
articles; the twenty-fifth anniversary of the death of George
Plekhanov, founder of Russian Marxism, was likewise cele-
brated with encomiums. The anniversary of Lenin's death was
marked annually with solemnity. Again and again press and
propaganda returned to the heroic period of Soviet wars against
Allied intervention and the world bourgeoisie. Only one thing
was in wartime forbidden: to speak openly of social revolution
in other countries. Socialism, to be sure, is the guarantee of
victory, but it is a purely Russian, Soviet matter. This was
offered occasionally in a rather comic, illogical, and maladroit
manner, as when, for example, Lenin was spoken of as the
creator of "Socialism in one country." In reality, "Socialism in
one country" had already been abandoned in 1939.[1] But now,
for diplomatic considerations, it was found necessary to emphasize this doctrine.

The "Internationale" ("Arise, ye prisoners of starvation")

1. See above pp. 16 ff.

was abolished as the official anthem in favor of the new neutral national hymn ("Great Russia has cemented forever the inviolate union of free republics . . . We will lead the fatherland to glory"). But the old anthem was reserved *expressis verbis* for use by the party. Both anthems are still used. One contains the seeds of nationalism, the other the traditions of Communism. Both anthems live peacefully side by side, but not without secret hostility.

The balance was on the side of the party, of Communism. Stalin, who always regarded his public speeches as presentations of a rounded teaching and not merely as diplomatic maneuvers, was very cautious. He never spoke in any of his speeches of the All-Slav movement or of the fraternity of Slav peoples. He always kept in mind that all his speeches, his every word, would be commented upon abroad, but—and this he considered more important—that they would also be discussed and analyzed in thousands of party study circles, in schools and universities; that he was destined to become part of a *Weltanschauung*. For this reason he avoided the danger of having his loyalty to Marxism-Leninism questioned even for a moment for the sake of a transitory political success.

In November, 1943, the *Propagandist* openly demanded action against two dangers existing on the ideological front. The first was "baseless cosmopolitanism," a synonym for Trotskyism. The other was "nationalistic prejudices and anachronisms." "We must not forget," wrote this official journal, "that efforts in these directions may bring us some injury"!

Rigid adherence to Communist ideology was the antidote used against nationalistic deviations in recent years. This antidote was accentuated to the degree of a mania—on orders from above, of course:

"The entire people must remain loyal to the end to the Socialist ideas which have found expression in the life of Soviet society."

"The Soviet people defend their Socialist fatherland."

"Socialism contains within itself gigantic forces, and mankind has now entered a stage of development holding out the promise of brilliant possibilities." This old phrase of Lenin's was reprinted by the *Bolshevik* in 1943.

Has not the course of the war confirmed—all papers, magazines, lecturers now asked—the importance of Socialism in Russia, has not Socialism saved itself from defeat? How could Russia have defended herself if, despite all difficulties, the program of lightning-like industrialization had not been put into effect? Could private industry have evacuated scores of plants to the east, for example? Would the villages have supplied the necessary foodstuffs if not for Stalin's reforms? "Without the collectives," wrote Professor M. Mitin in October, 1943, "we could not have provided food for the country and the Red Army, and raw materials for industry. The collectives system makes possible the solution of all difficulties that arise in connection with supplying the Red Army and the country with food and industry with raw materials." Even the patriotism of Soviet soldiers, it was now repeatedly asserted, is the conscious patriotism of men defending their Socialism.

After the War

THE defense of a country by its army, and even heroism and sacrifices, are in no way tantamount to an approval of that country's political and social system. The British army fought magnificently, but the majority of its members appear to have been opposed to the wartime political leadership, as numerous polls and the elections of 1945 demonstrated. As far as Germany was concerned, it is doubtful whether the majority of the German army was genuinely National Socialist.

This is even more true with regard to Russia. The period of great military victories in Russian history was at the end of the eighteenth century: it was the period of Suvorov. This was precisely the worst period of the cruel serfdom, which reached its extremes under Catherine II. But those peasant serfs, humiliated and tortured at home, displayed marvels of heroism when mobilized into the army. There is no parallel between the state of the people's welfare and its exploits in war. It does not exist now as it did not exist in the past. Very important is the quality of military organization, the patriotism of the military intelligentsia, and the capacity and readiness of the Russian soldier to endure hardship and privation.

The Soviet government, however, drew quite different conclusions from its military successes. It considered its victories as a popular referendum in favor of its policies. Generalissimo Stalin won the war—therefore the soundness of all things Stalinist was evidenced. The reins had to be tightened again. No retreat! No concessions, no weakness!

And, by implication, no democracy! During four years the Soviet press had preached the "alliance of democracies" against fascism. Divergencies among the "democracies" had been passed over in silence. Now, on the contrary, these differences were stressed more and more. Old formulas reappeared: "theirs is a capitalist democracy, ours—the only real, Soviet democracy." But isn't your system a dictatorship, the foreign press kept asking. Yes, Moscow replied, we are a dictatorship and a democracy at the same time; ours is a "dictatorial democracy." It is a higher political system than that of political liberties.

Historical reminiscences were discarded; Suvorov and Kutuzov were once more relegated to the archives. Instead, the age-old Leninist formula of "capitalist encirclement" made its way anew into the Soviet limelight. Russia was indeed encircled—by Soviet satellites. Nevertheless, the mere existence of capitalist powers was considered a potential menace. The army was slowly being demobilized, but in contrast with the war-weariness evident elsewhere, Soviet leaders espoused the slogan of "strengthening the Soviet Army." This slogan dominated not only the military press but also mass meetings, manifestoes of the Communist party and national parades.

The Great Purge which started in the summer of 1946 meant a new streamlining following the "ideological retreat" made during the war. This purge was not so bloody as that of 1936–38, but it soon became no less universal, extending to every social and political aspect of Soviet life. In certain regions 90 per cent of the lower officials were removed from their posts. Laxity in restoring kolkhozes (in cases where they had disintegrated or been disbanded by the Germans) was severely criticized. State publishing houses were ordered to revert to the party line, theaters were reprimanded for continuing to present foreign or old plays, classical figures of Soviet literature had to disappear. In only two fields has the wartime retreat not been stopped: privileges and hierarchism in the Red Army were still considered necessary, in view of the growing international tension; and limited freedom of religion was maintained—for the benefit of Soviet policy in the Balkans and elsewhere.

The great retreat had ended. A new "Socialist offensive," on the way since the late 'forties, reached its peak in 1952 and early 1953, when the Ministry of State Security (actually controlled by Lavrenti Beria) was itself officially reprimanded for laxity and a new, extensive purge was inaugurated. One of the features of the purge was the arrest of sixteen Soviet doctors. The accusations against the doctors and the methods of extracting "confessions" were reminiscent of the Great Purge of 1936–38.

In the midst of these developments and on the eve of the instituting of new sweeping actions which were ominous for many leading persons of the regime, Stalin died. The purge operation was halted, Beria was restored to a high place in the government, and after the great strain and anguish there was a measure of temporary relaxation.

This was not followed, however, by substantial liberalization of internal conditions within Russia, as we will see in a later chapter.

Chapter 8. THE TWO MAIN DEVIATIONS

Trotsky and Trotskyism

"Stalin feared popular movements in Europe. Stalin did not want revolutionary explosions. He turned his back on world revolution." Dissident Communist factions of various hues and tendencies, and many noisy semi-Communist groups, have accused and continue to accuse the Russian party of treason to Communism—to world revolution. Among them Leon Trotsky and his group have played the leading role. It was Trotsky who declared, beginning in 1924, that Stalin would betray the Communist cause and all the traditions of Leninism, that he would abandon internationalism for nationalism. Have not facts confirmed the treachery?

Similar sentiments were expressed by others during the war, but with a positive estimate of Stalinism and its evolution. It is, indeed, fortunate, said these people, that Stalin abandoned international Communism; to our great satisfaction he quit fomenting revolutions in other countries. By confining himself to matters of internal Russian interests he became a national Russian leader; and it is much easier to find a common language with nationalism than with revolutionary Leninism.

"It was but natural," declared Congressman John E. Rankin in the House of Representatives on January 26, 1944, "that when Stalin came into power and got rid of the Trotsky crowd he should open the Churches and restore freedom of worship. Stalin is a gentile, and Trotsky was a Jew. When Stalin got into the war things began to change. He got rid of the commissars . . . he restored the insignia. Stalin not only did that but he changed some more of Trotsky's crazy stuff. Trotsky had organized the Comintern. Stalin broke up the Comintern. He said, 'We are no longer afraid of the rest of the world. We are convinced we can get fair treatment at the hands of our allies.' "

In Moscow, however, it was denied that either of these two views—Trotsky's or Rankin's—has any basis in fact. Moscow declared: "Stalin is the Lenin of today." Stalin, they said, is a true disciple of classical Communism, the perpetuator of its cause, the outstanding champion of world revolution today. The Communist opponents of Stalinism are themselves traitors and betrayers of high principles. Had their policy prevailed, defeat would have been certain.

In this strange controversy the voice of official Moscow was closer to the truth. The policy of old Communism had assumed a new coloring under changed world conditions but it remained basically unaltered. Even more, Stalin's policy was the only possible Communist policy under the circumstances. Any other policy would have led to either an internal or an external defeat of Communism. Whether this would have been good or bad, no other road was open to Communism.

The differences between Stalinism and Trotskyism were vastly exaggerated in the public mind. These differences did not arise from a conflict of Communism versus capitalism, or internationalism versus nationalism. The hostility between the two and the ruthless suppression of Trotskyism in Russia should not be taken as a measure of their differences. On the contrary, conflicts between two closely related tendencies, competing for influence over the same social elements, are frequently more bloody than any others.

The inspiration for many of the achievements of the Soviet government under Stalin came from the arsenal of Trotskyism. A great deal of the activity of the Soviet government has actually received the approval of the Trotskyist opposition, although this approval was frequently veiled in polemical phrases. Stalin's program of rapid industrialization and collectivization, for instance, was taken from the "platform" of the Trotskyist opposition, but only after the suppression of the opposition at the end of the 'twenties. The authors of this policy were Trotsky, Zinoviev, and Preobrazhensky, who as early as 1923–24 maintained that the continued coexistence of private (peasant) economy and state economy was an impossibility and demanded that the Socialist economy of the state "devour" the private sector.

After he had exiled Trotsky and removed Zinoviev from his responsible post, Stalin explained before a party congress why Trotsky's program had been impossible of realization earlier. "What would have happened," asked Stalin in June, 1930, "if we had listened to the 'leftists' of the Trotsky-Zinoviev group, and had opened the offensive [i.e., the campaign of collectivization] in 1926–27? We would have surely failed in this task."

Later, when the cruel and ruthless methods employed in "de-kulakization" became known, and especially with the onset of the terrible famine of 1932–33, the opposition assailed Stalin for the too rapid tempo of collectivization, contending that the operation should have been extended over a longer period. But this was only belated, irresponsible criticism from the sidelines.

An official declaration by five hundred members of the opposition in 1929 declared quite justly that "many of the ideas, slogans, formulations of our platform have become the official property of the party."

The destruction of the opposition, marked by exilings and executions, was denounced by the members of the opposition as a violation of their "elementary rights." It appeared that democracy had no more ardent supporters than the Communist opposition. Victims of ruthless suppression, they demanded liberty and accused the government of practicing "bloody violence," of promoting a "caricature of Socialism," of "degeneration." But the democracy they were demanding was only a replica of the existing system; all they really wanted was that the "ins" change places with the "outs."

"The opposition demands party, trade union, and Soviet democracy," wrote Trotsky. But the "freedom of organization" demanded was to be within the framework of dictatorship. Trotsky never explained how he proposed to square this circle. His own friends were then already demanding a purge. They demanded a breach with the "right Communists" and "acceleration of the tempo" of economic reconstruction. Had the opposition come to power it would have been compelled, though unwillingly, to apply the very same terroristic methods which it was then denouncing. Otherwise it would not have retained power.

Incidentally, the authorship of the institution of forced labor armies, this blacklist phenomenon of contemporary Soviet reality, does not belong entirely to Stalin and his associates. It was Trotsky who in the early 'twenties proposed the creation of forced labor armies of millions to be utilized by the Soviet government as it pleased. They could be moved from place to place and would serve as an important instrument of Socialist construction. To be sure, it had not occurred to him to make them a feature of the penal system. Trotsky was also the author of mass mobilization of peasant labor: "Our industrial life will acquire elements of militarism." And, indeed, after completing its maneuvers in 1920, the Third Army was sent to work in the Ural forests and on railway construction. The Fourth Army was assigned to harvest work in the Ukraine. It was decided also to create a new labor army in the Ukraine.

"When we start labor mobilization on a large scale," Trotsky wrote, "to draft hundreds of thousands and millions of peasants into production, we shall not be able to mobilize them with the help of trade unions; we can accomplish it only by military measures. They will be organized in companies, battalions, with strict discipline."

The Kronstadt uprising in March, 1921, put an end to these projects and compelled the introduction of the NEP. But ten years later these ideas, which had never disappeared from the thinking of Russian Communism, were again brought forward, strengthened by the experience gained in the Solovetsky and other concentration camps, and were made the basis of the system of mass forced labor.

On international problems Trotsky likewise shared the ideas common to all brands of Communism, including Stalin's. After Hitler's rise to power, when the contours of the coming war had become apparent, Trotsky was convinced, as were Stalin and the entire Comintern, that "in the event of victory France and England will do all they can to save Hitler and Mussolini." For fascism and Hitlerism were regarded by Trotsky, as they were by the official leaders in Moscow, as representing the last stage of capitalist development. All Communism has maintained (and continues to maintain) that there is a historical law according to which liberal and democratic capitalism becomes transformed, at a certain stage of its development, into a totalitarian capitalist regime, i.e., into fascism; and fascism can be transformed only into a Soviet regime. "Decayed democracy" and the old capitalism cannot replace fascism, for that would be as incongruous as the reverse transformation of the butterfly into a cocoon.

"How could the victory of the decaying democracies over Germany and Italy liquidate fascism?" asked Trotsky. "This would be contrary to socio-historical laws." This is precisely the theory held by official Moscow Communism.

Trotsky severely criticized the Moscow government when it signed the Soviet-German "treaty of friendship." What Trotsky criticized, however, was not the government's effort to preserve neutrality in the European war but only the treaty with Germany. What was necessary, Trotsky declared, was to remain neutral, without signing any treaty that would make Russia "Hitler's commissary." This was all very good, militant, but irresponsible criticism, for Stalin had no other choice. Germany did not and could not believe the Soviet government's promises. To be sure of Russia Hitler needed a whole system of treaty guarantees, of economic obligations, territorial dispositions, and "spheres of influence." Without these neither side could feel secure. Not wishing to participate in the war on the side of France and England, Stalin had to sign a number of treaties with Hitler, thus becoming "Hitler's commissary." It was a case of "either or." Trotsky's criticism was unreal. *La critique est aisée, l'art est difficile.*

Trotsky leveled the same criticism against the Soviet attack on Finland at the end of 1939. While criticizing the war on Finland he maintained that "once having been begun it should have been carried to the end, that is, to the Sovietization of Finland. Stalin had promised this but failed to carry it out." That was what Trotsky wanted. At one time during the Finnish war Trotsky believed that the Red Army had succeeded in kindling a civil war in Finland, a belief based upon erroneous reports from Moscow. He declared with satisfaction: "The Red Army is expropriating the big landowners and is introducing workers' control, preparatory to expropriation of the capitalists." The above quotations demonstrate clearly how mistaken is the belief that Trotsky based his plans and hopes only upon revolutionary movements in other countries, while Stalin was allegedly satisfied to operate with the Red Army as a national Russian instrument. Trotsky welcomed the revolutionary role of the Red Army in Finland.

There was no fundamental difference between Stalin and Trotsky as regards the "premature peace with Finland." It must be remembered that the Finnish campaign of 1939–40 had threatened to drag Stalin into a great international military conflict. On this point, too, the difference between the two men was not so much one of political principle as of the different circumstances in which they found themselves: the difference between a political leader and a brilliant but irresponsible critic.

On the basis of the historical record we can now strike a balance in the argument about "world revolution." In this argument Trotsky does not emerge the victor. He accused

Stalin of strangling the revolution, of being narrowly nationalist, of lacking faith in the power of the movement, of cor-
rupting "fraternal parties" into instruments of his own policy.
He asserted that with a different policy in Moscow the world
revolution would have greater chance of success. Today it is
quite clear that the failure of world revolution to materialize
in the period between the two World Wars was due to the
absence of adequate revolutionary sentiment within the respective countries themselves. Wherever revolutions did occur in
the period between 1918 and 1925 they petered out. The big
Communist parties in Germany, France, Czechoslovakia had
hundreds of thousands of members, but they were without
adequate revolutionary fervor; these countries had not reached
that hopelessness and despair which alone drive peoples to
revolution.

It was possible to instigate revolutionary outbreaks, and this
was done from Moscow in Germany in 1923, in Estonia in
1924. But these outbreaks were easily suppressed and left behind them only disillusionment. It was possible to bring in
arms, money, instructors, ideas from the outside, but one thing
it was impossible to import—a revolutionary sentiment. Without it the revolutionary drama becomes *opéra bouffe*. Neither
Stalin nor anyone else had the power to conjure up the spirit
of revolution from beneath the earth of Europe at that time
while other quite different political ideas dominated the situation. Communist outbreaks could only provoke anti-Communist fury.[1] What they might have provoked was a European

1. For years Trotsky had expected revolutionary outbreaks and he saw
the signs of revolution in places where there was not the slightest justification for such hopes. This was quite in harmony with the spirit of official
Communism. He merely compromised himself with his predictions. When
a strike wave swept France in 1936 Trotsky wrote in the New York *Nation*
(July 4, 1936), "The French revolution has begun . . . We must prepare
ourselves. The industries and factories will elect their deputies . . . we must
prepare for a victory. Soviets everywhere? Agreed. But it is time to pass from
words to action." The *Nation* illustrated Trotsky's article with a reproduction
of Daumier's "Last Council of the Ex-Ministers." The ministers are shown

alliance, headed by Germany, for possible war against Russia. This would have brought not victory for world revolution, but the defeat of the Soviet government.

Trotsky was right in one respect, however. The entire outside world, and particularly the revolutionary elements, were frequently repelled by the reality of the Soviet system, which was so different from the promises of the early Soviet period. The wholesale violence and terrorism that prevailed cooled sympathies, and crippled the activities of the Communists abroad. Supporters of the Soviet regime were able to accept these features during the stormy period of civil war in Russia, but the subsequent years of peaceful economic construction brought many protests. Repellent also was the profound poverty of the Russian people—despite all the successes of industrialization—and, finally, the new class distinctions that arose, provoking the perplexing, deadly question: Is it really worthwhile making new Soviet revolutions only to raise to power a new ruling caste? Trotsky was right when he pointed to Soviet reality as the most important antirevolutionary factor.

But his criticism of the internal policy of the Soviet government, so eagerly accepted by politicians and publicists of various schools, was very superficial. He blamed Stalin for the "absolutist bureaucracy" in power in Russia, for the development of an "unbridled oligarchy." He protested against the privileges enjoyed by the "higher-ups" and Stakhanovites. He perceived in the social structure of Soviet Russia a "monstrous perversion of the principles of the November revolution." For these reasons, beginning with 1933–34, he saw salvation only in a new revolution, which he termed (incorrectly) a political but not a social revolution: the overthrow of the "party bureaucracy" and a return to the creative mainsprings of Leninism.

---

terrified and running away as the door opens and a good-natured, fat figure of the Revolution in Phrygian cap enters.

But this Marxist, who had always denied the accidental in history and had always emphasized the primary role of historical laws, who attributed secondary importance to the role of the individual in the historical process, never answered the fatal question: Why did the Soviet revolution culminate in the rule of an "oligarchy," of a "bureaucracy"? He vented his wrath upon Stalin and upon the seizure of power by the "Stalinist clique." But this was not convincing: how did Stalin manage to fool all the forces of the proletarian party? Trotsky refused to see the natural, logical development from universal equalitarianism at the beginning to the "new oligarchy" at the end. For this reason he left everybody in a state of perplexity. Suppose it were possible to have a new revolution à la Trotsky, is there any guarantee that the new regime would not follow the very same course of development as Stalin's?

Trotsky looked upon the emergence of class distinction as a "degenerative" process, but it was the natural accompaniment of the economic restoration of Russia and, fundamentally, constituted progress. The somber aspects of that process, the blood spilled, the executions and concentration camps, were, of course, the product of the policy of a given government and would not necessarily inhere in a program of state and economic reconstruction under all conditions. But Trotsky's program to have the country return to the initial stage of a formless, classless Soviet society was essentially reactionary.

The "oligarchy" and the "bureaucracy" became for Trotsky the chief enemy. They embraced the entire new class of Soviet employees and the new intelligentsia. With a mechanical conception of history, he saw in the new high-salaried class a new *ruling* class. This was then and still remains quite untrue. What he did was to apply to Soviet society Lenin's division of all society into a "privileged top" and a "toiling population":

"Twelve to fifteen million privileged and 160,000,000 people who are profoundly dissatisfied."

In Trotsky's theory Stalin was the representative of the

twelve to fifteen million privileged, and he, Trotsky, the ideologist of the toiling millions, or, at any rate, of the working class. He summoned the toilers to revolt against the privileged. Everything was turned upside down.

In reality Stalin's government was not and is not the government of the class of Soviet employees, but has lived in open or concealed hostility to that class. If that class were to come to power it would bring relief to the country, Trotsky's theories to the contrary notwithstanding. And the "uprising of the toilers," if it were victorious, would drag the new intelligentsia down once more to the lower level of the masses, and would lead in turn, through another painful process, to the formation of new higher classes.

But without losing sight of the distinctions between official Communism and Trotskyism, it is important to remember that Russia in Trotsky's time had in embryo all the elements of the future Stalinist state. If after Lenin's death Trotsky had been included in the "triumvirate" that succeeded Lenin, and if in his conflict with Stalin he had managed to seize strategic positions and to achieve victory, it is almost certain that Trotsky would have been compelled by circumstances to do everything that Stalin has done in his thirty years of reign. With his distrust of the peasantry it is natural to suppose that Trotsky would have resorted to Stalin's collectivization program to solve the grain problem. The ruthless methods used in the struggle against the kulaks would not have repelled Trotsky; he had fully approved these methods during the period of the "Committees of the Poor" in 1918. From the very beginning Trotsky had rejected democracy for the non-Communist population. The internal party struggle (against "Stalin's faction"), becoming more acute from year to year and marked by purges and repressions, would have brought any leader of the dictatorship to the point of general liquidation of political opponents. Trotsky himself would not have been able to retain power without the use of these methods, if he wished to avoid a return to "decaying democracy." And he was opposed to any such return.

Trotsky's efforts to rebuild the Soviet economy and the Soviet state would of necessity have generated a new "bureaucracy" no less speedily than one developed under Stalin. No other Soviet leader was as inclined by character and belief to the system of hierarchical subordination as Trotsky when he was at the height of his power. No one accorded such privileges to his bureaucratic associates as did Trotsky in the period of the civil war and universal equalitarianism. It was Trotsky, as already stated, who devised the classic program of militarization of labor, and the idea of the state-apparatus, brought to realization later by Stalin, was rooted entirely in Trotsky's conceptions.

Trotsky, like most Russian Communists, was moved by deep antagonism to Britain and by only slightly less antagonism to the United States. A firm and stable alliance with the democracies against Hitler would have been as impossible under Trotsky as it has been under Stalin before the Hitler attack. He, too, was opposed to participation in any great European war, and he would have tried to maintain neutrality in the war of 1939.

To prepare the country for war Trotsky, like Stalin, would have embarked (though perhaps unwillingly) upon the restoration of "national-Russian traditions." Just as he was the true creator of the new Russian Army, Trotsky would have had to restore ranks and decorations in the army, and adopt many other features of the "Russian Thermidor" which he so bitterly denounced from his foreign exile.

Fata volentem ducunt, nolentem trahunt. The iron logic of facts is stronger than the strongest of men. It was this logic that, for a certain time, transformed "the greatest enemy of Soviet Russia," Winston Churchill, into an ally and collaborator; the antimilitarist Stalin into the builder of Russia's greatest

ment are now in France. Who knows whether the French Government, together with the Belgian, Dutch, Polish and Czechoslovak may not be compelled to seek refuge in Great Britain?

"I do not believe for a moment in the realization of Hitler's plans for a Pax Germanica and world domination. New nations, and not only European, will come forward to bar his road . . . But before his hour strikes much and many will be wiped out in Europe. Stalin does not want to be among them."

Trotsky declared prophetically: "Only a new world coalition will be able to break the German Army through a war of unprecedented proportions."

Trotsky combined a capacity for objective evaluation of historical events with utopian "Trotskyist" conceptions and unrealizable prognoses of world revolution. Toward the end of his life, however, doubts had begun to penetrate his soul. As though arguing with himself, he wrote sadly in October, 1939:

"If the November revolution does not find its continuation in the course of this war or immediately thereafter in any of the advanced countries . . . we shall undoubtedly have to raise the question of reexamination of our concept of the present epoch and its moving forces.

"Have we really entered an epoch of social revolutions?"

THE TITOIST HERESY

TROTSKY'S murder in 1940, the East-West alliance of the war years, and Stalin's assumption of the role of builder of a huge new Communist world led to a considerable weakening of the old non-Stalinist Communist factions, Trotskyism among them. Since 1948, however, another nonconformist Communist party, the Yugoslav party, which likewise accused Moscow of retrogressive "evolution," has attracted general attention and for a number of years has remained persistently in the limelight.

Vigorously anti-Stalinist, the course taken by Tito differed from Trotsky's in more than one respect, the first point of difference being that the Yugoslav Communist party was a party in power. As the party of the government it could not afford the luxury of irresponsible propaganda and free gestures. Tito's followers could not embrace Trotsky's negative and contemptuous attitude toward "socialism in one country": what Tito, with a great deal of pride, was engaged in was precisely the "building of socialism" in one country; moreover, his "one country," much smaller than Russia, would be, under the Trotsky concept, even less appropriate for the isolated venture; in this respect the Yugoslavs accepted the teachings of Stalin rather than Trotsky.

Prolonged coexistence and organic collaboration with the capitalist powers was another issue on which Titoism deviated from Trotskyism. Never outrightly denying the possibility of coexistence, Trotsky was more skeptical on this issue than Stalin; he advocated, at least on paper, a more vigorous anti-capitalist, revolutionary course of action. Here again the party in power in Belgrade could not follow the Trotskyite line, especially after Yugoslavia lost the protection of Moscow. Surrounded by suspicious neighbors and closely watched by a great power, it was happy to be left in peace; its salvation lay in the financial and military assistance it could receive from the greatest of those very "capitalist powers."

Tito himself could not openly adhere to the Trotskyite camp. A Communist of the younger generation, he had belonged to the most loyal of the Stalinist groups in the Comintern. In the years of terror, for example, when the purge of Trotskyites and other "deviationists" was under way, when the Yugoslav Communist leadership in Russia was imprisoned, when even Tito's wife was arrested as a Trotskyite (she has since vanished), Tito was not only not persecuted, but was nominated by Stalin to the post of supreme leadership of Yugoslav Communism. Under these conditions, it was proof of his extreme loyalty that he translated into Croatian Stalin's *Short Course,* which

appeared in 1938. Condemnation of Trotsky and the Trotskyites as the "scum of the earth," proclaimed hundreds of
times by the leaders of Yugoslav Communism at the time, was
making a rapprochement impossible.

Actually, however, Tito, Rankovich, Kardelj, Bebler, Pijade,
and their press have gradually, since 1949, produced a semi-
Trotskyite philosophy of Soviet evolution away from Communism. To them, not only Marx and Engels but Lenin, too, is of
the true prophets; Stalin was the villain, the perverter of the
legacy, the father of a "reactionary" policy, his "international"
a tool to block the progressive movements of mankind.

The Yugoslavs have maintained that the Soviet Union was
on its way to creating a true Socialist society but went in the
wrong direction when Stalin broke with Marx' precept that the
state must wither away: the power of the Soviet state has been
constantly on the increase and finally overpowered the people,
the workers, and even the Communist party itself:

"The development of the revolution in Soviet Russia [Tito
said] came to a halt; the workers' rights were entirely destroyed,
and the state went the way of state capitalism. Stalin has created
the most centralized state in history. The entire country of two
hundred million people possesses only one brain, that of the
Kremlin." [2]

The growing power of the state found expression in the
growth of bureaucracy, centralized administration, the police
system, the armed forces; it found expression also in Soviet
"imperialism" (as the Tito group now labels Communist expansion), in Stalin's reliance on the army and his faith in
armed force as the main instrument for the attainment of
socialism. Neglect of smaller nations, exploitation of its weaker
allies, and the growth of Russian nationalism were the other
elements of this retrogressive "evolution" of Soviet Communism under Stalin.

"Bureaucratic centralism," said Ales Bebler, "the power of

2. Vladimir Dedjer, *Tito* (New York, Simon and Shuster, 1953), p. 425.

the State machinery as opposed to the individual citizen, their Great Russian nationalism overshadowing the smaller peoples within the USSR, their interference in the life of their neighbors, their pressure and their threats against a small and independent country like Yugoslavia, their lack of good will in the field of international collaboration, as shown, among other instances, in the recent walk-outs from the United Nations organs—all these manifestations of Soviet policy have cast a shadow on the very essence of a doctrine, namely Marxism, which in our opinion is fundamentally democratic and in the best traditions of what we now call the West." [3]

Much of this criticism, while not always profound, was justified; much of it was only a repetition of what Trotsky had said before. But unlike the Trotsky faction, the Yugoslavs were in a position to try to prove that there is a better brand of Communism possible than that of the degenerated Stalinists. To fight pernicious bureaucracy and centralism, the Tito government introduced a kind of "workers' control" in industrial plants which was to replace the Stalinist method of centralized economic administration. "The withering away of the state," Tito stated in June, 1950, "starts first of all at its economic functions, in the management of production by the producers, in the gradual transfer of economic functions from the state to the working collective, though not by leaps and bounds, but gradually, since anarchy would arise otherwise." [4] Limiting the problem of democracy to the narrow field of elected shop committees, the Tito government was unable to cure its political troubles. For bureaucracy, a grave illness of our times, assumes huge proportions and becomes intolerable wherever its activity is protected by an omnipotent government, a regimented press, and the absence of free criticism. "Elections," if they are not combined with free criticism and offer no choice of program, are of no help. The Yugoslav experiment with

3. *Yugoslav Newsletter,* New York, June 12, 1950.
4. *Borba,* Belgrade, June 17, 1950.

elected shop committees can abolish bureaucracy at about the speed that a pump can bail out the sea. The same is true with regard to the other Yugoslav reforms of recent years, such as decentralization of administration by transfer of certain functions from Belgrade to provincial and district authorities, and the attempt to reduce numerically the size of the officialdom. The essence of a bureaucracy, its supreme role in the life of a nation, and its relationship with the people remain unaltered by periodic cuts in size, as has been proved more than once in Russia.

On the other hand, in the course of developing more and more anti-Soviet trends, the Yugoslav Communists began to embrace ideas of the freedom of the individual. This was a highly important departure from the theory of dictatorship. "There is nothing more convincing," Ales Bebler has stated, "than facts; we Yugoslavs have pledged ourselves to establish a historic fact of great importance: a Socialist state with the fullest freedom of the individual, liberated from servitude to other individuals and from the tyranny of the state, a Socialist state with a high standard of life and a high cultural level for all its citizens, a Socialist state with the fullest equality, both political and economic, of all the peoples and national minorities, a Socialist state preparing and achieving its complete identification with the people, and thus bringing about its own abolition as a machinery above the people." [5]

"There is no doubt," added Edvard Kardelj, "that free Socialist criticism, political and scientific, that contributes to the progress of Socialism, must be the law of every genuine Socialist country and that it must be granted a fitting place in the system of Socialist democracy." [6]

This was a most important set of ideas; in fact, the ideas in open contradiction to orthodox Communism, with its emphasis on the "collective" and the "masses" and the sacrifice of the

5. *Yugoslav Newsletter*, June 12, 1950.
6. *Yugoslav Review*, New York, *I*, No. 5 (1952), p. 7.

individual for the common cause. At this point Titoism came dangerously near to the general concept of democracy; had it put these ideas into practice, it would have demonstrated its ability to go the way of a democratic evolution.

Facts proved, however, that the scope of Communist evolution in Yugoslavia was limited, and that the stressing of free criticism and the freedom of the individual remained only pious promises. On September 10, 1953, Vice-President Moshe Pijade told the Yugoslav Parliament that the number of political arrests in the country amounted to 45,086 in 1948, 52,606 in 1949, 36,196 in 1950, 22,359 in 1951, and 15,484 in 1952. Political arrests have been on the decrease but even at their lowest level are an indication of the severity of the police system.

Tito himself set limits to the prodemocratic trends. "We wonder," he said, "why the West wants a multi-party system, why the West wants us to go backwards, to throw away what we have achieved. This would mean only a retrogression, a return to capitalism, the conversion of our country into a satellite of this or that great power. The first business of a revolution is the liquidation of the multi-party system." [7]

The Djilas affair of late 1953 served as the first test of the vigor of the new trends. Milovan Djilas, chairman of the Yugoslav Parliament, veteran Communist revolutionary, and considered the best choice to succeed Tito if the need arose, wrote a series of articles advocating less thought control and "free expression of opinions." In his criticism of the system of government of his country, Djilas called for more freedom within the ruling party, a demand tantamount to a demand for the right to build factions and groupings of a nonconformist type; he did not ask, however, for the right to legalize a second political party. At first the official press viewed Djilas' articles as another contribution to the general attack on the Soviet system, and printed them. The protests, however, became loud,

7. Dedjer, *Tito*, p. 420.

and finally Tito took the lead in an operation aimed at the suppression of Djilas and his ideas.

The operation was carried out in true totalitarian fashion. At the January, 1954, session of the Central Committee, called to discuss the Djilas affair, Tito acted as chief prosecutor; a number of staunch followers supported him; to make the picture complete, Djilas "repented." The decision of the Central Committee was to expel Djilas from the Committee, divest him of all posts in the party, and "give him a last warning." In addition, the leadership instructed the party hierarchy to avoid even purely personal contact with Djilas. Only one of Djilas' friends, Vladimir Dedjer, disobeyed the order. Dedjer, official biographer and close friend of Tito, had joined the ranks of the opposition. He was shelved as a member of the Central Committee and, removed from political activity, took a job as a lecturer in modern history.

Meanwhile Djilas granted a political interview to a *New York Times* correspondent in which he advocated the organization of a second party. On December 28, 1954, the Yugoslav Parliament revoked Djilas' immunity in order to make possible prosecution for "propaganda against the state and the people." In January, 1955, Djilas and Dedjer were convicted of waging "hostile propaganda"; Djilas was sentenced to 18 months in prison, Dedjer to 6 months. (In both cases the sentence was suspended for a probationary period.) In the course of the trial, Vice-President Kardelj reiterated the Yugoslav regime's opposition to any multiparty political system.

Both in ideology and in political practice Titoist Communism represented great progress compared to Soviet Stalinism. After its break with Moscow it discontinued its belligerent course against its neighbors and opposed the North Korean war offensive. In internal affairs it has permitted the dissolution of peasants' collectives and, within the framework of the dictatorship, reduced prosecutions and political terror. But the limits of dictatorship proved to be an iron wall which could not be breached.

The limited potentialities of a democratic evolution in Yugoslavia made a rapprochement with the Soviet Union possible. Soon after Stalin's death new ties were established between Moscow and Belgrade. The improvement in relations between the two regimes culminated in a visit of Soviet leaders to Belgrade in May, 1955, and the proffering of an apology by the Russians to Tito and his party. "Evolution" had materialized to a very modest degree.

Chapter 9. THE COMMUNIST PARTY
OF THE SOVIET UNION

AT THE BEGINNING of the first Russian revolution (1905), the Bolshevik party numbered from five to eight thousand members. At present it has some eight million party members, supplemented by sixteen million adherents of the Communist Youth League, a party auxiliary. From a paltry few thousand to nearly twenty-four million is a considerable growth.

Paradoxical as it may sound, the fact is that the governing element of the party, numerically speaking, has remained about what it was some thirty years ago. The real party, in its Bolshevik conception, consists as before of a few thousand members.

It is very difficult for a non-Russian to grasp the peculiar Russian-Communist view of a party. An American party is a great entity united by common political opinions but leaving room, at the same time, for new ideas and new leaders. Every few years an American party may witness a contest that determines its leadership, shapes its program, and offers its voters an opportunity to set its policies and its fate in one direction or another. Such a party keeps its ear attuned to the wishes of its followers and the electorate, to what its local politicians report, to polls, to changes in sentiment in the various states and districts. All this is the exact opposite of the Bolshevik concept of a party. Yet unless this difference is kept in mind it is impossible to comprehend much that goes on in Russia.

We will come closer to the question if we draw an analogy between the Bolshevik party and the officer corps of an army. The rank-and-file soldiers, comprising at times millions of men, are merely the material in the hands of the commanders. A few thousand officers, trained from youth and making it their career, constitute the nucleus of a modern army, which, when necessary, is transformed, through mobilization, into a vast force of many millions. When this army is again contracted to a minimum, a great part of the officer cadres may be maintained. The rebirth of the Germany Army after Versailles became possible only because the army was given the right to maintain four thousand officers.

Such was always the Bolshevik concept of a party: an officer corps which organizes its army; not a party according to the Western idea, which chooses its commanders. Soldiers do not choose their own generals.

The Bolshevik idea of a party is akin to the steel framework in modern architecture. The framework is erected first; then it is covered with bricks. Sometimes, even, the brickwork may be removed and a new building erected upon the old steel framework. To be sure, it is impossible to attain the objective without support from the masses, just as it is impossible to live in a structure consisting only of steel girders and rafters. But everything rests upon a framework. The party is the framework and the people are the necessary, but secondary, element.

Fifty years ago, as we have seen, the Bolshevik party (at that time termed the Bolshevik faction) consisted of a few thousand men and women, devoted to their cause. The great majority were not workers—in all probability there were more members from the ranks of the nonworker families than manual laborers. As the revolution developed, however, tens of thousands flowed into the various revolutionary parties, including that of the Bolsheviks. When the revolution had attained its high point—October–December, 1905—these parties, among them the Bolsheviks, had enrolled masses of people, with scores of organizations and countless sympathizers. Then, with the end of 1906, came the reaction; the revolution was soon crushed, and the years from 1907 to 1917 marked the last stable period of the tsarist monarchy. The masses deserted the revolutionary parties, and the Bolshevik party was reduced, too. In March, 1917, the tide of popular support began to rise again, once more filling the readymade party mold with human material, and by October, 1917, the Bolshevik party was the strongest of all the Russian parties.

As Bolshevism conceives it, a party is not a popular mass, and a popular mass is not a party. A party is solid, constant, a backbone; the people are unstable, changing, flesh and muscle. A party has a clear theory, a revolutionary conception; the people are subject to moods and hesitations. The party leads, the people follow. A party is a minority directing the majority. A party must not be too big; when it numbers millions it loses its stability and spiritual quality. It is possible to find a few thousand, perhaps a few score thousand firm, unbending enthusiasts, but millions cannot sustain this enthusiasm. From this flow all the difficulties of the present period, when the Bolshevik party has become an organization of millions.

At the dawn of the Bolshevik movement, when its foundations were being laid, no one could, of course, foresee this difficulty. The "people" to whom the small party appealed were, first and foremost, the industrial workers, who numbered in prerevolutionary Russia about two to three million. The Bolshevik leaders regarded them very dubiously. "An elemental labor movement," wrote Lenin, "can create and inevitably creates only trade unionism, and a trade-union policy of the working class is a bourgeois policy of the working class." The workers themselves, he wrote, cannot develop a Communist consciousness: "this can be brought only from outside."

By "outside" he meant a small party seeking to lead the workers but not necessarily consisting of workers. "The founders of modern scientific Socialism themselves, Marx and Engels, belonged to the bourgeois intelligentsia," wrote Lenin, just as the Communist movement [1] in Russia developed not as a movement of workers but as the "natural and inevitable result of the development of thought in the revolutionary-socialist intelligentsia." "Only from outside," he declared, emphasizing the word "outside," "is it possible to bring a new political consciousness to the workers." [2]

By "outside" Lenin meant an "organization of revolutionists essential to the carrying out of a political revolution." Such an organization "must embrace people whose profession consists of revolutionary activity." This profession must constitute their only or most important occupation, and for this reason, said Lenin, the party "must not be too broad." It must be an organization of directors of the revolution. "Give us an organization of revolutionists and we will turn Russia upside down!" Lenin exclaimed.

Such a party, he taught, must work in deep secrecy and preserve the strictest discipline. Its various organs must carry out without question the instructions of the higher authorities. The entire structure was actually made up as follows: a small group constituted the Central Committee, which had at its disposal an apparatus of agents and representatives; the agents selected local and regional committees from among party members. The system of centralization was applied to an extreme degree, buttressed by rigid discipline. But while there were many changes, for various reasons, in the composition of the Central Committee, one man remained unsupplanted at the head of all party organizations, committees, and editorial offices from 1903 to 1923. That man was Lenin. It was he who actually

1. Lenin spoke in this instance of the Social Democratic movement, which, in present-day terminology, should be translated to mean the Communist movement.

2. It must not be supposed, however, that Lenin placed particular hope in the intelligentsia. They were, for the most part, anti-Bolshevik even then, and adhered largely to the moderate parties. Lenin had in mind only the small group of Russian intellectuals whom he considered capable of forming the nucleus of an extreme revolutionary party.

picked the members of the Central Committee, thus being able, under the system of rigid centralism and discipline, to direct the entire party.

In this way, even at its beginning, the Bolshevik party structure led to the centralization of all leadership in the hands of its outstanding leader, while the small organization of revolutionists was the embryo of the *future state power*.[3]

The important role played by the party leader was accompanied by a worship of discipline unknown in any other party. Long before the various purges of the later period under the Soviet regime, the blind obedience expected from the party members was elevated to a high principle. The orders of the commander-in-chief must be implicitly obeyed. The intellectual life and ideological independence of the party members were considered much less important than unalterable, rigid discipline.

During that period—the period preceding the downfall of the tsarist regime, when the old foundations of the nation's political structure were being shaken—Russian youth was inclined to subject to criticism all traditions, without exception. Rebellious "nonrecognition of authority" was the symptom of the approaching storm; in place of the old authoritarianism there was criticism, respect for the "critically thinking individual," for spiritual and intellectual life. But Bolshevism fought these tendencies, taking the position that the authorities of the old world had to be overthrown, to be sure, but must be replaced immediately by new authorities; by new men, new ideas, to be followed without criticism, blindly, even without comprehension, perhaps, of the deeper, long-range aims of the leader.

3. When Lenin put forward this concept, the young Trotsky remarked prophetically in 1904: "In Lenin's scheme, the party takes the place of the working class. The party organization displaces the party. The Central Committee displaces the party organization, and finally the Dictator displaces the Central Committee" (*Nashi Politicheskiya Zadachi*, Geneva, 1904, p. 54).

For this reason, the Bolshevik party never required from the mass of its members any deep understanding of programs and principles: what was important was not so much the intellectual preparation on the part of the individual member as emotional devotion to and faith in the leaders.

LENIN'S PARTY

AT the time of the downfall of the tsarist regime in 1917, the Bolshevik party was a small group. In the new revolutionary atmosphere, however, the party's influence mounted rapidly among the workers and soldiers (because of its antiwar position—it was the only party opposed to the war) and within six months the membership leaped to 200,000.

That was the short period of Russian democracy, when the doors were opened wide for political debate and struggle; freedom of speech and assembly were fully utilized for its own purposes by the Bolshevik party, with its network of organizations covering the entire country and the entire front. In accordance with his general scheme, Lenin considered his task simple and natural: "Russia used to be ruled by 150,000 landlords," he wrote in August, 1917. "Why could not 240,000 Bolsheviks do the same job?"

At the time of the November revolution, as already indicated, the party had some 200,000 members.[4] In the next two years the party continued to grow, but slowly. First the Brest Litovsk peace served to cool the sympathies of many, and the subsequent civil war and armed conflict between the government and peasantry, which at moments had threatened to end in the overthrow of the government, slowed the influx of new members. In the spring of 1919 the party membership numbered 313,000.[5] Subsequently, however, after the liquida-

4. Official party statistics subsequently revised this figure, giving the number of party members at the time of the November revolution as even below 100,000. However, this revised figure is rather doubtful.

5. This number did not include, however, many regions situated at that time behind the anti-Bolshevik fronts of the civil war.

tion of Allied intervention and on the eve of the collapse of the White armies, the influx was resumed. The number of party members at the time of the Bolshevik Congress in 1920 had risen, according to official figures, to 612,000—an increase of almost 100 per cent, reflecting the victories of the Soviet regime.

Lenin's original scheme of party organization presupposed the creation of a small party of Communists, absolutely devoted to their cause, whereas, after the November revolution, the party was inundated by tens and, later, hundreds of thousands of people, who flocked to it from conviction, or from the desire to make a career, or from considerations of immediate material gain. The party swelled to huge proportions.[6] To be sure, it would have been possible to reduce its membership arbitrarily or simply to close the doors to new members. However, the great party mass now became the reservoir supplying thousands of people for the expanded apparatus of administration and state economy, and the admission of new members facilitated control of the state machinery. The party no longer resembled the staff of the commander-in-chief of a disciplined army. This was the period of a plethora of "intraparty discussions" on numerous questions, such as "the trade unions," "democratic centralism," etc.

All this was contrary to the classic conception of what a Bolshevik party should be. "The party is in a fever," declared Lenin angrily, obviously and properly concerned about the situation. But after his death the fever grew considerably worse. Only toward the end of the 'twenties, when political struggles in general came to a standstill, did a calm descend upon the party so far as its inner life and ideological activity were concerned.

6. This growth affected its composition. In 1918 according to official party figures, workers constituted about 57 per cent of the party membership; in 1919, 48 per cent; in 1920, 44 per cent; and in 1921 only 41 per cent. Even more striking were the figures of new members who joined the party in these years: in 1917, 56 per cent of the newcomers were workers; in 1918, 40 per cent; in 1919, 38 per cent; in 1920, 33 per cent; in 1921, 30 per cent.

Molding the Party

THROUGH purges extending over a period of two decades (up to the war) 1,500,000 to 2,000,000 people were expelled from the Communist party and the number of those who were refused admittance to the party was also very great. A party which at the beginning of the 'twenties numbered about 500,000 members subsequently expelled or refused admittance to numbers vastly greater than its former total membership.

At the base of this practice lay Lenin's old idea of a small Communist nucleus, whose task it was to organize whole peoples in military fashion in time of political storms. As we have seen, it was not the mass that was to impose its will upon the revolutionary leader but the leader who was to direct the mass. The people inside the party was something quite new. But inside or outside the party, the people remained merely the object of policy. It became necessary to regulate this intraparty popular mass, to remold the party as if the vast membership were so much clay, to give it the form best suitable to the realization of the aims of world Communism, the roads to the attainment of which were clear only to the small nucleus of leaders. The party had to remain an instrument in the hands of a chosen few, and this instrument, like every instrument, had to be constantly sharpened, ground, cleaned, and repaired.

The right of the leader to institute purges follows as the immediate conclusion from this conception.

The first general purge in the party occurred in 1921. Within a period of a few months nearly 30 per cent of the members were removed; of 585,000 members, 175,000 were expelled or found it wise to leave. This first experiment in the purge differed from subsequent ones in that almost none of the "purged" were arrested or made to suffer any other loss, most of them remaining at their former posts.

In 1925 the Central Committee again decided to remold the composition of the party within a period of two years: a minimum of 50 per cent of the membership was to consist of "workers-at-the-bench." By means of mass recruiting drives this was almost achieved by the end of the 'twenties, when 48 per cent of party members were workers. But this situation did not last long.

The general membership continued to grow as the growing state machinery required additional officials. In 1925 the figure had risen to 800,000, and in 1926 it was more than 1,000,000. In 1927 the number rose to 1,147,000, after a recruiting campaign instituted on the occasion of the tenth anniversary of the November revolution. Thus, in 1928, the party membership had expanded to 1,304,000. Finally, in 1930, a special "Lenin membership drive" was launched, resulting in the recruiting of 150,000 "candidates."

The second of the Great Purges took place in 1928. In the interval between the two there were smaller, partial purges, in 1924 and in 1926. In 1924 (after a not unusual outburst of party conflict marked by successes for Trotsky among students and in some organizations of government employees) the purges struck party cells in educational institutions and in government offices. In 1926 a purge was carried out in various rural party organizations. Roughly, the number of those expelled (and of those who left the party voluntarily, which was tantamount to expulsion) was as follows: in 1922, 45,000; in 1923 about 40,000; in 1924, 23,000; in 1925, 32,100; in 1926, 35,000; in 1927, 44,000; and in 1928—before the great purge—about 40,000. Thus, the number of those who were expelled or who left the party in the interval between the two great purges, or from 1922 to 1928, was approximately 260,000.

The end of the 'twenties was marked by bitter conflict between various party factions, and Stalin came out victorious. The Great Purge of 1929 was the natural consequence of this victory, being designed to strengthen the captured positions. The number of party members expelled was more than 160,-

000. Among those hit were the rural organizations, 15 per cent of whose members were driven from the party.

While expelling scores of thousands of old party members, the party centers were forcing the admission of new ones. Despite the great purge the party membership continued to rise. In 1929 it was 1,532,000 and in 1930, 1,852,000.

For millions of people this process was not so much acceptance of Communism as the disappearance in the masses of the population of any spirit of militant resistance to the regime. After the defeat of the liberal and conservative parties, after all other parties had ceased to function for a decade, the Soviet regime had acquired a peculiar stability and endurance —it became "legitimate" in a historical and political sense.

By experience extending over many years, the Russian people were taught to accept the idea that this Soviet-Communist regime was strong and stable, that it was hopeless to struggle against it. In the realm of international relations this consciousness of its stability led to the recognition of the Soviet government *de facto* and *de jure*; the process of recognition by various countries was extended over a period of ten to fifteen years. The average Russian, who had ceased to resist the Soviet government by 1919–20, began to realize, long before foreign governments did so, the iron power and peculiar stability of the new regime. All capacity for resistance vanished. This was to be even more true of the younger generation, for whom a non-Soviet regime was now as much of an archaism as would be a journey on horseback from New York to Chicago.

Soon ideological debates in the party came to an end. Opposition groups were smashed, and as the Soviet regime had become identical with Communism, so Communism became identical with Stalinism. Membership in the party or in any of its auxiliary organizations became a certificate of loyalty; frequently it was an essential condition to admission to an important job in industry or in the government. Those who sought advancement had to pass through party offices if they wanted to avoid many obstacles. On the other hand, the party officials made it their business to seek out ambitious, prominent men and women and bring them into the party: writers, engineers, military people, students with honor records, successful Stakhanovites. These were the elements the party needed—the new "notables" of Russia. To be sure, the party continued at the same time to admit simple folk, rank-and-file workers and soldiers, but this had already assumed a decorative character, being designed to demonstrate the regime's "tie with the people" or to confer a reward for service to the Soviet fatherland.

In the 'twenties, no one took seriously the constitutional rights and liberties guaranteed in the Soviet constitutions, but the bylaws of the Communist party, that other constitution, did have a certain real value. The political rights enjoyed solely by party members included that of participating in decisions affecting current problems and an indirect right to determine the composition of the government. Elections to party conferences occasionally took the form of genuine electoral contests. Party members at their meetings enjoyed a certain measure of freedom of speech. They had the right to bear arms. Arrest of a party member was inconceivable, except for extreme criminal offenses.

Subsequently, however, this constitution—the party bylaws —ceased to be observed. The political rights of party members disappeared with the liquidation of the opposition. Discussion of important questions at party meetings was abandoned, while the meetings became increasingly rare. From then on all voting at party meetings had to be unanimous. Thus, in this respect, too, in the matter of political rights, the distinction between the Communist and non-Communist masses disappeared. Henceforth a Communist could be not only expelled from the party but arrested for political reasons. The hundreds of thousands of those expelled from the party, and, later, the arrested party members, gave evidence of the fact that the qualitative distinction between the party membership and non-party mass had almost disappeared.

The consequence was the re-emergence of the old scheme: ten thousand devout Communists wielded the power in efforts to advance the Communist cause; behind them, with complete faith in their authority, without venturing to question or to criticize, marched several million people, displaying the emblems of the party and the Komsomol. All that was required of them was strict discipline and hard work. They constituted the transmission belts between the group of leaders and the vast bulk of the nonparty masses, who were supposed to toil in the sweat of their brows, in silent, patient expectation of the day when the sun, kindled by someone, would shine for them, too.

ALL the phenomena mentioned above had attained their full development in the 'thirties. Party conferences or congresses, having lost their importance, having become parliaments without an opposition, were being convoked at increasingly rarer intervals. Although the 1927 Congress decided that such party conclaves were to be convened at least every two years, three years elapsed before the next one. There was an interval of almost four years between the 1930 Congress and the next. Finally there was but one other party congress during the period preceding the war—in March, 1939. Thirteen years passed before the next congress of the Soviet Communist party was assembled, in 1952.

The purge begun in 1933 continued for several years. Nearly 200,000 members were eliminated from the party in the first year. It was expected that the purge would be concluded by 1935, and the announcement of a forthcoming restoration of normal party life was actually made. However, this did not happen. A new purge was launched in 1935, and with the summer of 1936 began the greatest and most terrible of all party purges (it coincided with the changed international situation). This continued until 1938, and in the army and navy until 1939. Many hundreds of thousands of party members were expelled; thousands were arrested and executed.

After the conclusion of the purge, Stalin informed the party congress of 1939 that the party membership had decreased by 270,000 as compared with 1934. The total of party members and candidates at that time, in the winter of 1939, was 2,478,-000. In September–October, 1939, the party membership exceeded 3,000,000. A year later it was 3,700,000,[7] and, in the spring of 1941, before Russia was plunged into the war, the figure was approximately 3,900,000. During the war the party continued to expand. By autumn, 1943, it had 4,600,000 members. At the end of the war it had 5,700,000 members. In the short span of four war years, despite the considerable losses in the war, it grew by about two million. In 1953 its membership had reached 7,000,000 and in 1956, 7,200,000.

STALIN AND HIS PARTY

How can this development be reconciled with the traditional Bolshevik concept of the party as a small directing group of devoted, enlightened Communists organized to lead the great nonpolitical masses?

It must be remembered that Stalin shared fully Lenin's concept of the party. Stalin saw in the masses "inertia and political indifference": [8] according to Stalin the party cannot properly, and therefore should not, amalgamate with the people or with the workers. It must be a minority composed only of "the best elements"; it must move in advance of its class. The party, Stalin maintained, must be a "political leader."

"The party must be the advance guard of the working class. . . . The party must absorb all the best elements of the work-

7. This figure included the new Communist organizations in the regions annexed to Soviet Russia between September, 1939, and July, 1940.
8. Stalin, *Works* (Moscow, 1947), *6*, 171–179.

ing class. The party cannot be a real party . . . if it cannot overcome the inertia and political indifference of an elemental movement. The party must stand in advance of the working class."

From this concept of the party Stalin's favorite analogy of a small general staff commanding an army of millions flows logically. "The party is the fighting staff of the proletariat," said Stalin. "The party must lead the proletariat into the offensive . . . and must direct the retreat if circumstances demand it."

Stalin continued to regard the working masses, even the millions within his own party, as an unstable human mass which could veer suddenly in the opposite direction; and he persisted in believing that the sole guaranty against its moving in a false direction lay in the enlightened Communist reason of the party leaders. His giving party cards to hundreds of thousands, bestowing party rights upon them, did not indicate any increase in his faith in the stability of the masses.

What Bolshevism once conceived as the principle that should govern the relationship between the small party and the people was now transformed into the governing principle operating within the party itself. The gigantic expansion of the party has transformed it into a huge body, but this party mass is not divided by an impenetrable gulf from the outside mass; both are politically dangerous, for both may "hesitate" in a moment of danger. The leaders remain the steel framework of the party structure.

Stalin's attitude toward this party mass was expressed again, in 1937–39, when the apparently unimportant question of admission into the party was again under discussion. In 1934 it had been decided that only those candidates were to be admitted who, having passed a course of political education, had "mastered the program and constitution of the party."

"Every party member must master the basic principles of Marxism-Leninism," declared Kaganovich, in those years the most powerful man next to Stalin, in explaining this require-ment.[9]

Three years later Stalin came out against this principle. What was required, he maintained, was not "mastery" of the party program but merely its acceptance, as had been the case in Lenin's time. True knowledge and understanding must be assumed to reside only in the upper spheres, where Leninism has been "mastered." For the party at large, however, this was not to be obligatory.

The party bylaws were again altered in 1939 in accordance with Stalin's views.

Thus the party membership has been divided into two parts: those who have "mastered" the program and policy of Com-munism, and those who merely "accept" it. The first are the leaders; the second include the useful workers, administrators, engineers, economists—elements essential to the life of the country, useful in their respective districts as long as they act in accordance with instructions.

Stalin has always been conscious of this difference. He has defined the Stalinist concept of the party as follows: "Three or four thousand men of the high command—the generals of our party. Then 30 to 40 thousand intermediate commanders: these constitute the officers' corps of our party. And further, 100 to 150 thousand of the leading elements of our party—these are, so to speak—the subaltern officers of the party."

Thus, according to Stalin's calculation, the governing ele-ments of the party numbered 150 to 200 thousand members, no more than 10 per cent of the party membership of that year (1937). Even so, one would hardly include all petty officers in the commanding elements of an army. Of the 30,000 to 40,000 party directors (the middle category), fully one-half are scat-tered throughout distant provinces, far from the main political

---

9. At that time this proposal was, of course, supported by Stalin. During membership purges, such as this one, the leaders were looking for oppor-tunities to get rid of many members, and failure to master the true teachings of Leninism was to serve as a point of indictment.

center. They have no part in the formation of party opinion. Only about 10,000 to 15,000 comprise the heart of the Russian Communist party. These constitute the real party.

By the end of the 'thirties, when the great purge was over, this new relationship between the leadership and the millions of members was firmly and finally established. The problem of a really small party, in Lenin's sense, inside the huge Communist party was solved. Now the party could proceed to enroll additional millions of members. It grew rapidly during the war. Bylaws were changed, conditions governing the admission of new members were eased as regarded members of the armed forces. If he was in uniform, a "candidate" could become a full-fledged member within three months; and the party was anxious to enroll all those soldiers and officers who had distinguished themselves, whether in battle or otherwise. Decorations and citations meant at the same time an insistent invitation to join the party ranks. The insistence was successful in virtually all cases.

The Real Party

THIS party kernel, the successor to Lenin's organization of "professional revolutionists," has grown very slowly over a period of decades. As we have seen, the underground organization of the Bolsheviks at the beginning of the 1905 revolution comprised about 8,000 persons, and it had about 23,000 at the beginning of the second revolution in 1917. In 1922, when the party membership had already exceeded 500,000, Molotov placed the number of "active party workers" at 15,000.[10]

An official census of the party personnel in 1927, including party "generals" and "officers," disclosed the following figures:

10. He gave the following figures: The Central Committee and its immediate associates in Moscow and in the provinces, 325 persons; these were the generals. Leading members in the provinces, about 2,000; party officials in the provinces and secretaries of individual cells, 13,000. These were the officers.

members of central, regional, and provincial committees, 3,500; minor leaders, 37,000.

Ten years later Stalin's report (just quoted) showed that the figures still held; there still were 30,000 to 40,000 "generals and commanders." His report was a convincing proof of how slowly the party kernel was developing, as distinguished from the influx of the party mass.

In 1939 Andrei Zhdanov presented the following report to the party congress giving the number of secretaries, i.e., of party employees, in charge of local organizations:

Secretaries and directors of regional and district divisions   843
Secretaries of lower party units 10,902
TOTAL 11,745

The party core itself is divided into various gradations. The authority of the leader is undisputed; after the leader, in point of influence, come the Politbureau (in 1952 it was renamed Presidium) and the administrative office of the Central Committee. The Politbureau-Presidium is the party's real brain; it numbers from 11 to 14 people including the deputies, elected from among the members of the Central Committee. Since Lenin's days the Politbureau-Presidium has been practically the government of Russia. The "Secretariat" of the Central Committee, with a few members of the Presidium at its head, is the nerve center of all political activity. Until 1952 the powerful Orgbureau dealt with internal problems of the party organization; among these problems appointments to and dismissals from public office were the most important. At times— such as during the purges—this activity of the Orgbureau was of great political significance.

The administrative office of the Central Committee is subordinated to the Presidium, but its importance is enormous. Its officials are not chosen by party conferences or congresses but hold office by appointment. Its importance is much greater than that of the small staff of executives and employees in the White

House, or at 10 Downing Street. It is not analogous to a premier's office, for there is another institution performing that function under the chairman of the Council of Ministers. The executive office of the Central Committee is an all-embracing administrative apparatus impinging upon all phases of government activity. It assembles material for the leaders' speeches, for government and party declarations, and important resolutions. It collects data pertaining to every prominent member of the party, and maintains complicated statistical records. The fate of many party leaders and rank-and-filers has been decided on the basis of material collected in these offices.

This institution also prepares projects dealing with collectivization, industrialization, purges, shake-ups, projects which are subsequently approved or rejected, as the case may be. Ministers and other high government officials come to the office of the Central Committee for instructions, for many officials in that office wield greater authority than do the ministers.

It should be kept in mind that the rank of minister (formerly people's commissar) in the Soviet Union cannot be compared in importance with that of a cabinet member elsewhere. There are several hundred ministers in Russia. Of these, only seventy to eighty reside in Moscow as ministers of the USSR or of the Russian Republic. Hundreds of others are ministers in the affiliated Soviet Republics. Only those ministers who also happen to be members of the Presidium, men like Bulganin, Molotov, and a few others, occupy positions of great authority.

Thus, hundreds of ministers scattered all over the country are conscious of the watchful eye of the administrative office of the Central Committee in Moscow. In practice, and contrary to the Constitution, they are responsible not to their respective parliaments (Supreme Soviets) but directly and indirectly to some specific division in the administrative office of the Central Committee.

The relationship between these leading party organs on the one hand and the Soviet government on the other is often misunderstood abroad, despite the fact that it has remained essentially stable. Members of the Soviet government (people's commissars or ministers) either are themselves members of the Presidium or are subordinated to a specific member of that leading party body. Governmental functions are actually divided among the members of the Presidium. The number of ministries (people's commissariats) has grown from twelve to over fifty in the course of the thirty-seven years of the Soviet regime, the main reason for this increase being the multitude of new economic functions. Groups of ministries are placed under the control of the real minister—a member of the Presidium.

In certain cases, a member of the Presidium performs functions that do not exist on paper and are not provided for in the Soviet Constitution. For a long time education, for example, was the concern of the various national republics, and there was no ministry of education in the constitutional government of the Soviet Union. Actually, however, the Presidium assigned one of its members to control and direct all the ministries of education in the various constituent republics. In this way the activities of all local and national educational institutions were synchronized and kept uniform. Autonomy exists only in the official Constitution. The party apparatus abolishes autonomy in favor of a high degree of centralization.

This system of government by division of portfolios among the members of the Presidium has been in existence for a long time. A reform, introduced in March, 1946, aimed to legalize it. At the head of the official Soviet government of about sixty members there were appointed nine men—one premier (Stalin) and eight vice-premiers. Unlike the other "simple" ministers, who are merely experts in their special fields, these nine men controlled their colleagues who were in effect subordinate to them. All nine of these men were members of the Presidium. In reality this meant that a small group of men, selected by the Supreme Leader from among the members of the party's Cen-

tral Committee, become members of the Presidium and constitute the real and official government as vice-premiers,
placed between the Leader and the rank-and-file ministers. In
the last months before Stalin's death, and again under Malenkov and Khrushchev, numerous reforms were undertaken to
alter the structure of the Soviet government. Essentially, however, the old pattern of relationship between members of the
party's Presidium and the ministers has been maintained.

At the beginning of the 'twenties the office of the Central
Committee comprised only 100 persons. In 1927 the figure was
650. This was subsequently reduced, and in 1929 the personnel numbered 375. Almost half of these were so-called "responsible workers." In the 'thirties the personnel was considerably
expanded, but the exact number was kept secret.

The office of the Central Committee consists of several di-
visions, each of which is charged with administering a special
sphere of government or party activity. There are the Secret
Division (later rechristened Special Division), the Distributive
Division (later Division of Cadres), the Division of Schools (a
Department of Education), the Division of Mass Campaigns
(collectivization, public demonstrations, etc.), the Division of
Propaganda and Agitation (press, radio, lectures), the Military
Division, and several economic divisions.

Even the party hierarchs look upon this office with great
respect not unmixed with fear. During the purges, for example,
the awe-inspiring Revisional Committee, having investigated,
as part of its duties, the personnel of the administrative office
of the Central Committee, humbly characterized its members
as follows:

"The apparatus of the Central Committee represents a firm,
ideologically galvanized organization, composed of tried and
theoretically accomplished Bolsheviks who have gone through
the school of struggle against class enemies and their agents
inside the party."

The principle of "collective leadership" proclaimed after

Stalin's death as a reaction against the late autocrat's tyranny
provided for more leeway and powers for each of the Presidium's members; to this extent the new principle was important. The basis of the Soviet system—supremacy of the Communist party over the Soviet government, with the party's
Presidium functioning as the actual government of Russia—
remained unaltered.

Thus the well-integrated and comparatively stable party
leadership rests, like the cupola of a great edifice, upon several
party columns: men of industry and leaders of agriculture,
education, foreign affairs, finance, and trade. But among these
columns there are two of primary importance: the Soviet Army
and the GB.[11] Their role and relationship will be discussed in
Chapter 10.

THE KOMSOMOL

THE Communist Youth League is a specific Soviet phenomenon. This league has played a very important role throughout
the entire history of the Soviet regime, and its development has
been symptomatic of the evolution of Soviet society.

By virtue of its sphere of activity the Komsomol has been
something more than an ordinary league of youth. It conscripted thousands of its members for fighting in the civil war,
sent thousands of youths to work in plants and factories, and
to wage political campaigns in the villages. Thousands of village offices were filled by Komsomol members, who also constituted a large percentage of the membership and officialdom
of local Soviets. The Komsomol is a political organization, and
has passed through all the phases of development which history
has bestowed upon its older sister, the Communist party: the
struggle of factions, expulsions, purges, arrests, executions; the

11. The designation GB is used here and below to embrace the names
of the secret police agencies which have succeeded one another—Cheka,
GPU, NKVD, MVD, MGB, KGB.

obligation to hear long political reports and vote unanimous approval of the government's policy. Thus, the Komsomol is but another party organization, or rather an auxiliary mass organization, which the party utilizes for various purposes and to a very substantial degree.

According to its first constitution, members of the Komsomol were to be youths between the ages of 14 and 23. Very soon it became apparent, however, that many, having reached the latter age limit, remained in the Komsomol instead of transferring to the party or joining the mass of nonpartisans. At one time, some 30 per cent of the Komsomol's membership consisted of such elements, aged even 30 and more. The point is that the Communist party was very strict in sifting candidates for party membership; there were the frequent purges, and frequent cessations of admission. Tens of thousands who desperately needed party membership cards preferred to be registered as youths, although in many cases they were men with large families and were approaching forty. The congress of the Komsomol in 1936 legalized this situation. Although it set the age limits for Komsomol membership between 15 and 26, it said that members might thereafter remain in the organization beyond the age of 26 but were to have no vote— only a voice. The limitation, however, did not make much difference.[12]

Founded in 1918, the Komsomol at first grew at a slower pace than did the party. The first year showed a membership of about 22,000, and the year following 96,000. After that, like the party, and for the same reasons, it began to grow rapidly, reaching 500,000 members by 1920. Simultaneously with the first party purge, the membership of the Komsomol was cut in half; in 1922 it was 247,000.

Then came a very rapid expansion. In two years the membership increased fivefold, reaching 1,140,000 in January, 1925. By that time, the principal features of the new political

12. In 1949 the age limit of 15 was lowered to 14.

situation had become apparent in the Komsomol—long before the appearance of analogous phenomena in the party.

Membership in the Komsomol had become the sole opportunity for advancement for young men and women, particularly
for the youth of the cities. Schools and higher educational institutions, although offering free tuition, took into careful consideration the party affiliation of applicants for admission.
Membership in the Komsomol became extremely useful—at
times indispensable—for entrance into a university or technical school. Workers eager to help their children get on in life
hastened to utilize the new opportunities; children of government employees and intellectuals naturally sought to complete
their education; even from the villages thousands flocked into
the schools. In addition to offering the advantages of facilitating
schooling and higher education, the Komsomol promoted ex-
cursions, maintained social clubs, provided evening entertain-
ments and dances. It arranged for visits to theaters and supplied
books. In short, the social life of young folk centered around
it, for no similar organizations were permitted to exist; and
young men and women who, naturally, did not relish isolation
from the world sought to join the Komsomol.

Unlike the party, the Komsomol set no great obstacles to
admission of new members, except for government employees
and intellectuals. There were no limitations for workers and
peasants; but out of fear of an influx of oppositionist elements
of the intelligentsia it was decided to create for employees and
intellectuals, constituting at that time a grade "B" class of
citizens, a special category of "candidates for the Komsomol";
for these there was instituted a probation period of a year and
a half before they could be admitted to membership. For a long
period there were about 100,000 such candidates.

In the cities the Komsomol was allotted a comparatively
modest role, that of auxiliary to the party, and the reservoir of
new material. In the villages its function was much more important. There, members of the Komsomol, individually and

in groups, frequently wielded authority over the nonpartisan peasantry; often they acted by appointment (although formally by "election") as chairmen of village soviets. Of 63,000 village administrations in Soviet Russia, members of the Komsomol ran about 6,000.

Before very long the Komsomol also became the center of intense political struggle. The discussions which subsequently shook the party raged in equal measure at Komsomol meetings. At such meetings Trotsky often won great victories, and Zinoviev at one period scored tremendous successes. In Leningrad, Zinoviev's satrapy, the Komsomol prided itself upon being the most powerful workers' organization.

The intention was at first to include in the Komsomol all young workers, for the purpose of "buttressing the composition" of the organization. Zinoviev related proudly in 1925 that 50 per cent of all young workers in Leningrad had joined the organization; in 1927 the percentage had risen to 73. Although this plan, of course, entailed the danger of admitting large numbers of non-Communists and even anti-Communists, one must keep in mind that by the middle of the 'twenties the Soviet regime had grown so strong and all other parties had been so completely crushed that the danger appeared to be very slight.

THE Komsomol continued to grow rapidly during the second decade of the Soviet regime, and overtook the party. Already in 1928 it had 2,070,000 members; in 1930 the membership rose to about 2,500,000; and in 1933 it mounted to 4,000,000. Like the party, the Komsomol halted its expansion at this point for several years.

By that time—the middle 'thirties—the position and function of the Komsomol had become fully established. Of its 4,000,000 members, some 700,000 were enrolled in higher and middle educational institutions. More than 100,000 were at work as teachers. More than 40 per cent were in the villages, and of these many were officials of state farms, and many others occupied administrative posts. About 1,000,000 were active in the collectives, combining their agricultural work with various functions of administration. Between 35 and 40 per cent of the organization consisted of young workers.

During this period, the central organs of the Komsomol stopped publishing statistics on its social composition in order to avoid the necessity of acknowledging its largely "non-proletarian" character. One could have cited, for example, the figures of new Komsomol members in the Moscow region for 1938–40. Of 208,522 such newcomers, workers represented only 36 per cent (76,000); government employees and students, 54 per cent (113,000); and peasant collectivists, less than 4 per cent (7,500). Thus at the end of the 'thirties, the Komsomol was no longer a "class," a "workers'" organization. There was no longer any need of regulating its composition artificially, for all members had become "loyal."

In 1936 Stalin decided to carry out an experiment which, if successful, was to be applied to other spheres. He determined to abolish all limitations of the admission of intellectuals to the Komsomol, of government employees and their children, and even of children of former capitalists and kulaks. On Stalin's personal orders, the congress of the Komsomol proclaimed the principle of equality for all who sought admission into the organization. The category of "candidates" henceforward was applied only to illiterates.

The growth of the Komsomol continued at an increased tempo. By 1939 the membership had reached 9,000,000; in 1940 it was 10,000,000; on the eve of the war in 1941 it was about 12,000,000.

At the outbreak of the Russo-German war there were about 40,000,000 persons of Komsomol age in Soviet Russia. Between 12,000,000 and 13,000,000 were in the cities, of whom 4,000,000 were in the Komsomol. Virtually the entire youth in many Soviet institutions, plants, educational institutions were Komsomol members. These were no longer the "advance guard" of youth but virtually the entire youth. At the same time, the Komsomol was shedding its old features of a militant, fighting organization.[13] It lost a great deal of its old Communist *élan* and became a universal, workaday organization devoted to practical everyday needs, such as education, advancement in jobs, and preparation for military service. The only political note that remained was the publicly avowed loyalty to the regime, regardless of the policies it might pursue.

Having rapidly grown during the war by recruiting members of the military forces and having reached a total membership of 15,000,000 in 1945, the Komsomol started to decrease in size as the demobilization went on. By 1949 the membership fell below 10,000,000; but then new efforts and new recruiting brought it to 16,000,000 in 1952.

The Komsomol's organization constitutes a guarantee of loyalty and blind obedience. Each local group elects, of course, its executive committee; the committee selects its secretaries, who direct the affairs of the organization. But the secretaries— and this is the important feature—must be confirmed by higher authorities in the hierarchic scheme. Thus, for example, the secretary of a Komsomol village group must be approved by the district organization—that is, by the district secretary of the Komsomol; but this district secretary must, in turn, have the approval of the regional secretary, whose existence depends upon approval of the secretary of the Central Committee. The secretary of the Central Committee of the Komsomol—"the Vozhd (Leader) of the Communist Youth"—is actually appointed by the leading organs of the Communist party: they consider in advance the composition of the Central Committee of the Komsomol, including the secretary. The party leadership

13. At the outbreak of the war the so-called "Pioneers," ages from 11 to 15, were an organization of 8,000,000 to 9,000,000; in the cities virtually all adolescents of these ages belonged to this preparatory school for the Komsomol. There were also the *Oktyabryata* ("Little Octobrists") ages from 8 to 11, comprising about 4,000,000.

can decide on removal of its leading officials. The secretary of
the Komsomol, nominated by the party and then elected
unanimously by the Central Committee of the Komsomol, con-
trols the regional secretaries, who, in turn, control the district
and local secretaries, and so on down the line. At the same
time, the party appoints one of its members to supervise
Komsomol affairs. In the period immediately preceding the
war this post was occupied by Andrei Zhdanov, one of Stalin's
closest and most trusted lieutenants.

Thus, the direction of the Komsomol, founded formally on
a democratic basis, proceeds actually in authoritarian fashion,
from above downward. The Komsomol became a government
institution administering the affairs of youth, as well as some
other affairs. Nothing would change if the government should
abolish by a stroke of the pen its bylaws with the congresses,
elections, membership regulations; the central and local administrations would remain and would continue to perform
their prescribed functions.

This process was accelerated with the outbreak of the war.
Many millions were mobilized, particularly the village youth,
who, as already noted, had been but little affected by the
Komsomol organizations. It now appeared useful to draw the
peasant-soldiers into the organization, which was developing
wide military-educational activity at the front. Now the Komsomol began to grow rapidly in the army, recruiting millions of
soldiers.

The thin partition which continued to divide the Komsomol
in the years immediately preceding the war from the non-
Communist youth was imperceptibly removed during the tem-
pestuous war period. Whole sections of the new army—recruits
as well as more seasoned soldiers—were incorporated in the
organization. On the occasion of its twenty-fifth anniversary
(October 29, 1943) the Komsomol addressed a greeting to the
Central Committee of the Communist party signed by 17,320,-
000 men and women. The peculiar character of the Communist

Youth League, its long battle against "backward youth," "religious prejudices," "peasant atavism," and "irresoluteness of the intelligentsia"—all this was no more. The type known to the world as a Komsomolets—the brazen, militant, swashbuckling fellow shaking his fist at the Pope of Rome and burning the effigies of "Kings and Churchills" in public squares—had become dissolved in the broad ocean of youth. Today a Komsomolets is a young Soviet citizen and, conversely, the young Soviet citizen is a Komsomolets.

The original social movement represented by the Komsomol, therefore, no longer exists. But the Komsomol organization remains: a network of committees, secretaries, organizers, who receive their instructions from above, from the highest authorities. The instructions pertain to schools, religion, and work in plants and Soviet institutions. Although they overlap the work of other government institutions, these organs continue to be considered essential because they are an additional means of assuring the loyalty of young citizens, of controlling their thoughts and conduct, of rewarding the worthy and punishing the guilty.

Chapter 10. THE ARMY AND THE SECRET POLICE

Two KINDS of armed forces have existed in Russia throughout the Soviet period: the army and the police. The police was a political force, the army was nonpolitical. The police was a tool of the party, the army was an object of its activity.

The history of the Soviet period, all the shifting policies and slogans, all turns and zigzags are reflected in the history of the Red Army. The main problem of the Russian revolution, the relationship of the people and the government, finds expression in the relationship of the army and the party, of the commanders and the GB. Persistent effort to expand the "proletarian kernel" as a guarantee of the army's obedience; the creation of party organizations in the army, embracing chiefly the commanding staff; the efforts of the Komsomol to recruit young privates; lecture programs, operation of Communist "political grammar" schools, and publication of a score of newspapers mark the history of the Red Army. Other methods used were the frequent mysterious removals of officers, leapfrog promotions, and purges, small and great.

The two principal instruments used in keeping check on the army were the Political Administration and the GB. The Political Administration, a department of the party's Central Committee, operated through thousands of its civil officials (under their various titles, such as "political commissars," "military commissars," "political workers," "party organizers," and others). The activities of the GB often were secret, and the identity of many of its chiefs and thousands of informants was not known to the army. The party commissars and the GB worked of course in close collaboration.

254

Each of these elements developed rapidly in the past fifteen years. The Red Army and its officer corps grew in numbers and quality. The number of Communists among the officers was constantly increasing but so was the danger confronting the party in the army. The "political personnel" in the army was 14,000 in 1925 and increased to 34,000 in 1939. In 1925 it appeared that no outside control would be necessary once all the commanding posts were occupied by party members. In 1938, however, when this goal was achieved, the army was covered with an unparalleled network of control and punitive organizations. At the beginning of the 'twenties less than 2 per cent of the Army rank and file belonged to Communist organizations, and the government had to keep close watch upon the "potential counterrevolutionists in uniform." In 1939 half of the Army's and two-thirds of the Navy's rank and file were members of the party or of the Komsomol.[1] But the government, nevertheless, found itself compelled to keep an even more careful eye upon the armed services.

Not for a minute did the party leaders forget the history of Napoleon and Cromwell, and every conceivable political instrument was put to use to forestall the possibility of an analogous development in Russia—that is, the rise to political leadership of some revolutionary hero who would discard the revolutionary process with the aid of a revolutionary army.

After the revolutionary years, as popular political activity declined, the soldier mass became more obedient and politically amorphous. Its capacity for political initiative diminished and with this diminished also the threat to the security of the Soviet system emanating from the army rank and file.

What did appear dangerous, or potentially dangerous, were elements of the government-employed intellectuals. Red Army officers, "military intellectuals," were part of the large class of

1. In 1939 Marshal Klimenti Voroshilov revealed that more than 50 per cent of the Army rank and file belonged to the Communist party or the Communist Youth League. In the Navy the percentage was 67.

state officials. Whenever the government accentuated its policy against the Soviet intelligentsia, the relations between the regime and Army officers reflected a similar tension.

Intellectuals in officers' uniform, even active members of the Communist party, of "Old Bolsheviks" assigned to military posts, often used to become infected with the spirit of opposition after some years of work; at times they joined various opposition groups (in most instances the Right Opposition in the party), and they were frequently subjected to punishment. One of the most talented Soviet military leaders, Marshal Mikhail Tukhachevsky, at one time joined the Right Oppositionist circles of the Communist party. He was executed in 1937, together with seven other Soviet military leaders, when a conflict arose over the restoration of the hated "commissars" in the Army.[2]

The great expansion of the Communist party did not make the established regime feel secure about the army any more than about the civil organization of the country. But the outward forms of conflict assumed other features. The Army was opposed no longer to the party but to its only armed rival, the only other force possessing rifles, tanks, and military airplanes, to the institution that checks the Army, reports on the Army, purges the Army, arrests Army leaders for political motives—

2. During the wartime alliance with Russia, much was written about the so-called "treason trials" of Marshal Tukhachevsky and other generals, as well as of nonmilitary Communist leaders. The former American Ambassador, Joseph E. Davies, who had witnessed the trials in Moscow and had reported on them critically to the State Department, now voiced a new faith in the fairness of the purge and the trials. He was followed by scores of writers and politicians who suddenly became apologists for Soviet justice. In this way the purges and "liquidations," though a part of prewar history, have remained a subject of passionate discussion down to the present time. No facts were advanced in support of the new pro-Soviet version; the only aim was to please the Moscow authorities and to strengthen the ties with Russia by means of an unworthy sacrifice of moral and human principles. The attitude toward the trials remains the acid test for measuring a writer's understanding and knowledge of Russian affairs. Those who believe in the treason (pro-German activity) of Tukhachevsky, Zinoviev, Bukharin, Trotsky, and hundreds of others belonged in one of two groups: either they were simply naïve and ignorant, or they were propagandists.

an institution occupying a position above the Army, and which has an army of its own. This is the GB.

THE GB is the purest Communist organization of all. Nowhere is the percentage of Communists so large, nowhere is the ratio of "nonpartisans" so low. All executives and nearly all employees of the GB are party members, carefully checked and sifted, clear of any oppositionist taint. Only the complete solidarity of the GB with the high party leadership makes possible the existence of the Soviet state; this constitutes the first prerequisite of its stability, a fact which permits of no deviations. The slightest ideological deviations, even suspicion of heresy on the part of a member of the GB, has invariably and inevitably led to his liquidation. The entire development of the Soviet state, from the romantic chaos of the early years to the confident stability of the latter period, has been closely bound with the strengthening and expansion of this institution.

In the past the GB, too, had been the scene of raging ideological differences, when groups of its agents in the corridors of this police fortress had engaged in heated discussions about Socialism in one country and the course of the Chinese revolution. There were many years when a party card had served as a guarantee against molestation by the GB. But all this has long passed. At first singly, then in hundreds, later in many thousands, once privileged party members began moving under convoy across prison corridors and through transfer points into the forests and tundras of distant regions. All discussion about the Chinese revolution has long ceased and no longer does anyone at the Lubyanka Headquarters venture to differ with the powers-that-be.

The small, weak, temporary Extraordinary Commission of 1917 (the original Cheka) has developed into a permanent institution, which has overtaken all others in its phenomenal growth, including the expansion of industry and the rate of collectivization. Only shamefacedness on the part of the regime prevents the publication of the facts and figures concerning this speedy and brilliant development. Bureaucracy and its red tape exist in other spheres of the regime but not in the GB; other Soviet institutions are charged frequently with lack of initiative, but there is plenty of initiative in the GB; in other institutions bustle and restlessness interfere with quick decisions, but the actions of the GB proceed always with lightning-like speed and are invariably productive.

The GB is not a political police in the ordinary sense of the word.

There is no economic enterprise outside of Russia, private or public, the scope of whose operations approaches the economic sweep of the GB. The network of schools administered by the GB would do honor in its size to any small country. Great "popular movements," such as the antireligious campaigns, have been carried out under the direction of the GB. The GB constitutes the actual government of entire regions in the east, where the local authorities exercise but a shadowy authority. Unlike the practice in all other countries, all places of imprisonment in Russia are not within the jurisdiction of the ministry of justice but under the authority of the GB. This applies also to the various Corrective Labor Camps and Labor Colonies mentioned in Chapter 6. Many building projects, for example, such as the construction of highways, canals, etc., come under the authority of the GB. Its budgets have therefore been tremendous, increasing from 482,000,000 rubles in 1933 to 3,000,000,000 in 1937. Together with other projects (in particular the construction of highways and railroads) the figure was as high as 4,000,000,000 in that year.

During the war period, 1941–45, other functions were added to the GB. Contrary to the system in vogue in all other countries, all war prisoners were immediately transferred from the authority of the Red Army into the hands of the GB, and all war-prisoner camps were administered not by the military but by the police. For this reason, organizations of war prisoners, such as the Free Germany Committee or the Union of German Officers, were formed on the initiative of the GB, on orders, of course, of the higher authorities. All decisions taken by these German organizations and all their resolutions had to pass the censorship of the GB. Finally, its wartime functions included the supervision of many military and engineering projects.

An important function of the GB is still checking on the Army. This function is performed through the long-established Special Division, created solely for this purpose. All military commissars under their different titles, and other political officials attached to the armed forces, are obliged to report regularly to the Special Division, either directly or through the so-called PUR—the Political Administration of the Soviet Army. Attached to the Army for the purpose of watching the conduct of officers (at first former White officers and later all officers), these officials furnish the Special Division with information concerning sentiments in the Army, current talk, and "conspiracies." Upon this information the Special Division carried out the purges in the Army.

The GB has its own not inconsiderable army. At first this was termed Special Service Detachments (*Chon*). Later it was changed to Internal Security Troops (*Vokhr*) and Special Troops. These consist of troops selected not only for their physique but for their loyalty. Thirty years ago they comprised only a few thousand; during the peasant uprisings local party members had to be used to augment their forces. To avoid this in the future, the size of the GB army was expanded. At the end of the 'twenties, with the beginning of the collectivization in the villages, which was accompanied by widespread revolts, these troops were increased to 60,000. Official Moscow sources reported subsequently, over a period of years, that the GB had an armed police of 58,900 men.[3] These figures soon became obsolete, although officially Moscow continued to quote them

3. Divided as follows: frontier guards, 28,150; frontier troops stationed in their own home territories, 17,240; escort troops, 13,200.

for ten years, up to the outbreak of the war. Foreign correspondents in 1936–37 estimated the forces under command of
the GB at 250,000. This figure, given in reports passed by the
censorship, is closer to the truth. During the war, it reached
600,000, and this number has only slightly decreased. The GB
forces constitute a real army, with their own officers, artillery,
and even aviation. They are better paid than the Army. The
famous secret weapon *Katyusha* was not entrusted to the Red
Army, but whenever it was brought to the front or transported
back it was handled by the GB army. The privileges enjoyed
are so great that during the war the GB army has been sent to
the front only in particular instances and for short intervals. This
army represents a revival in many respects of the prerevolutionary Corps of Gendarmes, whose function was also that of
political security guards, and which during the first World War
had aroused so much resentment by its comfortable situation in
the rear that with the outbreak of the revolution the demand
arose: "The gendarmes to the front!" However, the gendarmes
of that period comprised an insignificant force compared with
the troops of the GB.[4]

But the power of the GB does not rest merely upon these outward attributes of authority. More significant, perhaps, are its
unseen tentacles, which embrace a larger number of people
than its army. Every member of the Communist party, no matter
where he may be working, is obliged to keep the GB informed
of everything he sees and hears that may be of interest. That this
is no mere "moral obligation" has been demonstrated by the
fate of hundreds of Communists who for reasons of carelessness
or because of humane considerations had failed to report on
their relatives. In addition to the general obligation impressed
upon the millions of party members, thousands of special Communist informers have the direct task of gathering information
on various aspects of social life and informing the GB; these

4. After the liquidation of Lavrenti Beria a part of the GB army, it appears,
was transferred to the jurisdiction of the Soviet Army.

operatives are present in every institution, office, plant, and scientific society.

Many thousands of nonpartisans perform the same function, diligently and without pay. These are persons who once had an unpleasant contact with the GB; they have been permitted to remain at liberty on condition of serving as regular informers; they are instructed to follow their usual occupations, without changing their mode of life in any way, to visit as usual their friends, schools, meetings, but to present reports about them. What is the number of such informers? Perhaps the GB itself does not know.

This army of spies presents a special problem. Their social position in the circle of their friends and acquaintances does not change when they become informers of the GB, although not infrequently those in whose circles they move become aware of their function; they cannot very well be excluded from these circles, first, because of fear of repression, and, secondly, because the matter is altogether an everyday phenomenon. The potential presence of informers in every nonpolitical group, at every entertainment, in every house committee is accepted as a matter of course. Thousands of these informers themselves undoubtedly dream of an opportunity of quitting their activity, of seeing the day when their shameful reports concerning their relatives and friends go up in flames. And, conversely, they would be horror-stricken if the archives were to be opened and their work given publicity. All this is material for some future Shakespeare.

Soviet scientists of world reputation, frequent participants in international congresses; writers whose works have been translated into many languages; suave and polite diplomats, Soviet pedagogues who teach the young the basic truths of morality; doctors with large practices; and many other figures of various degrees of importance would gladly give everything they own, down to the last shirt, if they could only destroy the handiwork of their sheer, animal cowardice. This might be called, in ordinary times and places, the moral degradation of some individuals; but how can the characterization be applied to a mass phenomenon? How can we expect heroism to be a mass phenomenon?

Both the volunteer informers and the paid squealers, the thousands of the victims and prospective victims, the purged and the expelled, the exiles and their families, all those who out of elemental fear of the GB will not venture to utter a word of criticism, desire what to them appears to be the impossible—the disappearance of this institution and its entire system.

Among these passionate dreamers Communists occupy a very prominent place. They, too, have been painfully whipped, and the very name GB has filled them with no less terror than it has their nonpartisan associates. They, too, have opened the summons to appear before the GB investigator with horror regardless of whether or not they knew themselves innocent; all that has yet been written about this drama is but a pale shadow of the truth. Communists, too, have been exiled by the thousands; they, too, have rotted in distant places; they, too, have been renounced by their wives and children. When permitted to remain at liberty, they, too, in shameful fear, have woven informers' tales about their chiefs and subordinates, their school friends, their intimates. And because of their diligence and enthusiasm, their pains and their services they quietly, sullenly, passionately hate the GB.

Such are also the sentiments of the rest of the population, civil and military. This has been true before and it is true now, after Stalin. There is hardly a family that has not lost someone in the war; and there are few families who at one time or another have not paid their tribute to the Moloch GB. Some friends and relatives have stood under the hail of German bullets at the front, others have been imprisoned in concentration camps, where they died young of hunger and disease, toiling at forced labor. Some officers landed in the hell of German captivity, others were removed and demoted as a consequence of reports by the ubiquitous agents of the GB.

Many observers and very many Russian Communists have more than once expected a decisive conflict between the Army and the GB; predictions of such a conflict were heard even during the war. So far these expectations and predictions have proved unfounded; but the first fortress which may fall as a consequence of the combined efforts of the Army and the people, as soon as the first rays of spring begin to alter the rigorous landscape, will not be the party, not even the collectives, but the incomparable, majestic, unique monolith resting upon inhumanity, slavery, abomination, and death—the GB.

Chapter 11. THE NEW RELIGIOUS POLICY

WHEN the Calvinist King of France, Henry IV, found himself hard pressed in his conflict with the French Catholics and it appeared difficult to take Paris, Henry, that prototype of political "realists," declared that *"Paris vaut bien une messe"* ("Paris is worth a mass"): he embraced Catholicism and the capital opened its gates to him. Was it worth sacrificing ponderable interests for the sake of vague ideology? asked the realistic king.

During the war many people imagined that something similar was happening in Russia in the field of religion. They read of brilliant church services in Moscow, of the reopening of closed churches, of the election of a patriarch, of the government agreeing to the restoration of churches wrecked at the front, of the solidarity of the Orthodox clergy with the government in all questions concerning the war—and they imagined that "the great realist in the Kremlin" was emulating the policy of his French prototype, and that before long Russia would have either complete freedom of religion or that the Orthodox Church would be restored to the position it occupied before the revolution in 1917.

Moscow, on the other hand, did all it possibly could to strengthen the impression that there was a genuine restoration of religious freedom. In conceding an inch to the church Moscow sought to make the world believe that it was granting a mile. Nothing pleased Moscow more than the belief cultivated by the foreign press that Russia was returning to her traditional roads:

"Bright with candlelight and the splendor of clerical garb,

264

THE NEW RELIGIOUS POLICY

the church presented a magnificent spectacle, perhaps as magnificent as it has ever witnessed. It was like a page from ancient Russia . . ."

A page from ancient Russia! As though by accident the author of this report from Moscow, Maurice Hindus, used a phrase which Moscow was eager to have used. During the war it wanted to spread the belief among all inside and outside the country who prefer the old Russia to the new that "a page of ancient Russia" had turned up again amid the Soviet metamorphoses, that Russia had turned her back on her Communist ways, substituted bishops for Marxists, conservatives for revolutionists, and transformed her government from an instrument of world revolution to a bulwark of world stability.

The history of the religious policy of the Soviet government exposes the error of this conception, so widely current because human beings are so prone to forget the recent past. The true meaning and character of the evolution Russia has undergone on this question may be clearly discerned in the tortuous history of Soviet religious policy.

Russia has experienced no less than three violent outbursts of the antireligious movement, of persecutions and the closing of churches, in the thirty-eight years of the Soviet regime. And three times, after each outburst, have come periods of relief, of moderation, of compromise.

The first big wave of antireligious persecutions, which had already begun during the civil war, struck the church in the period of the NEP, 1921–23. While some concessions were being made to private economy and many observers had imagined that a return to "ancient Russia" was impending, the "revolutionary offensive" continued in the sphere of religion. Arrests and executions of priests assumed a mass character. "Freedom of conscience" as guaranteed by the Soviet Constitution had no real significance beyond propaganda aims. Paragraph 13 of the first Soviet Constitution provided:

"The church is separated from the state, and freedom of religious and of antireligious propaganda is recognized for all citizens."

"All citizens" (not only the workers) were accorded the right of religious propaganda. Yet the years following adoption of the Constitution were a period of ruthless persecution of religion. Religious propaganda was rigorously suppressed.

The Constitution, adopted in 1924 and drafted with great care on the basis of previous experience, separated the school from the church but reaffirmed the phrase concerning the rights of citizens to religious propaganda. Paragraph 4 declared:

"To assure the workers of true freedom of conscience the church is separated from the state, and the school from the church, and freedom of religious and antireligious propaganda is recognized for all citizens."

In explanation of the Soviet government's policy on questions of religion, Stalin declared in his interview with an American labor delegation in 1927:

"The party cannot be neutral in respect to religion, it wages an antireligious propaganda against all religious prejudices because it stands for science . . . There are cases of party members interfering with the full development of antireligious propaganda. It is good that such members are expelled."

The persecutions in the first period of Soviet antireligious policy reached their zenith in 1923. The execution of the Catholic priest Budkiewicz provoked an international conflict, with particularly serious consequences to Soviet Russia's relations with England. The Soviet government found it wise to make concessions. Its religious policy experienced a shift. The persecutions were moderated and the remaining open churches were permitted to function.

The antireligious movement was halted in part. The Union of Militant Godless, founded in that period, continued to function, supported by the Komsomol, and the distribution of antireligious literature continued, but the persecution of priests was considerably alleviated.

By that time the basic feature of the subsequent antireligious movements—from the end of the 'twenties to the war—had become crystallized. These movements ceased to be as popular and spontaneous as in the first ten years of the revolution, and assumed in all their alternating outbursts and recessions an artificial character. The population, especially the youth, continued to display a lively interest in religious and antireligious problems; supporters of religion declined in number. But the original fervor ("we will climb up to heaven and disperse all the gods") had abated, the sensational digging up of relics of saints was over. The international effect of Soviet religious policy moved the government, for its part, to put the brakes on antireligious stunts.

The principal center of the antireligious movement was in the GPU, which had a special division concerned with religious problems whose task it was to accelerate or moderate the pressure, as need required. In later years the Union of the Godless worked in close contact with and under the direction of the GPU.[1]

The moderation of religious persecutions in the middle and late 'twenties gave rise to some hopes, but in 1929–30 came collectivization, and the attitude of the government toward the church experienced a radical change. The local church constituted an important element in village life, and the attitude of the clergy toward the collectivization was known to be hostile. The entire course of internal policy swung to the left, and many promises previously given were wiped out in a moment. Mass closings of churches were resumed, many priests were exiled, wholesale arrests were under way everywhere. The persecutions were soon extended to the cities; in 1932 priests were exiled from the cities in batches as "nonworking ele-

1. The official book *The Komsomal and Antireligious Propaganda* (Moscow, 1937) contains many observations like the following: "Cells of the Union of the Godless frequently confine their activity to distributing membership cards in the Union of the Godless.
"Godless members of the Komsomol have become too tame."

ments." The severe repressions continued for several years. The aforementioned Paragraph 4 of the Constitution was revised as follows by the Congress of Soviets in 1929:

"In order to assure the workers of true freedom of conscience, the church is separated from the state and the school from the church, and freedom of religious worship and of antireligious propaganda is recognized for all citizens."

From now on there was to be freedom only for antireligious propaganda but not for religious propaganda. Believers were accorded only "freedom of religious worship," which meant the right of priests to perform services but no more.

In July, 1930, the Communist Party Congress decided to intensify the antireligious propaganda.

How difficult was the position of the representatives of the church and how great were the concessions they were obliged to make for their self-preservation may be seen from the interview given by the Metropolitan Sergei in February, 1930, and published by the entire press under the signatures of two metropolitans, two bishops, and two other prelates:

"QUESTION: Is there persecution of religion in Russia?

"ANSWER: There never were persecutions of religion in Russia . . . True, some churches were closed, but this is not done on the initiative of the government but by will of the population, in some instances even by decision of the believers themselves.

"QUESTION: Is religious propaganda permitted in the USSR?

"ANSWER: Religious services and sermons are not forbidden. The teaching of religion is permitted."

The next question concerned repressions and cruelties practiced against priests.

"ANSWER: All this is pure invention, slander. We have had no limitations placed upon the administrations of our church organs to date." [2]

Only in 1934–35, after collectivization had been completed

---

2. The details of this interview, historic in its way (published in *Izvestia,* February 16, 1930), are told in William Henry Chamberlin's *Russia's Iron Age* (Boston, Little, Brown and Co., 1934), chap. 31.

and the international situation required that the Soviet government embrace the policy of collective security and support of the League of Nations, did the government again moderate its church policy. Mass persecutions ceased. Antireligious processions were forbidden.

Once more official pronouncements declared: "We do not persecute religion by any means. We demand from church parishioners that they refrain from interfering in politics. The old clergy, bound to the old regime, would not abandon its struggle against the Soviet power, and it was necessary for us to resort to repressions. But now they have apparently turned their faces in our direction—and the church is free." This was almost literally a repetition of the arguments used in the 'twenties, which had been followed by new outbursts of repressions.

Meanwhile, the new Constitution, drafted in 1936, in this period of religious liberalism, did not signify a return to Lenin's formulas. It again excluded religious propaganda: "Freedom of religious worship and freedom of antireligious propaganda is recognized for all citizens."

On the other hand the new Constitution abolished the civil disabilities imposed upon "nonworkers," which had applied also to priests. The right of franchise in elections to the Soviets (even the right, on paper, of being elected) was accorded also to priests. However, the significance of these constitutional reforms was negligible.

At the end of 1937 came a new wave—the third—of persecution of religion. This was the period of the Great Purge. More than ten thousand religious parishes were closed according to Professor N. S. Timasheff.[3] Severe repressions descended upon priests, with arrests, exile, imprisonment in concentration camps, and executions. The old trite accusations of espionage, industrial sabotage, and all the other crimes attributed at that time by the NKVD to many others were directed also against priests.

In 1939, with the conclusion of the purge, the repressions

3. *Religion in Soviet Russia,* New York, Sheed and Ward, 1942.

against priests ceased. Another period of tolerance ensued. It continued until the outbreak of the war with Germany.

In 1940 the observance of Sunday was restored with the reestablishment of the seven-day work week. While there were some repressions of priests in the new regions annexed to Russia, the general policy was a cautious one.[4] To avoid misunderstanding, the Central Committee of the Communist party was now moved to remind its members that they were forbidden to practice religion.

AND so the history of the period of 1918–41 follows a torturous line. Periods of severe repression alternated with spans of relative tolerance. For the religious policy was only part of the general internal policy with its ups and downs. But with the end of each span of repression, the surviving representatives of the church would begin to console themselves with the hope that a profound evolution had taken place in the ideology of the government, and that the new rights accorded to the church would remain inviolate.

The graph on page 271 records the changes of Soviet policy on religion. The line indicates the years and the measure in which the government altered its policy. It is to be observed that at no time did a turn favorable to religion win all the ground lost by the church through previous repressions. Before the war only a few of the closed churches were permitted to reopen and exiled priests were not given their liberty. A new generation of priests was not permitted to develop, and in many instances laymen, and occasionally women, served as substitutes for the clergy. The right to publish the Bible was not restored, nor was it permitted to import it from abroad, even if it was sent free.

At the time of Hitler's invasion of Russia, after twenty-four years of the Soviet regime, Russia had:

---

4. In Bessarabia priests were ordered in December, 1940, to move into the interior of Russia. In Riga churches were closed at Christmas, 1940.

   28 bishops—a decrease of 75 per cent since 1917.

5,665 priests—a decrease of 90 per cent since 1917.

3,100 deacons—against 15,210 in 1917.

4,225 churches—against 46,457 in 1917.

   37 monasteries—against 1,026 in 1917.

Regarding the attitude of the population toward religion, Soviet sources noted before the war that about two-thirds of the village population and approximately one-third of the city population, that is, about half of the population, considered

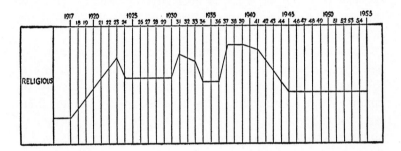

themselves as adhering to various churches. These figures are from a census taken in 1937. Because they showed a surprisingly persistent devotion to religion, they served as the motive for a new antireligious campaign, begun in 1937 and halted at the beginning of 1939.[5]

The war brought great relief for religion and the church.

The principal reason for the new reforms lay in the religious

---

5. Because many feared to answer the question "believer" or "nonbeliever" in the census, little value must be attached to the final figures. The Soviet press has contended that believers had little genuine faith. The *Komsomolskaya Pravda* received the following letter in 1937 from a person who had taken the entire course of antireligious propaganda:

"We repudiate the writings about God and we assert that there was not and there is not any such person. This fact has been established on the basis of scientific data concerning the origin of man as well as the origin of the universe. But what interests me is another thing: Do sorcerers and conjurers really exist and what is the power they possess by which they corrupt people and transform them into swine, dogs, etc.? You may, perhaps, deny this, but these are facts."

sentiments preserved by the population, particularly in the villages. It was possible to ignore them when the government had to do with industrialization and purges, but when the peasants were mobilized for a life and death struggle it was necessary to take a "step backward" and adapt the policy to the needs of "backward elements." A situation, involving as it does great popular activity, particularly in matters concerning the war, has compelled a retreat from the straight Communist line on the ideological front. The concessions granted during the war were specifically a compromise with the Russian peasantry. This was the first and most important motive of the reforms. The first but not the only one.

For a number of years before the war the Nazi government had encouraged the activities of Orthodox prelates and priests resident in Germany and consisting almost exclusively of émigrés from Russia. Hitler appropriated money for the construction of an Orthodox cathedral in Berlin; nineteen Orthodox churches received government appropriations for repairs. All this was by way of preparation for the great political campaign which developed immediately after the invasion of Russia by German troops.

In the occupied regions a number of Orthodox priests declared their support of Germany and prayed for the success of the German arms. Some high dignitaries of the church went over to the German side. Attention has already been called to the church leaders of the wartime in occupied territories and the blessing they conferred upon the German Army. The Germans paid particular attention to the church in the Ukraine. By conferring favors upon it they sought to wean it away from Moscow, and in this respect they had some success. Their second aim was to obtain support of the church against the Vatican; in this respect they were not so successful. Not until the end of 1942 did the Germans become rather cool toward matters concerning the Orthodox and Ukrainian churches.

The anti-Soviet policy of the Orthodox clergy in the occupied regions of Russia was an important factor in determining the policy on religion pursued by the Soviet government during the war. It was wise to come to the "defense of religion" in the struggle with heathen Hitlerism. German propaganda sought to create a great European bloc against "Godless Bolshevism," and Moscow replied with a counterblow: defense of religion against the heathen, revival of the patriarchate, and restoration of churches destroyed by the Germans.

One of the motives for a change in Soviet religious policy was the effect which the antireligious policy as pursued over a long period had created in neighboring, allied and enemy, countries. The religious beliefs of the populations constituted an obstacle to the policies recommended by Moscow for the various national movements (in which Communists were to play the directing part). In Yugoslavia members of the Orthodox Church constituted half the population (more than half among the Serbs); in Bulgaria they were two-thirds; in Rumania, two-thirds; in Greece, 99 per cent. The "All-Slav Meetings" in Moscow were appealing to the national sentiments of the Slav peoples; Orthodox religious leaders were in a position to appeal also to non-Slav peoples, such as the Rumanians and Greeks. It was natural, therefore, to combine the All-Slav propaganda with Orthodox propaganda.

Moreover, there were a number of political problems presenting a source of disagreement between Russia and her allies on which an authoritative nongovernment voice, the voice of public opinion, expressing itself in support of Russia would be more effective than the Kremlin's. On the question of the second front, for example, the Orthodox Church spoke out with determination in support of the government's position. Many other such questions might arise in the future.

IMMEDIATELY after the beginning of the Soviet-German war the highest church authority in Russia, the Metropolitan Sergei, declared his support of the war in the name of the church. At a solemn service in Moscow on June 29, 1941, he prayed for success of the Russian arms.

In September of the same year the *Godless* and the *Antireligionist* ceased publication. In America and other countries this was interpreted by some as the consequence of intervention by President Roosevelt through Averell Harriman, who at that time had made his first visit to Moscow as an official representative. Harriman did talk about the matter to Stalin. But as indicated above, there were many other extremely important reasons for a change in Soviet religious policy.

On the anniversary day of the November revolution the Metropolitan Sergei hailed Stalin as "the divinely appointed leader of our armed and cultural forces leading us to victory." Metropolitan Nikolai of Kiev wired Stalin wishing him a long life. A week later came the sensation of his appointment as a member of the Commission of Inquiry into German Atrocities. The churches participated in war-fund drives.

Very soon, in February, 1942, the Metropolitan Sergei, who had been evacuated from Moscow to Ulianovsk (the former Simbirsk) issued a manifesto against the Orthodox priests who had gone over to Hitler and were forming an "independent" church in the Ukraine. He pointed out that the leader of this movement, Bishop Polikarp Sikorsky, had previously pledged allegiance to the Soviet government. The Metropolitan Sergei threatened the renegades with excommunication and called upon the Orthodox faithful to repudiate them.

Then followed another sensation. The church leaders—for the first time since the revolution—published a book in Russian on religion entitled *The Truth About Religion in Russia.* Expensively printed, despite the difficulties experienced by the printing industry in wartime, and richly illustrated, this book sought to prove that religion was free and that, in general, there had never been any persecution of religion in Russia on the part of the government. Any unpleasant developments that had occurred had been due to the activities of the Union of the Godless and not of the government! (As already indicated, this loyal interpretation had been used as a defense mechanism by the clergy since 1930.) Despite its loyalty and patriotism, however, this book was not distributed through book stores. It was circulated only among Soviet grandees and institutions abroad. It is worth noting that it was printed in the printing shop which used to print the *Godless*. Apparently the NKVD division which had previously directed the antireligious propaganda was now directing the proreligious activity behind the scenes. No doubt the very same persons did both jobs.

On Good Friday, 1943, the Metropolitan Sergei read over the radio an address to the Orthodox population of all countries, but directed particularly to the Serbs, Czechs, and Greeks. Naturally, it had previously been approved by the government.

The biggest moment in the history of the Orthodox Church came in September, 1943. The government permitted the election of a Patriarch. On September 4, 1943, Stalin, in the presence of Molotov, received the 76-year-old Metropolitan Sergei, who was accompanied by two other metropolitans. This was followed immediately by announcement of the restoration of the Synod, composed of six men, and of the election of Sergei as Patriarch. The day after his reception by Stalin the new Patriarch demanded a second front, addressing the following sharp remark to Russia's allies:

"We Russians are the world's most patient people, but the cup of our patience is overflowing."

At the same time a conclave of nineteen metropolitans, archbishops, and bishops made public a manifesto declaring:

"There are individuals found among the clergy and laymen who, forgetting the fear of God, have dared to build their own welfare upon the misfortune of all. They meet the Germans as welcome guests, enter their service and sometimes go so far as direct treachery, betraying their brethren to the enemy, as, for example, guerrillas and others who are sacrificing their lives for the country.

"Everyone guilty of treachery to the common cause of the church and desertion to the side of fascism as an enemy of God's crucifix will be deemed excommunicated; and if he be bishop or priest he will be unfrocked. Amen."

The Patriarch was given the use of one of the finest houses in Moscow, formerly occupied by an official German delegation. Churches began to be restored, particularly in territories cleared of the Germans. Churches previously reopened under the Germans continued to function. The Alexander-Nevsky Monastery was restored; Troitsko-Sergiev partly so. The former, where Suvorov was buried, experienced a flow of visitors, and military men were ordered to kneel before his grave.

At the beginning of 1944 training of new priests was permitted. Establishment of the Orthodox Theological Institute was authorized, as were also various theological courses. Contrary to the new practice in universities, tuition was free, but students could not be below eighteen years of age. High taxes levied from church buildings were lowered considerably.

Finally, in order not to compromise the church with a connection with the NKVD, a separate government Committee on Affairs of the Orthodox Church was set up to act as liaison between the church and the government. In June, 1944, the Soviet government decided to create an official committee dealing with the affairs of all churches.

SUPPORT of the clergy became necessary also in the Soviet opposition to the Vatican, which continued to play a very important role in the European war.

The Vatican's moral influence was thrown entirely on the anti-Hitler side of the scales, particularly after 1939, when Catholic France, Poland, and Czechoslovakia fell under German domination. But unlike other anti-Nazi powers—Britain and the United States—the Vatican, as a spiritual power, could not think of collaboration with the Soviet government without a radical change in Soviet religious policy. The Vatican could not simply forget, as did the temporal powers, the activities of Communism in all countries, the religious persecutions which had held sway in Russia only five years before, the fate that had been inflicted upon Catholic priests in Spain, and similar events.

For this reason the Vatican remained not only an anti-Nazi but also an anti-Communist power. It could afford the luxury of such consistency because it had no armies and navies of its own, did not concern itself with strategy, and was not trying to solve problems of first and second fronts. Foreseeing the defeat of Germany, the Vatican feared the spread of Communist, antireligious movements in Europe and adopted, therefore, a very cautious attitude on the question of collaboration between non-Communists and Communists in liberated territories. The Vatican had thus become a great anti-Soviet force during the war, during the very period when the Soviet government had hoped to expand its political and intellectual influence in Europe.

To stand in its old position of unstable legalistic "freedom of conscience" was not wise for the Soviet government. It was advisable to bring into action another religious power against the Vatican, a power that would wield greater influence in the Christian world in matters of religion than could the Soviet government. The Orthodox Church, and particularly the figure of the Patriarch, stood out as the proper authority for this purpose.

With improvement of relations between Soviet Russia and her allies (after the Moscow and Tehran conferences) at the end of 1943, the Vatican appeared as Moscow's sole serious opponent in the anti-Nazi camp.

On February 1, 1944, *Izvestia* again assailed the Vatican. "The Vatican's foreign policy," wrote the official organ, "has earned the hatred and contempt of the Italian masses for supporting fascism. The disgraceful role the Vatican played in Hitler's and Mussolini's Spanish adventure is widely known. The Vatican emerged in the role of a supporter of armed intervention."

The foreign policy of the Soviet government was thinly veiled behind an apparently theological dispute which otherwise would seem quite incomprehensible in wartime. Patriarch Sergei attacked the very principles of the Papacy, in April, 1944. "The uninterrupted presence of Christ in the church," the Patriarch wrote in his *Journal of Moscow Patriarchate,* "and the spiritual marriage between Christ and the church make inconceivable the concept of an intermediary between the two such as a vicar on earth." He concluded with a hint of a political nature: "I could conceive of a union of churches around some chief who could not be a vicar of Christ but a bishop of some world capital."

In 1944 a new feature appeared, however, in the attitude of the Soviet government to the Catholic world. The territories with a prevailing Orthodox population were reoccupied by the Red Army in the first months of that year, and the Soviet troops stood at the gates of Catholic countries: Lithuania, Poland, Czechoslovakia. In the Balkans and in Austria the influence of the Catholic Church was strong, too.

Everywhere the influence of the Vatican stood in the way of Soviet foreign policy. The struggle between Moscow and Rome was mounting. More than once attempts at reconciliation were undertaken; they proved unsuccessful. In the belt of nations bordering on prewar Russia in Europe, the Catholic churches might become the nuclei of national movements for political independence; it was natural that anti-Soviet feelings sometimes were widespread among Catholic parishes in the middle zone of Europe. The Soviet government, however, is the last to tolerate any opposition to its policies.

With the war approaching its end and even more so since the termination of the war, considerations of foreign policy began to prevail in the attitude of the Soviet government toward the church.

In 1941–43 domestic motives primarily had guided the Soviet leadership in its relations with the church: the fight against the influential pro-Nazi clergy as well as the need of encouraging the people through non-Communist, religious leaders in wartime was paramount. The Orthodox Church responded to the demands of this situation. Summarizing its functions during the war, Patriarch Alexei said: "The main achievement of the Orthodox Church in the years of war was its demonstration to the entire world of its unity with its Government . . . It works together with the Government, it aids it, follows its appeals." [6] The messages and sermons of the Orthodox clergy were directed against Hitlerism and the Orthodox priest-traitors; they readily adopted the use of the word "fascism," strange and alien to the vocabulary of the Russian Church, and execrated traitors. And they glorified the Soviet leaders to high heaven. "Before the New Year," Patriarch Sergei said on the anniversary of the November revolution in 1943, "let us ardently pray for our divinely protected country and for its authorities, headed by our God-sent Leader!"

In December, 1944, in preparation for the future cession of Carpatho-Russia to the Soviet Union, a delegation from Orthodox churches in eastern Czechoslovakia arrived in Moscow. In June, 1945, the new Patriarch Alexei, the former Metropolitan of Leningrad, who had succeeded Sergei in February, 1945, visited Orthodox churches in Egypt and Palestine. In October, 1945, he made a trip to Soviet Georgia. Two months earlier, Metropolitan Nikolai was in Paris with the political mission of rallying as many former émigrés as possible around the Soviet government. He had considerable success, and the Patriarch publicly praised his accomplishments. Soon afterward a reconciliation was achieved with the Orthodox Church in Yugoslavia. Early in 1945 a Soviet church delegation went to Bulgaria to terminate the church schism there in a manner favorable to Moscow. Archbishop Alexei was in the United States in November, 1945, but was not so successful as his colleague in Paris in uniting the Orthodox churches. In the spring of 1946

6. *Izvestia,* May 12, 1945.

Patriarch Nikodemus of the Rumanian Orthodox Church visited Alexei in Moscow. In May, 1946, Patriarch Alexei went on an official visit to Bulgaria. In July, 1948, a galaxy of Greek-Orthodox leaders arrived in Moscow to take part in a church celebration; among them were, in addition to metropolitans and bishops from Russia and the satellites, the highest Orthodox dignitaries from the United States, Central and Western Europe, and countries elsewhere.

When the Soviet government launched its campaign to re-annex the Kars and Ardahan region from Turkey, Gregori Peter XV, head of the Armenian Church, declared in favor of incorporating Turkish Armenia into the Soviet Union.

Assisted by the Orthodox clergy, the Soviet government developed great activity in Jerusalem to regain both property and prestige. The old Russian Palestine Society, which was founded about a hundred years ago and had accumulated considerable property in Palestine, was revived in 1952 under the name of the Palestine Archaeological Society. Its ecclesiastical envoys soon came to Jerusalem to claim all the rights and privileges of the prerevolutionary society. Large sums were expended for repair of church property in both Israel and Jordan. Large quantities of religious books were distributed; aged monks and nuns were taken care of. The Soviet envoy in Israel and his staff attended church services regularly.[7] At the same time Russian priests visited Nazareth, the Arab-Christian center, and established contact with Armenian and Syrian "sister churches." In July, 1950, the Lebanese government recognized the legality of Soviet claims to old Russian properties.

Finally, the postwar Orthodox church gave considerable assistance to the propaganda drives of the Soviet government. Church leaders have taken part in the so-called peace congresses, given their signatures to "manifestoes," and thrown all their authority behind campaigns to prohibit use of atomic

7. *New York Times,* August 22, 1952.

weapons. The government has used the church as one of the most important and effective arms of its foreign policy.

Just as important as this diplomatic activity was the fight of the Soviet clergy against the Vatican after the end of the war. The Soviet leaders as well as the press accused uncompromising Rome of collaborating with fascism and inviting a new war with Russia. While the Moscow radio accused the Vatican of "continuing their efforts to save fascism," the Moscow Patriarch publicly blamed the Vatican for "trying to absolve Germany of the responsibility for all war crimes." The Vatican replied through encyclicals and interviews in its own press, denying that the Catholic Church had ever supported or encouraged Hitler's war against Russia. On the other hand, it enumerated acts of Soviet terrorism against the Catholic clergy in Soviet-occupied territory and asked for the protection of Catholic as well as non-Catholic displaced persons who did not wish to return to eastern Europe. Now the political role of the Vatican grew even more important, since it fell in line with the policy of the United States and Great Britain.

Patriarch Alexei wrote a letter to the Ruthenian Church asking for its adherence to Moscow. The first response was cool. About the end of 1945, Soviet authorities arrested all four Ruthenian bishops and deported to Siberia more than one-fifth of the Ruthenian priests.[8] On March 8, 1946, the Uniate Church Assembly, consisting of 216 delegates (clergy as well as lay persons) sent a message to Premier Stalin—not the Patriarch— in which it stated that after 350 years of oppression the Ukrainian population of the Carpathian lands had regained moral freedom under the Soviet regime and now wished to "return to the bosom of the Holy Russian Orthodox Church of our forefathers." This action involved two to three million Uniates.[9]

8. N. S. Timasheff in *Religious News Service*, New York, March 22, 1946.
9. The Eastern Polish Regional Association in London published a statement in which it termed the above address of the Uniates "the result of ruthless pressure by the Soviet Union upon members of the Greek Uniate

Subsequently thousands of Catholics fled from the east to the American and British zones in Germany.

By the end of the war, Georgi Karpov, head of the State Council on Orthodox Affairs, stated, there were something over 16,000 Orthodox churches functioning in Russia, compared with about 50,000 before the revolution. In addition, there were 89 monasteries and convents, which existed as a kind of kolkhoz. At Easter, 1946, church bells rang for the first time since the revolution. In subsequent years measures were taken to increase the number of young people training for the priesthood. In 1954 there were two theological academies and eight seminaries engaged in training; students were recruited mainly from among the sons of priests. At present (1954–55) about 55 churches are ministering to a population of over 6,000,000 in Moscow and vicinity; in Leningrad, 14 churches are serving a population of over 3,000,000. The majority of newborn infants are being christened. Solemn services attended by thousands and numerous declarations by church leaders have created the impression that the Soviet government has entered upon the road to complete religious liberty, even to the extent of encouraging religion.

While these changes in Soviet policy were broadcast everywhere in the world and taken by many as proof of Soviet evolution toward democracy, the Soviet government was taking measures to counterbalance its risky operation by other moves. In 1944, three years after atheist propaganda had been virtually stopped and antireligious publications had ceased to appear, the Central Committee of the Communist party adopted a resolution dealing with "scientific-educational propaganda" which meant the resumption of antireligious propaganda. In the fol-

---

Archdiocese of Lwow and the dioceses of Przemysl and Stanislawow." It stated that the "Metropolitan of Lwow, Msgr. Slipyi, and the Bishop of Stanislawow, Msgr. Chomyszyn, died in prison in Kiev." It also reported that Msgr. Latiszewskij, Bishop Adjutant of Stanislawow; Msgr. Lakota, Bishop Adjutant of Przemysl, and two bishops adjutant to Lwow "had been deprived of their liberty."

lowing year, 1945, the Central Committee repeated its order to increase the "scientific-educational work" against religion.[10] In 1947 a new Society for the Dissemination of Political and Scientific Knowledge was founded. In subsequent years, assisted by the party and abundantly financed, it developed antireligious activities all over the country, issuing millions of leaflets and pamphlets every year and arranging thousands of lectures. Of course, *Pravda* commented, the Stalin Constitution has proclaimed freedom of conscience, which implies the privilege of performing religious services, yet "freedom of conscience does not mean that our social and scientific institutions are neutral regarding religion."

Dissemination of "scientific knowledge" was merely a new, less offensive title for an activity that had been carried on throughout Soviet history. Soon antireligious societies bearing the same names emerged in the satellites.

The antireligious drives were viewed as urgently necessary because during the early postwar years notions had begun to spread in Communist circles that the party was about to make peace with religion. In 1946, for example, a Komsomol (Communist Youth) meeting adopted a resolution of the prewar type prohibiting Komsomol members from attending church services. Promptly *Young Bolshevik* (Nos. 5–6) attacked the resolution from a liberal viewpoint: nobody should be expelled, it said, from the Communist youth organization for reasons of religious belief. The top leadership of Komsomol considered the matter important enough to call for a sharp reprimand of *Young Bolshevik*: "A young person cannot be a member of the Komsomol if he is not free from religious convictions"; this would mean "compromising materialism with priestism and idealism, a retreat from Marxism." From that time on, and fairly regularly, antireligious articles have been appearing in the Young Communist press and in Army newspapers. Their theme is always

10. *Pravda,* June 29, 1948 and *Large Soviet Encyclopaedia,* 2d ed., Vol. 2, 512.

the incompatability of Communism and religion. From time to time the Central Committee of the Communist party and *Pravda* have devoted attention to antireligious propaganda, regularly stressing the urgent need to increase antireligious activity and admonishing that such activity must be conducted on the propaganda level without recourse to physical suppression. On November 10, 1954, Nikita Khrushchev signed a new instruction to this effect:

"Whereas in relation to the state, religion is a private matter, and therefore the church is separated from the state, the Communist party, which bases itself on the only correct, scientific world outlook—Marxism-Leninism—and its theoretical foundation, dialectical materialism, cannot adopt an apathetic, neutral attitude toward religion, an ideology which has nothing in common with science." However, "it is stupid and harmful to cast political doubt on Soviet citizens because of their religious convictions. Profound, patient, skillfully arranged scientific atheist propaganda among believers will help them in the long run to free themselves from religious delusions. On the other hand, administrative [i.e. penalizing] measures of any kind and insulting attacks on believers and clergy can only do harm, can only lead to strengthening and even intensifying their religious prejudices.

". . . The Party Central Committee considers it wrong that many party organizations have held aloof from daily guidance of scientific-atheist propaganda and do not show concern for the careful selection of propaganda cadres. Articles in the press, lectures, and reports are frequently allowed to be made by people who are ignorant in science and in questions of atheist propaganda, and sometimes even by hack workers who mainly know only anecdotes and tales about clergymen."

Resurrected and comparatively free since 1942, the Orthodox Church in Russia was given a new constitution that differed considerably from the previous one adopted in 1917. In 1917 the All-Russian Church Assembly (*Sobor*) adopted a constitution based on democratic principles: all believers who were regular churchgoers formed the church community which had the right to choose church officials; the assembly of representatives thus chosen, together with the representatives of the clergy, had the right of choosing the bishop for the respective region; the All-Russian Church Assembly of Bishops together with the representatives of the rank-and-file clergy and the church communities had the right of choosing the Patriarch. In February, 1945, a new constitution abolished the principle of clerical elections. Now the Patriarch had to appoint the bishops, and the bishops appointed the priests. In this way the Patriarch obtained complete control over the personnel of his churches.

Actually, however, his authority was greatly limited. Simultaneously with granting permission to elect a Patriarch, the Soviet government created a new agency to supervise the church. This was the State Council on Orthodox Affairs, appointed on October 8, 1943, by the Council of People's Commissars.[11] This Council was headed by Karpov and his three assistants. The Council stands above the Patriarch and the metropolitans. It is an agency of the Soviet government; its head, for a number of years, belonged to the GPU-NKVD, whose religious section conducted the antireligious campaigns over a considerable period.

Karpov's office constitutes the link between the church and the Soviet government. Karpov publicly stated that he is a member of the Communist party and therefore an atheist; so long as the government considers it necessary, he will collaborate with the churches and assist them—but no longer than that. No important decision of the Patriarch becomes effective until endorsed by Georgi Karpov. When the Patriarch travels across Russia to important church conferences he is accompanied by Karpov. Every priest in Russia knows that Karpov is the actual master of church affairs and acts accordingly.

In a political system such as that of Russia, every local church

11. Later, other churches were similarly subordinated to Karpov.

parish, however small, is feared and distrusted by the authorities. Each parish lives its own life and must, perforce, exhibit differences of opinion on various questions. A police government is bound to suspect that a church parish may be transformed into a cell of discontent and opposition. Church autonomy is a dangerous thing, however efficient the system of espionage within it. For this reason, and not only because of the shortage of priests, the number of churches remains limited, and a system of checks and double checks prevails. The new State Council immediately created a dense network of its own agencies covering the entire country. After a short time Karpov reported that he had more than one hundred representatives in all regions and provinces and "they in turn have their representatives in the local Soviets, and these maintain contact with local church affairs." [12]

As a political maneuver in the grand style, the church reforms carried out by the Soviet government were successful. This was one of the political acts that are justly responsible for Stalin's reputation as a realist; it was an intelligent step toward shifting a part of political responsibilities to the clergy of the Orthodox Church. It was shrewd to let the church appeal to the recalcitrant neighboring nations and useful to have it fight the Vatican.

However, the method of accomplishing these plans was often blunt and primitive. Instead of creating the impression of a free and strong religious movement in Russia, the frightened and terrorized clergy went rather far in their adjustment and subservience to the state agencies. There was too little dignity, too much servility. Stalin was praised, of course; but this was done in grossly exaggerated forms; even Karpov, the police commissar, rated a deep bow from the church leaders. When Karpov was awarded the Order of the Red Banner, he received congratulatory messages from most of the bishops and many other

12. Robert Casey, *Religion in Russia* (New York, Harper and Brothers, 1946), pp. 178–186.

clergymen. When a new theological seminary was inaugurated, the first greeting to be read to the assembly was a telegram from Karpov.

For Stalin the church found even finer epithets and greater attributes of virtue. "Above all," Patriarch Alexei said, after the victory over Germany, "let us thank God for sending us wise men to lead our country and for heading it by the divinely chosen genius leader, Iossif Vissarionovich Stalin, who to this day has led our fatherland to success and will lead it in the future to unprecedented glory." Metropolitan Nikolai wrote in 1944 that "in our leader the faithful along with the rest of the country recognize the greatest of men that our country has given birth to . . . He combines in himself the best and the highest, the profoundest wisdom, a paternal heart, and the genius of mastery."

The Patriarch instructed all churches to pray "for the well-being and flourishing of the God-sent leader of peoples of our Christ-loving country."

It has been almost a tradition in the Orthodox Church for centuries that its heads are clever realists. Russian church leaders appraise the situation in all its complexity. Their apprehensions are great lest the proreligious zigzag of Soviet policy end soon and they be obliged to exchange their splendid robes for the prisoners' frock. While foreign visitors become enthused about the "freedom of conscience" in Russia, Russian church leaders protect their reputations and unduly stress their loyalty. They are always on guard. They are far from happy about their own lot and the lot of the churches in Russia.

It has also become clear that separation of church and state has no basis in fact under a political regime such as exists in Russia. Under Soviet conditions, the church cannot develop its activities if the state does not assist it: under such circumstances the restoration of churches without the help of the state's economic organs is impossible. It is impossible to obtain the ornaments and habiliments necessary for services without the co-

army; passionate patriots of old Russia into a group of Russian traitors in Berlin. Cruel facts would have compelled Trotsky, had he been in power, to adopt the policy which he assailed. Of course, outwardly the policy would have been given a different coloration. There would have been other phrases, other slogans, a different terminology. Trotsky would have known how to paint his policy in bright hues, he would have been more generous in the number of public appearances, and he would have lent much brilliance to his political actions. But the substance would have been the same.

OCCASIONALLY, when he was not embroiled in his conflict with Stalinism, Trotsky was able to manifest a farsightedness and a gift of prophecy which place him in the first rank of the political figures of the period between the two wars.

In 1938 Trotsky wrote that "the social bases of the Soviet regime [planned economy and state ownership] would resist the test of war," although in the event of war he expected great political changes in Russia. In the spring of 1939, when the entire world waited from week to week for the signing of an Anglo-Soviet treaty against Germany, Trotsky wrote that "an agreement with Hitler would signify security of frontiers" for Stalin, and that by signing such an agreement Russia "could systematically supply Germany with almost all raw materials and foodstuffs she lacks."

Even more remarkable were Trotsky's predictions concerning the course of the war, expressed in those early months when France appeared powerful and Russia and the United States barricaded themselves behind the walls of neutrality. Trotsky did not believe in the power of France, or in the weakness of Germany. Nor did he, however, foresee a German victory.

"The international propaganda which hastens to picture Hitler as a cornered maniac is very stupid," he wrote. "The situation is still very far from that.

"The Polish Government and the Czechoslovak Govern-

operation of government agencies. The printing of books and magazines in Russia requires not only money but also the active collaboration of various government agencies. The Synod, the Patriarch, the Theological Institute, and the rest can be housed only with the assistance and at the will of the government.

For this reason the church is not actually separated from the state in Soviet Russia. Living by the grace of the government, the church faces the risk of losing its new privileges at any moment; hence it is compelled to cooperate with the government politically, and at times church leaders find themselves in an undignified position. They accept many compromises in order that the churches may be permitted to function. But at the same time they are forced to swallow many bitter pills.

For several years now a kind of balance in church affairs has been maintained. Bloody persecutions have ceased, a limited number of churches are open and conduct services undisturbed; the Bible has appeared in print. The church remains the only non-Leninist, ideologically nonconformist organization in the Soviet Union. Yet for its right to exist it pays with heavy assistance to government policies, mainly those in the field of foreign affairs. The Greek-Orthodox Church is the privileged one; the Moslem Church is in an inferior position, and the Catholics and Jews are the worst treated as far as church affairs are concerned. This differentiation in treatment accorded to different religious groups, under which first place is accorded the Orthodox Church and the position of the Jewish group has deteriorated, is reminiscent of the prerevolutionary state of affairs.

The church does not play a great role in the social life of Russia today. But the history of religion in Communist Russia and of its religious policy illustrates glaringly the nature of the political system and the conditional character of the political shifts.

PART THREE: Foreign Policy

Chapter 12. THE SOVIET CONCEPT

Words must have no relation to actions—otherwise what kind of diplomacy is it? Words are one thing, actions another. Good words are a mask for concealment of bad deeds. Sincere diplomacy is no more possible than dry water or wooden iron. JOSEPH STALIN.

STALIN thus expressed his conception of diplomacy in 1913. Of course, he added the adjective "bourgeois" to qualify the substantive "diplomacy." His idea of international politics concurred with that of Charles Talleyrand, who had said, a century earlier, that "language has been given to man to conceal his thoughts."

No government or political party has ever offered the world as many precise theses, platforms, manifestoes, and programs as did the Soviet government and its party. From this wealth of material the deep roots of Soviet policy can be discerned and its growth traced. But in the late 'thirties this frankness was abandoned for its opposite, and Talleyrand's concept became the basis of political strategy. There was nothing enigmatic about the philosophy, plans, and program of Lenin and Trotsky, or of Stalin in earlier years. But in the last two decades silence has become golden and the schemes are the carefully guarded secrets of an intimate circle.

CERTAIN basic conceptions persist in Moscow's ideology. Nothing has altered in the Soviet attitude toward capitalism—it remains convinced that capitalism is dying. As official Moscow sees it, the coalition of the Soviet Union with capitalist states during the war did not constitute evidence of the stability of capitalism; on the contrary, the war demonstrated the truth of the old Bolshevik axiom that "the long drawn-out crisis of world

291

capitalism" must assume the forms of a great catastrophe. Millions of lives must be sacrificed because capitalist society can find no way out of "the inherent contradictions" arising from private ownership of the means of production, no solution to the "clash of imperialist powers" struggling for world domination. The enormous sacrifices the USSR was compelled to make during the second World War and the sacrifices it would have to make if a new world war should break out are due to the antagonism between capitalism and Socialism. A new world war will end in a new victory for the anticapitalist nations and further contraction of capitalism or its final destruction.

The main features of all of these Communist theories include the concept of declining capitalism and the inevitability of imperialist conflicts in this era; the first World War and the Russian revolution of 1917 marked the beginning of the crisis of world capitalism.

The first period of this crisis lasted about six years. In Europe, and especially in central and eastern Europe, it was a time of storm and stress, of direct Communist struggle for power. It ended with the victory of Socialism in one country and retreat of revolutionary forces everywhere else.

The second period, from 1923 to 1928, was one of apparent convalescence for capitalism; according to Stalin, this represented the "relative stabilization" of bourgeois society in the economic and political fields. However, this period differed from previous periods of capitalist stability and expansion; it was brief and insecure and culminated in the worst crisis ever known. The depression of 1929–33 gave new proof of the inability of decaying capitalism to solve any of its fundamental problems.

The third period, from 1929 to 1937, was characterized by mass unemployment, bankruptcy, declining production, economic and political instability. Capitalism was in its death throes, Stalin reiterated in speech after speech.

The widely publicized and systematic analysis of "the general crisis of capitalism" ended at this point. Between 1917 and

1937 Moscow had sought the widest possible distribution of its many publications, giving in endless theses and programmatic manifestoes a full explanation of Communist concepts and Soviet policies. The second half of the 'thirties was, on the surface, a period of Soviet efforts at collaboration with the democratic capitalist countries through the League of Nations, and pacts with France and other powers. Silence became necessary now. "Words are one thing, action another. Good words are a mask."

It is not difficult, however, to find in fragmentary speeches and ideas expressed by the late Soviet leader and his closest collaborators the links between the ideology of all the preceding "periods" and that of the ensuing fourth period. Moscow interpreted world developments as follows:

Between 1937 and 1941 the capitalist countries, having failed to overcome their internal crises and increasing antagonisms in international relations, were being swept inexorably toward a world war. According to Stalin, the first skirmishes of this second World War began in 1937–38. German troops occupied Austria in 1938; they took possession of the Sudetenland, then the rest of Czechoslovakia, and, finally of Poland. The civil war that was raging in Spain was also a war of the German-Italian alliance against Britain and France. In Asia the war began in 1937 with Japan's attack on China.

Communists everywhere followed Stalin's lead in characterizing this phase of the war, and the next phase during which Germany occupied most of western Europe, as a strictly imperialist conflict. It was presented as a new attempt of Germany, Italy, and Japan to force a redivision of the world's colonies, markets, sources of raw materials, spheres of influence. Both groups of imperialist powers sought world domination. "The progressive elements of mankind" could not sympathize with either of the contending power groups. Hence the Soviet Union was justified in her neutrality.

A new period began at the moment Germany violated her pact of 1939 and invaded Russia, on June 22, 1941. An entirely different and nonimperialist force was then drawn into the war, which altered everything. The war assumed a dual character on June 22. The imperialist struggle for world hegemony continued; the entry of Japan and the United States only made it global. But the belligerency of the Soviet Union added to this imperialist rivalry the struggle for the preservation of the Socialist fatherland against fascism and imperialism. This dual character of the war led to the coalition of the Big Three; the USSR entered into this alliance to protect Socialism; Britain and the United States entered it because they were unable to crush German imperialism alone. The capitalist countries sought to utilize Russian military forces for their own national self-interest, but they hoped that German and Soviet armies would mutually exterminate each other so that neither would again become decisive factors in European affairs. The Kremlin remained as suspicious as ever of Anglo-American motives.

The period since 1945 is another part of the accumulating crisis of capitalism. Its main trait is, according to the Communist theory, the disintegration of the world entity into two "world markets," one Socialist, the other capitalist. The fact that China and the European "people's democracies" have broken away from the capitalist system and together with the Soviet Union have formed a united camp aggravates "the contradictions of capitalism" and sharpens the general crisis. The danger of a new war is increased in view of the strong position of the "monopolists" in the United States. In the Communist view it is likely that the abolition of capitalism will be completed in three world wars, two of them behind us, the third still ahead.

IN the course of the second World War the Soviet policy of "Socialism in one country," with its apparent emphasis on Russian nationalism, its praise of tsarist heroes, its seeming abandonment of the hope of world revolution, won laudatory comment from high places abroad. But since the war, this policy has been replaced by a new one.

For as Moscow sees it, the policy of "Socialism in one country" was correct during periods of revolutionary defeat, of relative stability of capitalism, but this policy, "which brought incalculable advantages" to the cause of Communism, in Stalin's phrase, came to a natural termination in 1939, when the world was plunged into a new holocaust and a new dynamic period of history began.

September, 1939, clearly set the demarcation line; for the first time in nineteen years Soviet troops crossed the European frontier into foreign territory. In the course of the next year, a series of countries and territories—Estonia, Latvia, Lithuania, eastern Poland, northern Bukovina, and Bessarabia—were "liberated, with the aid of the Red Army, from the yoke of their fascist regimes." Soviet regimes were established, with nationalization of the local economy. Socialism was now triumphant in more than one country.

This expansion of the sphere of Socialism, which continued for about a year, reached its prewar limits in July, 1940.

A new push took place at the end of the war—far into central and southeastern Europe. A new empire emerged, thus surrounding its kernel, the Soviet Union (with a population of over 200 million) by belts of dependent nations with a total of nearly 100 million. Between 1945 and 1949 the successful Communist offensive in the Far East, greatly aided by Moscow, ended in the emergence of a Communist China and Communist North Korea; in 1954 North Indochina, too, emerged from war as a Communist state. The total population of the three Far Eastern "people's republics" is not known; it is claimed to be about 650,000,000 but is probably closer to 400,000,000 or 450,000,000.

That a third of mankind now lives in Communist-ruled countries is seen, by Soviet eyes, as the highest achievement of the era of the second World War.

Suspicion and Mistrust

THE widespread tendency to explain the puzzles of Soviet policy —for example its antagonism to the West—as being motivated by suspicion and mistrust is founded on error. Nor is it any more correct to assume that Soviet actions are based on constant fear resulting from the Allied military intervention in Russia in 1918–19.

It is not true that the Russian people have a peculiar distrust of foreigners and that they view them with more suspicion than does any other nation. During the century before the revolution, the number of Russians going abroad and of foreigners coming to Russia grew by leaps and bounds. Thousands of Russian intellectuals, students, and merchants, as well as members of the old nobility, regularly visited western Europe. Vienna, Paris, the French Riviera, Baden-Baden, the German university cities —each had its Russian colony. Foreigners came to Russia by the thousands but never had occasion to complain about the attitude of the people; they sometimes had reason, however, to complain about the attitude of the police. Austrian, German, and English businessmen as well as journalists were highly regarded in Russian circles. Men of Western science were often better received in Russia than in other countries.

It is necessary to dissipate this strange inculcated theory about the general distrust of foreigners in Russia. During the war thousands of Allied soldiers and officers had the opportunity of meeting members of the Russian Army, but it is doubtful that one of them was able to confirm these alleged traits of Russian character. They often complained, however, about the attitude of Soviet authorities who considered every foreigner a potential or actual spy. But this attitude is part of a premeditated system and not a feature of the national character.

The presentation of Soviet foreign policy as dictated by the fear of foreign intervention belongs in the same category of manufactured theories. Here again the Russian people are pictured in a psychologically anomalous state—something like the hydrophobia of a man who had almost drowned in his early childhood; like a dog that is afraid to walk past a house whence a brick once had dropped and hit him. Actually the Russian people as well as the Soviet leaders are reasonable, calculating, normal men, and their actions are not in the least motivated by recollections of events that took place three or four decades ago. How little this recollection matters is evident in the differentiation made by the Soviet government in its attitudes toward the United States and France. During the military intervention in Russia, France was by far the more active in supporting Generals Denikin and Wrangel and the Polish offensive; the United States, on the other hand, helped Lenin's Russia against Japan. During the past decade, however, the relationship between Moscow and Paris has been much better than that between Moscow and Washington.

The protection of the "security" of the Union, as the main motive behind Soviet foreign policy, is nearer to the truth. Yet it is not security in the usual meaning of the word—that is, the safeguard of frontiers from attacks from without. This need of security in the usual sense would not explain Soviet policy in Iran or in Manchuria or Yugoslavia. The Iranian border, for example, is the most secure among all the borders of Russia. During the 120 years of the present status, no war or even threat of war ever arose from this side. (Only when the Russian Army disintegrated, in 1918–19, did foreign troops appear in the Caucasus.) So long as a normal armed force exists in Russia, no other power will venture upon any suicidal and nonsensical aggression against Russia through the deserts of Iran. The same applies to the borders of China in Mongolia.

In Soviet conception, security has a different meaning. There is no security for Communism in Russia so long as there exists a non-Communist world. Real security will not be achieved until Communism becomes the universal system of our globe.

Stalin wrote in 1938: "Can Socialism victorious in one country regard itself as fully secure against the danger of a military invasion and therefore against attempts at restoring capitalism?" And he answered:

"We would be in a position to say that the victory [of Socialism in the Soviet Union] is complete if our country were situated on an island and if it had not many other [capitalist] countries around it. But since we live not on an island, but in a "system of states," a considerable number of which are hostile to the land of Socialism, thus creating the danger of intervention and restoration, we say openly and honestly that the victory of Socialism in our country is not yet complete.

"This problem remains to be solved . . . It can be solved only by uniting the serious efforts of the international proletariat with the still more serious efforts of the entire Soviet people."

Security, in this sense, is identical with the overthrow of non-Communist political and social systems abroad. The security of the Soviet Union is proportionate to the extent of Soviet territories, protectorates, and colonies. Complete security is identical with the complete triumph of the world revolution.

Good-natured and well-meaning people in the West readily consider "legitimate security" a road to a far-reaching agreement with the Soviet government. They do not suspect, however, that this kind of "security" hinges on the defeat of their own nations and governments.

THE roots of this policy lie in the following ideology: The widening of the realm of Communism is a boon not only for Russia but also for humanity; world-wide Communism is the only guarantee against want, war, and the humiliation of man. Social revolution is the road to world-wide Communism. Great wars are an integral part of the social-revolutionary process. Since 1917 every great war has served—and every great war in the future will serve—to enlarge the extent of Communist control.

"During the war of 1914–18," V. I. Lan, Stalin's loyal commentator, wrote in 1934, "the victorious November revolution raised the banner of labor over one-sixth of the globe. The second World War will spread the workers' rule to one-third, to a half, maybe even to a greater part of our planet."

Mr. Lan was only popularizing Stalin's conceptions. More than once the Soviet leader had explained his concept of the significance of great wars in an age which he terms the long period of social revolution. In 1934, a long time after he had proclaimed the concept of "Socialism in one country" and had been falsely presented to the outer world as a narrow-minded but modest Russian nationalist, he told his party congress that the "inevitable" war in which Russia would be involved "will lead to a complete defeat of the aggressors, to revolution in a number of countries of Europe and Asia, and to the overthrow of the bourgeois-landlord governments in these countries." [1]

"Things are moving toward a new imperialist war," Stalin continued:

"The war will certainly unleash revolution and put in question the very existence of capitalism in a number of countries, as was the case in the course of the first imperialist war . . . Let not the gentlemen of the bourgeoisie blame us if on the morrow of the outbreak of such a war they miss certain ones of the governments that are near and dear to them, and who today are happily ruling "by the grace of God" . . . If the bourgeoisie chooses the path of war, then the working class in the capitalist countries, reduced to despair . . . chooses the path of revolution. That means that a revolutionary crisis is maturing and will continue to mature."

At the Congress of the Communist party in 1939 the delegate Biryukov said that in case of war:

"The armed forces of the Soviet Union, in the East as in the West, will be met everywhere as liberators of mankind from capitalist slavery and fascist reaction. The rear echelons of the

1. Stalin, Report to the 17th Congress of the Communist Party of the Soviet Union, 1934.

capitalist armies will be in flames. Hundreds of thousands and millions of toiling men will arise against their enslavers. The capitalist world is pregnant with Socialist revolution. . . . [This will be] the last, the decisive struggle. Long live the general of the legions of the international proletarian revolution, our leader, our pride and glory, our own Stalin!"

BIRYUKOV, like Stalin, was wrong in his anticipation of popular movements but right in his prediction of the sovietization of other nations.

One of the top Soviet leaders and a close associate of Stalin, Lev Mekhlis, even developed a strategic plan combining future war with an "increase in the number of Soviet republics" throughout the world.

"If the second Imperialist War," he said in 1939, "should turn its point against the first Socialist state in the world, military actions must be transferred to the territory of the enemy, and we must fulfill our international obligations and increase the number of Soviet republics."

How firm the hold of this theory was upon the leaders of Soviet Russia became obvious in 1940. Early in August of that year Molotov appeared before the most brilliant and enthusiastic session of the Supreme Soviet to present the three Baltic Republics and Bessarabia as new members of the Soviet family. With pride in his party and with contempt for the outer world, he explained:

"The capitalist world will have to move over a bit and make room."

The results of the second World War seemed to confirm Stalin's expectations and predictions. As far as Europe is concerned, there were no great popular revolutions in the traditional sense—with no military aid from the outside. The only attempt at bringing one about—in Greece—was a failure. But this fact seemed of no great consequence: now the force of the Soviet Army, reviving the weak local Communism, became the vehicle of the social revolution, and in this sense the success was enormous. In Asia, especially in China, the great postwar up- heavals were more of the popular-revolutionary type than they were in Europe, but even in the history of the Chinese civil war and the emergence of the Communist government in Pe- king, Soviet aid, Soviet-controlled stores of arms in Manchuria, and Soviet strategic and diplomatic guidance proved to be most essential, even decisive.

ARE WARS INEVITABLE?

THE future, too, appeared to Stalin as fraught with military conflicts and great wars; on this issue he adhered to the old Leninist tenets. As if replying to the many questions addressed to the prophet concerning the further struggle for Communism, Stalin said in his speech of February 9, 1946, that new wars will be unavoidable:

"The uneven development of the capitalist countries leads in time to sharp disturbances in their relations, and the group of countries which consider themselves inadequately provided with raw materials and export markets try usually to change this situation in their favor by means of armed force."

Here Stalin developed a theory of the causes of wars which was certainly wrong in regard to the last two great conflicts. What is important, however, is his conviction and prediction that the same historical "law" will remain in effect in the near future:

"Perhaps the catastrophe of war could have been avoided if there existed the possibility of periodic redistribution of raw materials and markets between the countries in accordance with their economic needs, by means of coordinated and peaceful decisions. But this is impossible under the present capitalist de- velopment of world economy."

Stalin again, as in 1939, expected the capitalist powers to clash in war; and he expected that in one way or another Russia will be drawn into the conflict that may again develop into a struggle for the aggrandizement of the Soviet world. His main aim for the next years was the strengthening of military forces and military industry. The new Five-Year Plan was therefore centered around the so-called "heavy industry" and "metallur-gical industry" as a preparation for war, in direct continuation of the prewar plans. After the fulfillment of three Five-Year Plans, Stalin said,

"Our country will be insured against any eventuality. Per-haps three new Five-Year Plans will be required to achieve this, if not more."

In fifteen, twenty, or twenty-five years, according to Stalin, the Soviet state will be completely secure; this means to Stalin that it will be stronger than the other powers taken together. Only such a superiority of force constitutes security. When this superiority is achieved, every conflict will end in favor of the Soviet Union. And there will be no reason for it to retreat, yield, give ground, and be reconciled with the existence of capitalist governments. After fifteen to twenty-five years the social revolu-tion will be nearly complete, the goal will be accomplished. Such was Stalin's theory on Communism and war in the last, the postwar stage of his leadership.

To the great majority of men, war is an evil: it brings death, destruction, and moral degradation. Communism views war in a different light. To the Communist leadership war is often a grave illness of a young organism from which the body emerges stronger and more beautiful; war means the unsettling of all traditional, stable relationships; it leads to the acceleration of development and the growth of new revolutionary (pro-Soviet) forces.

The first germs of this theory emerged as far back as 1904, when during the Russo-Japanese war a dispute arose between Lenin's party on one hand and the Mensheviks and Social Revolutionaries on the other, concerning their attitude toward war. The Russo-Japanese conflict was extremely unpopular—probably the most unpopular war in all history. As a consequence of Russia's defeats, revolutionary developments were precipitated at a high speed. "Peace at any price" or "immediate peace" were the slogans of the non-Bolshevik parties. Lenin opposed this program; he frankly admitted that he wanted to see the war prolonged. He said: "The cause of Russia's freedom depends greatly upon the military defeats of autocracy . . . The Russian people have gained by the defeats." The war, he said, is certainly a calamity; but it is wrong to base a policy "on this trivial reasoning."

Out of these discussions there grew later Lenin's program for the transformation of "imperialist wars" into civil wars. And, in turn, the great socialist revolution which, for Lenin, began in November, 1917, was fraught with the prospect of international wars. He was prepared for a long period of revolutionary struggles intermingled with wars, and wars developing into revolutions. "The history of revolutions, of profound conflicts," he said, "teaches that wars—a series of wars—are inevitable . . . All the inevitability leads to a combination of the several states of civil wars with revolutionary wars." And he repeated:

"There has been no great revolution in the world which was not connected with wars."

Stalin expressed the same idea when, after Lenin's death, he said that the "epoch of world revolution covers a whole strategic period which may occupy years or even decades. In the course of this period there will occur, nay, must occur, ebbs and flows in the revolutionary tide."

The role of war, according to Stalin's concept, grew in proportion to the decrease of revolutionary upheavals.

In 1924, after Lenin's death, and five years after the first World War, it appeared to Stalin that a certain stability in the international fabric had again been achieved. During the comparatively stable period after 1923 Russia succeeded in keeping her new social-political system. The stability ended in the 'thirties, when new wars loomed on the historical prospect. The second World War was therefore not entirely unwanted by Stalin's followers. The Stalin-Hitler pact of 1939 was obviously an encouragement to the Berlin government to start the war. The expectation that in the course of the war other nations would undergo social transformations and join the Soviet family of nations was certainly present in the complex calculations which determined the course of Soviet policy for a number of years.

As was the case after the first World War, the first years after the second World War were to Communism a period of instability when the rich political and social harvest must be reaped. This was the essential meaning of Soviet postwar policy. It was not aiming at another war, and it would recoil before a real threat of war, but every grain and every blade that could be gathered without immediate military conflict had to be brought into the Soviet barns and granaries. If diplomatic conflicts emerged out of this activity, they could be taken in stride. If outside economic help to Russia was denied because of this activity, this was no reason to abandon the achievement of great political tasks which would become impossible of fulfillment in a few years when a new temporary stability may set in.

In this period of fifteen to twenty years between the end of the war and the moment when the Soviet Union is expected to become the strongest power in the world, the relationship between the Great Powers is conceived by Moscow thus:

France, Germany, Japan, and Italy have ceased to be great powers, and measures have been taken to make the re-emergence of the most dangerous among them impossible.

Of the two remaining great capitalist powers—the United States and Great Britain—the latter not only is the weaker but also was undergoing internal crises that may culminate in its disintegration.

The crisis of the British Empire was grossly exaggerated in Soviet eyes. Economic rivalry between the United States and

Great Britain certainly existed, but it, too, was seen out of all proportion in the Soviet perspective. As a result of these concepts and exaggerations, Moscow still expects a deepening of American-British divergencies.

Soviet antagonism to Britain was one of the most stable and constant elements in Soviet ideology as well as in the policies of the Soviet government. The Soviet attitude toward France, Germany, the United States, and Japan underwent changes in the years between 1919 and 1939; zigzags, rapprochements, and deteriorations in relations characterized this period. However, the hostility toward England, often bordering on hatred, was almost uninterrupted.

Stalin explained: "English capitalism was, is, and will be the most vicious strangler of popular revolutions . . . The English bourgeoisie has always stood in the front ranks of those who crushed liberating movements of mankind." [2] "Great Britain heads world reaction," he proclaimed in a resolution of the Communist International on May 29, 1927.

As for the relationship between the United States and England, Stalin said:

"The principal of these conflicts is between the United States and England. After the principal conflict comes the secondary . . . between America and Japan, between Germany and France, between England and France, and so forth." [3]

On another occasion Stalin made this statement: "The one basic problem [is] the problem of the struggle for world hegemony between England and the United States . . . The star of England is setting, the star of America is rising. What is this basic conflict fraught with? It is fraught with war. When two giants collide, when this globe is too small for them, they try to measure their strength, they try to solve the vexing question of world hegemony by means of war." [4]

In the 'thirties, in expectation of German aggression, treaties

2. Stalin, "On the Menace of War," *Pravda*, July 27, 1927.
3. Stalin, *Problems of Leninism* (1931), pp. 494–495.
4. Stalin, Speech of July 13, 1928.

of friendship and alliance were concluded between Moscow and Paris. No such treaty was signed between Russia and England. In the summer of 1939 negotiations for a treaty with England proved futile. The antagonism toward England rose even higher between September, 1939, and June, 1941, when England was termed "aggressor" and "warmonger."

Then, for a period of four years, a wartime coalition with Britain became imperative for military reasons. Open attacks against "British imperialists" had to be avoided. Molotov even signed a twenty-year treaty of alliance.

No sooner had the war ended than the former emotions and attitudes were resurrected with new strength. The greatest activity was now displayed by the Soviet government in the areas which have traditionally been part of the British sphere: Iran, Turkey, the Mediterranean, Greece. Independence won by India was hailed in Moscow mainly because it weakened Britain. The evacuation of Egypt was supported primarily because it meant a loss to the British Empire. The withdrawal of British troops from Syria and Lebanon was strongly supported by Moscow. Britain's loss was Moscow's gain.

Contraction and weakening of the British Empire did not, however, yield the fruits that Moscow had hoped to reap. The vacant seat of the strongest world power went to the United States, which since about 1945–46 has taken leadership in the non-Communist world.

NEW PATTERN OF THE WORLD REVOLUTION

AT this stage the new pattern of world revolution became obvious once again. From Karl Marx, from Friedrich Engels, from the Socialist International, and from his Russian teachers, Lenin had inherited the old classical concept of the transformation from a capitalist to a Socialist society. Depending on her history and the contemporary social setup, the theory went, each country, sooner or later, enters a period of political tension which more often than not assumes forms of political violence. At the end of this revolutionary path will stand a society renovated in a political as well as in a social sense.

However, the bell does not toll for all nations at the same time; rather, revolutions will develop without logical or geographical regularity. Today they will flare up in central Europe, tomorrow in the Far East, then in America, then perhaps in Europe again, and so on. This drawn-out process of social revolution will be like summer lightning at night, flashes occurring in any part of the darkened sky without visible order—in the north and south, east and west, in an apparently chance sequence. Only at the very end of this protracted critical stage will the great transformation, engulfing the whole globe, be completed and the battered strongholds of capitalism replaced by the edifice of Socialism.

Even after Lenin and his party had attained power in Russia, this concept prevailed for a long time. Russia's influence in world affairs was based on ideology rather than on force, and Lenin saw no reason to credit the first Soviet country with more than secondary importance in the conflict between the old order and the new. His Russia was poor and weak, its army badly trained and badly supplied. He looked to other nations not only for economic assistance but even for new revolutionary initiative. He saw Russia as only the source of inspiration and a haven for its standard bearers.

Lenin died without revising the inherited concept. Trotsky, who died sixteen years after Lenin, remained faithful to it until his very end.

The Stalin doctrine, which had been ripening since the first stage of Soviet history, deviated from these concepts. Stalin had seen the first Communist government in Hungary suppressed by Admiral Horthy while his Russia stood by unable to help. A little farther to the west a Communist government had emerged in Bavaria; no outside assistance had been forthcoming and it had been destroyed. On the other hand, wherever the Red Army had been able to arrive in time and fight, the chances of a Communist victory had greatly improved. Independent Georgia had been quickly transformed into a Soviet republic in 1921; so was the "Far Eastern Republic" when the Japanese withdrew in 1922. Socialist transformation would be successful—Stalin drew the conclusion for himself—only if and where the military force of the first Soviet fatherland could be brought into the fighting.

In other words, only revolutions in areas adjacent to Russia could be assisted to the extent necessary to achieve victory. Once transformed into Socialist organisms, these territories could either be formally incorporated into the Soviet Union or, for special reasons and for a certain time, allowed to retain their formal status of sovereign nations. "History has shown," Stalin said, "that single nations, if they adopt the Soviet system, are not able to live as separate units while imperialism reigns outside the Soviet sphere, and to defend themselves successfully without the economic and *military assistance of the adjacent Soviet republic.*" A year later Stalin announced that "access to the Soviet Union is open to all Soviet Republics: to those that exist and those that will emerge in the future."

By this concept the role of Russia—the Russian state, Russia's military power, Russia's government—is raised to such a height that Russia overshadows all other nations, great or small, advanced or backward. Russia is the great center of the expanding Socialist community. There is no longer any trace of the old theory of spontaneous and irregular social revolutions. In the new conception the Socialist world spreads like an ink spot on blotting paper. The role of popular movements, barricades, and revolutionary fighting diminishes almost to the vanishing point. The military might of the great Socialist Fatherland now does the job.

The notion of Russia's new grandeur and decisive role in the abolition of capitalism makes it necessary to preserve her from all danger, and this is the other side of the medal. To the adherents of this doctrine Russia's downfall today would be a catastrophe. To prevent this, and for this purpose to make concessions to foreign powers, is just as reasonable and necessary as it is to expand by leaps and bounds when the possibility offers.

Once the Soviet Union fulfills its duty and creates a group of satellite nations, these nations become endowed with the traits, privileges, and obligations of their Soviet creator. Born into the world with Soviet help, they subsequently themselves assume, under Soviet guidance, the same functions in regard to a further group of nations. The Soviet Union represents the founding fathers of the Communist nations; the European satellites and China are the second generation; Indochina, Korea, and East Germany are the third generation. The new generations of Communist nations are expected to play the obstetrician's role in respect to their neighbors—Thailand, Burma, India, and West Germany. Projected into the Western Hemisphere, this strategy implies that no frontal attack would ever be made against the United States (except, of course, in a great war); instead, an operation beginning somewhere in Latin or Central America, and aided by the older generation of Communist nations, would have to reach the borders of this country from the south.

BECAUSE, in the Communist concept, revolutions now in process are component parts of a great revolutionary era, and because revolutions frequently develop into wars, the Soviet government did not demobilize its armies after the war to the extent that the other powers did. Its army in Russia and its occupation forces in Germany, Poland, Rumania, Hungary, and (until 1955) Austria far exceeded in size the military forces of all other nations combined. Moreover, Moscow supported the rearming of the satellites, and those that had been in the German camp were urged and helped to rearm far beyond the limits set for their armed forces in the peace treaties.

Under these conditions and with these expectations Moscow could not support any plans for true disarmament. Since the days of Lenin it has been a sacred precept of Communism that an "armed proletariat" is the first requisite of Communist progress (armed proletariat meaning arms for insurrection in a "capitalist country" and arms and armies in a "Socialist nation"). Genuine disarmament, therefore, has been out of the question, and the aim of Soviet disarmament propaganda was only to slow down the arming of the political enemy. Openly if permissible, or by ruse or secrecy if not, the relative strength of the armed forces of the "Socialist camp" had to increase. Stalin provided an eloquent formula for this combination of peace-loving propaganda and bellicose policy:

"There is a glaring contradiction between the imperialists' policy of piling up armaments and their hypocritical talk about peace. There is no such contradiction, however, between the Soviet government's preparations for defense and for revolutionary war and a consistent peace policy. Revolutionary war of the proletarian dictatorship is but a continuation of revolutionary peace policy 'by other means.' " [5]

Thus, without reverting to its prewar size, Soviet military forces actually remained, during the first postwar decade, on a war footing, quantitatively exceeding all other armies combined. Their armament was increased and improved from year to year; Soviet aviation rivaled that of the United States in both quantity and quality; a new sizable navy was created. At great cost and sacrifice atomic weapons were produced and perfected.

The same considerations determined the Soviet course in the new United Nations organization which emerged in 1944–45 as a product of the wartime alliances and served, in Soviet eyes, as an excellent rostrum for popularizing its policies rather than as a means of international negotiation. The United Nations was never accepted in Moscow as a barrier to an armed expansion of the Soviet bloc of nations. In 1950, for instance, on the eve of the North Korean attack, the Soviet delegation to the

5. Theses of the Sixth World Congress of the Communist International, 1928.

United Nations simply walked out on a slight pretext to forestall an expulsion similar to their expulsion from the League of Nations in December, 1939, when Russia attacked Finland.

THE FUTURE WAR

BUT the war foreseen by Moscow under Stalin and later under Khrushchev was quite different from the type of East-West conflict Westerners have envisaged in the last few years. Before Stalin's death Moscow was saying a new war was "inevitable," that wars cannot be abolished so long as "capitalism remains the predominant form of economy." But the third World War, Moscow said, will be a war between capitalist nations and not one between the Soviet bloc and the Western powers; the pattern of the first two world wars, which began as wars among capitalist nations, will be maintained in the third. In such a war the Soviet Union will, at least in the beginning, remain neutral.

The Moscow view of the contours of this future war was as follows: The present solidarity of the Western powers is only transitory. New antagonisms are rapidly developing between the major capitalist power, the United States, and the minor powers, Britain and France, because the former is taking advantage of the latter. In addition, Germany and Japan, at present controlled and partially occupied by the United States, will rehabilitate themselves and become anti-American. The conflict will lead to a war between the United States and her capitalist opponents. In the process, or toward the end of the war, the Soviet Union may take an active part in the fighting in order to increase the number of Soviet republics.

Stalin's plans were not entirely convincing to his collaborators: Is there *really* a war in the making, they wondered, other than a conflict between "capitalism" and "Socialism"? One of the skeptics was Eugen Varga, dean of Soviet economists and close student of the international scene. Varga saw no indications of impending serious conflicts between the "capitalist"

nations, while everything pointed toward a possible fight between East and West. Stalin replied to Varga and the other
doubters:

"Some comrades hold that, owing to the development of new
international conditions since the second World War, wars between capitalist countries have ceased to be inevitable. They
consider that the contradictions between the Socialist camp and
the capitalist camp are more acute than the contradictions
among the capitalist countries . . . These comrades are mistaken . . . Capitalist Britain, and after her, capitalist France,
will be compelled in the end to break from the embrace of the
U.S.A. and enter into conflict with it in order to secure an independent position and, of course, high profits. Let us pass to
the major vanquished countries, Germany (Western) and
Japan. These countries are now languishing in misery under the
boot of American imperialism . . . Yet only yesterday these
countries were great imperialist powers and were shaking the
foundations of the domination of Britain, the U.S.A., and
France in Europe and Asia. To think that these countries will
not try to get on their feet again, will not try to smash the United
States 'regime' and force their way to independent development,
is to believe in miracles."

The Soviet leadership naturally endorsed Stalin's theory, and
in October, 1952, the Party Congress, following Malenkov's report, approved it as a matter of course. Neither Stalin's death
nor the accession of new men to power has changed the official theory that the future war will be a war between Western
powers. As for the strategy of the Soviet Union, this was outlined by Stalin in 1925 (but not made public until 1947): "If
war breaks out we shall not be able to sit with folded arms. We
shall have to take action, but we shall be the last to do so. And
we shall do so in order to throw the decisive weight in the scale,
the weight that can turn the scales." [6]

6. Speech at the Plenum of the Central Committee of the V.K.P., January
19, 1925. In a public report made in May of the same year, Stalin cam-

In the end Varga capitulated. Left out in the cold as a consequence of his deviations and removed from his post on an economic magazine, he finally did what was expected of a loyal Communist. Varga recognized, says the record of the discussion in the Institute of Economics, that he was wrong. "While speaking of his work Academician Varga admitted that he was mistaken in assuming that under the present conditions, in connection with the extreme aggravation of the contradictions between imperialism and Socialism and the extreme preponderance of the U.S.A. over other capitalist countries, Lenin's thesis of the inevitable wars between capitalist countries becomes obsolete. 'I admit,' stated Academician Varga, 'that I was wrong in this question. Comrade Stalin gave sufficiently exhaustive proofs of the inevitability of wars between capitalist countries at the present stage.' " [7]

Long after Stalin's death this theory was reiterated in the official *Soviet Encyclopaedia:* "The policy of the American imperialists aims at the attainment of world supremacy. This inevitably leads to the aggravation of contradictions between imperialist states; the most acute struggle goes on between the American and British imperialists . . . So long as imperialism exists wars between capitalist nations are inevitable." [8]

In the last sentence of the above quotation the emphasis was on *between capitalist nations;* a military conflict between "the camps of Socialism and capitalism" may or may not be inevitable. This easing of the old rigid view of the "inevitability" of a new great war was Stalin's reluctant concession to the general antiwar sentiments in Russia. Somewhat later, under Khrushchev, this concession assumed the proportions of a new doctrine, as we shall see later.

---

ouflaged his strategy in an interesting way: "Needless to say, if our country is attacked we shall not sit with folded arms, we shall take all measures to unleash the revolutionary lion in all countries of the world. The leaders of the capitalist countries cannot but know that we have some experience in this matter."

7. *Voprosy Ekonomiki,* Moscow, No. 12, 1952.
8. Vol. *29,* p. 468 (November, 1954).

THE facts of postwar history have already shown the weak point in this political philosophy. Anglo-American relations have improved, and opposition to Soviet expansion has led to the emergence of firm associations of non-Soviet powers. Arming of the Western powers and rearmament of Germany create a force which, if integrated, is greatly superior to the military power of the Soviet bloc.

DURING the last years of his rule, from 1948 to 1953, Stalin maintained his policy of continuing the expansion of the emerging Socialist empire without directly involving Russia in a war. By February, 1948, with the coup in Czechoslovakia, the belt of Soviet satellites in Europe had reached its limits; the next step would have to affect West Germany. In the summer of 1948 Stalin proceeded to cut West Berlin off from West Germany, an operation expected to succeed by a threat of Soviet arms, yet without the actual use of armed force. The blockade, countered by the American airlift operation, proved a failure and ended in a restoration of the status quo.

At the same time Stalin ostracized Communist Yugoslavia. In Stalin's view—and in line with the only logical Communist concept—the family of "Socialist nations" is a single camp preparing and prepared for conflicts, campaigns, small and large wars. A military camp, it must be cemented by strong discipline allowing no deviations, disagreements, or discussions in the face of the enemy. When Tito displayed independence, Stalin tried to engineer an internal upheaval in Yugoslavia; the attempt failed. Again Stalin faced the alternative of recognizing his defeat or sending an army against Yugoslavia; again he refrained from using his *ultima ratio,* with the result that Communist Yugoslavia, though damned by the new Communist International (the "Cominform"), remained independent.

With Yugoslavia's defection, the ties between the Greek Communist insurrectionists and the Soviet world were broken.

The Greek civil war ended—another failure for Stalin's policy of aggression without the use of military force.

Thus, beginning about 1949, a paradoxical situation of unbalanced equilibrium existed in Europe. No new acquisitions for the Soviet empire were possible without a military offensive, and a military offensive was too dangerous. Stalin's attention was focused on the Far East, where more leeway for Communist expansion existed and where the United States had no foothold on the continent except in the southern part of Korea. Manchuria, where the railways, industry, and southern ports were in Soviet hands, became the base of extensive operations. Greatly aided by the Soviet Union, Chinese Communist guerrilla forces gradually expanded over the whole country, while a new Communist army was organized in North Korea under Soviet instructors and with the aid of Soviet arms.

At this point Stalin tried out his new method of aggression against South Korea, with the prospect and intent of expanding into Japan. The onslaught began in June, 1950. Successful at the outset, the North Korean armies had to retreat before the American forces almost to the Manchurian border. Then the Chinese Communist army, advised by Soviet generals and supplied by the Soviet government, entered the war. It met with only partial success; having restored the pre-1950 situation, it was not able to proceed further and defeat the American armies.

The aging and stubborn Stalin refused to compromise on secondary issues of an armistice, and the war continued without prospects of success until his death, just as the Communist war in Indochina continued with arms from Russia and her satellites and with direct aid from Communist China.

Chapter 13. SOVIET POWER
AND COMMUNIST
MOVEMENTS

TWO LINES of development were decisive for the course of Soviet foreign policy in the 1950's, first under Stalin and, to an even greater degree, after his death.

1. The substantial growth in the power of the Soviet Union.
2. The decline of Communist movements in the Western world.

The "contradiction," as Moscow would say, of these two trends is the root of Soviet policy—a policy which mixes intransigence with "coexistence," massive rearmament with attempts to make use of the "breathing-spell."

THE INCREASE in Soviet power has been spectacular. In the two world wars Russia was in no position to operate without military and economic aid from Western allies; left to her own resources she was no match for her foes. Soviet power in the second World War combined Russian manpower with overseas lend-lease. Moscow emerged a victor in 1945 as a result of Western assistance. Now the situation has changed.

Anticipating the possibility of an East-West conflict, the Soviet regime has devoted enormous energies and resources to new types of industry and to military stores which could support a prolonged war against the West. It has been attempting to organize a self-sufficient military economy in its orbit. This attempt underlay both Stalin's last Five-Year Plans and the Khrushchev-Malenkov controversy over "heavy industry."

Soviet success has been considerable. New weapons and new

316

inventions have been introduced, new plants and railroads constructed, aviation perfected, and a formidable intelligence network maintained. Food reserves, at the time this is written, must be sufficient to last a large army at least a year.

Russia today is more powerful than any nation of continental Europe and in many respects is on a par with the United States. But in power terms the Soviet Union is virtually isolated, despite a number of small allies. The West is a *combination* of great powers, and though Russia is strong compared to any one of them, she and her allies are weak compared to the Western alliance which comprises six great powers.

For several centuries now a group of powers has defined the contours of world politics; their relations have decided the course of history. These powers have included Britain, France, Prussia-Germany, Russia, and a few others. In the many wars among them, the nations that were defeated soon rose again. Humiliated in 1815, France was a major power again within five years; the same was true after 1871. Defeated in 1918, Germany came back in less than two decades; now we are again witnessing her resurrection after the collapse of 1945. Russia experienced incomparable catastrophe during the first World War and the civil war of 1918–20. But, even with the devastation of the first World War, Soviet power today greatly exceeds that of prerevolutionary Russia. Against a background of perpetual change—frontiers moved backward and forward, treaties imposed and broken, armies mobilized and demobilized —the stability of the Great Powers has remained a constant.

A few other nations in Europe were Great Powers for a time, only to retreat again: Sweden, Holland, Spain. One power, weak because of its multinational tensions, has disappeared completely: Austria-Hungary. At the end of the last century Italy joined the select company of major nations. And, finally, two non-European nations have entered the ranks of Great Powers: the United States and Japan. Today seven drivers sit at the wheel of the political chariot: Britain, France, Germany, Italy,

Japan, Russia, and the United States. (Communist China does not belong in this list.) Of these, six constitute the Western bloc of nations, outnumbering the Soviet Union 6 to 1.

Every Soviet leader realizes this basic Soviet weakness and understands that Moscow cannot hope for military success if she must defeat the combined power of the others. On the balance of arms and armies, the West greatly outweighs the East. The Soviets believe that an additional factor can redress the balance: the Communist movement in the West or East.

THE older Soviet leaders remember and every Soviet schoolboy has studied the "armed intervention of fourteen nations" in 1918–19 against the weak Soviet Republic, and how that assault ended. This chapter of Soviet history serves as a classic illustration of "international solidarity": the popular movements in London and Paris under the slogan "hands off Soviet Russia"; the political crises in the Western nations; the mutiny of the French fleet in the Black Sea; and, finally, the total collapse of intervention followed by official recognition of the Soviet government. This Soviet triumph resulted from the combination of Soviet resistance with pro-Soviet pressure in the West. Either of these factors alone could not have succeeded.

The interaction of the two forces—Soviet power and Communist movements abroad—has continued since. The world-Communist response has not always been so strong as Moscow has wished, but in every Soviet maneuver left-wing activity abroad was an element in Moscow's calculations. (We are wrongly told that Stalin, having evolved into a Russian nationalist, began to despise the Communist International. Although he treated a number of foreign Communist personalities with contempt, he never disregarded the movement as such).

The Communist world abroad was considered important even to purely Soviet needs, especially those relating to war and peace. Russia's salvation in a war with a strong enemy would be the rising of the workers against the capitalist aggressor. At its

conference in April, 1925, the Soviet Communist party stressed
that its policies depended on the progress of international Communism: "The dictatorship of the proletariat in the USSR needs
help on the part of the international proletariat." It blamed
those party leaders who, in their "nationalist narrowness," were
inclined to disregard the interdependence of the Soviet system
and the "worldwide proletarian revolution." A new war, Stalin
predicted in 1934, "will be certain to unleash the revolution."

Whether the democratic powers would aid Russia against
Nazi Germany appeared doubtful to Moscow; on the other hand,
the Kremlin felt certain that the response of the Communist
world would be forceful and decisive. When Nazi Germany attacked Russia in 1941, Moscow was very disappointed that
"the workers" throughout Europe remained silent and passive.
The Comintern, which meanwhile had begun to impede the
new Grand Alliance, was dissolved, though a department of
the Central Committee of the Soviet Communist party continued to carry on its main functions.

Although the Communist movement abroad proved too weak
to prevent the anti-Soviet war or to quell it at its start, in other
ways world Communism rendered great services to the Kremlin
during and after the war. Pro-Communist groups in Berlin with
access to the strategic plans of the High Command relayed them
to Moscow. The Soviet intelligence apparatus in Switzerland,
in which the German Rudolf Rössler-Lucy was the star per-
former, was a little Comintern in itself: Its head was the Hungarian Alexander Rado, its chief worker the Briton Alexander
Foote, its other important figures included a Pole and several
Swiss. Soviet speed in manufacturing an atomic bomb was the
product of another international Communist effort: Pertinent
information and, in certain cases, samples were supplied in
1943–46 by the German Klaus Fuchs, the Briton Allan Nunn
May, the Italian Bruno Pontecorvo, the Americans David
Greenglass and Clarence Hiskey, and others. Western Communism has assisted and can continue to assist Soviet foreign

policy in a variety of ways. Though the basic principles of Communism remain constant, the vigor of each important Soviet step depends to a large extent on those factors and developments abroad which we summarily term Western Communist public opinion.

A democratic government's policies depend largely on public opinion at home. The Soviet government cares little for public opinion at home but, in planning long-range world operations, is attentive to the reaction of broad left-wing circles abroad; these must supplement, as we have seen, what is lacking on the scale of power relations.

DECLINE OF THE COMMUNIST MOVEMENT IN THE WEST

HAD SOVIET Communism retained the freshness and vigor of its youth, its leaders would now step forward with the bold though painful statement that after the second World War "capitalism" has again reached a high degree of stability, that revolutions are on the ebb, and that Soviet policy must be oriented accordingly. But new ideas and bold statements have become abhorrent in Moscow; Stalin's heirs, like Stalin himself, prefer confusion to frank acknowledgment of failures and defeats.

Unlike the first postwar period of 1918–23, there were no popular revolutions in Europe or America after the second World War. Moscow has tried to represent the upheavals in the satellites since 1944 as popular revolutions, but even these ended in February, 1948, when a Communist government took over in Czechoslovakia. Since then, an adverse trend has prevailed. The civil war in Greece ended in a defeat for the Communists, and Finland and Iran remained independent.

More than once, Stalin's circle tried to spur the Western Communists to greater revolutionary activity—in vain. "The main danger for the working class at this moment," declared the first conference of the new Cominform (1947), "lies in the underestimation of its own strength and overestimation of the force of the imperialist camp." Andrei Zhdanov, Stalin's deputy, castigated the French and Italian Communists for being too cautious; a short while afterward the Communist leaders in those countries, thrown out of the coalition government, retreated without a fight.

According to the Communist concept "capitalist stabilization" is to some degree reflected in the strength of Communist trends in the population. And the fact is that the deterioration of Western Communist movements has attained significant proportions since the war. Communist party membership in nine countries of Western Europe has changed as follows between 1946 and 1954: [1]

	1946	1954
Austria	150,000	60,000
Belgium	100,000	30,000
Denmark	60,000	16,000
German Federal Republic	300,000	125,000
Great Britain	60,000	34,800
Luxembourg	3,000	500
Netherlands	50,000	33,000
Norway	40,000	7,500
Sweden	60,000	30,000
Total (nine countries)	823,000	336,800

In these countries the Communist parties have declined to virtual insignificance. In two other countries they have lost heavily but continue to play a vital political role: France and Italy.

	1946	1954
France	850,000	450,000
Italy	2,300,000	1,700,000
	3,150,000	2,150,000

Communist deterioration is just as remarkable in the Western Hemisphere. The United States Communist party, which

1. *Strength of the International Communist Movement*, Senate Committee on Foreign Relations, October, 1953; May, 1954. Two papers on postwar Communism, by S. Wolin, *Free Europe*, March and July, 1955.

has never been a mass movement, declined from 85,000 members in 1947 to 54,000 in 1950 to 25,000 in 1952. In four leading countries of Latin America, Communist membership went as follows:

	1947 (claimed)	1954 (est.)
Brazil	130,000	60,000
Chile	50,000	40,000
Mexico	25,000	5,000
Peru	35,000	10,000

"The combined strength of the Communist parties in Latin America amounts to less than 250,000. Ten years ago, it was estimated at 350,000, and the parties polled an aggregate of about one million votes in various national elections." (In Argentina, the only exception to this trend, the Communist party grew from about 30,000 in 1947 to 40,000 in 1954.)

There are no Communists at all in the parliaments of Britain and West Germany. In the Netherlands, Belgium, Austria, Norway, Sweden, Denmark, and Switzerland, Communists occupy from 2 to 6 per cent of seats, in France 23, in Italy 24. Eloquent as they are, these statistics do not convey the full measure of Communist deterioration. Hand in hand with the disillusionment of those who have turned their back on Communism in the postwar decade, a process of emotional enervation has been going on among the faithful. Zeal and force—Communism's strength in its younger years—have vanished in the Western nations; no general strikes are attempted, no barricades are set up, street demonstrations are dared only under solid police protection. . . .

The Soviet leadership is confident that this state of affairs is only temporary, that a new tide will "inevitably" follow the ebb. Meanwhile, however, the ebb is the reality and the rest is hope. Drawing its conclusions from this state of affairs, the Soviet government has been devoting increased attention to Asia and Africa while stressing the "coexistence" theme for Europe and America.

Chapter 14. SOVIET POLICY AFTER STALIN

THE THAW AND ITS LIMITS

THE FIRST EFFECT of Stalin's death, in March, 1953, was a certain relaxation in Soviet home affairs, economy, relations with the West, and relations with the satellites. The change was not planned and occurred almost automatically. So great had been the tension in the preceding period that a sigh of relief followed the late leader to his mausoleum. The legacy which his heirs received was beset with problems; a dead end had been reached in home affairs as well as in foreign policies. The hopeless war in Korea continued. On November 24, 1952, three months before Stalin's death, Andrei Vyshinsky had announced Moscow's refusal to support the principle of voluntary repatriation of prisoners of war. Despite the large-scale "peace campaign," all roads to relaxation in the international arena were closed. The cold war continued unabated.

A serious crisis in relations with the satellites was approaching. Stalin's concept of a Soviet empire maintained by Soviet armies, secret police, trials and executions, began to crumble the moment the aged leader disappeared from the scene. Under his pressure the satellites, in addition to maintaining Soviet armies on their soil, had to pay tribute to Moscow in the form of "mixed companies," reparations, Soviet trade mediation, and high salaries to Soviet "advisers." Yugoslavia was an irritant: here was a Communist-controlled pro-Leninist government, strong and independent, which was free of the burden of oppressive tribute and enjoyed abundant help from the West. Must

323

the "people's democracies" reconcile themselves to the humiliation of being tributaries of Moscow?

Stalin's "Socialist" empire, which in some respects resembled
the ancient Roman Empire and which would inevitably have
reached a crisis sooner or later, was in danger when Stalin died.

In home affairs the new great purge was in the offing. The
all-powerful Ministry of State Security, controlled by Lavrenti
Beria, had been officially reprimanded for laxity, and the arrest
of the "sixteen doctors" had been announced. The actual number of arrests was not reported, but the affair was only a small
part of a new great drive under way.

Under the Malenkov-Beria regime (March-June, 1953) the
relaxation extended to many fields of Soviet policy. Measured
by Western standards this was modest, but by Soviet standards
it appeared the inauguration of a new era. The arrested doctors
were released and vindicated; a partial amnesty was proclaimed;
the nationality policy took a more liberal course in regard to the
minorities. Stalin's name disappeared almost entirely from both
official pronouncements and the newspapers, while the term
"collective leadership," indicating a change from the personal
dictatorship of a severe and suspicious leader, sounded appealing. No sooner had Stalin been buried than new efforts to settle
the Korean conflict began; four months later the armistice was
concluded. Sensing the change in the Soviet climate, Winston
Churchill proposed a "summit" conference to sound out the
new Soviet leadership; the parley did not materialize, however,
because Washington felt it was premature and because Churchill himself fell ill soon after.

The fresh breeze from Moscow reached the Communist
parties of the satellite countries, eased their tensions, and for
a time at least put an end to the extremes of Soviet regimenta-
tion. Uniformity in economic matters became less rigid; in
Hungary a "rightist," Communist more pro-peasant group was
permitted to come to power; in China pressure on the peasants
to enter into collectives eased. Sensing a change in the political

climate, the workers of East Germany started a vigorous strike movement which was about to develop into a great popular uprising. After the movement was put down by military force, Beria's protégé in Berlin, Wilhelm Zaisser, was removed from his post of Minister of State Security.

Beria himself was arrested and charged with a number of fictitious crimes. Along with a number of codefendants he was executed in December, 1953.

Obviously the old architecture of the Soviet empire was obsolete. The great edifice would have to be re-cemented by economic sacrifices on the part of the Soviets or it would start to crumble and no amount of Communist discipline would be able to preserve it. The alternatives before the Soviet leadership were either to become reconciled to a shrinking of the empire, with Soviet progress ultimately centered on Russia's historic soil, or to hold fast to the great "achievements," ease the economic yoke of the Communist allies, give them more assistance, stimulate their industrialization, and, by sacrifices if necessary, compete with the potential Western help. This was the fateful issue in 1953–54. In essence it was the old problem in new attire: worldwide Communism, or the interests of Russia as a nation; and the government was vacillating between the extremes.

The removal of Beria, while it did not mean an immediate end to the relaxation, nevertheless diminished it in scope and intensity. Nikita Khrushchev, new first secretary of the Communist party, whose star rose as Beria's declined, was collaborating with Georgi Malenkov, the prime minister, within the framework of the new "collective leadership."

The spirit of *détente* found expression in a new program, approved by the party's leading bodies in the summer of 1953, a few months after Stalin's death, and announced by Malenkov on August 8: all attention was to be focused on His Majesty the consumer. There was to be less heavy industry and less armament, more light industry and more food; taxes levied on the peasants were to be cut. "Two or three years," said Malenkov, "are required to fulfill the program of a considerably improved standard of living." "Two or three years" became a slogan that was repeated almost daily in the schools, in articles, and over the radio, a slogan to which Malenkov's career was closely tied.

For the kolkhoz peasants Malenkov promised concessions to their "bourgeois instincts." To increase food production he lowered taxes levied against the tiny private plots of the peasants; the average of 600 rubles a year in taxes was reduced to 300; tax arrears were canceled; delivery quotas were reduced. In October, 1953, Malenkov proclaimed that "under Socialism trade is the basic form of distribution and will remain so for a long time." For the city population 40,000 new stores and 100 large department stores were to be built in 1954–56; 508 new kolkhoz markets were to be created in the cities and towns.

In foreign trade the Malenkov government tried to follow a similar course—consumers' goods instead of "means of production." Four billion rubles (one billion dollars) of food and consumers' goods were to be bought abroad, one-third of it from outside the "people's democracies." Industries controlled by the defense and aviation ministries were ordered to produce a quantity of metal bedsteads, refrigerators, and bicycles. "The Soviet people are entitled," Malenkov stated in August, 1953, "to demand from us, and in the first place from the industries of mass consumption, goods of high quality."

Hope of relaxation ran high among the millions of the rank and file, and the party leadership whipped up this hope, sometimes to the point of enthusiasm. Communist youth was strongly affected by the new optimism: more freedom combined with economic prosperity would serve as proof of the superiority of Communism over all other social-economic systems.

Ilya Ehrenburg, the highly official, praised, and decorated Soviet writer, significantly called his new novel *The Thaw* [1]— spring has not yet arrived but is approaching. One of Ehrenburg's characters was general manager Ivan Zhuravlev, an effi-

1. *Ottepel,* published in Moscow in 1954.

cient man of the Stalin era bent on 100 per cent fulfillment of industrial plans but unconcerned about the poor living conditions of his workers. At the end of the story Zhuravlev is removed from his post. Another character in the novel is Vera Sherer, a physician who had been persecuted during the anti-doctor campaign but was now happily vindicated. (At the height of that campaign a group of workers, Ehrenburg relates, sent her a pot of flowers.) "In my youth," recalls another character, "I read an article by Gorki in which he said we must have our own, Soviet, humanism. The term has somehow disappeared, but the task remains . . . It is time to fulfill the task . . .

"These are the last of the winter days. On one side of the street there is still frost, and on the other heavy drops are falling from the icicles."

A prominent member of the party's Central Committee, Alexander Korneichuk, a playwright and loyal propagandist for the party, wrote a play, in the vein of the Ehrenburg novel, entitled *Wings*. One of the unsympathetic characters is Gordei Dremliuga, chairman of the local Soviet. Imbued with the old Stalinist spirit, he is proud of his great work, which consists of receiving and forwarding instructions, giving orders, and reprimanding. His chief method of operation is coercion, arrest, jail. Dremliuga's antagonist is the newly appointed party secretary, Piotr Romodan, a man of education, humaneness, and concern for the well-being of the population. He is concerned about cows, butter, milk, meat, and, of course, corn: "The price of potatoes," he notes, "is higher than that of imported bananas." "Shall we continue," he asks, "to make speeches about the radiant future and pay no attention to the needs of men today?" Soon, he tells his sister, "there will be great changes in the life of the kolkhozes; the people ask questions, and the party, the government, prepare new laws." Coming from a member of the Central Committee, this statement sounded like a pledge. Romodan's wife, Anna, a doctor, was arrested by the GB for having been a "collaborator" during the German occupation, but is later vindicated. The old Stalinists are grumbling: "Before, everyone felt uneasy when one [a high official] rose on the platform; they sensed the authority . . . Now everybody relaxes and chatters . . . They don't recognize authorities, are not afraid of anything . . ."

Such was the general climate of relaxation in the early post-Stalin era.

THERE has been more than one political springtime in Soviet history, but never did expectations rise so high as they did following Stalin's death. As time went on, however, the broad river of hope narrowed to a streamlet of small reforms. The story of this development is important for an understanding of the post-Stalin stage in Soviet evolution.

Malenkov's pledge to show results in "two or three years" could not be fulfilled, least of all in the field of food and agriculture. His concessions to the peasantry were timid ones (timidity has always been the curse of "rightist" Communism). What the Russian peasants needed was at least an increase of their individual land holdings, which were limited to 0.2 to 1.2 acres. It is not to the credit of the Stalin heritage that in a country which endures unending food crises, no farmer is permitted to keep more than one cow, and only 55 per cent of the peasants own their cattle. Forcible limitation of the peasant's "private enterprise" has been at the root of the permanent scarcity of food products in the Soviet Union.

Yet "rightist" Malenkov and his group were not prepared for great leaps forward. Afraid of criticism, charges of "rightism" and breaking with Communist tradition, they made only minimum concessions, which proved to be ineffectual. The reputation of the leadership suffered; the national economy did not improve. By the end of the first of Malenkov's "two or three" years his star had begun to dim. At the same time the more orthodox Nikita Khrushchev was embarking on a grand-scale counteroffensive.

By nature and by past experience Khrushchev was antagonistic to Communist moderation and "rightism." Clever but unsophisticated, dynamic but not a great historical figure, poorly educated, a believer in slogans about "traitors" and "warmongers," a mixture of Communist realist, cynic, and dreamer, he won notoriety in 1950 when he came out publicly with one of his grand chimeras—a plan for the wholesale resettling of millions of Russian peasants who would be moved from their villages into a small number of "agrocities." The purpose was to overcome the "eternal backwardness" of the Russian farmer and at the same time abolish the many vestiges of private farm economy. Khrushchev's plan, despite its appeal among Stalinist circles, was rejected when it met with protests on the part of certain Communist leaders.

After the beginning of 1954 Khrushchev had wielded more power than Malenkov and his group. Malenkov was gradually pushed back to the subordinate position which Soviet premiers like Rykov in the 'twenties and Molotov in the 'thirties had occupied in relation to the secretary of the party's Central Committee.

Meantime the official press had started to build up Khrushchev as a hero of the civil war and one of the greatest leaders of the Soviet-German war. While Malenkov was condemned to silence, the first secretary developed into a somewhat too prolific speaker. He lectured the Congress of Soviet Architects on how to build houses; he gave advice at conferences of agronomists; he instructed industrial managers. He was abundantly voluble, of course, on every political issue in the plenary sessions of the Central Committee; he spoke to foreign visitors on matters of foreign policy. This was all reminiscent of the Stalin universality.[2]

2. While visiting a shipbuilding plant in Yugoslavia in May, 1955, Khrushchev could not refrain from giving advice to the workers on the most efficient methods of shipbuilding. A few months later a *Pravda* correspondent humbly reported from Belgrade (September 5, 1955) that the plant "begins to shift to more advanced methods, as Comrade Khrushchev advised."

In his final attack on Malenkov, a few days before the latter's resignation, Khrushchev revived nearly forgotten phrases of the 'thirties: his opponent's views, Khrushchev said, are a "regurgitation of rightist deviation, regurgitation of views hostile to Leninism, views which Rykov, Bukharin, and their ilk once preached."

"Capitulators," *Izvestia* fulminated. "Class enemies," said *Trud*. The grand-scale drive against the "rightist deviation" inflamed the Communist world. In Hungary the party's Central Committee announced that the reasons for the serious difficulties in the country were to be found in the "rightist deviation," in the "anti-Marxist, antiparty and opportunist attitude." Prime Minister Imre Nagy, the main rightist culprit, had "duped the working class by demagogic promises." Nagy and his rightist faction were accused of nationalism, of belittling the significance of the Soviet Union, of a false economic policy, and of a tendency to reduce the role of the Communist party. Nagy became "gravely ill." At about the same time it was announced in Peking that Kao Kang, member of the Chinese Politburo, and Jao Schu-shih, a rising star in the Chinese Communist firmament, had been revealed as "rightists" whose purpose was "to pave the way for the restoration of counterrevolutionary rule." They had become "agents of imperialism and the bourgeoisie." Both leaders were expelled. Kao committed suicide; seven others were purged. Reporting on these developments, the Communist press of all other countries approved the new antirightist trend and joined in passionate condemnation of the deviators.

The conflict in Moscow ended in a showdown in February, 1955. Nikolai Bulganin, a loyal subaltern, obtained the premier's post, while Khrushchev actually and openly assumed supreme leadership; Malenkov, who during his premiership had loyally carried out all the decisions of the Presidium, was not thrown out, only relegated in rank.

The gradual ascendancy of Khrushchev and the eclipse of Malenkov in 1954 signified the victory of orthodox Communism over the "rightist trend": not one step back from the limits of socialist expansion attained in 1944–50. Belts must again be tightened, the Soviet "consumer" must be dethroned and light industry again be relegated to second place.

AFTER almost two years of half-hearted moderation in international affairs, the party leadership, under the rising Khrushchev, entered on the new course, once again resuming the Great Offensive. The new course was not a simple reversion to Stalin's type of offensive, which in its last stages proved ineffectual and too provocative. The Khrushchev concept developed from the premise that capitalism, far from being exhausted or on the verge of collapse, was still rather powerful and in the present state of affairs could not be attacked head on; that new large-scale Communist revolutions would be out of order under the present circumstances; that therefore the worldwide Offensive of Communism, which must continue despite the opinion of the "rightists," would have to apply methods other than those applied during the last era of Stalinism. Two new political devices were outstanding in Khrushchev's arsenal.

The first related to the world of the backward nations of Asia and Africa, which had only in the last decade been liberated from dependence on European metropolises and was still harboring antagonism to the West. Very largely non-Communist, the new intellectual strata of India, Indonesia, Burma, and the Arab world viewed distant Moscow as a lesser danger than London, The Hague, and Paris; they were often lured by Soviet economic performance, which was pictured to them in exaggerated colors.

From its very beginning the Soviet government had tried hard to attract to its fold the "colonial and semicolonial" nations; the first great appeal was made as early as 1920, at the memorable Congress of Baku. Although its efforts to build a Communist movement in Asia and Africa had been not unsuccessful in the 1920's and 1930's, all attempts to bring about political upheavals proved futile. The second World War and the easy Japanese victory over the white man in Asia were the first phase of a quasiemancipation. Since 1949, China has taken over from Moscow propagandistic (but not political and military) leadership. Under the coleadership of Communist China, with Moscow guiding the effort in the background, the Bandung Conference of the nations of Asia and Africa, in April, 1955, marked the beginning of a new anti-Western offensive.

While the Communist movement, as we have seen, suffered considerable losses and defeats during the postwar decade, its retreat was more pronounced in the West than in the Orient, and some time must pass before forces and developments which have resulted in this diminution of Communist power will begin to tell in Asia and Africa. Required to give up the offensive in the West, Moscow pressed it in the East with redoubled effort, replacing anticapitalist with anticolonial slogans, with the aim of achieving leadership over the world of neutral nations. The creation of an alliance of "Socialist" and neutral nations against the West—a prerequisite of new victories in the long drawn-out process of the world revolution—is the program of the offensive.

Secondly, Khrushchev's foreign policy implied a new economic offensive against the West. The attempt to compete with the "capitalist powers" in the economic field, in addition to competing with them as political forces, was a new element in Soviet policy. The effort was rooted in the Communist view of the postwar evolution of colonialism and imperialism and the position of the United States in the Western world.

The conventional methods of colonization and empire building, according to the new Communist theory on which Khrushchev's foreign policy is based, heretofore had consisted of the use of military force; colonies were conquered and kept within the framework of foreign empires by means of a monopoly or superiority in arms. But the United States, the last to arrive on the colonial scene, having to compete for colonies with the old empires, turned to other methods and slogans: while trying to detach colonies from their old masters, the United States stressed independence; it tried to achieve its aims through its superiority as a capital-exporting and industry-building nation. In Communist eyes, the most important document of American imperialism was President Truman's Point Four program: "American imperialism carries out an adventurous policy of achieving world predominance by means of increasing its colonial expansion and subjugating peoples under the guise of 'agreements' relating to financial, technical, and military aid (as, for example, Point Four of the Truman program.") [3]

This notion of a new "imperialism" is intended to replace the old Lenin theory which, in the face of the recent developments in Asia and Africa, has nearly collapsed. The picture of the United States as the main present-day colonizing power is also wrong to the point of being absurd. What Moscow intends to derive from this concept is a new course in foreign policies. If America is able to build up its "colonies" by means of "financial, technical, and military" aid, without taking over the regimes of semi-independent nations, why should not the powerful Soviet Union try to counteract with a similar program? If nations of all continents are in danger of losing their independence because of American economic penetration, why should not the Soviet Union proceed to save the most endangered among the "neutral" nations?

Similarity is, of course, relative. Soviet assistance, Khrushchev well knew, could not assume the proportions of American assistance. Besides, the Soviet government under Khrushchev did not want or intend to maintain its own industrial companies abroad from which profits and dividends, flowing to Russia, would appear to Communist eyes as "exploitation of backward peoples"; it preferred to grant long-term loans which

3. *Large Soviet Encyclopaedia,* 22 (2d ed. 1953), 38.

would enable local governments to acquire the industrial units (a program possible only if the loans were small and repayable). To gain popularity and a more favorable public opinion than that engendered by the "greedy capitalists," Moscow added another attraction to its offer, namely a low interest rate (usually 2 per cent).

All of this was made possible only because the Soviet government has absolute rule over the Russian economy. Only by keeping the living standard of the Russian people at a minimum could Russia achieve surpluses for use in its foreign aid operations. No other nation with such a low standard of living could export goods and "technical help" in substantial quantities, nor could it, while itself paying higher interest rates to foreign banks, afford to write off losses. It is true that the Soviet economy has made great strides in the last few years, and that it is this progress which has enabled the Soviet government to enter into these spectacular operations. The progress, however, has been one-sided and of a peculiar kind: it has been restricted to one small group of industries, while other branches of industry have been neglected. Because military considerations have taken priority in the Five-Year Plans, the metallurgical and war industries have expanded tremendously; the aviation industry has progressed satisfactorily; water dams and electrical power projects, which increased the power of the central authority over the nation, have been built. On the other hand, food industries, housing construction and textile manufacturing have lagged seriously. This is why the Soviet government offered its backward-nation clients mainly metallurgical plants, dams, and arms. This type of one-sided progress is so closely tied up with basic Communist policies that even Communist China, now only in the first stages of industrialization, in the summer of 1955 sold 60,000 tons of rolled steel to Egypt in exchange for cotton.

Maintaining the stability and integrity of the new Socialist realm in Europe and Asia was another principle of Khrushchev's foreign policy. Efforts were made to surround the Soviet satellite area with a belt of neutrals, so that now as the satellites protect the various frontiers of the Soviet Union, the neutrals protect the satellites.[4] West Germany and South Korea were the main Communist targets in Stalin's days. Now Moscow recognized West Germany and was prepared to recognize South Korea.

The slowdown in Soviet expansion must be compensated for by a closer consolidation of the Soviet bloc. Formal sovereignty notwithstanding, the subordination of the satellites to Moscow will become more complete. Moscow's supremacy over the satellite armies and economies, concealed behind a maze of treaties and a tight screen, was formalized in May, 1955, by the Warsaw treaty, which put the satellite armies under the command of Soviet Marshal Ivan Konev. Equally important was another section of the same treaty which set up a joint Political Consultation Committee of the Soviet Union and its satellites.

For many reasons formal abolition of the satellites' sovereignty had to be postponed. But Stalin demonstrated several times how a nation could be completely subjugated while her "independence" was being advertised. Following Stalin's lead, his successors made a few moves calculated to stress the fictitious "independence" of the subordinate peoples: the return of Manchurian railways to China, the redelivery to Bulgaria of four, and to Rumania of twelve, mixed companies, etc.

The United States remained the main enemy of the Soviet bloc because, far from settling any basic issues, "coexistence" was only a stalemate. On most world issues the Soviet regime continued to feel the resistance of American power. Although extreme Stalinist forms of propaganda (like the germ-warfare and potato-bug charges) were dropped, anti-American agitation did not abate. NATO, SEATO, the Balkan Alliance—all international combinations potentially dangerous to Moscow—remained targets of Soviet attack.

4. The situation is made clear in the maps on pp. 336, 337.

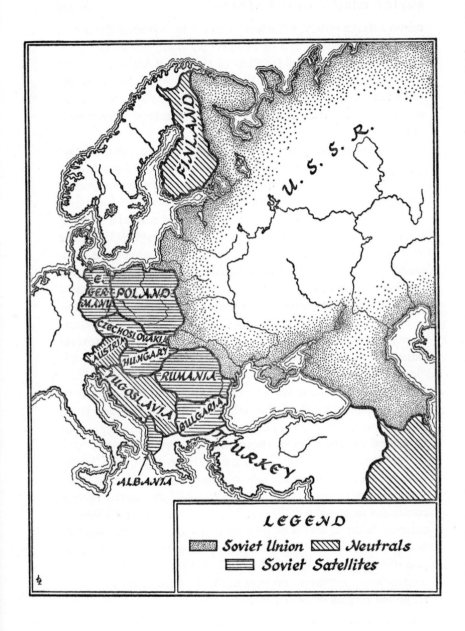

LEGEND
Soviet Union   Neutrals
Soviet Satellites

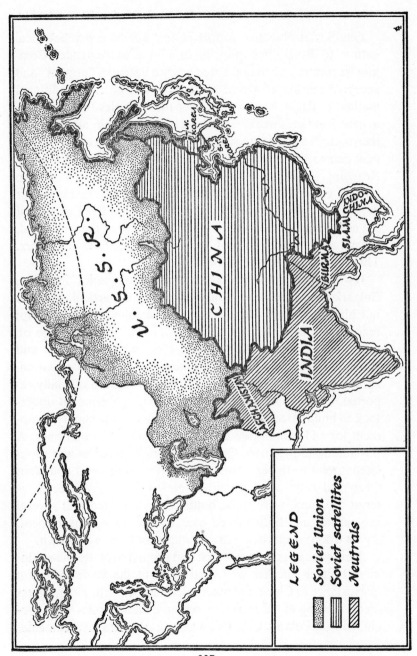

One Soviet objective in this period was of a psychological nature: to dispel the impression of a huge, overextended Communist empire and to make that empire instead a "normal" and accepted feature of world politics. It has been a traditional method of Russian expansion over the centuries to advance to a new frontier, break resistance, withstand all attacks, and then make it a constant feature of the landscape. As time passed, new generations grew up to replace the old political leaders. Reaching maturity under new circumstances, they began to take for granted what their fathers had vehemently resented. For more than a decade now, Eastern Europe has lived as part of the new Soviet state formation. The resistance of the free world, fervent at the start, will cool off as one decade follows another. This is what the Soviets hope and expect.

It was not enough to abolish the "mixed companies" in China, Bulgaria, and Rumania. Industrial programs, particularly those in China, were to be pushed by means of abundant Soviet help; rearmament of China and the satellites was likewise to go on with Soviet assistance. In October, 1954, when Krushchev and Bulganin went to China at the head of a Soviet delegation, agreements were signed of which eight have been officially reported. Under these agreements the Soviet government undertook to build fifteen large industrial plants and to supply equipment for 141 other large units and hundreds of small ones. A Soviet long-term loan to China of 520 million rubles was stipulated; credit to the extent of 400 million rubles and abundant "technical help" were promised. New railways, of special interest to China, were to be built. It was reported that several submarines had been turned over to the Peking government. Soviet troops occupying Port Arthur were to be withdrawn.

Assistance in atomic research and supplying of atomic equipment became another very costly part of the Soviet program of assistance to China and other satellites. In April, 1955, agreements relating to aid in atomic research and supplies were concluded with Poland, Czechoslovakia, East Germany, Rumania, and China. It was this program that secured China's loyal collaboration with Moscow and paralyzed, for a time at least, all anti-Soviet trends among the Communist leadership of China.

SOVIET GRANDEUR

THIS Soviet concept of *grandeur*—the intense rivalry with the United States in arms and economy, the claim to the role of wealthy leader of half the world, the pretense of functioning as a capital-exporting nation—was a paradox, in view of Russia's quite recent hunger for foreign aid and foreign capital. Moreover, *grandeur* demanded rivalry with the West among the neutral nations, too.

In 1954 the Soviet government proposed to build a steel plant in the Bhilai region of India. (Britain and the United States were assisting the Indian metallurgical industry.) The Soviet-Indian agreement signed on February 2, 1955, provided for a twelve-year 400-million rupee (about a 100-million dollar) credit. To the Soviet people the loan meant that during the first few years of the credit period the steel plant in India would be built at the expense of the Soviet consumer.

Moscow offered Burma machinery, factories, and a sports stadium to be built by Russian technicians; the offer was accepted. In Afghanistan, Soviet agencies built factories and grain elevators. In India, Soviet technicians were expected to assist in the development of the oil industry. The Yugoslavs received a Soviet offer to supply blueprints and licences for the manufacture of MIGs on Yugoslav soil. The most spectacular gesture was the Czech-Egyptian arms contract, which was concluded, of course, with Moscow's blessing; in this case Soviet economic expansion was coupled with a far-reaching strategic plan. It was characteristic of the new situation that Soviet activity finally moved to the countries of the "dark continent," where the Communist element was either weak or altogether absent. Neither social programs nor even "liberation of a colonial nation" was behind arms aids to such nations as Egypt.

One after another, big loans have been granted to the three Asian People's Democracies, each loan equivalent to a sizable quantity of goods taken away from the Russian producer and consumer. Many thousands of Soviet "advisers" roam the satellites in Europe and Asia. They are dispatched to build Socialism on the Soviet model, to synchronize all the political, military, economic and police activities of this world of twelve nations. A special department of the GB in Moscow supervises the army of "advisers" throughout Soviet Eurasia.

Besides the great cost of maintaining a Communist bloc of nations, there is a Soviet armed force which in its present dimensions is imposed on Russia by the same set of conditions (namely, the overextension of the empire). A great part of heavy and light industry work exclusively for the Army's needs. Of the so-called "consumer goods" the lion's share goes to Army stores.[5]

Finally, there is the grave problem of the manpower shortage. The 120 million gainfully employed Russians are not equally divided between men and women. The striking disproportion which existed just before the war (7 million more women than men) was increased by Russia's war losses, predominantly male: 7 million on the battlefield, millions in captivity, other millions at home. Of those who survived the war, hundreds of thousands are disabled. Of the remaining Russian men, somewhere between 4 and 5 million are absorbed by the Army, Air Force, and Navy; other millions are engaged in transporting, equipping, feeding, and arming the military services. In peacetime this disproportion results in lowering Soviet economic

5. The rise in the Soviet military budget may be seen from the following figures:

1932	1.3	billion	rubles	(3.4%	of	total	budget)
1940	56.7	"	"	32.5%	"	"	"
1950	82.9	"	"	20.1%	"	"	"
1952	108.6	"	"	23.6%	"	"	"
1953	110.2	"	"	20.8%	"	"	"
1954	100.3	"	"	17.8%	"	"	"
1955	112.1	"	"	19.9%	"	"	"

levels. What would happen, however, in a war, when most of the remaining men would be called to service? In both world wars the Russian Army was able to draw on millions of peasants, while huge imports from Britain and the United States helped replenish the warehouses. Today the peasantry consists, in the main, of women and old men, and no substantial help from the outside can be expected.

The huge, richly equipped military force is the minimum required to protect the overextended Soviet empire. Driven to absurd extremes, this empire saps Russia's blood and paralyzes all its national functions. By its extent the empire arouses apprehension; by its methods of gaining security it provokes animosity; by its very existence it helps powerful opposition blocs to form abroad. History shows that the overextension of a national organism can be as pernicious as impotence.

Realization of the grandiose program meant new efforts, new strains, new burdens. This essentially political development was expressed, in Russia, in economic terms—as a reversal to the granting of priority to "heavy industry." The buds of the first post-Stalin program died before they had a chance to blossom.

"Heavy industry" was an economic pseudonym for a new, grandiose scope to foreign policies which in turn required a new course in home affairs.

It has been a particular trait of Russia's history throughout centuries that her rapid expansion, absorbing all available resources and forces, proceeded at the cost of the people's freedoms and their well-being. Tender sprouts of political liberty and of a new standard of life were frozen under the icy cover of foreign-political exigencies. It is tragic that the dilemma was progress or expansion, and that history gave priority to the second at the expense of the first. The same, *mutatis mutandis,* was the case in the Soviet era. Priority of world-shaking projects over material well-being; attacks and crusades even in peace time; belligerence; and far-reaching goals—all dominated Soviet policy under Lenin, Stalin, and Khrushchev.

Without realizing how very old and deep-rooted was his concept of a strong but poverty-stricken nation, Stalin, entering upon the hard path of industrialization and collectivization, expressed it in a speech before Soviet industrialists on February 4, 1931:

"It is sometimes asked whether it is not possible to slow down a bit in *tempo,* to retard the movement. No, comrades, this is impossible. It is impossible to reduce the *tempo!* On the contrary it is necessary as far as possible to accelerate it. This necessity is dictated by our obligations to the workers and peasants of the USSR. This is dictated to us by our obligations to the working class of the whole world. To slacken the *tempo* means to fall behind. And the backward are always beaten. But we do not want to be beaten. No, we do not want this!

"Incidentally, the history of old Russia is the history of defeats due to backwardness. She was beaten by the Mongol khans. She was beaten by the Turkish beys. She was beaten by the Swedish feudal barons. She was beaten by the Polish-Lithuanian 'squires.' She was beaten by the Anglo-French capitalists. She was beaten by the Japanese barons. All beat her for her backwardness, for military backwardness, for cultural backwardness, for governmental backwardness, for industrial backwardness, for agricultural backwardness. She was beaten because to beat her was profitable and could be done with impunity . . .

"In the past we did not and could not have any fatherland. But now that we have a working-class government, we have a fatherland, and we will defend its independence. Do you want our Socialist fatherland to be beaten and to lose its independence? If you do not want this, you must put an end to this backwardness, as speedily as possible, and develop genuine Bolshevik speed in building up the Socialist system of economy. There is no other way. That is why Lenin said during the November revolution: 'Either death, or we must overtake and surpass the advanced capitalist countries.' . . .

"We are fifty to one hundred years behind the advanced countries. We must cover this distance in ten years. Either we do this or they will crush us . . .

"Must we justify the hopes of the world's working class; must we fulfil our obligations to them? Yes, we must if we are not hopelessly to disgrace ourselves. Such are our obligations, internal and international.

"You see, they dictate to us a Bolshevik *tempo* of development."

This program, although based on an entirely mistaken theory (actually Russia has gained more victories than she has suffered defeats, and it was only because of this that she was able vastly to expand her realm over the centuries) was the basis of Stalin's foreign policies; modified and refurbished, it was again put into operation under Khrushchev.

Khrushchev's course on the home front was emphatically antirightist. Whereas Malenkov had tried to appeal to the "bourgeois instincts" of the Soviet peasants, Khrushchev's emphasis was on the state farms and kolkhozes. His program for solving the acute food problem was one of great projects, each of which would normally require years of meticulous preparation and cautious experimentation and would be slow of realization. About 100 million acres of virgin land (in addition to the approximately 40 million acres ploughed in 1954) were to be made available for agriculture during the next several years. Hundreds of thousands of technicians, administrators, and laborers would have to be brought in and resettled in the barren places. The new land to be cultivated had been lying fallow, because of climatic and other conditions, since before the revolution. But Khrushchev was impatient, and the economic situation was making rapid reforms imperative. His program was to increase food and fodder production by 50 per cent in five years (instead of Malenkov's imprudent "two or three years"), mainly by organizing new state farms and expanding kolkhozes. Where new state farms were to emerge there would be no hamlets or villages; with "agrocities" on his mind, Khrushchev spoke only of "settlements" and "rural cities" and not of the traditional Russian *derevnya* or *selo*. Grand-scale economic transformation was a constant element in Khrushchev's plans.[6]

Corn (maize) became one of his pet interests, and corn growing was to be greatly expanded. The grain had not been unknown in Russia; in the southern provinces it had been cultivated for a long time, as it has been in certain regions of southern Europe. Special conditions of temperature and moisture have regulated the expansion of corn growing in every country, including the main corn-producing country, the United States. But now "we even have proof of growing of corn in Yakutia" [near the Arctic Circle], Khrushchev stated; corn growing in Russia, he said, had to be rapidly increased to eight times the present production. The corn program, accordingly, was pushed vigorously in the traditional "campaign" manner, with rewards for successful administrators and punishment for failures. The satellites, always attentive to what is going on in Moscow, followed suit. Immediately after Malenkov's fall, government leaders in Poland, Czechoslovakia, Rumania, Hungary, and Bulgaria announced that large areas would be allotted to corn growing.

Sweeping gestures became typical of Khrushchev's mode of action. Disappointed over the failures of the collective farms, he proceeded to shift their leading personnel by the thousands. Since "all prerequisites have been created in our country for prosperity in agriculture," the cause of failure could lie only in inadequate personnel. Therefore a purge of the administration of the kolkhozes—although without terroristic overtones —was another of Khrushchev's grand operations. Of the 90,000 kolkhozes, no fewer than 30,000 had been assigned new "chair-

6. The harvest of 1955 on the virgin lands, because of adverse climatic conditions, was bad, as this was feared and predicted by many agronomists.

men" (i.e., managers) by the end of July, 1955. The new chair-men—if further proof is needed of Khrushchev's antipeasant tendencies—were recruited not from among peasants or agrono-mists already working in agriculture but from the cities, mainly from industry. *Pravda* was frank when it compared the sweeping operation with some of Stalin's most ominous campaigns.

Addressing the 20th Congress of his party in February, 1956, Nikita Khrushchev acted as the recognized actual head of both party and government. He stressed the fact that under his rule, in obvious contrast to Stalin's era, the Presidium has started to function regularly, and that Khrushchev's report, his program, and even certain alterations in the official Communist theory were the product of the collective work of the supreme body of the Soviet Communist party.

The revision of Lenin's theories which Khrushchev proposed was indicative of the beginning of chipping off the old phi-losophy rather than of the development of new theories. He warned against the interpretation of "Lenin's thesis of the decay of imperialism in a simplified fashion"; he did not substitute for it, however, a new philosophy which would reconcile the tremendous progress of the West in the last decades with the obsolete theory of "decaying" capitalism. He accepted Tito's thesis that, contrary to the old Leninism-Stalinism, there exist various roads, even peaceful roads, to Socialism, and that civil war is not the only path of a collectivist transformation. He stretched out his hand to Socialist parties and in the case of certain countries accepted the view that parliaments may help transform "backward" societies into Socialist ones.

These concessions to moderation, these retreats from ortho-dox Communism, symptomatic as they are, did not mean a real moderating of Soviet policy. While Khrushchev's pro-nouncement scarred the rounded monolithic theory of old Communism, it did not smooth the way to a happier coexistence of the various nations. In practical foreign affairs Khrushchev remained as aggressive as ever. Carried away by his notion of

Soviet-Communist *grandeur,* he tremendously and dangerously exaggerated the power of his own camp and minimized the force of his adversaries. According to Khrushchev—and here he followed in the footsteps of Stalin—the West is hopelessly torn by crises and dissensions, of which the antagonism between the United States and Britain is the most important. In the face of this great weakening of capitalism, war between the Soviet world and the West is no longer inevitable: the Socialist transformation of the remaining capitalist countries may now be achieved without military conflicts. In this respect Khrushchev paid tribute to the genuine and general antiwar sentiments which exist in Russia among all strata of the population. But his aggressiveness in foreign policy, and the preservation of many vestiges of the old internal policies, did not augur well for Russia's evolution in the near future.

It would be a mistake, however, to assume that the ascendance of Khrushchev has meant simply a return to Stalinism. It did not. Stalin's era, a separate chapter of Russian history, was closed forever. Though gradually restored to an honorable place, and even quoted, Stalin occupied last place among the gods in the Communist pantheon. Many acts of his which had been accepted with a shrug of the shoulders, which had evoked surprise at home and had made Russia a laughing stock abroad, were being undone. The ridiculous claims that practically every invention and discovery of the world had been made by Russians were no longer put forth. Contempt for the West—"it is not becoming to bow before the West"—was succeeded by a flow of Soviet delegations going abroad to study progressive capitalist economy. The Soviet claim that Russia "single-handedly" defeated Germany in the second World War was likewise dropped, and the role of the Western allies was stressed. At home, scientific charlatans of the type of Trofim Lysenko, formerly favorites of Stalin, were dethroned. The grim GPU-NKVD, now renamed the Committee of State Security, had less power than under Stalin; the government tried, if reluctantly, to introduce some reforms and create at least the impression of a new legality. And considerable numbers of labor-camp inmates were released. Repudiation of Stalin's policy toward Yugoslavia, recognition of the Bonn regime, and withdrawal from Austria marked the new Soviet course under Khrushchev-Bulganin.

However, all reforms and improvements were kept within narrow limits. So long as the urge for a new empire prevails, no large-scale determined evolution toward a new mode of life can be expected. Zigs follow zags; ups follow downs. Progress or expansion, the old dilemma—this curse of the people of Russia has remained in force, and grandiose expansion has remained precept number one.

In this way, international issues disrupt Soviet internal affairs and infringe on the priority of the "transition to Communism." It would be erroneous to assume that these developments are hidden from Soviet sight. On the contrary, every ranking member of the regime knows that the narrow limits of Soviet progress at home are imposed by the situation of the USSR in the family of nations—a situation dictated by the precepts of Communist expansion rather than by the security needs of the Soviet people.

Elephantiasis

Although both the West and the Soviet government prefer the status quo to open fight, the present configuration of Europe and Asia bears within it the seeds of bitter conflict. Western Europe today is merely the densely populated, highly civilized hinterland of Communist Eurasia; it lives in eternal danger and fear, its capitals only a few hours march from the enemy frontiers. In Asia, too, Thailand, Laos, Hong Kong, and other areas must reckon with the possibility of invasion year after year. In the Middle East, Iran, at the very least, is threatened. If some day the Soviets again launch a satellite attack, they can arm their satellite with atomic weapons. Europe's free nations, under these circumstances, insist on the presence of American troops; Japan, too, would feel endangered if all United States forces departed. The United States cannot feel secure in such an atmosphere; it will feel threatened by any advance of Soviet might. For only a thin belt of free nations separates us from ominous face-to-face encounter.

Later on, other nations will assume major roles, among them Germany and Japan. As rehabilitated democratic powers, more intimately concerned with Russian issues, they may in fact take over the initiative and somewhat ease the burden which today falls so heavily on the United States. Yet if all these efforts fail, "coexistence" will end in a storm.

Is it possible that Moscow, in the foreseeable future, will enter the path of peaceful retreat? In its present political and personal composition, as the executive committee of the most orthodox of Communist parties, the Soviet regime will balk and resist; it may even prefer a conflict to consistent retreat. Nevertheless, the changes and trends unleashed by Stalin's death have not yet reached their limit.

The Soviet government is at all times two things. It is, first, the regime of a major nation obliged to care for its own security—what we usually call a national government presiding over national interests. At the same time, the Soviet regime is guided by a party and a philosophy with a set of its own goals and programs. Sometimes these two functions coincide; sometimes they conflict.

Russian national interest and that of the Communist movement coincided, for example, in the wartime alliance with the West against Nazi Germany. In a case of this kind, it was easy for the Soviet leaders to cloak the Communist course in national (immensely popular) clothing. When national interest has conflicted with that of Communism, however, the first as a rule has been subordinated to the second. In domestic affairs the most striking examples were the forcible farm collectivization and the Great Purge. In the international field the present overextension of the empire is contrary to Russia's legitimate national interests.

Superficially, one might imagine that there is no better defense for a country than a strict control over its neighbors north and south, east and west. Actually, this concept—realized in ancient Rome and Napoleon's France—is fallacious. Geography and political factors set limits to the expansion of every nation. This is especially true in modern Europe. As soon as a nation transgresses these limits, the historic laws which affect cohabitation on a multinational continent begin to tell.

From the viewpoint of Russia's national interests, the complex structure of her empire necessitates sacrifices and expenses which can be borne only with the greatest of strain. The huge rearmament, the unprecedented size of her armies, the feverish race for nuclear weapons, the effort to become a major naval power, rearmament of the satellites, the extensive railroad and industrial building abroad—all these policies have been imposed on a poor country ravaged only recently by the most terrible war in its history. Not only do such policies doom the Russian people to a level of perpetual misery but they involve innumerable conflicts abroad and bear the seeds of apocalyptic war. Postwar Russia is suffering from elephantiasis. Contraction, rather than expansion, of the empire is dictated by Russia's true interests.

On the other hand, the Communist concept of an ever-growing Union of Soviet Republics dictates a policy of new aggrandizement. So long as Stalin could create satellites and wage satellite wars with success, this course provoked few doubts and little opposition in the Kremlin—except among a few farsighted leaders like Maxim Litvinov. Now, however, easy victories are over and future prospects are dim, despite some spectacular moves and sensational gestures.

Thirty or forty years ago Russian Communism was one of the waves in a world-wide troubled sea of revolutions. Today Communist Russia looms as a high and mighty rock in the midst of a drying sea. In a way the nearly four decades of Soviet history may be viewed as a very slow process of divorce of the Russia which is a part of World Communism and the Russia which is a new postrevolutionary national formation. The painful evolution still in its beginnings will not be completed without a resounding fight at the top of the Soviet regime. Today the old world-revolutionary trend, although dimmed and anemic, still prevails. As new tendencies crystallize, the two components of Soviet policy—Russian national interest and Communist *Weltanschauung*—will tend to become divorced in Soviet minds and actions. In the end the first must prevail, though not without grave internal crises.

Chapter 15. THE MAIN ISSUES

OF THE MULTITUDE of postwar international problems of Soviet policy those of four areas stand out as the most delicate and intricate: Germany, China, Yugoslavia, and the Middle East.

RUSSIA AND GERMANY

FOR more than two hundred years Russia has had two policies toward Prussia-Germany: to reduce it to impotence or to join it when it was very strong. Prussia-Germany, similarly, alternated between predatory wars against Russia and intimate alliances with her. This source of policy has been rooted in two facts which still obtain: (1) Germany's geographic position between Russia and the West, and (2) generally superior power of the West. Britain has been invincible for centuries; Britain and France together were stronger than any single power in Europe. Thus Russian opposition to Britain and France often involved alliance with Germany. After Peter the Great there was no Russian Tsar or Soviet ruler who could be termed consistently pro-Western; more than one was pro-German.

Russo-German relations have developed as follows. In 1760, during the Seven Years' War, Russian troops occupied Berlin; they were withdrawn after a short time. New ties soon connected Russia and Prussia, namely the partition of Poland, in defiance of the West. When Prussia later became Napoleon's ally, Russian troops again entered Berlin. After Waterloo, Russia and Prussia were partners in the Holy Alliance, and during much of the nineteenth century Prussia maintained at least a benevolent neutrality toward Russian affairs. Toward the close of that century a definite Russo-German rapprochement seemed under way. But Berlin's cementing of ties with the Hapsburg Empire, St. Petersburg's chief antagonist in the Balkans, threw Russia into the arms of the Western coalition, which led directly to the anti-German alliance of the first World War.

The pattern continued under the Soviets. Lenin's regime signed a humiliating treaty with Germany at Brest-Litovsk. A few months later Germany was defeated by the West. It was not long before a new Russo-German cooperation arose, directed primarily against Poland; it was expected to materialize into a military alliance against Poland and France. This expressed itself primarily in secret rearmament, as the Soviets helped Germany circumvent the disarmament clauses of the peace treaties. Having borne rich fruit for both sides, the secret Russo-German agreements remained in force until 1934–35, when Hitler, set on war with Russia, ended them.

Yet within four years the Russo-German combination re-emerged, again directed immediately against Poland and against the West more generally. But when Hitler invaded Russia in 1941, Stalin moved into close cooperation with the Western powers.

There were, of course, periods when Russia's attitude toward Germany and the West was not so sharply defined, when the prevailing "normal relations" were neither affectionate nor belligerent. Considerable trade went on, ships journeyed between the ports, embassies accomplished their modest tasks, tourists traveled in both directions. Such periods were at times fairly prolonged. This was the case in the era of the Franco-Russian alliance, from 1891 on. With Britain in "splendid isolation," the Franco-Russian pact did not disturb the friendship between the Hohenzollern and Romanoff monarchs or the collaboration between their two governments. In 1934–35 Stalin also tried to establish a kind of equilibrium with Germany and France. After his pact with Laval, he made constant overtures to Berlin, which Hitler rejected until the summer of 1939.

There has been a certain regularity in these Russo-German

conflicts and alliances. The two powers cooperated either when both were very strong—and then their alliance was predatory—or when both lay prostrate and aided each other's recovery. The first type of cooperation took place in the late 1890's, when Russia and Germany, in a move against Britain, attempted to seize Chinese ports; and in 1939, when the two prepared to divide Poland. The second type of cooperation prevailed in the 1920's, when both Russia and Germany had to organize new military forces almost from scratch.

On the other hand, Russo-German cooperation proved impossible if one party was strong and the other weak; in this situation the weaker party feared the other's domination. This is what happened in 1918, when mighty Germany dictated peace terms at Brest-Litovsk. Likewise, in 1945–50, when Moscow was in a position to impose its will on Central Europe, it annexed part of Germany to Russia, part to Poland, and after a few years set up still another part as a Soviet satellite, the German Democratic Republic.

This time, however, Russian occupation of German territory meant more than it had in the past. This was no simple military action calculated to impose certain conditions, and then to return the nation to its legitimate government. This was the final achievement of a cherished old Communist dream: a Soviet Germany, a new Socialist Republic, the Western rampart of the glorious Communist family of nations.

So long as Stalin's offensive continued, East Germany was merely the nucleus of a future, much greater German satellite which would further penetrate the West and ultimately help to detach the last free continental nations from the maritime powers. The new resistance of the West did put an end to this dream, at least for the time being.

It is the Communist (as distinguished from the traditional Russian) component of Soviet foreign policy which prevents the return of the occupied areas to a free German government. After more than a decade of "Socialism" such a step would involve the restoration of the liberal order; the German Communist *gauleiters* would be discharged; a significant "expansion of capitalism" would ensue. All of this makes it difficult for Moscow to take the only logical course.

The implications of yielding East Germany are greater than meet the eye. As a united Germany gained power and influence, at least two Soviet satellites, Poland and Czechoslovakia, would feel its pressure. Both these countries acquired substantial German territories in 1945 and expelled their populations. New agreements between Russia and a united Germany could only be at the expense of these two nations. In sum, German unity would involve a formidable retreat by world Communism from its present positions.

This is, then, the key issue: At stake in East Germany is not so much Russian security (which history shows can be assured in more than one way), but the security of Communist achievements. In Communist eyes, any solution of the German problem must prove Moscow's devotion to the lofty cause and its determination to resume the offensive once conditions change.

Refusing to yield East Germany, the Soviet regime is attempting to normalize its relations with West Germany through mutual recognition and trade. As time goes on, Moscow hopes to find ways and means of luring Bonn into the same type of Russian policy as Gustav Stresemann conducted thirty years ago, i.e., impartiality in conflicts between Russia and the West. Thus in the Soviet scheme of things "capitalist Germany" will be neutralized, while "socialist Germany" will remain firmly Communist.

But this scheme will not work again. The barrier is Germany's different postwar situation. In the Weimar era (1919–32), Germany had lost no territories to Russia, had not been partitioned in favor of the East, had not been forced to pay reparations to any Eastern power, was not menaced by the Soviet Union. On the contrary, all the pressure on Weimar Germany came from the West; thus Berlin welcomed support from Mos-

cow. Now the shoe is on the other foot: The Soviet empire is
the main threat to Germany's existence, and West Germany will
continue in the Western camp so long as its East remains de-
tached. Thus Moscow can gain German neutrality only at the
expense of its satellites.

On the other hand, if two Germanys continue to exist, the
trend toward unification, formidable today and sure to grow
stronger, will become a source of dangerous conflict. Military
conflict between the two Germanys might some day become
inevitable. Perhaps Russia and the Western powers, fearing
each other and fearing all-out war, will refrain from military
intervention. In that case the German civil war would embody
the interests and hopes of the two worlds, and its outcome would
decide the fate of Europe.

COMMUNIST CHINA

IN the nineteenth century China's destiny was forged in her
south and central regions—in Canton, Shanghai, or Nanking.
But the key to modern China is Manchuria, which since the first
decade of this century has rapidly outstripped every other part
of China in both economic and political importance. As the
era of British and French influence, centered on the southern
and central ports, came to a close, Russian and Japanese penetration of China proceeded through Manchuria. In the early
1930's the first Soviet efforts to resist Japan likewise developed
in Manchuria. Strategically located, rich in minerals, with a
prospering agriculture and a rapidly burgeoning industry, Manchuria was the economic base for Japan's wars in the 'forties.
A few years later, under Soviet occupation, it was turned over
to the Chinese Communists as a base for their operations against
the Nationalists. (One of the greatest wartime errors of the
United States was to permit unilateral Soviet occupation of
Manchuria in 1945; had it been placed under temporary four-
power occupation, the postwar history of East Asia would have

been very different.) Today, Manchuria is the Soviet gateway to China and the most important link in the chain which binds Peking to Moscow. It is actually under a Soviet-Chinese condominium; the Manchurian authorities are intimately linked to the Soviet government and there are no less than 50,000 Russians in Manchuria.

China's dependence on Moscow has been dangerously underestimated in the West. The Soviet press, which since the 'thirties has tried to hide Russian ties to the Chinese Communists, today plays down the essence of the relations between Moscow and Peking, attempting to groom China as the independent leader of all Asia. And this fiction has found its way into much Western political literature.

Yet according to a United Press report on October 14, 1953, there were 80,000 Soviet advisers in China. Their number had almost doubled in a year. In September, 1952, there were 45,000 advisers, broken down about as follows: 12,000 army, 4,000 air force, 3,000 navy, 5,000 political advisers, 10,000 technicians, 4,000 railway specialists, 6,000 economists and teachers. In 1952 the cost of Soviet advisers was estimated at $52 million; it obviously has risen since then. The Voice of America has estimated the number of Soviet advisers in China at 80,000 to 100,000; the *New York Herald Tribune* on August 3, 1953, put the "over-all strength of Soviet advisers, trainers and teachers in China" at 112,000; Formosan sources gave an estimate of 30,000 in November, 1953.

"This new leadership which has replaced the traditional Chinese gentry," says Richard L. Walker in his *China Under Communism*, "has developed a vested interest in maintaining the present relationship with the Soviet Union as a source of strength and as a justification for rule. Their high positions and prestige, their investment of time and effort, their language training, their jargon, their past crimes against their fellow Chinese: all these are to a great extent bound up with the maintenance of the Soviet tie. Each highly placed official facing the new problems involved in the central direction of all phases of life in China probably draws comfort and assurance from the idea that there is in the Soviet Union his counterpart on whom he can rely for direction and aid." [1]

One must also remember that in 1945, persons who had studied in Russia formed 57 per cent of the membership of the Central Committee of the Chinese Communist party; and at present many children of Chinese Communist leaders are students in Russia.

Doubtless there are disagreements between the Soviet and Chinese Communists, just as there are disagreements between the Russians and the Communists of the East European satellites. What matters, however, is that these disputes are settled in favor of Moscow if Moscow insists. Manchuria and China depend on the Soviet Union for the training, equipment, and strategic guidance of armed forces; for diplomatic protection and support; for industrial development. The moment Peking authorities refused to accept an important Soviet demand, Manchuria would be in danger of being cut off from the rest of China and reconstituted as an independent People's Republic. The rest of China, deserted by Moscow, would be doomed as a Communist nation. Perhaps history will take this turn some day; meanwhile, the gloomy prospect of isolation from Russia serves as a deterrent to the Peking Communists and helps keep them in line.

We can hardly expect any real solution of Far Eastern problems in the near future. Years may pass before Moscow's hold on China is substantially weakened and Japan acquires any great independent influence on East Asian affairs.

YUGOSLAVIA

ANTI-TITOISM had been a gloomy obsession of Stalin, and as long as he ruled, there was no possibility of reconciliation with Tito. With Stalin's death in March, 1953, his personal hatred of

---

1. Richard L. Walker, *China under Communism* (New Haven, Yale University Press, 1955), p. 275.

all things Titoist ceased to have an influence on Soviet policies, and now Moscow had to settle the question of what attitude to assume toward Belgrade in the new era of "coexistence." Would Tito continue to maintain close relations with the West or would he agree to return to the Communist fold?

Titoism and the Soviet attitude toward Titoist heresies are important questions because there is not a chance that Communism as the prevailing faith of intellectual circles in a country like Russia can be immediately replaced by a hitherto despised and abolished Western philosophy of "formal democracy." Not even a serious political and ideological crisis could transform Communism and its social concomitants, its hatred of the strong and rich, and its history of rebellion against the old empires into a component of a civilization that only a short time ago was viewed as a capitalist hell. But Titoism represents the first cracking of the ice in the frozen Communist river, and the new Soviet attitude toward Titoist heresy is the first jarring of the foundations of orthodox Communism.

Up to 1947–48 no Communist party had been more extreme in its belligerency and anti-Western attitude than Tito's Communist party of Yugoslavia. No sooner did Tito assume leadership of the "partisans" in the war against Germany and Italy than his deviations from the Moscow line began; the deviations, however, were always in the direction of the left. While Stalin, allied with the West during the wartime emergency, sometimes tried to temper the revolutionary, antimonarchical and anticapitalist trends among his adherents, Tito, who disliked compromise, disregarded orders and stirred the revolution by all the means at his disposal. No other Soviet satellite displayed as much revolutionary zeal as the ruling group in Yugoslavia; its attitude was uncompromising, its conflicts with the Western allies bitter. In 1946–47, when Stalin's expansionism reached its peak, Tito was outdoing his master. The Yugoslav leadership combined the elementary belligerency of revolutionary Communism with the lack of experience of political neophytes.

During that period the Yuogslav Communist heads were full of the noisy slogans, crude lies and half-truths that have constituted the ideological content of world Communism since the war: that the United States is ruled by warmongers; that the West strives to abolish the independence of small nations; that the West represents "capitalism"; that human rights are a hypocritical slogan and democracy a fraud; that even the Socialist parties of Europe are a phalanx of scoundrels and traitors. The truth of these ideas was still to be tested when the break between Moscow and Belgrade occurred.

When the break came, Stalin at first expected that the "working class" of Yugoslavia, meaning the Communist party, would rise against Tito; faced with the alternatives of Stalin or Tito, could there be any doubt as to whom they would choose? Contrary to Stalin's expectations—and orders—"the masses" defied him and chose Tito. Now the Kremlin expected that in accordance with Communist theory the Western powers would stage a political upheaval in Yugoslavia, encourage the old Yugoslav parties, and restore capitalism, as they had done in Hungary in 1919, when Bela Kun's Communist regime was overthrown by Allied forces and replaced by the government of Admiral Horthy. To teach his Communist satellites a lesson, Stalin was prepared to throw Yugoslavia to the capitalist wolves —and what a triumph it would have been for him if the Western powers had attempted a restoration of the old Yugoslavia by force of arms!

What actually happened was the opposite of what Stalin had expected: the United States came forward with abundant help for the independent Yugoslav Communist government, even covering up many an absurd Yugoslav economic experiment. The hundreds of millions of dollars granted the small country over a period of six years saved it from economic ruin and political subordination; the United States helped to arm a military force that matched in power the military forces of Yugoslavia's satellite neighbors. All this of course was contrary to the teachings of Leninism-Stalinism, in particular the precept that alliance of a small nation with the "imperialists" means enslavement, exploitation, poverty, and restoration of capitalism.

Yet Moscow did not relent. A sacred principle was at stake which if violated would make obsolete an important component of Stalinism. Stalin's new interpretation of the course of events was that "the imperialists" did not need to engineer political upheavals in Belgrade, since Tito's government had transformed itself into a subservient, pro-imperialist, abject type of regime, and Yugoslavia had lost its independence when Tito turned to and obtained help from the West.

"The Tito gang are turning Yugoslavia into a virtual colony of Wall Street and the City. They have already plunged the country into financial servitude, and are now asking for new oppressive loans from the American usurers . . . Tito's Trotskyite crew have come to be one of the shock battalions of present-day piratical imperialism, to whom the instigators of war assign the most sordid tasks. The special characteristics of these agents is that they try to represent their service to dollar imperialism as Marxism and Communism." [2] "The Tito clique have undertaken to assist the American intervention-mongers and their menials in Athens in their war against the Hellenic Democratic army." [3] That is to say, an independent Communist government cannot exist if it does not march in unison with and obey the directives of Moscow and the Cominform.

The testing of this basic precept of Stalinism continued, however, and led to rather unexpected results. After Stalin's death, when Lavrenti Beria's influence was growing in Moscow, diplomatic relations between Moscow and Belgrade were restored; the Soviet satellites soon followed suit. Border incidents almost ceased; trade agreements were signed; "cultural relations," represented mainly by visits of "delegations," were resumed. These elements of "normalization" were easier to achieve than

2. *New Times,* June 22, 1949.
3. *Ibid.,* August 3, 1949.

the establishment of a proper relationship between the Soviet and Yugoslav Communist parties. For the term "collaboration" has in this connection a deeper meaning than it appears to have. Implementation of the Soviet satellite status of a nation is achieved by the machinery of Communist parties and the Comintern-Cominform. The independence and sovereignty of the People's Democracies, which do exist as a legal pattern, are only understandable against the background of "collaboration" of the Communist parties. Moscow's invitation to Belgrade to "collaborate" was tantamount to a suggestion to Tito that he resume the satellite condition, though a bit eased since Stalin's death.

This was the crux of the Yugoslav question. If true collaboration between the Soviet and Yugoslav Communist parties was in sight, a new Comintern could emerge, the Moscow-Belgrade conflict would soon be forgotten, and progress on the road to Communism could be resumed. If, however, solidarity should prove impossible, Titoism would further corrode the flesh of orthodox Communism. To the Soviet and satellite believers everything hinged on the answers to the questions: what precisely had occurred in Yugoslavia during the years of the Stalin-Tito antagonism? Had the country been "marshallized" by American dollars? Had it become a colony of Washington? Had it restored capitalism? And did it continue to combine—in the "typical fascist way"—political oppression and one-party rule with exploitation of its toiling people? Or was Tito's claim true and was his country independent and noncapitalist? If this were so, how had Tito, contrary to all the laws of Marxist-Leninist science, performed the miracle of preserving independence and building Socialism with help from the capitalist powers and in bitter opposition to the fatherland of Socialism and the People's Democracies?

The leadership of Soviet as well as international Communism was obviously divided on this issue. Vyacheslav Molotov, since the deaths of Zhdanov and Stalin the only remaining member of the generation of Soviet intellectual leaders and theoreticians, sensed the dangers implied in concessions to the Yugoslav doctrine. Having learned the value of firmness and consistency from his recently deceased leader, he still viewed Tito as a deviator and the guilty party in the conflict of 1948, since he had refused to comply with the orders of the supreme command. In his report of February 8, 1955, made during the period when the Moscow-Belgrade climate was mellowing, Molotov reiterated the old accusation that it was Yugoslavia and not Stalin, Beria, or the Soviet leadership in general that had "deviated from the positions assumed in the first years after the second World War." This reaffirmation of the old thesis that the Kremlin is always right was a renewed challenge to Tito, who reacted to it with vigor. In his speech of March 8 he charged that Molotov's statement was misleading, that it was Moscow and her satellites who should admit their faults: "Mr. Molotov's reference to Yugoslavia in his statement to the Supreme Soviet does not correspond to reality . . . I believe this is an attempt to withhold the true facts from their own people with a view to harming us." [4]

It was indicative of the divided attitude of the Soviet leadership that *Pravda* was ordered to publish Tito's rebuke to Molotov without a word of criticism. Tito's reputation among Communist leaders of the Soviet army did not stand high, particularly since Tito's refusal, despite all "normalization," to join the military bloc of the Soviet satellites and submit his military force to the command of Soviet marshals. In November, 1954, the Soviet government invited all European governments to a conference the purpose of which was to create a system of collective security—the initial phase of the "Warsaw pact." Only the satellites agreed to participate; Tito, cautious and wiser after his experience as a Soviet satellite, and consistently avoiding unilateral ties with either side, proposed a postponement of the parley. The conference, which was held on the

4. *Yugoslav Review,* 4, Nos. 2–3, February–March, 1955.

eve of the visit of the Soviet delegation to Belgrade, ended, as was expected, in the appointment of a Soviet marshal to head all military forces of the Eastern bloc.

Writing on the anniversary of V-E Day in 1955 about the contributions of various nations to the victory over Germany, Marshal Georgi Zhukov, Soviet Defense Minister, accorded a prominent place to Tito's guerrilla forces. Soviet marshals— men of lesser official rank, such as Vasili Sokolovski, Alexander Vasilevski, and Ivan Bagramian—sided with Molotov, however, and minimized the value of the Yugoslav resistance during the war. In his list, published in *Red Star,* of the nations which were "liberated" by the Soviet army (the phrase sounded like a deliberate provocation of the Titoists), Marshal Sokolovski placed Yugoslavia near the bottom; Marshal Bagramian, in *Komsomolskaya Pravda,* and Marshal Vasilevski, in *Izvestia,* gave Tito a similar rating.

The decision to send a delegation to Belgrade and formally apologize for the crimes of Stalin represented a rejection of the orthodox attitude toward Tito heresy by the "collective leadership." Logically enough, Molotov did not accompany the delegation. *Pravda* officially acknowledged Tito as a builder of socialism and Yugoslavia as a socialist nation:

"The fact that in Yugoslavia public ownership of the basic means of production prevails; that the main classes there are the working class and the working peasantry, which have militant revolutionary and patriotic traditions; that there exists between the peoples of the two countries a long-established and deep-reaching community in the realm of culture and thought; and the fact that the working people in the USSR and in Yugoslavia have the same basic interests, the interests of the international working class movement, and the same ultimate aim of the working class—all these facts prove that there exists a solid foundation for broad, comprehensive cooperation between the Soviet and Yugoslav peoples." [5]

5. *Pravda,* May 18, 1955.

More than once during their stay in Yugoslavia and subsequently, the Soviet leaders referred to Yugoslavia as a country on its way to Socialism. By implication they acknowledged not only the blunders (actually committed by Stalin) but something even more important, namely that the Communist government of a small country can live and thrive even if surrounded by capitalist wolves, and that its independence, which it had nearly sacrificed to win Soviet protection against "reaction and imperialism," was restored the moment it broke with Moscow and turned to Washington.

It is impossible to exaggerate the importance and impact of this new perception of the Soviet leadership. Since Lenin's days it has been one of the highest principles of Communism and the Comintern that only strict discipline and submission to the supreme leadership in Moscow can save a Communist country from counterrevolution; that therefore the new Communist International must break with the traditions of its predecessors, curtail the autonomy of the national parties, and introduce an unprecedented degree of centralized rule. In line with this reasoning, Moscow had appointed and dismissed Communist leaders of other countries, purged them, condemned them to death; it had maintained "instructors" and other kinds of agents who could tell national leaders what and what not to do; it had sent arms to one country and withheld them from another. After the hypocritical dissolution of the Comintern in 1943, Moscow continued along this, the only Leninist, course. (In the United States the dismissal of Earl Browder, actually carried out by Jacques Duclos on Stalin's orders, occurred in the era after the dissolution of the Comintern.) Within a few years the new Cominform ("Information Bureau") emerged as the iron hand which was to hold together the Communist movement all over the world.

Now the Soviet government was itself placing in question this fundamental thesis of Communism. No discussion of the Tito issue appeared in the Soviet press, but in Paris a Molotov-type Communist leader, Etienne Fajon, secretary of the

French Communist party, tried to salvage what could be saved of Stalin's anti-Titoist politics. There was nothing wrong—Fajon wrote in *Humanité* (June 8, 1955), after the Belgrade parley—with the Cominform's anti-Titoism of 1948, but only with the 1949 thunderings (meaning the resolution, which had used stronger language than in 1948), which had been inspired by the traitor Beria: "The resolution on the situation in Yugoslavia," Fajon said, "which was elaborated by the Bureau [Cominform] in 1948, contained a kind of criticism which is absolutely normal . . . Such criticism is a Communist tradition." Only the second resolution, he said, "that of 1949, is faulty and inadmissible because it is based on false documents forged by Beria."

One after another, fragments continued to crumble from the loaf. If a Communist nation can survive isolated from the great fatherland of Communism, the question arises: Where is the wisdom in dividing the nations of the world into a "capitalist" and a "Socialist" camp? Does not Tito's position between the camps indicate that something is wrong with the orthodox philosophy? On June 22, 1955, *Pravda* reprinted an interview with Koca Popovic, the Yugoslav foreign minister:

"We are not inclined to divide governments and countries into a capitalist and a Communist group. Such a simplified classification, made with the help of labels which are used variously by various people, does not lead toward correct interpretation and understanding of the complex social system that exists in the world." [6]

What is the road to Communism? The old Leninism-Stalinism never asserted that Communist strategy and tactics should be uniform for all countries. On the contrary, it acknowledged that differences and peculiarities in the historical development of various nations make a universal tactical plan impossible. It did, however, demand coordination of the diversified parties

6. There was no special reason for *Pravda* to reprint, without comment, a statement made by Popovic in San Francisco. The leading Soviet newspaper was, of course, not in sympathy with Yugoslav heresy, but in printing the statement it set out the problem provocatively.

—the coordination to be the responsibility of the supreme head-quarters of international Communism. By means of such co-ordination the Communist family could present a picture of unity. In the international Communist movement the individual parties are segments of a single extended front line maintained by the will and brains of a supreme command. The segments of the front do not necessarily attack or retreat in unison; operations at various points may differ—at one point cavalry is called for, at another infantry, and at a third artillery. Yet there is no "autonomy" behind these strategical differences—each party is part of a single general plan.

In this concept of a supreme command there was great political as well as propagandistic force. Its simplicity was so attractive that thousands of inflamed Communists swallowed it whole.

The Yugoslav view was that international Communism has already achieved such force and standing that it cannot be over-thrown from the outside by military means; that the "capitalist powers" are not preparing for aggressive war; that, in any event, a war policy cannot be imposed on a Communist nation if its people do not accept it. Centralization is a means of forcible expansion; independence of small nations is the basis of con-solidation. What do the Russians want—forcible expansion or stability? During the Soviet visit to Belgrade in May, 1955, Khrushchev expounded the old thesis that progress is meas-ured by the expansion of the Soviet-satellite realm and criti-cized Tito's "reformist" views of the Socialist parties. He proved to be uninformed and confused about the real situa-tion in the world. Tito, enlightened and sophisticated, answered Khrushchev "in terms of some of the facts of life about the West of which Khrushchev had proved himself woefully igno-rant." [7]

7. *World Today* (August, 1955), p. 311. In this connection it is interesting to note that soon after the return of the Khrushchev group to Moscow, a new research project was launched—a study of the specific traits of capitalism in our time.

While the Soviet leadership and the Soviet press, obviously confused about the fundamental issues, remained silent, the Yugoslavs took another bold step away from Leninist-Stalinist orthodoxy. When the Soviet guests had departed, the Belgrade *Kommunist* published a long "theoretical" article by a ranking leader, Veljko Vlahovic. Obviously addressing the conservative minds of Moscow, the author called for realization of the great changes that have occurred in recent decades and which make a revision of Communist tactics imperative: the death of the old colonialism, the growing role of the state in national economy, the role of small independent nations, the changes brought about by the use of atomic power. Under these conditions, Vlahovic said, the old theory of "two blocs," capitalist and Socialist, becomes obsolete; moreover, it is wrong to assume that there is only one road to Socialism. The moderate Second International is dead, but the Cominform is also dead. A new alliance of "workers parties," which will embrace Socialist as well as Communist parties, must emerge.

After October, 1954, when Edvard Kardelj, the Yugoslav theoretician, started on a trip which took him over all of Western Europe, there was considerable progress in rapprochement with the Socialist parties of the West. In a report made after his return, Kardelj expounded the heretical thesis that in the "highly developed" Western nations the labor movement moves toward Socialism by evolutionary, not revolutionary, means. Happy to see the Cominform split up, and ignoring the dictatorial and terroristic phase of Titoism, some Socialist leaders in Germany, France, Norway, and Britain became friendly, perhaps overfriendly, with Tito's envoy. Tito thus compensated for his rapprochement with "leftist" Moscow by friendly gestures toward "rightist" Western Socialism. In his projected International (which is hardly likely to materialize) Tito chooses for himself the same central position that he tries to assume in international affairs—a position between the two blocs.

No real agreement between Moscow and Belgrade on the

fundamental issues of Communism was reached, and Tito's return into the satellite fold was therefore out of the question. Since there was no agreement, a number of current problems remained unsolved and the frontiers of the Soviet bloc remained where they were, namely at the line which divides Hungary, Rumania, and Bulgaria from Yugoslavia. The withdrawal of Soviet occupation troops from Hungary and Rumania was therefore postponed and the large armies of the three satellite neighbors of Yugoslavia were little reduced, despite the fact that they far exceeded the limits prescribed in the peace treaties.[8]

An abyss, though not so wide as before, continued to divide the Soviet family from Yugoslav Communism. In his Karlovac address two months after the Soviet visit to Belgrade, Tito stressed Yugoslavia's particular path of "Socialist development": "Although we are a Socialist country, we have no intention or wish to be affiliated with any bloc. We wish to be an independent country. Setting our country as an example, we want to ascertain whose method of building a Socialist society is better, theirs or ours . . . We shall not take a single step back from our friendly relations with the Western countries." Tito's statement paralleled Khrushchev's summary of the Belgrade negotiations. We wish you luck, Khrushchev told the Yugoslavs, if you think that your practice is good, but "as far as we are concerned we will, I believe, use our own methods."

Unable to reach its great goal of reaffiliating Yugoslavia with the Soviet family of nations, Moscow scored, however, a number of substantial gains, of which the most important was Tito's open adherence to the group of "neutrals" and antagonism to the "power blocs." The situation during the Stalin era, when Yugoslavia closely approached the West and entered the violently anti-Soviet Balkan Alliance, gave way, in 1955,

8. The total armed forces of the three satellites amounted to 730,000; at the present writing they are reduced by 78,000 (about 11 per cent). The limit provided in the peace treaties is 70,000 for Hungary, 138,000 for Rumania, and 65,500 for Bulgaria, a total of 273,000.

to a certain estrangement between Belgrade and the West and a considerable weakening of Yugoslavia's ties with Athens and Ankara. It was clear, however, that when Tito's independence was at stake, there were limits to his vacillations.

In August, 1955, Moscow indicated its readiness to give Yugoslavia designs and permission for construction of MIG jets; Tito rejected the offer. The dispute between Washington and Belgrade over the American privilege of inspection of arms in Yugoslavia, which had produced considerable nervousness, was settled by Robert Murphy of the State Department during his visit to Belgrade in September, and subsequently it was agreed that the American military staff in Yugoslavia would be increased from forty-four officers to sixty. While Moscow granted Yugoslavia credits and loans averaging $28 million a year for the next three years, the United States agreed to furnish far more substantial economic aid.

Yugoslav relations with Soviet satellites, for a time at least, remained cool, however. In Bulgaria a number of army officers were arrested for harboring pro-Yugoslav attitudes, while Tito hinted at "free Balkans." Yugoslav leaders attacked Czechoslovakia and Hungary, in particular the Hungarian supreme chief, Matyas Rakosi, and Tito rejected an invitation from the Rumanian premier to send a delegation to the celebration of the Rumanian national day.

This hostility of the satellite leaders toward Tito abated; it would have been impossible had unanimity prevailed in Moscow. Neither Rakosi nor Gheorgiu-Dej—nor any other of the satellite gods—would have dared to show unfriendliness to the Yugoslav regime if this had been contrary to clear-cut instructions. The fact that in the face of a certain improvement in Soviet-Yugoslav relations, animosity still reigned among the other members of the bloc proved that behind the scenes in Moscow, Paris, and Peking, a divergence of views continued, and that still unsolved was the crucial problem: What should be the role of a "people's republic" and how much independence may it possess? Satellite or sovereign nation? Component of an empire or independent organism?

THE NEAR AND MIDDLE EAST

IN the framework of Soviet foreign relations the countries of the Near and Middle East fall into two groups: (1) Russia's direct neighbors, and (2) all other nations. This distinction between direct neighbors and more distant lands has been decisive in Soviet postwar policy.

As we have seen in the preceding parts of this book, directly adjacent territories served as avenues of Russian expansion. Unlike the great empires of the West, Russia has always been landbound. While Britain, France, Spain, Portugal and the Netherlands acquired lands in far-off continents and islands in all the seas and oceans, Russia developed as a massive land unit. Because of her lack of ports, industrial backwardness, and inability to enter into rivalry with the other empires in naval power, her attempts to imitate the other type of imperial expansion (for example, her efforts to gain influence in Malta in the Mediterranean and Hawaii in the Pacific) failed completely. But she was successful in incorporating, one after another, neighboring territories in the west, south, and east.

These factors conditioning Russia's growth have remained in force during the Soviet period of her history. Her spectacular expansion after the last war and the growth of her spheres of influence have been exclusively territorial; not even in the most successful period of her expansion, 1944–48, did she acquire any overseas possessions. Since the war the Soviet Army has remained the largest in the world, but the Soviet Navy has lagged far behind the navies of America and Britain. It was characteristic of the Soviet pattern of imperial growth that Stalin's efforts to gain a foothold in weak Spain should end in failure but that he should be highly successful in acquiring influence in huge adjacent China. This is the reason why the distinction must be made between on the one hand the three Middle East neighbors of the Soviet Union—Turkey, Iran, and Afghanistan —and on the other the group of Arab nations and Israel.

Having surrounded herself along the entire perimeter from the Baltic to Korea with belts of satellites, the Soviet Union created a strategically ideal situation. The only break in this tier of satellites occurs in the Middle East. Here independent Turkey, Iran, and Afghanistan are in a position to resist and, if necessary, enter anti-Soviet coalitions. The first aim of Soviet policy in the Middle East is to put an end to this situation.

In his attempt to subdue Turkey and Iran after the war Stalin once again started at the point where the old Russian Empire stopped. At the end of the war he demanded a military foothold in the Dardanelles; he planned an expansion of Soviet Georgia and Soviet Armenia to the south by annexation of Turkish territory—the same program that had animated the Tsar's government during the first World War. Now, in 1945, Turkey's independence and territorial integrity were saved only by the resistance of London and Washington. It was logical and natural that in 1951 Turkey should join NATO and become a firm anchor of that international organization in the East. Moscow protested violently in the press and through diplomatic channels, and in fact in its note of November 30, 1951, made an outright threat against Turkey: the policy of Ankara, the Soviet government said, "will cause serious damage to the relations of Turkey and the Soviet Union," and "the responsibility for the results of this policy will fall entirely on the Turkish government." Deep animosity toward Turkey continued in Moscow.

In the era of "peaceful coexistence" following Stalin's death Moscow approached the Turkish government with suggestions. In July 1953 Russia officially withdrew all claims to Turkish territory. In a note calculated to make a dramatic impression on Turkey and the West, Moscow said:

"In the name of the maintenance of good neighborly relations and the strengthening of peace and security, the Governments of Armenia and Georgia consider it possible to renounce their territorial claims against Turkey.

"Insofar as it concerns the question of the straits [the Dardanelles] the Soviet Government has reconsidered its opinion on this matter and holds that it is possible to insure the security of the U.S.S.R. from the side of the straits on conditions equally acceptable both for the U.S.S.R. and for Turkey. Thus the Soviet Government declares the Soviet Union does not have any territorial claims whatsoever against Turkey."

The attempt was of no avail. Skeptical of Moscow's oral and written promises, Ankara refused to take the path of rapprochement and the relations between Moscow and Ankara have continued cool to this day.

Soviet policy toward her neighbors left them with only two alternatives: to become satellites or enemies. Like Turkey, Iran, too, resisted the alternative of becoming a satellite.

More than a century ago, imperial Russia, in her drive to the south, acquired from Persia the territory of Azerbaidzhan (including oil-rich Baku); since that time she has made intermittent efforts to penetrate the remaining territory of the Persian kingdom. Encountering British resistance, Russia found the means to a compromise, and in 1907 North Persia was recognized as a Russian sphere of influence, while Britain obtained its sphere in Persia's south.

Later events erased the contours of this northern sphere and destroyed Russian privileges in Persia. After more than two decades, however, Stalin resumed where the old thread had been broken. At the end of the second World War, while his armies occupied northern Iran, Stalin attempted to transform the large territory into a new Soviet satellite and the nucleus of an even larger Iranian People's Republic. In 1946 a satellite government was set up in Tabriz, and the Soviet army remained in Iran after the date of the agreed upon withdrawal. As in the case of Turkey, forceful opposition on the part of Russia's allies, supported by a *démarche* in the United Nations, helped Iran to maintain her territorial integrity.

Soviet influence did not diminish, however, after this failure; Iran's attempts to find a path to the West were blocked more than once. It was harder for Iran to join the Western fold than it had been for Turkey.

First, the Soviet-Persian treaties of 1921 and 1927 hung like a Damocletian sword over the Iranian government. According to these treaties, if other powers should try to use Iranian territory as a *place d'armes* against the Soviet Union or the latter's allies, the Soviet government "will be entitled to send its armies to the territory of Persia in order to take the necessary measures for its defense." The interpretation of this provision is up to Moscow; in a favorable situation—for example, at a moment of international complications elsewhere—the Soviet government could make use of this unusual privilege to reoccupy a large part of Iranian territory. This is why Iran cannot, if it wanted to, join NATO.

Second, a strong anti-British movement developed in Iran. Supported by the not insignificant Tudeh (Communist) party, and directed primarily against British oil concessions, the movement, which reached its peak in 1952, was a genuinely popular one.

In 1952–53 it seemed that the Soviet government, frustrated in its frontal attack in 1946, would soon enter the Iranian scene as a friend, supporter, and ally of the anti-British regime of Mohammed Mossadegh. To strengthen its alliance with Mossadegh and bring the Tudeh party to power, Moscow even sacrificed its lucrative but unpopular fish and caviar concession in Iranian waters, for it could gain more than commercial advantages if its political blueprint should become reality.

After the spring of 1953 Mossadegh was supported by the Tudeh and Moscow. Iranian Communist leaders, condemned four years before by a military tribunal, were acquitted. Soviet-Iranian trade discussions ended in a trade agreement. Finally, the Shah, symbol of the anti-Soviet, pro-Western orientation, was forced to depart and Iran was about to become a republic —in this case the first stage on the road to becoming a "People's Democracy."

Soviet expectations were shattered when the anti-Soviet trend in Iran gained the upper hand in August, 1953, and General Fazoliah Zahedi replaced Mossadegh and arrested him. Refusing to reconcile itself to the defeat, the Soviet embassy in Tehran (which is in a position to act with less restriction than Soviet embassies elsewhere) tried hard to impede the oil negotiations between the Zahedi regime and the new consortium of eight Western countries. In September, 1954, before the ratification of the new oil agreement, the Soviet embassy actively supported a Communist army plot to overthrow the pro-Western government. The attempt failed.

The hardest blow to Soviet policy in Iran was Iran's joining of the Turkish-Iraqi pact in October, 1955, which implied that faced with the alternative of satellite or foe, Iran had chosen the second because she abhorred the first. Against the background of considerable Soviet success in the Middle East in the 1950's this was a heavy blow to Soviet prestige and interests.

The Soviet press reacted violently to Iran's defiance of Soviet demands. *Pravda,* in an editorial of October 13, 1955, stated that "by its adherence to the Baghdad military pact Iran enters a dangerous path," and that its policy "does not hold any promise of good." At the same time Vyacheslav Molotov told the Iranian ambassador in Moscow that Iran's joining the Baghdad coalition "is incompatible with the interests of peace and security in the Near and Middle East and is in contradiction to the good-neighbor relations between Iran and the Soviet Union and the well-known treaty obligations of Iran."

THE third Middle-Eastern neighbor, little Afghanistan, is in a different position. In this country the West is gradually losing one advantage after another in favor of Moscow. Because Afghanistan has no ports and can be reached by the Western nations only through Pakistan (or eastern Iran), her trade with the West is small, while her permanent border troubles with pro-Western Pakistan almost automatically draw her nearer to Russia. In Afghanistan more than in any other Middle-Eastern country, Russia symbolizes economic progress. During the last few years Moscow has taken pains to impress this backward country by its industrial accomplishments: Soviet engineers are building oil dumps, roads, grain elevators, and factories and supervising the paving of the streets of Kabul; numbers of Soviet technicians are working in the country; and an oil pipeline from Russia is to be built by Russian technicians.

For her permanent disputes with Pakistan, Afghanistan is seeking arms, and here again she turns to Moscow. Czechoslovakia has offered arms to Kabul, and when the agreement relating to arms shipments materializes, Afghanistan will be closer than ever to the Soviet camp. Trying to avoid far-reaching international complications, the Soviet government refrains from outrightly transforming Afghanistan into a People's Democracy and incorporating it into its sphere, although it has the power to do so. At a favorable moment, when the attention of the world is diverted to another spot, Moscow will be in a position to use some pretext to move in and start "protecting" Afghanistan against her southern neighbors.

ROUGHLY half of the 100,000,000 population of the Near and Middle East live in the countries described above as Russia's neighbors. The other half, numbering approximately 45,000,-000, comprise the Arab nations and Israel, the latter with a population of close to 2,000,000.

In marked contrast to its attitude toward the neighbor countries, Moscow does not at present view the nations of this second group as potential satellites and will not do so as long as the present world situation remains unchanged and no new great conflict breaks out. Membership in the Soviet family of nations is not being planned now for any of the Near- and Middle-Eastern nations of this second group, and they are not faced with a choice between being satellites or free nations.

The dilemma facing these countries is rather one of partisanship with the Western bloc or neutrality. The supreme goal of Soviet policy in this part of the world is to detach one small nation after another from the alliance with Britain and the United States. Moscow will not be satisfied until the anti-Western neutralism which now prevails in South Asia is embraced by the independent Near and Middle East. In this area the Soviet methods of influencing governments and peoples are more subtle, friendly, and helpful, and the reaction to the Soviet démarches is therefore more conciliatory. The nations of this area do not feel directly menaced by aggression on the part of the Soviet Union; they have a free choice. Communism, although alive in both the Arab and the Israeli worlds, is too weak to be a threat; in these areas Moscow fosters movements of a national type in which the "evils of capitalism" are overshadowed by "anti-imperialist," anti-American, and anti-British slogans. In its search for anti-Western support the Soviet government is prepared to ally itself with any antidemocratic monarchy and any dictatorial, even racist, regime, and to approve any bellicose trend, if such action would help to detach one or another nation from a pro-Western orientation.

When the Arab League emerged after the war, it was violently attacked in the Soviet press as a "stronghold of reaction" and a tool of British policy. In the contest between the Arabs and Israel in 1947–48, the Soviet government favored the partition of Palestine and the creation of an independent Jewish state despite its anti-Zionist attitude because this would weaken Britain. Later this gesture was used as proof of the farsightedness and progressivism of Leninism-Stalinism on national issues. As time passed, however, a careful balancing of the Arab and Israeli sides was becoming more and more difficult.

Soviet envoys in the Arab countries were ordered to avoid friction with the Moslems, make regular visits to mosques, and stress the affinity between certain religious groups of the Soviet Union and those of Asia and Africa. The Orthodox clergy, too, assisted in the grand-scale Soviet drive to win strongpoints in the Middle East, as we have seen above.[9] On the other hand, the Soviet position vis-à-vis the state of Israel, essentially a matter of foreign policy, became interwoven with internal issues, namely the regime's attitude toward Jews and Zionism in Russia. As the tensions of the cold war mounted and antagonism toward the West began to overshadow all other problems in Moscow, Stalin's government saw the Jewish population in Russia as the bearers of pro-Western trends and Western ideas and even as partisans of the Western type of democracy. How closely international affairs were tied up with internal policies became obvious when a large Jewish crowd in Moscow, in defiance of the government, staged an enthusiastic demonstration in honor of Golda Meyerson, the first Israeli envoy to Moscow.

Never expressing his real attitude toward Israel in so many words, Stalin in 1948 began to step up his anti-Jewish drive at home and abroad, merging his personal dislikes with the worldwide objectives of a movement of which he was the leader. As persecution of Jews mounted in Russia, all pro-Israeli trends and activities in the Soviet Union as well as in the satellites were violently suppressed. In February, 1953, three weeks before his death, Stalin broke off diplomatic relations with Israel, using as a pretext the bombing of the building housing the Soviet mission in Tel Aviv, for which, of course, the Israeli government was not responsible.

After Stalin's death Soviet policy toward the Arab nations and Israel changed slightly. In the first months of confusion,

9. See pp. 280 ff.

diplomatic relations with Israel were resumed (July, 1953) and the fight against Zionism in the satellites abated. The period of weakness and the attempts at conciliation, usually associated with the name of Georgi Malenkov, did not last long. When Malenkov's star faded (after mid-1954) and Khrushchev took over leadership, new vigor was instilled into Soviet foreign policy. "Priority for heavy industry"—the formula under which Malenkov was dismissed and Bulganin took over the premiership—actually meant the inauguration of a foreign policy which, while avoiding direct military entanglements, actively competed with the West in the task of industrializing and arming backward countries. At the same time export of arms to anti-Western governments was fostered. Moscow itself refrained from trade in arms, preferring to use the satellites for this delicate job. Among the satellites only two, East Germany and Czechoslovakia, were able to produce and export modern equipment. Since German arms would have been highly unpopular abroad at this time, the war industry of Czechoslovakia (the expanded Skoda works) served as the Soviet base in the munitions trade.

The Bandung conference of 29 Asian and African nations which took place in April, 1955, about two months after Malenkov's dismissal, accentuated the anti-Western slogans. On April 16, 1955, the Soviet government published its statement on security in the Near and Middle East, which, while it contained no new ideas and outlined no new political positions, marked the start of a new grand-scale diplomatic and political offensive.

The Soviet offensive centered around Egypt, the leading Arab nation. Britain had erroneously assumed that accession to Egyptian demands and withdrawal of British forces from the Suez Canal would pacify the Arab world and reduce the fever of nationalism that had taken hold of the Egyptian intelligentsia in the last few years. The British-Egyptian agreement signed in 1954 provided for the evacuation of British forces in the comparatively short period of twenty months, so that after a long era of British troops on Egyptian soil this Arab nation would have regained complete independence. The Soviet government, however, had made abundant use of the mounting nationalist feelings in Egypt and proved to be more far sighted than London. Egypt did not, after the conclusion of the agreement with Britain, abandon its anti-Western position; indeed, it moved closer to the Soviet Union.

Working hard behind the scenes, the Soviet envoys in the Middle East accomplished a great coup in the summer of 1955 in piloting a coalition of three Arab nations—Egypt, Syria, and Saudi-Arabia.[10] Against internal and external objections—in particular on the part of Iraq—Egypt and Syria signed a "defense pact" on November 7, 1955. The material basis of the pact was the supplying of arms by Czechoslovakia to the two Arab nations, on financial terms agreed upon with the help of Soviet diplomatic representatives.

In its effort to lure Egypt from the West and demonstrate the advantages of collaboration with Moscow, the Soviet government, in the summer of 1955, arranged for wide-scale trade operations in favor of the Cairo regime. Communist China bought Egyptian cotton in the amount of 8 million Egyptian pounds ($23,000,000). In a similar operation, Czechoslovakia traded Czech arms for Egyptian cotton and rice.

When the Egyptian-Czechoslovakian arms deal became known and the world press attacked Moscow for its dangerous venture in the Middle East, official Soviet publications reacted in a characteristic way. Defending Czechoslovakia and Egypt and stressing the latter's "sovereign right" to buy whatever arms it wants wherever it wants to, the Soviet press never so much as mentioned whom the Arab nations were arming against and what kind of war was in the making if supplying of arms to Egypt in considerable quantities should continue for a considerable time. Pretending to "fight for peace" everywhere, in-

10. Because of Iraq's position close to the Soviet border it has remained outside of the Arab coalition sponsored by the Soviet Union.

cluding the Middle East, the Soviet press did not mention Israel as the target of the Soviet arms supplies. If a war should break out in this part of the world, the sympathies of the Soviet regime, although never stated explicitly, will be on the Egyptian-Syrian side; insofar as assistance can be given without risk of outright involvement in war, the two Arab nations, rather than Israel, will enjoy Soviet help.

It would be an exaggeration to say that by its policy in the Middle East Moscow was intentionally setting the stage for a world war. On the other hand, Moscow would not be unhappy to see the outbreak of a local war between local forces in which superiority would lie with the anti-Western bloc. And when the day arrived for settling the conflict, the Soviet government would expect to be invited to participate and have a voice in the settlement negotiations, as she had in the case of the settlement of the Korean and Indochinese wars.

A few years ago Vyacheslav Molotov stated that there is no international issue or territory in which the Soviet Union is not interested. For a long time Soviet Russia has been excluded from the Mediterranean and the Middle East. Its aim now is to obtain a place in the African sun and secure a foothold which it can strengthen in the future.

CONCLUSION

UNLIKE MOST ANIMAL ORGANISMS, the social organism is capable, when necessary, of growing a new organ to replace one that has been cut off. When in the course of the social revolution in Russia the head—the intelligentsia—was cut off, a new one began to grow. The painful process is still going on, although today the agony is somewhat diminished. The rise and consolidation of a new leadership in such a nation as Russia has been an important event in history, an event that has provoked protracted tensions on a world scale.

At the beginning of the Soviet era only a small minority of the intellectually upper strata belonged to the Communist party, and these were found mainly at the highest levels. Thirty years ago only the top leaders of Soviet institutions, economic units, and military bodies were required to be members of the party, and these occupied posts as heads of the commissariats, members of their executive bodies, directors, rectors of universities, chairmen of Soviets. The middle and lower posts in the administrative and economic organization were filled by men who did not belong to the party. As the party grew and the old intelligentsia disappeared into the abyss, the personnel at all levels, from the highest to the lowest, were more and more often Communists—that is, members of the party.

Today a significant majority of party members are, as they used to say in the old days, of the "petty bourgeois" type—individuals who have no great aims, who do not devote their lives to pursuit of an ideal but rather seek comfort for themselves and their families, who accept human failings, weaknesses, egotism. These Russian Communist-"Philistines," who comprise 90 per cent, if not more, of the membership of the party, bear little resemblance to the old, inflexible Communist fighters, fanatics, and idealists.

Yet this large mass of Communist-"Philistines" cannot be considered a potential anti-Soviet force. Given their past, their ascent into the ranks of the intelligentsia, the privileges they have won, and the measure of prosperity they enjoy, they owe a debt to the revolution. If there had been no November upheaval, they (or their fathers) would be serving today as shepherds, blacksmiths, common day laborers, or dock workers. In each of their lives a miracle has occurred. They are bound to the Soviet state more by instinct than by reason. They know little about the "world proletariat"; they would find it difficult to explain why it was necessary to close all private shops in the country of the Soviet and drive the peasantry into the kolkhozes. But if they are dissatisfied, and they are often dissatisfied with many things, their desire is not to abolish but to change the order which reared and fed them.

They dream of order, of personal security, of doing away with purges, of liquidating "liquidation," but at the same time they are true opponents of all the old parties, which to them are a symbol of the era when they and their fathers lived in filthy huts, went barefoot through the village, and ran errands for the local merchant. By instinct they are against a constitutional or absolute monarchy, not because they are republicans by conviction but because the monarchy and the Tsar symbolize the system which had to perish in order that they might live. This does not mean that they are completely devoted to their government, but it does mean that those in Russia or abroad who might suggest a restoration of old institutions would find no affirmative response in these circles.

They are not passionate Communists and in no way "internationalists," but some ideas, snatched by Communism from the treasure house of humanism and distorted, have entered their blood and serve them as principles: an "exploiter" is a sinister person, "the people" great, and a "usurper" a dark figure in world history. Often they are unaware that exploitation flourishes around them, that usurpation of power is an everyday occurrence in their country, and that the principles of morality which they recognize are daily violated in Russia.

If the pressure should one day be lifted, this large stratum of Russian society would remain on top and would immediately begin the march toward power, but it cannot be transformed into an anti-Soviet force. The soul of these millions is not a *tabula rasa* on which any desired text can be impressed. These people have less brilliance, less daring than the old Leninists-Stalinists; they make fewer sensational gestures; they are less excitable; but there is still a pale, faded reflection of the ideas and theory of the November revolution.

This layer of Russian society represents the potentially largest political force in the country, a force which at a moment of crisis could find itself stronger than the highest authorities, the old commanders, the secret and public police, and, of course, stronger than the restless, perplexed, and inarticulate masses of peasants and physical laborers. This impersonal mass of Communist intelligentsia, which belongs to no faction, has no theory, does not link itself to any opposition leader— these millions of "average" people in the ruling party who penetrate every crevice of the "apparatus"—could speak in a voice louder than the Trotskyism, Bukharinism, and other "isms" of the days when Soviet leaders clashed over ideological issues, routes of world revolution, and Marxist-Leninist texts.

The era of Soviet youth is approaching its end.

"There are no more devoted servants of the Soviet system," a former prominent Communist wrote, "than the youth of both sexes, 14 and 15 years of age, who are recruited yearly in contingents of 400,000, chiefly out of the villages, and trained for industrial work. For this promotion, for being sent to the city, for their hopes, they thank the leaders; they are devoted to such a degree—and this is no exaggeration—that if the Leader demanded their lives, they would make the sacrifice." Following recruitment, there come, for these youth, the years in the Komsomol, school, training, Stalin's *Short Course,* and the concepts of the "world working class" and its "oppression," its "hatred of capitalism," its "unending revolts," and the "corruption and venality" of all other parties in the world except the Communist party. The Komsomol member absorbs this doctrine and takes it with him into the army, or, if he is lucky, into a *Vuz,* an institution of higher learning. But then comes the job, the party, the family; after come the experiences of life. Doubt begins to beset him. He begins to understand that the newspaper is not always truthful and that the party secretary says what he is ordered to say. At work he is nagged and reprimanded without cause; occasionally there is a summons from the secret police. Doubt turns into skepticism. Disbelief grows, though it is kept hidden. In his soul there is neither Leninism nor world Communism, nor is there anything to take its place.

As the intelligentsia has changed, so has the language of the journalists and officials who write for it. A comparison, for example, of recent issues of *Pravda* and *Izvestia* with those of the 1920's reveals significant differences in terminology. Three decades ago the phrases "class" and "class interests" were used abundantly; today they are out of fashion with respect to conditions inside the Soviet Union and are rarely used to describe developments in the outside world. The terms "social revolution" and "world revolution," which were the subjects of passionate internal disputes in the 'twenties and early 'thirties, have disappeared, and the term "revolution" itself is used less frequently than before.

The terms "proletariat" and "proletarian" are almost entirely out of use. Karl Marx, their originator, used them as synonyms for "working class," but imparted to them a distinct revolutionary shading. Later these terms were used by the

Socialist world, and of course by the Bolsheviks, until approximately the 1930's. Today they have almost disappeared. Even the term "bourgeois" appears infrequently in the Soviet press.

"Dictatorship of the proletariat," another slogan inherited from Marx and in earlier days used at every opportunity, is falling into oblivion; the word "dictatorship," which in the texts of Lenin is used in conjunction with "workers and peasants," has vanished from use both in this connection and separately.

The term "toilers" has replaced "workers"; even in official statements "Soviets of Toilers" has replaced the obsolete "Soviets of Workers' Deputies." This evolution in terminology of course implies no essential change, but to the Russian ear fine shades of difference are important. The old Russian Populism, which rejected Marxism and the class struggle as a universal explanation of history, clung to the term "toilers" as a synonym for "the people," a phrase which in the purely Russian sense comprehends the millions of people who toil at physical labor. Against Populism and its terminology the fathers of Russian Marxism, including the young Lenin and his generation of Bolsheviks, waged a merciless war. They believed that not all "toilers," but only "proletarians," could form the basis for a revolution.

If, today, official Soviet terminology reverts to the usages of Populism, this of course implies emphasis on the fact that "class antagonisms" do not exist within Soviet society, and that, on the contrary, "for the first time in history" the classes have been fused into one harmonious mass of toilers. But behind this attempt at "scientific" explanation lies the pressure of the need of the average Communist, after decades of wrangling, purges, and tension, to settle down at last to a more peaceful, more comfortable life. This pressure, rather than any specific orders from above, is the reason why the term "toilers" has gradually, almost imperceptibly, crept into that section of the Soviet press which reports on political events abroad, where, it would seem, the "workers" must continue to wage intense struggles, and where the term "toilers," according to Lenin, serves to soften, or "lubricate," and thereby lessen, the intensity of social antagonisms.

While in these linguistic metamorphoses there is of course a great deal of strategy (words can be sacrificed if necessary), the terminological reform goes far beyond petty deceptive maneuvers. It is significant when, in the political arena, words are discarded and new words come into use. The new generation uses a new terminology, and the older generation absorbs it in order to keep in step with the times. The new terms and the new forms of expression reflect the changing situation and are related to the changing psychological needs.

It is significant that the term "democracy," in all its variations, is in abundant use in Russia; as a matter of fact, it is used more frequently in the Soviet Union than in the West. This is not indicative of any inclination on the part of the Soviet leadership to make real concessions to the principles of democracy. Yet in the 1920's and 1930's this term seldom appeared in Soviet literature and in the daily press. When it was used, it was preceded by the ridiculing adjectives "formal" or "bourgeois." Today, to the degree that the term "dictatorship" is being withdrawn from circulation, "democracy" is becoming a catchword—a stratagem, but symptomatic nevertheless.

For understanding the changing world of Soviet Russia it is essential to realize that the Soviet era of Russian history cannot end in an upheaval of the type of the November revolution. The idea that a new social revolution is in the making, in which not only the political power, but the ruling stratum as well, will go down, must be abandoned.

As was mentioned, only the English Revolution of the seventeenth century and the French Revolution of the eighteenth century are comparable to the upheaval in Russia. Each of these three revolutions was propelled by a fanatical popular movement which had an enormous—although exaggerated and naïve—faith in the possibility of transforming this vale of tears and sorrow into the promised land. In the civil wars which in all three instances accompanied the social overturn, whole strata of society that had long dominated various spheres of life quickly passed into oblivion. In their places rose others, sprung from the "lower orders," comprising men who had earned their laurels by talent, ability, initiative, and devotion to the new order. In England and France the destruction of the prerevolutionary intelligentsia (using the word here in its conventional sense) was a by-product of the revolution—that is, the revolution did not consciously set itself the task of systematically creating a new upper layer of society. In Russia, on the contrary, the dislodging of groups of "bourgeois origin" by the *Vydvizhentsy* ("promotees") was a distinct element of the overturn and was systematically waged by the state power. The renovation of the upper strata went significantly further in Russia than in either France or England. In England, where the aristocracy was being continually renewed, it emerged from the upheaval of the seventeenth century as an amalgam of the remnants of the old with the newcomers who had successfully pushed themselves forward during the years of the revolution. In France, even after the return of the émigrés, and even after the foreign intervention, the restoration was short-lived, and the new strata which had arisen during the revolution soon resumed their place on the commanding heights of French society. In Russia the process went even further.

In this succession of the ruling social strata is perhaps hidden the true meaning of a revolution.

In Russia and abroad many have written and many have quarreled about the "achievements" of the upheaval in Russia. Everybody agrees about the "achievements" that had a negative character: the disappearance of the large landed estates, the abolition of national discrimination, the destruction of the monarchy, and so on. It has not been so easy, however, to indicate the positive and enduring effects of the changes wrought during the revolutionary period. Universal education? Russia had already started on the road toward this before 1917. Improvement of medical care for the people? This also had begun before the revolution. What, then, are the lasting changes brought about by the profound upheaval in Russia?

It is ironic that thousands of the "men of October," those who were the potential new privileged layers at the top of the social pyramid, honestly believed that they were conducting a war against inequality, and that "the people" were coming to power. As a result of their passionate efforts and great sacrifices, a social system emerged which was like neither the one they overthrew nor the one they wished to create.

In all probability a change in the composition of the ruling strata similar to that which has occurred in Russia will be the main content of the social transformation in the satellite countries. At the present time, when only a few years separate the "Socialist order" from the old "capitalism" in these countries, there still survive, at the bottom of the different layers, somewhere between the layers, or in jail, a majority of the old elements. In the satellites neither the social nor the physical liquidation have had the mass character that they have had in Russia, nor has the terrorism been so cruel or so pervasive. The larger the Communist party in a given satellite nation, the more quickly will it occupy the key positions, crowd the remnants of the old strata out of the governmental, economic, and cultural apparatuses, and replace them with others plucked from the masses. It would seem that this process has gone farthest in China and least far in Czechoslovakia. There is little doubt that within a certain period the old classes in the satellite nations will be so devastated and rendered so impotent that it will not be possible even to think of a restoration of the old society. At that point a political overturn—

that is, the liberation of a satellite from Soviet control—will not signify the restoration of the old social groupings.

The English, French, and Russian revolutions were profound mass social revolutions, as distinct from political revolutions in which the consequences of the upheaval are less radical and in which the masses play a lesser role. The profundity of a revolution is measured by the degree of popular activity. The fact that in all three cases civil wars occurred in which newly created mass armies were victorious indicates how deeply into the masses the revolutionary spirit had penetrated. In contrast, the European revolutions of 1848, which burst out in the winter and by summer of the same year had already gone into a decline, were purely political movements. Even in France, where the old monarchy was overthrown in 1848, the sweep of the revolution did not parallel the storm of sixty years earlier. In terms of profundity, mass participation, and radicalness, the Russian revolution occupies, whether for good or bad, first place on the many-runged ladder of revolutionary upheavals.

The more profound a revolution, and the greater the part in it of the "man in the street," the "masses," the less likelihood is there of its being repeated. Generations must pass, memories be obliterated, disappointments forgotten, before the faith of the masses in the miracle-working power of a great upheaval can again begin to move mountains. A political overturn, which does not require the kind of spiritual force, idealism, and faith that a profound revolution must first possess, can occur every thirty years in a given country, as has happened in France, for example; a social revolution occurs once in ages.

A great revolution bursts into flame when, counterposed to "the people," there exists a ruling group, long separated from it, which has created for itself legal and material privileges. Once, long ago, this group itself emerged from the lower ranks of society—the soldiery, hirelings, grooms, courtiers, petty and impoverished princes. Having raised themselves to the heights and isolated themselves further from the rest of the people, the new upper layers, in a process stretching out over centuries, create their own way of life and legal titles to power and wealth. The Soviet bureaucracy is undoubtedly developing in this direction, and in time, if political events do not interrupt the development, will transform itself into a privileged social stratum. At present, however, this evolution is at its very beginning. In these Soviet bureaucrats who have "arrived" the people still recognize their own plebeian line. A popular movement against the "new nobility" cannot arise so long as the people and this "nobility" continue to feel a bond between them.

It is true that the Soviet government does not rest on a popular majority, that there is great dissatisfaction among the people, and that the first serious political crisis could give expression to these feelings of dissatisfaction. Yet the primitive formula of "people against government" cannot be applied to the Russian situation. The Soviet government rests on its own party and the Komsomol, with a combined membership, as we have seen, of about 24,000,000—that is, at least 20 per cent of the adult population. They are the government, but still part of "the people." The "masses" themselves, however, lack everything—clear ideas, a program, leaders. Their flare-ups and revolts, of a local character, are easily crushed. These flare-ups, symptomatic of the general condition of the country, do not threaten the system. Every man having the slightest capacity for anything better than physical work is drawn out of the "masses" and into the upper ranks; given the constant shortage of adequate personnel, this is still the rule, not the exception.

The first phase of the second World War, and in particular the period from October to December, 1941, was a test for the Soviet regime. The political machine began to jam, and discipline slackened seriously; antigovernment talk was heard here and there; plundering of warehouses and banks occurred; some were eager for the entry of the Germans. But out of all this no movement developed that could seriously shake the Stalinist regime. There were moments in October, 1941, when it seemed that the foundation of the state power itself was shaky and that an armed mob bursting into the Kremlin might have put an end to the Soviet system. But such a group— that is, a group with political leaders and political aims—did not appear. This was another indication of how little the situation had ripened for a popular revolution.

The last great attempt to call out the masses against the Soviet government was the White movement of 1918–20. The civil war of those years gave the answer to the question of whether the Russian revolution was to be a profound or a superficial one. If a victory of the Whites had been possible, it would have meant a renovation of not more than 10, 15, or 20 per cent of the upper layers of Russian political and economic society; on the whole, the old groups would have remained on top. Had a victory of the Whites been possible, it might have saved Russia from many delusions and errors. The victory of the Reds signified that of the old groups there remained (for a time) a small group—20 to 30 per cent— that later was absorbed into the new ruling group. History decided in favor of the latter variant. The defeat of the Whites was the final verdict: the entire prerevolutionary elite was condemned to destruction.

The order of battle of 1918–20 cannot be repeated. From the time the White movement was defeated, a "united front of anti-Communist forces" in Russia has remained a phrase without meaning.

But would not a new war, if one should break out, be the vehicle by which the formula of "people against the state power" could be restored to life? Will there not develop in case of a military defeat, a large popular anti-Communist movement, apart from and despite the new ruling strata?

The defeat of France in 1813–15 did indeed lead to the restoration of the monarchy, but not as the result of internal political upheaval; it was rather the result of foreign intervention. The prerequisites were not only a complete rout of the army but occupation of the capital as well. Under Russian conditions, particularly since the experiences of the second World War, such a development is almost inconceivable. If the Russian Army should suffer a defeat, Russia's adversaries would refuse to be drawn deep into the country, to suffer the fate of the Germans when they marched into the endless steppes and forests of Russia, beset on all sides by guerrillas, and paid a heavy price in casualties. A series of military defeats can release new internal forces and provoke a political crisis, but even military defeats cannot open the sluices of popular revolt and convert a political crisis into a social revolution.

A government may be overturned in a week; a new constitution may be proclaimed in one day; laws of the greatest importance and appropriations of billions may be enacted in a short time. In the social sphere it takes only a few years to make a successful merchant of a poorly educated peasant, or turn a locksmith into a mechanic or a mechanic into an engineer. Talented men have risen to be ministers in a few years. But to restore the brains of a whole nation takes more than a year and more than a decade. The creation of a new intelligentsia is a slow, painful process, and there are no artificial means whereby its development can be hastened. This is an aspect of the revolutionary process that is not revealed in any official statistics.

Hundreds of thousands of young Russians have entered the universities and technical schools, with the result that the percentage of those who have had the advantages of "higher education" is greater than at any time in the past and continues to increase rapidly. The authorities try, of course, to hasten the regeneration of the intelligentsia by formal education, films, radio, and books. And a hunger for learning exists among the hundreds of thousands who recognize their own backwardness, lack of education, and lack of skill for the performance of responsible work. Although progress is being made, the quality of the new scientists, artists, teachers, writers, and diplomats is still poor.

The tiresome repetition and abuse of the word "culture" in Russia is symptomatic of both the government's desire to educate the intelligentsia and the hunger of the people for learning. As used at present, the term covers everything from cleanliness in the home to rules of polite behavior, from reading and writing to the latest fashions, from foreign languages to correct spelling. There are "cultured behavior," "cultured curtains," "cultured recreation." In this word the great yearning to attain the manners of a real intelligentsia and the heights of knowledge finds its expression, as does also the pitiful awareness of backwardness. The Soviet press is full of articles on the duty of every citizen, especially the Communist, to "improve himself" and to continue learning.

The mass of Soviet students and teachers are still on a lower level generally than their prerevolutionary predecessors. Often they remain half-educated all their lives. We meet these semi-intelligentsia as writers on Soviet newspapers and magazines; they come to the West as diplomats and delegates, often surprising their colleagues from other parts of the world by their mediocrity. They often believe that their forebears invented everything; that Americans spread bacteria and kill babies; that in America the unemployed die in the streets; and that acts of terror are used in the West to win in parliamentary elections. New political writers are not conspicuous. Novelists like Tikhonov, Simonov, and Fadeyev appear in the pages of *Pravda* as political writers. Mikhail Zoshchenko became very popular because in his short stories he pictured the new world that was rising out of the depths of the human mass, its upward strivings, and its impotence to conquer its past. "I am a semi-intellectual," a Zoshchenko hero says proudly, unaware of the irony in his words. But he is right to boast, this hero, for a great deal of effort and energy was expended to transform an illiterate into a half-educated man.

The mass production of half-educated people out of illiterates is a tremendous task, but if a new stratum of superior intelligentsia is to be created, the task must be performed. It may take another generation to accomplish it, but it must be accomplished. And a long period of time is required, perhaps as long as it takes for one generation to replace another, before the need for political freedom grows up within this stratum. It takes decades for the myths to start to fade. The new order created by the heroic generation is taken for granted by the new generation; prose replaces poetry; criticism replaces enthusiasm. Gradually the new generation begins to grope its way toward ideas of law and freedom.

The pattern of social evolution which requires a succession of generations is better understood in this country than elsewhere. The first generation of immigrants from Europe remains spiritually rooted in European soil and carries over into the new country its tastes, customs, habits, and even political parties. The second generation still speaks its European languages, retains many of the views of its parents, and begins to take root in the new soil; the third generation is "pure" American, with new opinions and new tastes and manners in personal and social life. This pattern of evolution appears to be rooted in human nature and apparently cannot be altered.

Once before in the Soviet land the new generation was ready to rise, speak out, and demand. This was in the middle 1930's, when the old Bolsheviks were beginning to die out and the young ones were approaching power. The prerequisites for a transformation were present: the political atmosphere both inside and outside the party was astir with heretical ideas. Then came the Great Purge, which drove hundreds of thousands out of the party and "liquidated" the young heretics.

New people had been drawn into the apparatus to replace those who had been purged. For these half million new people who were brought into the body of the "intelligentsia" and quickly elevated to influence and material prosperity, the social revolution took place not thirty-eight but only fifteen years ago. Their cycle began later, and they are still "first generation." This process of purge of old groups and recruitment of new groups into the intelligentsia prolonged the life of the government for many years.

But no purges, no police operations, no iron or other curtains can stop the process of natural growth and maturing of the people of a great nation. Impediments can delay, postpone, and retard. They cannot abolish the laws of nature or those of history. Russia, reshaped and transformed and longing for freedom, will embark upon new paths leading to liberty and security for herself and the other nations of the world. The road is long, dark, beset by pitfalls and frustrations. Progress is painful. But at the end stand a better Russia and a better world.

SOURCES

FROM the extensive literature and abundant material on Soviet Russia only those sources are listed below which have been quoted or otherwise directly used in this book.

PART I. SOCIAL REVOLUTION IN RUSSIA

CHAPTER 1. THE NEW SOCIAL STRUCTURE

Lenin, *Works,* 3d ed. Vol. *19,* 37 ff.; *20,* 133 ff.; *21,* 233, 438; *24,* 102, 185–186.

Decrees of the Soviet government, November 12 and December 16, 1917.

Vserossyiskaya Konferentsiya RKP, 1922, *Bulleten,* Moscow, 1922.

Stalin, *Voprosy Leninizma,* 11th ed., pp. 462–495.

Mitin's speech at the 18th Congress of the Communist party, in *Stenograficheskii Otchet 18 S'yezda.*

N. Bukharin in *Bolshevik,* 1925, Nos. 9–10.

THE NEW SOCIAL CLASSES AND THEIR INCOME:

The statistical yearbook *Sotsialisticheskoye Selskoye Khozyaistvo,* 1939.

Statistical yearbooks, *Sotsialisticheskoye Stroitelstvo,* 1934, 1935, 1936, 1939.

Statistical yearbooks, *Trud,* 1934, 1936.

Professor S. N. Prokopovich's *Bulleten Ekonomicheskovo Kabineta,* Praga, 1935–38, and his *Quarterly Bulletin of Soviet-Russian Economics,* Geneva, 1939–43.

Gosplan, *Kontrolnye Tsyfry,* 1926–27, 1929–30.

Problemy Ekonomiki, 1940, No. 7, Pisarev, *K Itogam Perepisi.*

Voznesensky's report at the conference of the Communist party in *Bolshevik,* 1941, No. 34.

Gosplan, *Narodno-Khozyaistvennyi Plan na 1936,* Moscow.

POPULATION PROBLEMS:

Wolf and Mebus, *Statisticheskyi Spravochnik po Ekonomicheskoi Geografii*, Moscow, 1928.
Tsentranoye Statisticheskoye Upravrelnie, *Statisticheskyi Spravochnik*, 1928.
Tsentranoye Statisticheskoye Upravrelnie, *Trudy*, Vols. *8, 18*.
Sautin in *Bolshevik*, May, 1940.
League of Nations, *Future Population of Europe and of the Soviet Union*, Geneva, 1944.
Stalin's speech, December 3, 1935, in his *Voprosy Leninizma*.
League of Nations, *Statistical Yearbooks*.
Statistical Yearbooks, *Sotsialisticheskoye Stroitelstvo*, 1936, 1939.
N. Timasheff, *The Great Retreat*, New York, E. P. Dutton, 1946.
American Journal of Sociology, 1948.
Frank Lorimer, *The Population of the Soviet Union*, Princeton, Princeton University Press, 1946.
A. Vagts in *Journal of Politics*, Gainesville, Fla., July, 1945.
F. Notestein in *Atlantic Monthly*, June, 1946.

CHAPTERS 2 AND 3. THE NEW UPPER CLASSES

COMMUNISM AND THE INTELLIGENTSIA:

Lenin, *Works*, 3d ed. Vol. *10*, 207 ff.
Stalin's speeches, June 23, 1931, January 7, 1933, November 25, 1936, in his *Voprosy Leninizma*, 11th ed.
———— report at the 18th Congress, in *Voprosy Leninizma*.
Kaganovich's report at the 17th Congress, in *Stenograficheskii Otchet 17 S'yezda*.
Molotov's speech at the 18th Congress, in *Stenograficheskii Otchet*.
Resolutions of the Central Committee of the Communist party, July, 1928, in *VKP v Rezolutsiyakh*, Vol. *2*, Moscow, 1940.
Vladimir Tchernavin, *I Speak for the Silent. Prisoners of the Soviets*, Boston, Ralph T. Hall, 1935.

RAPID INCREASE OF THE NEW CLASSES:

Gosplan, *Piatiletnii Plan*, Moscow, 1930.
Yearbooks, *Sotsialisticheskoye Stroitelstvo*, Moscow, 1934, 1935, 1936.
Ekonomika Sotsialisticheskoi Promyshlennosti, Moscow, 1940.

N. Voznesensky, *The Fourth Five Year Plan*, Moscow, 1946.
Large Soviet Encyclopaedia, 2d ed. Vol. *12*.

CHAPTER 4. THE WORKING CLASS

Review of Economic Statistics, Cambridge, May, 1954.
S. M. Levin and N. I. Antonov, *Organizatsiya zarabotnoi platy v chernoi metallurgii*, Moscow-Kharkov, Gosudarstvennoye Nauchno-Tekhnicheskoye Izdatelstvo Literatury po Chernoi i Tsvetnoi Metallurgii, 1950.

CHAPTER 5. THE PEASANTRY

Lenin, *Tezisy po Agrarnomu Voprosu*, 1920.
Stalin's speeches, May 28, 1928, October 19, 1928.
Stalin's report at the Plenary Meeting of the Central Committee, April, 1929, in *Voprosy Leninizma*.
Planovoye Khozyaistvo, 1938, No. 9, and 1939, Nos. 5, 7, 9.
Izvestia, May 22, 1938, and March 29, 1941.
Plan, November, 1936.
Sotsialisticheskaya Rekonstruktsiya Selskovo Khozyaistva, 1940, Nos. 11–12.
Sotsialisticheskoye Zemledelie, December 22, 1938, June 5, 1940.
Altaiski, *Dokhody v Kolkhozakh*, 1937.
Bolshevik, Moscow, 1946, No. 5.
Kolkhozy vo Vtoroi Stalinskoi Pyatiletke, 1939.
S. Prokopovich, *Ekonomicheskogo Bulleten*, Kabineta, Praga, 1935–38.

THE PEASANTS AND THE COMMUNIST PARTY:

18th Congress of the Communist party, 1939, speeches by Patolichev, Andreyev, Mikhailov, Chernousov, and Shtykov.
Kaganovich's report at the 17th Congress.
10th Congress of the Komsomol, speeches by Kossior, Andreyev, and Kosarev.
Partiynoye Stroitelstvo, 1934, No. 1; 1937, No. 12; 1941, No. 6.

THE PEASANTRY IN WAR:

Bolshevik, decrees of the Soviet government, 1942, No. 7–8; 1943, Nos. 7–8, 15–16.

Information Bulletin of the Soviet Embassy, Washington, February 10, 1944.

CHAPTER 6. FORCED LABOR

I. L. Averbakh, *Ot Prestupleniya k Trudu,* Moscow, 1936.

J. Littlepage and D. Bess, *In Search of Soviet Gold,* New York, Harcourt, Brace, 1937.

John Scott, *Behind the Urals,* Boston, Houghton Mifflin, 1942.

S. Firin, *Itogi Belomorstroya,* Moscow, 1934.

Insarov, *Baltiisko-Belomorski Vodnyi Put,* Moscow, 1934.

Lilian Mowrer and Olga Kochanska, *Arrest and Exile,* New York, William Morrow, 1941.

Vladimir Tchernavin, *I Speak for the Silent. Prisoners of the Soviets,* Boston, Ralph T. Hall, 1935.

Tatiana Tchernavin, *Escape from the Soviets,* London, H. Hamilton, 1933.

Victor Kravchenko, *I Chose Freedom,* New York, Charles Scribner's Sons, 1946.

S. Mora and P. Zwerniak, *La Justice Soviétique,* Rome, 1945.

Boris Souvarine, *Stalin,* New York, Alliance Book Corporation, Longmans, Green, 1939.

Leonard E. Hubbard, *Soviet Labor and Industry,* London, Macmillan, 1942.

G. Besedovski, *Den Klauen der Tscheka entronnen,* Leipzig, Grethlein, 1930.

Sotsialisticheskii Vestnik, Paris, 1938, No. 24.

Jerszy Glicksman, *Tell the West,* New York, The Gresham Press, 1948.

Antoni Ekart, *Echappé de Russie,* Paris, Hachette.

The Dark Side of the Moon, New York, Charles Scribner's Sons, 1947.

Jules Margolin, *La Condition Humaine,* Paris, Calmann-Levy, 1949.

Gustav Herling, *A World Apart,* London, William Heinemann, 1951.

Margarete Buber-Neumann, *Als Gefangene bei Stalin und Hitler,* Munich, Verlag der Zwölf, 1949.

Elinor Lipper, *Eleven Years in Soviet Prison Camps,* Chicago, Henry Regnery, 1951.

Joseph Scholmer, *Vorkuta,* New York, Henry Holt, 1955.

Brigitte Gerland, *Die Hölle ist ganz anders,* Stuttgart, Steingruber Verlag, 1955.

Wilhelm Starlinger, *Grenzen der Sowjetmacht,* Würzburg, Holzner-Verlag, 1955.

B. Yakovlev, *Kontsentratsionnyie Lageri SSSR,* Munich, Institute for the Study of the History and Culture of the USSR, 1955.

PART II. THE SOVIET SYSTEM

CHAPTER 7. THE SO-CALLED EVOLUTION OF COMMUNISM

LENIN AND STALIN AS POLITICAL REALISTS:

Yevgeni Pashukanis, *Marx i Proletarskoye Gosudarstvo,* Moscow, 1933.

Emil Ludwig's interview with Stalin, December 13, 1931.

D. Manuilsky in *Bolshevik,* 1944, No. 1.

COMMUNISM AND THE STATE:

Lenin, *Works,* 2d ed. Vol. *14,* Pt. II, *Gosudarstvo i Revolutsiya* and *Uderzhat-li Bolsheviki Gosudarstvennuyu Vlast.*

―――― *Works,* 3d ed. Vol. *18,* 81 ff.; *22,* 291 ff.

Stalin, *Voprosy Leninizma,* 3d ed., pp. 702 ff.

Bukharin and Preobrazhensky, *Azbuka Kommunizma,* Saratov, 1920.

STALIN AND HIS PARTY IN THE WAR:

Stalin's speeches, particularly July 3, 1941, May 1, 1942, November 7, 1943, and Stalin's Order of the Day, May 1, 1943, in *Soviet War Documents,* Washington, 1943.

A. Kursky in *Bolshevik,* October, 1943.

K. Kuznetsov in *Propagandist,* 1942, No. 9.

A. Fadeyev in *Propagandist,* 1943, No. 21.

MARXISM―LENINISM IN THE WAR:

Nekotorye Voprosy Prepodavaniya Politicheskoi Ekonomii, in *Pod Znamenem Marxizma,* No. 7–8, 1943.

A. Makhanov in *Propagandist,* 1942, No. 3.

Leading article in *Propagandist,* 1942, No. 7–8.

G. Alexandrov in *Propagandist,* 1942, No. 19–20, and in No. 5, 1943.

Leading article in *Propagandist,* 1943, No. 11–12.

P. Pozdnyshev in *Propagandist,* 1943, No. 13.

Leading articles in *Propagandist,* 1943, Nos. 14 and 18.

M. Mitin in *Propagandist,* 1943, Nos. 19–20.

Leading articles in *Bolshevik,* 1943, Nos. 22 and 23–24.

Alexander Shcherbakov's Report, January 21, 1943, in *Propagandist,*
1943, No. 2.
Istoriya VKP, Kratki Kurs, Moscow, 1938.

CHAPTER 8. THE TWO MAIN DEVIATIONS

Bulleten Oppozitsii, 1929–40, particularly Nos. 5–6, 75, 81, 82–83.
Trotsky, *Nashi Politicheskiya Zadachi,* Geneva, 1904.
Stalin, Reports, December 27, 1929, and at the 16th Congress of the
Communist party, in his *Voprosy Leninizma,* 11th ed.
Trotsky, "If World War Comes Again," *Yale Review,* 1938, No. 4.
———— *Works,* Vol. *15, Vseobshchaya Trudovaya Povinnost.*
Vladimir Dedjer, *Tito,* New York, Simon and Schuster, 1953.
Yugoslav Newsletter, New York, June 12, 1950.
Yugoslav Review, New York, May, 1952.

CHAPTER 9. THE COMMUNIST PARTY OF THE SOVIET UNION

Lenin, *Works,* 3d ed. Vol. *25,* 578 ff.
Stalin, "Ob Osnovakh Leninzma," in his *Voprosy Leninizma,* 1939.
Stalin's speech, March 3, 1937, in *Bolshevik,* 1937, No. 7.
VKP v Tsifrakh, published by the Central Committee of the Communist
party, twice a year until 1928.
Perepis RKP, published by the Central Committee, 1922.
Vserossiiskaya Konferentsiya RKP, Moscow, 1922.
A. Mitrofanov, *Itogi Chistki Partii,* Moscow, 1930.
Stenograficheskii Otchet 16 S'yezda, reports by Vladimirsky and Kaga-
novich.
Stenograficheskii Otchet 17 S'yezda, reports by Vladimirsky and Kaga-
novich.
Stenograficheskii Otchet 18 S'yezda VKP, speeches of Zhdanov,
Biryukov, Mekhlis, and Shatalin, and the report of the Mandate
Commission.
Boris Meissner, *Russland im Umbruch,* Frankfurt a.M., Verlag für
Geschichte und Politik, 1951.
———— *Die kommunistische Partei der Sowjetunion vor und nach dem
Tode Stalins,* Frankfurt a.M., Institut für Europäische Politik und
Wirtschaft, 1954.
Alexandre Ouralov, *Staline Au Pouvoir,* Paris, Les Iles d'Or.
Merle Fainsod, *How Russia is Ruled,* Cambridge, Harvard University
Press, 1955.

Komsomol:

Molodezh SSSR, Moscow, 1936.

Balashov, *Komsomol za Desiat Let*, Moscow, 1928.

Sotsialisticheskoye Stroitelstvo, 1936.

O. Mishakova, in *Propagandist*, 1943, No. 18.

S. Ostriakov, *Chto Trebuyet Komsomol ot Komsomoltsa*, Moscow, 1937.

Otchet 10 S'yezda Komsomola, Moscow, 1936, report by Kossior.

Chto Reshil 10 S'yezd Komsomola, Moscow, 1936.

CHAPTER 10. THE ARMY AND THE SECRET POLICE

Voroshilov, *Stat'i i Rechi*, Moscow, 1936.

Komplektovaniye Krasnoi Armii, Berlin, 1926.

G. Agabekov, *Cheka za Rabotoi*, Berlin, Strela, 1931.

Yevgeni Dumbadze, *Na Sluzhbe Cheka i Kominterna*, Paris, "Mishen," 1930.

Essad-bey, *OGPU*, New York, The Viking Press, 1933.

W. G. Krivitsky, *In Stalin's Secret Service*, New York, Harper and Brothers, 1939.

Report on Court Proceedings, Trial of N. Bukharin and Others, Moscow, 1938 (in English).

D. Fedotoff White, *The Growth of the Red Army*, Princeton, Princeton University Press, 1944.

N. Sinevirski, *Smersh*, Limburg-Lahn, Grani.

Alexander Orlov, *The Secret History of Stalin's Crimes*, New York, Random House, 1953.

CHAPTER 11. THE NEW RELIGIOUS POLICY

William Henry Chamberlin, *Russia's Iron Age*, Boston, Little Brown, 1934.

Religious News Service, New York, March 22, 1946.

Large Soviet Encyclopaedia, 2d ed. Vol. 2.

N. S. Timasheff, *Religion in Soviet Russia*, New York, Sheed and Ward, 1942.

Stalin in *Izvestia*, September 15, 1927.

Komsomol i Antireligioznaya Propaganda, Moscow, 1937.

Russian Orthodox Journal (in English), Philadelphia, March, 1943.

Robert R. Casey, *Religion in Russia*, New York, Harper and Brothers, 1946.

PART III. FOREIGN POLICY

Stalin's speeches of July 13, 1928, and November 7, 1941; his *Pravda* article of July 27, 1927, "On the Menace of War."

Theses of the Sixth World Congress of the Communist International, 1928.

Voprosy Ekonomiki, Moscow, 1952, No. 12.

Large Soviet Encyclopaedia, 2d ed. Vol. *29*.

S. Lozovsky in *Bolshevik*, July, 1941.

Stalin, *Voprosy Leninizma*, Moscow, 1931.

Stalin's reply to Ivanov, February 12, 1938.

Richard L. Walker, *China under Communism*, New Haven, Yale University Press, 1955.

Max Beloff, *The Foreign Policy of Soviet Russia*, 2 vols. London, Oxford University Press, 1947–49.

Nazi-Soviet Relations, 1939–1941. Documents from the Archives of The German Foreign Office, Department of State, 1949.

Gustav Hilger and Alfred G. Meyer, *The Incompatible Allies*, New York, Macmillan, 1953.

Vneshnyaya Politika Sovetskogo Soyuza, 1941–48, 5 vols. Moscow, Gosudarstvennoye Izdatel'stvo Politicheskoi Literatury.

Index

Academicians, trial of, 47
Administration of Propaganda and Agitation. *See* Communist party of the Soviet Union
Afghanistan, 339, 371, 375
Africa (African), 322, 331–333, 377 f., 380
Agabekov, Georgi, 402
Agriculture: mechanization, 26–27, 29
Agrocities, 329, 344
Alexander II, 115
Alexander-Nevsky Monastery, 276
Alexandrov, Georgi, 198, 201, 400
Alexei, Archbishop, 279
Alexei, Patriarch, 279–281, 286
All-Russian Church Assembly. *See* Sobor
All-Slav Meetings, 273
All-Slav Movement, 202, 273
All-Union Commissariat of Trade. *See* Ministry of Trade, USSR
Altaiski, 398
Alter, Victor, 130
America, 26, 85, 87, 92, 307, 309, 320, 322
American Civil War, 12
American Federation of Labor, 164
American Journal of Sociology, 31, 397
Andreyev, Andrei, 398
Andronov, 194
Anglo-Soviet treaty, 217
Ankara, Turkey, 369, 371 f.
Anti-Communist movements, 44 f., 52, 136, 140, 212, 249, 277, 297, 298, 391
Antireligionist, 274
Antonov, N. I., 398
Arab nations (Arabs), 280, 331, 371, 375–380
Arab League, 376

Archangel, USSR, 144, 151, 156
Arctic, 146 f., 157, 344
Ardahan, 280
Argentina, 322
Arman camp, USSR, 160
Armenia (Armenians), 140, 371, 372
Armenian Church, 280
Army (Red Army), 2, 32, 52, 144, 146, 185, 196 f., 203–205, 209, 211, 216, 246, 254–262, 274, 278, 283, 294–297, 299 f., 307–310, 323, 338, 340 f., 362 f., 368, 370, 372, 392, 402; abolition of ranks and insignia, 11–12; restoration of them, 184; discipline, 12; losses in second World War, 33-34; early defeats by Germans, 36; officers as part of new intelligentsia, 55; mobilization of workers, 101; bravery, 121; one conception of its purpose, 186; in theory, the army of the dictatorship of the proletariat, 200; history of Soviet period reflected by changes in, 254; instruments of control, 254; party members in, 255; Army intellectuals as potential danger to regime, 255–256; treason trials, 256 n.; GB as rival, 256–257; the PUR, 259; conflict with GB, 263; as vehicle of the social revolution, 300–301, 307–308
Asia (Asian), 137, 140, 299, 300, 312, 314, 322, 331–334, 340, 347, 355–357, 377 f.
Asiatic people, USSR, 41
Athens, Greece, 360, 369
Atlantic Front, 39
Atlantic Monthly, 397
Atomic Weapons, 310, 319, 338, 345, 348 f.